THEY HIT AND HIT AGAIN, LEAVING THE ENEMY STUNNED.

"At five minutes to two the skyline behind us exploded. A broad curtain of yellow flames lifted to the sky and stayed there, lighting the bare landscape around us. Rumbling and thunderous explosions followed one another throwing up more flames. Drums of gasoline, projected upward, burst in mid-air, blazing globes of fire that floated slowly down. A moment later a rolling wall of heavy, billowing smoke, lit to a fierce red by the fires burning on the ground, had taken possession of half the horizon and reached to the sky. It seemed incredible that the petty manipulations we had done so quietly in the dark could result in such a glorious catastrophe . . .

"We felt slightly awed and very powerful."

POPSKI'S PRIVATE ARMY

THE BANTAM WAR BOOK SERIES

This series of books is about a world on fire.

The carefully chosen volumes in the Bantam War Book Series cover the full dramatic sweep of World War II. Many are eyewitness accounts by the men who fought in a global conflict as the world's future hung in the balance. Fighter pilots, tank commanders and infantry captains, among many others, recount exploits of individual courage. They present vivid portraits of brave men, true stories of gallantry, moving sagas of survival and stark tragedies of untimely death.

In 1933 Nazi Germany marched to become an empire that was to last a thousand years. In only twelve years that empire was destroyed, and ever since, the country has been bisected by her conquerors. Italy relinquished her colonial lands, as did Japan. These were the losers. The winners also lost the empires they had so painfully seized over the centuries. And one, Russia, lost over twenty million dead.

Those wartime 1940s were a simple, even a hopeful time. Hats came in only two colors, white and black, and after an initial battering the Allied nations started on a long and laborious march toward victory. It was a time when sane men believed the world would evolve into a decent place, but, as with all futures, there was no one then who could really forecast the world that we know now.

There are many ways to think about that war. It has always been hard to understand the motivations and braveries of Axis soldiers fighting to enslave and dominate their neighbors. Yet it is impossible to know the hammer without the anvil, and to comprehend ourselves we must know the people we fought against.

Through these books we can discover what it was like to take part in the war that was a final experience for nearly fifty million human beings. In so doing we may discover the strength to make a world as good as the one contained in those dreams and aspirations once believed by heroic men. We must understand our past as an honor to those dead who can no longer choose. They exchanged their lives in a hope for this future that we now inhabit. Though the fight took place many years ago, each of us remains as a living part of it.

POPSKI'S
PRIVATE ARMY

LIEUTENANT COLONEL
VLADIMIR PENIAKOFF
D.S.O., M.C.
"POPSKI"

BANTAM BOOKS
TORONTO • NEW YORK • LONDON • SYDNEY • AUCKLAND

This edition contains the complete text
of the original hardcover edition.
NOT ONE WORD HAS BEEN OMITTED.

POPSKI'S PRIVATE ARMY

A Bantam Book / published by arrangement with
Thomas Y. Crowell Publishers

PRINTING HISTORY
Originally published in Great Britain
as Private Army
Bantam edition / September 1980
2nd printing . . . May 1988
Drawings by Greg Beecham.
Maps by Alan McKnight.

PRINTED IN THE UNITED STATES OF AMERICA

KR   11 10 9 8 7 6 5 4 3 2

CONTENTS

PART IV ITALIAN PARTISANS

INTRODUCTION

THIS is the story of what happened to me in my middle age between the beginning of the year 1940 and the end of 1945. Up to the times I am writing about I had found little contentment, and I believe that my contemporaries had the same sterile experience; but during these five years every moment was consciously happy. My excuse for asking strangers to read a book mainly about myself is that they may be interested in the record of events that led me and a few friends to considerable happiness.

My tale is of war and hard work and enterprises, sometimes stirring but more often ludicrous; of sudden reversals of fortune; of people in high places who were not ruled by convention and others who were; of lowly men of foreign nations whose devotion to our cause exceeded our own; of bloodshed and violence, but more of cunning and deceit and high spirits and the pleasant cudgeling of brains and then again more hard work; above all of friendship.

Only to the fools among the men of my generation will the realization come as a surprise that we liked war.

Of my first forty-five years there is little to be said that is relevant to this story. I was born in Belgium to Russian parents of an intellectual type now extinct: they showed an old-fashioned turn of mind in having me taught English as my first language and later by refusing to send me to school, which they considered inadequate. For years I had never less than three tutors who pumped knowledge into a precocious brain; as well as music, riding, and fencing masters.

From this rarefied atmosphere I passed in 1914 to a Cambridge college, a precious intellectual prig, with high scientific ambitions, and conscientious objections to war. I left at the end of my fourth term to enlist as a private in the French Army. I was in a hurry and couldn't face the months of training I would have had to go through had I applied for a commission in the British Army. The French were obliging: eleven days later I reported to my battery, a fully fledged gunner. It all ended with twelve months in hospitals and convalescent camps, and I was invalided out of the army shortly after the 1918 armistice.

I had gone practical and, turning my back on a donnish career, I trained as an engineer. I worked hard at a succession of jobs in which I didn't believe much and in 1924 I settled in Egypt where I devoted many years to the manufacture of sugar. In the meantime I married and had two children, read, traveled, made a few friends, flew a plane, and motored in the desert in an indestructible Model A Ford, rudely nicknamed The Pisspot, of which more later.

I had developed a curiosity about the desert; as a mere hobby at first, then more and more in earnest, I spent most of my spare time knocking about the wastes of rock and sand that stretch on both sides of the Nile valley. In the early years I traveled on a camel, then in my car which I had adapted to this purpose. Forming plans of exploration in Arabia, which in the early thirties still offered rich rewards to the explorer, I set about to teach myself in the hardest possible manner. Traveling generally alone, navigating my car with a sun compass and by observation of the stars, as a mariner does at sea, after a few years of practice I knew that when I came to undertake real exploration I would not have to face any fundamental difficulties that I had not yet experienced.

In the spring of 1939, I began to prepare for a trip to Oweinat, an isolated mountain peak that springs up to six thousand feet out of a flat desert, 700 miles to the southwest of Cairo. In my mind this trip was to be the last of my experiments: it never came off because war, breaking out in Europe, set me to other things.

Ever since my early days at Cambridge I had loved England with a somewhat ridiculous fervor; now that she was threatened by smooth German bullies I had to take a hand in the war. I soon found that there were obstacles in the way: my ignorance of the technicalities of war, my age (I was forty-three), my waistline which tended to expand, but mainly my nationality, for I was a Belgian, a neutral, and under no circumstances would I be employed so long as my wretched country kept out of the war.

The Germans solved my problem on May 10, 1940, by

invading the Low Countries, but it was not till the following September that I got commissioned as a Second Lieutenant in His Majesty's Forces. I got round the Medical officer, who was young and, I suppose, romantic, by laying my cards on the table with false candor. At my age, I said, and with my special qualifications, my ambition was to be posted to Intelligence; an office job, to be sure but in which I hoped to make myself useful. I knew my limitations and that there was not the remotest possibility of anyone thinking of employing me in a fighting capacity. Middleaged men, however, have their vanities: mine was to be passed as fit in the highest medical category. It couldn't do anybody any harm, so perhaps he would see his way to put me down as A 1. He smiled and agreed that an office job was indeed my obvious destination; he gave me a cursory look over and filled the forms as I had suggested.

Thus armed and bringing to the notice of the proper persons my knowledge of Arabic and my experience of the desert, I got myself posted to the Libyan Arab Force, a body of Senussi Arab volunteers, which was then being raised with the intention of training it for guerilla warfare.

Our men were drawn from the tens of thousands of refugees, survivors of Graziani's planned massacres, who had succeeded in escaping from Cyrenaica to Egypt.

Alone, isolated from the outer world, they had fought for nineteen years against the Italian invaders with weapons and ammunition captured from the enemy. The struggle continued with varying fortunes until 1929, when, General Graziani having massacred more than half the population, the Arabs at last ,submitted to the foreign conqueror. Now they were eager to take up once more the fight.

I can't claim that the Libyan Arab Force fulfilled the expectations of our men—or my own. Four battalions, of which I commanded one, moved into Cyrenaica after it had been liberated for the second time. Their role turned out to be that of a police force. When the Germans under Rommel pushed the British out once more, the commander of one of our battalions let himself deliberately be overrun, fought for a while in the enemy rear, and eventually marched it back to our lines, two hundred and thirty miles through enemy territory. Two men who will appear frequently in this story distinguished themselves in this difficult operation: Bob Yunnie, a Scottish insurance agent, recently commissioned after serving one year in the ranks, and an Arab officer, Sa'ad 'Ali Rahuma, an old scoundrel to be sure, cantankerous, vain and untruthful, but a man with a great knowledge of the ways of his own people, and immense cunning.

My own battalion had a small share of rear-guard fighting. When it was ordered back to Egypt, I left it by a friendly arrangement, and attached myself to an armored car regiment, the King's Dragoon Guards with which I did some patrolling. But all too soon it was also ordered to Egypt for a refit, and I found myself back in the Libyan Arab Force. I succeeded, however, in getting myself appointed to command a new detachment called the Libyan Arab Force Commando and from that moment I never looked back. This was in the early spring of 1942.

POPSKI'S
PRIVATE ARMY

NORTH AFRICAN DESERT

Miles

| 0 | 50 | 100 | 200 | 300 |

— P.P.A.'s Route   ～～ Wadis   ▲▲ Escarpment

--- Easonsmith's Route   ⌁ Sand   o Wells & Tombs

----- Motorable Tracks   ❀ Marshes

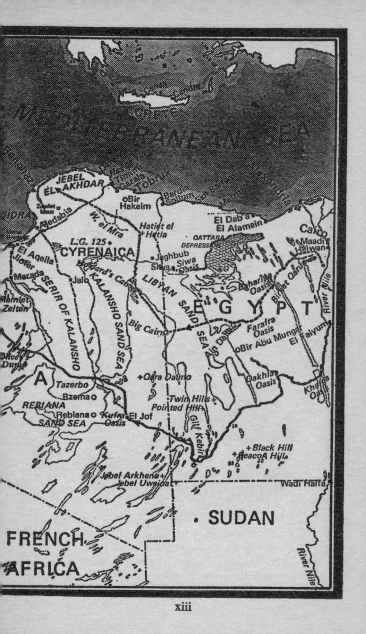

Vladimir Peniakoff

PART I

THE SENUSSIS

1

MY OWN PLANS

AFTER my return from Cyrenaica and my brief service with the K.D.G.'s I knew what I wanted to do: it was to build up a network of intelligence covering the Jebel Akhdar from Derna to Benghazi (now held by the enemy) —to take control of the friendly Arab tribes in that area and, as a minor object, to destroy enemy gasoline dumps. I wanted to blow up dumps only when it would seriously embarrass the enemy at a critical moment and on a large scale; I was completely opposed to undertaking minor acts of violence such as raids and ambushes on isolated trucks or individual soldiers. I considered such small operations to be of no military usefulness whatsoever, and their only possible result would be reprisals on our friends the Arabs and the upsetting of my intelligence organization.,

The Arabs as a source of information had not been untapped. The Long Range Desert Group (L.R.D.G.) ran regular motor patrols in the desert to the south of the Jebel Akhdar: they occasionally left a couple of Arabs at some spot and picked them up again on their return trip three weeks later with such information as they had been able to collect from local gossip.

My aim was to collect intelligence—continuously—over the whole of Axis-occupied Cyrenaica and to be myself on the spot to appreciate the implications and the credibility of the information brought in—to check on news of importance and, if necessary, go and see with my own eyes—to direct and co-ordinate the work of my informants, and to pursue and develop promising clues. I wanted to present the Eighth Army headquarters, not with disconnected pieces of information, but with a co-ordinated picture of the enemy position in Cyrenaica kept up to date day by day.

At that time the German-Italian front line was at

Gazala, west of Tobruk. Their supplies came by road from the ports of Benghazi and Tripoli, respectively three hundred and eight hundred miles in the rear. Their supply dumps and reinforcement camps were placed in the area extending from Benghazi to Derna, the fertile mountainous heart of Cyrenaica which I call, by an extension of the local usage, the Jebel Akhdar—the Green Mountain. Keeping watch on the Jebel Akhdar I would be able to inform the Eighth Army of the supply position of the enemy, and of their movements of troops and equipment.

To achieve my plan I wanted to establish myself permanently in enemy territory and take with me only a small number of Arab soldiers as a personal bodyguard and to handle stores and run errands. Some of these men would be trained in demolitions to form a small striking force for eventual operations against gasoline dumps. For my communications I required two radio sets and British signalers to work them. The bulk of the intelligence work would be done by local Arab civilians. To the intelligence

L.R.D.G. Chevrolet 1½ ton truck

officers at the Eighth Army I gave a hint of what I proposed to do and asked them to keep an eye on my reports; to get the support of the Libyan Arab Force I concealed my hand and spoke only of demolitions.

The indifferent success achieved by the Libyan troops that had gone out to Cyrenaica had already caused the disbandment of one of the five battalions, and further retrenchments were likely. The officer commanding the force hoped that small spectacular stunts by his newly formed Commando might, if properly advertised, help to avert the axe and thus preserve some substance to his command.

Middle East Headquarters, whose sanction was requested for the scheme, were equally favorable for the reason that at a stage in the war when major reverses were following one another in a depressing succession, any positive achievement, even very small, was welcome to maintain morale. The spirits of staff officers need more watching over even than those of the rank and file, for they know too much. I am sure my friends at the Middle East Headquarters expected me to provide them with tiny but picturesque successes that would, for a while, take their minds off our big failures in the desert and in Greece. Thus Libyan Arab Force Commando was formed to provide me with the men I wanted for my own schemes.

In fact I was provided with more men than I thought I could employ, but I kept my own counsel and selected, from the whole force, twenty-two Arab other ranks,* one British sergeant to look after them and one Arab officer, all volunteers. Thus, though I was overstaffed, I made a small call on the slender resources of British personnel in the Middle East, an argument to which headquarters were very sensitive.

The Arab officer I had asked to accompany me was Lieutenant Sa'ad 'Ali Rahuma and he had accepted eagerly: he liked me and he liked even more the prospect of becoming a man of importance among his own people.

Everybody helping, my preparations proceeded happily. The whole party received training in demolition work: loud bangs went off day and night in the neighborhood of Mena Camp, and many a forty-gallon drum of gas went up in flames. Sa'ad 'Ali revealed a surprisingly accurate

*Other ranks refer to noncommissioned officers and privates.

knowledge of detonators, primers and fuses, which, added to the fact that he admitted having spent much time in Palestine, led me to suspect that, after he had fled penniless from Cyrenaica following on the Italian pacification in 1931, he had made a living by hiring his services to the Palestinian Arab terrorists. Which was indeed what he had done, as he told me on a later occasion, and a very good living he had made of it, on French gold.

By the end of March, 1942, my little party was ready. Minute as it was, my new command was independent and it was for me the fulfillment of eighteen months of training and waiting. I valued it above its intrinsic importance as a promise for the future; I felt confident that with such a start I should, with good management, be able to keep myself on active operations, without a break, till the end of the war, which I put at ten years hence.

The possibility that I should survive that long seemed remote, and as, while I remained a soldier, I had no use for a private life, before leaving Egypt I set about arranging my affairs on the assumption that I would never come back to be a civilian.

My two young daughters had been evacuated to South Africa the preceding summer and were at school in Durban. I made for their maintenance elaborate financial arrangements which took into account the possibility of an enemy occupation of the Middle East, and then dismissed them from my mind for the next few years. My wife, with whom I had been on terms of friendly disagreement for a long time, was living in Cairo doing a job of a very secret nature at the Middle East Headquarters. We arranged to divorce and got through the proceedings quite easily, through the friendly offices of the Belgian Minister in Egypt.

I sold my car, gave away my civilian clothes, sent to the Red Cross such of my books as I thought might suit hospital patients, and piled up the remainder with pictures, letters and the rest of my belongings into two rooms.

Ties all severed, family responsibilities shaken off and forgotten, and material belongings reduced to the contents of a bedroll, an army pack and two haversacks, and of course the still undefeated Pisspot, I set out cheerfully to fight the war on my own.

The Pisspot ended its career in Matruh, where it was handed over to workshops for a minor repair while I proceeded to Jaghbub with my men. When I returned a few days later to collect it, a friendly young officer said: "I have done you a good turn. That car of yours was not desert worthy—it was not even road worthy, and anyway it was a civilian type. I have returned it to Base as being 'beyond local repair.' Here is your permit: you can get a new car from El Fayed." I thanked him kindly for his good intentions, but the permit of course was of no use to me, as the poor old Pisspot was my private property and not an army vehicle at all. Thus it ended ingloriously, on a scrap heap in Egypt.

2

WADI BUMA

IMPROVISATION and dash are foreign to my nature, unknown risks make me uncomfortable: I am never so happy as when I can spend my time making cautious preparations. Slow and unhurried, I have of course many times deliberately let golden opportunities slip by, unused, because I didn't feel ready for them; but, on the other hand, every one of my enterprises has had some measure of success, and my losses have always been low and easy to make good.

A set plan, worked out to minute details is not what I mean by preparedness: on the contrary, there is no more formidable obstacle to success. What I like to do is to go myself beforehand over the country and get the feel of the plains, the mountains and the valleys; the sand, the rocks and the mud. At the same time, I listen to the local gossip, find out who commands the enemy and what are his pastimes—who my friends are and how far they are prepared to help me and what are the presents that will please. Then, when I come back later with my men to carry out my evil schemes, I can let the plan take care of itself. If I have got a picture in my mind of the general conditions and a clear view of what I want to achieve, if I know roughly what there is over the next hill and the one after, I needn't worry: a workable plan of action will present itself to my mind when required—with no painful striving.

This will explain why, having brought my party as far as Jaghbub Oasis, I left it there to proceed on a preliminary to the Jebel with only Sa'ad 'Ali Rahuma, one Arab called Hamed, and a stock of cigarettes, tea, sugar, calico to be used as goodwill gifts and curren-

anyone who had business in enemy-occupied Cyrenaica booked a passage on the Long Range Desert Group "Bus Service" to the enemy's back door. The Jebel Akhdar, the Green Mountain ranges, run parallel with the Mediterranean coast, one hundred and seventy miles from Derna to Benghazi. They rise abruptly from the sea in precipitous rocky cliffs, to reach a maximum altitude of nearly three thousand feet, then drop in a succession of ranges of decreasing height to the great inland desert plain, fifty miles south of the coast. The northern slopes which receive a fair rainfall (I have even seen a thin covering of snow at Beda Littoria on a January morning) are covered in evergreen oaks where the forest has not been cut down for the Italian agricultural settlements. Going south the trees grow stunted and scarce, to be replaced by scrub and finally by scanty desert bushes along the dry wadi beds. Farther south again the gravelly sands and rocks are barren, with only a few clumps of bushes here and there, flowering and sweet smelling during the short spring and dry the rest of the year.

This inner desert, completely uninhabited, stretches over eight hundred miles of hills and rolling plains to the high peaks of the Tibesti Mountains, where a few primitive tribesmen pasture their flocks—then another eight hundred barren miles to Lake Chad in French Equatorial Africa. Isolated in the waste, five hundred miles from the coast, the tiny Cufra (Kufra) Oasis lies in a depression where, having flowed underground one thousand miles from the equatorial rain belt, sweet water wells up and irrigates palm groves and gardens of millet.

Debased town Arabs live in stone houses in the coastal towns, Benghazi and Derna, and inland at El Merj, which the Italians call Barce, in its rich, red, cup-shaped plain. The remainder of the Jebel and the foothills to the south are the home of the true nomads, who pitch their tents from well to well as they follow their grazing flocks. Except along the trade routes to the oases of Jalo and Cufra, they never wander into the southern spaces where their cattle would find neither pastures nor water.

These truly desert wastes were used for their travels by the Long Range Desert Group. I have avoided tiresome initials so far but this unit will appear often in my story and it will be called L.R.D.G. Its full designation Long Range Desert Group appears now for the last time.

The L.R.D.G., having solved many problems of desert

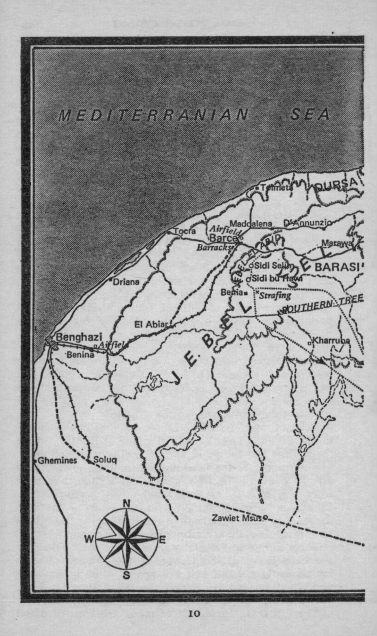

MEDITERRANIAN SEA

Tennet

DURSA

Tocra

Maddalena

D'Annunzio

Airfield
Barce

Marawa

Barracks

E BARASI

Driana

Sidi Selian

Sidi bu Hawi

Benia

Strafing

SOUTHERN TREE

El Abiar

J E B E L

Benghazi

Airfiel

Kharruba

Benina

Ghemines

Soluq

N

W   E

S

Zawiet Msus

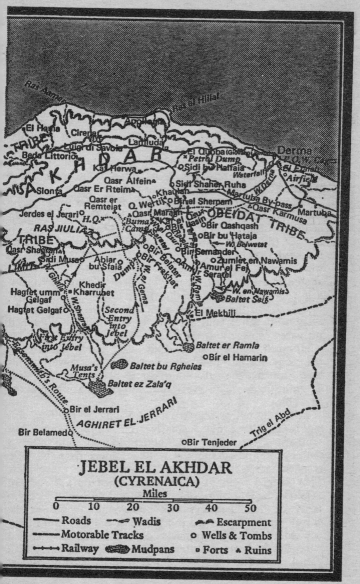

JEBEL EL AKHDAR
(CYRENAICA)
Miles

| 0 | 10 | 20 | 30 | 40 | 50 |

—— Roads   ⌒⌒ Wadis   ⌒⌒⌒ Escarpment
- - - Motorable Tracks   o Wells & Tombs
•⌒•⌒• Railway   ⌒⌒⌒ Mudpans   ▫ Forts   ⌂ Ruins

II

travel and navigation, ran their motor patrols from Egypt
to Tripoli, twelve hundred miles, with a soul-satisfying
regularity. Except through enemy action they had never
lost a truck nor missed a rendezvous. A free, cheerful,
tireless, efficient body of bearded men, they were the most
pleasant companions I have ever had. I graded their
squadrons, drawn from various parts of the Empire, on a
scale of human excellence, which ranged from the New
Zealanders high on top through the Rhodesians and the
British Yeomanry down to the squadron drawn from the
Guards Regiments. The New Zealanders, farmers in civil
life, took easily to a roaming life in the desert. They had
from the first a resourceful, happy assurance and set a
standard which the others tried to follow.

Colonel Bagnold, a shy, scholarly man, had founded the
L.R.D.G. in the very early days of the war, with the help
of Prendergast, Shaw and Clayton, who had been with him
on his travels of exploration before the war. He had
invented a sun compass and adapted astronomical methods
which made navigation easy and accurate; his trucks,
altered and improved, could, with the help of steel channels (another of his inventions), drive over all the obstacles found in the desert. A condenser devised by him did
away with water consumption by the truck engines and
increased considerably the range of the vehicles.

His next brilliant achievement was getting the pick of
the army for his unit, and such was the power of his
leadership that he even contrived to fire Guardsmen with
an enthusiasm which overrode their customary ill-natured
squabbles.

L.R.D.G. patrols of five 1½-ton trucks, carrying five
men each, drove out regularly from Egypt through the
southern desert, their undisputed domain, and after a
journey of a thousand miles, like raiders from the sea,
reached undetected the coastal area held by the enemy.
They ranged from Tripoli to Lake Chad on a variety of
missions, mainly of reconnaissance and survey. The regularity of their journeys was occasionally upset by the
enemy, but such was the excellence of the men and of the
equipment that geographical obstacles and mechanical
breakdowns never interfered with their schedule. Each
patrol carried a radio set and remained in daily contact
with headquarters.

On the evening of April 25, 1942, five days out of Siwa

with Captain Hunter's patrol, I sighted the Jebel, a brown smudge on the northern horizon. The next morning we topped a low rise and trundled down into a plain covered in flowers and dotted with acacia bushes, the lower reaches of Wadi el Ghelta, near Hagfet Gelgaf. Sheep, goats and a few camels grazed the sweet-smelling brush, the first life we had seen since we left Siwa, three hundred and eighty miles away. We pulled up under cover of a steep wadi bank, a few hundred yards from a village of tents, and I sent Sa'ad 'Ali to talk to the Arabs.

An hour later he returned with half a dozen of them and we squatted on the sand in the shade of some acacia bushes. Sa'ad took me aside to advise me not to waste much time or treasure on our guests as they were men of no importance. Sa'ad 'Ali's appearance was ludicrous. He had the build of a jockey, wore an ill-fitting, soiled and crumpled British officer's tunic (with a dirty purple and white ribbon of the Military Cross) and slacks, his wizened, dark face under a cap-comforter, with brown monkey eyes vivacious, sharp and clever and a humorous smile that broke up his face in hundreds of creases and wrinkles. His wit was sharp; after he had scored a point he would break into a disarming silent laugh, mouth open like a child. His mannerisms were many and catching: and I still use a grimace to express playfully indignant surprise which I acquired from him.

Our guests, simple shepherds of an obscure subtribe, would in more prosperous times have worn colored braided vests and full-bottomed Turkish pantaloons, yellow elastic-sided boots and a white cloth turban wound over a brown felt skullcap. As it was, after two years of war and blockade, their apparel was mostly of ragged castoff garments from the three armies which had marched up and down their country. Their dignity was only saved by the jerd, a rectangular piece of woolen material fourteen feet long and four feet across, which every Arab of Cyrenaica wraps nobly round his body, toga fashion. Sa'ad 'Ali once said: "The Italians showed us in a film the glory of the Romans. *We,* obviously, not *they,* are the true descendants of the ancient Romans for we still dress as they did." And he was quite right, for the jerd *is* a toga.

I passed cigarettes round to our guests, who helped themselves with a lightening of their solemn countenances, but Sa'ad 'Ali, who is a desperate smoker and couldn't suffer any waste of our not too abundant stock of tobacco, lifted his voice in formal tones and said: "Your Excellency the Major, honored friends, brethren! Our guests here are distinguished sheiks of the Barasi tribe; true Arabs and good Senussis all, they do not smoke. They would not appear discourteous and refuse their host's gift but I think the major will not want to embarrass them by insisting that they light obnoxious cigarettes. All peoples have their customs and what is right and decorous for Englishmen can be unseemly for Senussis." The faces of our guests fell at the homily and with lordly gestures they handed back their cigarettes to Sa'ad, who collected the booty with an air of veiled distaste. He then turned to me and gave one of his infernal grins.

Hamed, our retainer, brought forth an enamel teapot the size of a fist, filled it to one quarter with tea leaves, then up to the brim with water, and put it to boil on the embers of a fire of dry twigs. The tea glasses, stemless and the size of small old-fashioned liqueur glasses, he disposed on a tray, side by side in a row. When the pot boiled over and hissed on the embers, he filled the glasses, pouring deftly from high up in one continuous motion. He then poured back the contents of the glasses into the pot and put it to boil a second time. The process was repeated twice; he then took a sip from one of the glasses, smacked his lips, and poured all the glasses back into the teapot for another boil. Filled again with the by now dark brown and frothy infusion, the glasses were handed round in order of precedence, with much polite disputation between myself and my guests as to who should be served last. The order finally achieved was: guests in order of seniority—myself —Sa'ad 'Ali—Hamed—retainers down to the last camel boy ('but not the children).

While we slowly sipped the hot tea, with sucking noises as loud as we could achieve without burning our lips, Hamed poured a handful of sugar over the leaves in the pot, filled up with water and boiled it once more with the same ritual. This second round was served out, and while it was being consumed Hamed added more sugar to the pot, stuffed it full of dry mint sprigs, topped up with water and gave it three more boilings. When the third round had been disposed of our duty to the guests was complete and we sat back on our haunches and talked business.

This tea drinking was not only for me a ritual of hospitality: I got to like the hot, astringent, sweet beverage so much that, guests or no guests, as long as our supplies allowed, I drank it two or three times a day. Particularly welcome it was at the end of a hungry night's riding, when it dispelled weariness and cleared the brain. My British companions on later excursions nearly all took a fancy to it and Arab tea drinking became a necessity more imperious than tobacco. I won't try to describe the taste of this drink but I should say that it has nothing in common with our English tea and it does not perform the same function.

Washing up after this very first of our tea parties Hamed tripped and sent flying five of our twelve glasses. They fell on rock and were smashed. This clumsiness set Sa'ad 'Ali against Hamed once and for all: "The man is no good," he said, "who can't be trusted with tea glasses. He is a fool and no soldier and will only get us into trouble." He turned out to be right in his judgment.

We got no other information from our guests than this: that no enemy patrols had come their way at all this season, which was no surprise to us, for no occasion could have brought them to this backwater. Of the gossip from farther north these Arabs had no knowledge whatever, and with a small gift of tea and sugar we left them to their cattle.

That afternoon, April 26, the L.R.D.G. trucks took us as far as they could go up the rocky foothills and left Sa'ad 'Ali, Hamed, a British officer called Chevalier and myself amongst the wild boulders of Wadi Shegran.

Thirteen rocky, broken miles to the north of where we stood, at Jerdes el Jerari, the enemy had a small post connected by a motorable track with Slonta on the southern tarmac road, along which drove most of the German supply trucks. Barce, Beda Littoria, and Derna were the main Italian towns in the Jebel; the area between the northern and the southern road was sprinkled with Sicilian farming settlements and army camps, and most of the forest had been cleared in such a way that we could venture there only with extreme caution. But to the south of the southern road the country, being wild and poorly provided with tracks, was seldom visited by the enemy. Again between the northern road and the coast, where the escarpment plunged down to the sea, the warlike Dursa tribe kept their country fairly free of Italian or German troops. Ninety-five miles to the west were our own lines extending from Gazala to Bir Hakeim.

We had, however, a friend much closer than that: Wadi Shegran had been used for a long time by the L.R.D.G. as a back door to the enemy positions. John Haselden had been picked up here the preceding November after the unsuccessful attempt on General Rommel's life at Beda Littoria, and three weeks before my own arrival Major Chapman had been left here with two British radio operators to investigate the possibilities of a commando raid on the traffic of the northern tarmac road. According to an arrangement made on the radio, he had posted an Arab to contact us in Wadi Shegran. This man, whom we found driving a small flock of sheep and goats, told us that Major Chapman had established himself in a canyonlike wadi less than an hour's walk away, and undertook to go and fetch him. Chapman, long and lanky, had been a schoolmaster in Cairo until he joined the army, leaving in Egypt a wife and three small children about whom he worried ceaselessly. With a studious, academic mind and a hypochondriacal disposition, he suffered nonsense from nobody, and applied himself with no delusions of glamor to the tasks he had set himself.

He arrived in the dark of the night and was rather disgruntled: the Shegran-Slonta line of approach had been overworked, the Italians had heard rumors and were very nervous. In particular a man called Selim, of the Barasi tribe, who had been our main contact in this area, was strongly suspected by the Italian commander at Slonta of helping the British and had been interrogated by him several times. Selim himself turned up the next night and confirmed the bad news. He had been questioned once more by the Italians on his pro-British activities that very day and he was taking a very dangerous step in visiting us. I immediately saw that it was unfair to compromise him any further and I decided to break new ground.

Sa'ad 'Ali approved: he distrusted the Barasi anyway. Full of prejudice, his words were: "The Barasi are all informers, let us go to the Obeidat"—the largest and most powerful of all Jebel tribes whose territory extends from Lamluda to beyond Tobruk in the east. At very first light Sa'ad set out on foot by himself to find transport, leaving me with Hamed and the stores amongst the boulders of the

Shegran. Chevalier, who had come out to help with the projected commando raid, stuck to his original plan and went into hiding in Chapman's canyon waiting for an opportunity to be guided north to the road.

In the evening Sa'ad returned with three decrepit, ragged Arabs leading a horse, two camels and a donkey. Avarice alone had induced them to hire out their broken-down animals, and they studiously ignored the fact that I was a British officer. Sa'ad wouldn't remain where we were one moment longer: he hustled and bustled, our small stores were loaded on the unwilling animals and off we went in the night. I rode the horse, with a back-breaking Arab saddle, Sa'ad 'Ali perched himself on the donkey on top of an enormous bundle—the rest of the party walked.

Past Sidi Musa our cross-country journey took us, a gray sheik's tomb, then under the cliffs of Ras Juliaz where we entered the forest, climbing all the time. Dawn found us near Qasr er Remteiat, a ruined Roman—or perhaps Greek—castle on a hilltop which gives its name to the district. Here Sa'ad 'Ali called a halt in a clearing of the forest, a wide meadow dotted with bushes and cut deeply by dry watercourses lined with trees. I appreciated the cunning choice of the camping site: the watercourses were deep enough to give us good cover and shade, and anyone approaching us from the woods would be in full view across the clearing. We paid off our guides and their beasts, and they slunk off and were gone in a moment in the early twilight. We kept the horse, however, having found it vigorous in spite of its sorry appearance. A few pounds of tea and two lengths of calico were the price paid for our mount, cheap enough indeed, but it had the Italian Army brand and was a dangerous possession for a poor Arab.

We sipped our tea; Sa'ad 'Ali scratched himself and said: "I haven't had a wash since we left Siwa, I am itchy all over. Now is the time for a bath." With a grubby towel and a cake of soap from his haversack, he disappeared over the bank, to come back after an hour shaven and shiny. Hamed followed then to perform the same function. I thought that so much cleanliness was against the rules of the game and I felt there was something vaguely heroic about an eight days' growth of beard, but Sa'ad wouldn't have it and insisted that Hamed on his return should take me to the well for a wash.

Starting on each side of the broad top of a hill were two low dry-course stone walls: they ran down the slope at a converging angle to meet after a few hundred yards over the mouth of a cistern hewn out of the rock and lined with masonry. When the torrential winter showers fall the walls act as the sides of a funnel to collect and guide the rushing waters down the hillside into the cistern. Thousands of these cisterns are dotted over the Jebel, nearly all of Roman build and some of them as large as the inside of a fair-sized house. They are the only water supply in the whole of the mountains for there are no true wells, nor, with the exception of the Wadi Derna, any permanent running streams, and the inhabitants are entirely dependent on them to water their cattle and for their own drink. Yet the labor-hating Arabs have let their Roman cisterns fall into disrepair, save a very few.

When I started undressing Hamed left me, with a can and a length of rope, at the square opening to the cistern, and went and squatted with his back to me at a little distance, for these Arabs are modest and would not be seen in their nakedness. In time I nearly reached to the Arab standard of cleanliness but, in common with all my British companions, I never could quite rid myself of the fancy that these frequent washings took something away of the romance of our boyish adventures.

As I had put myself entirely in Sa'ad 'Ali's hands there wasn't much I could say when, returning to camp, I found him not furthering warlike designs but preparing to bake bread. Though not at all religious—I seldom saw him pray except in company and then very perfunctorily—Sa'ad had all the good Senussis' distaste for tinned food—infidel food—and would consume it only in the most extreme emergency. Hence his resolve to bake bread. He scraped a hollow in the ground, lined it with flat stones and lit a blazing bonfire over it of dead tree branches. On a flat rock he mixed his flour, water and salt, kneaded the dough, slapped it and banged it, white to the elbows and grinning like a cheerful devil. When the fire had burned itself out to embers he scraped the stones clean, put flat round cakes of dough on the hot stones, and covered them again with embers. He then seemed to lose interest, walked away, busied himself with other things and finally lay down under a tree and dozed off. Suddenly he jumped up, called to Hamed: "The bread is ready!" and they both scraped off the embers hurriedly lest the critical moment be passed and the bread burned. The loaves, about a foot across and two inches in thickness, were pulled out and set to cool. The outer crust, black and charred, had to be scraped off: the bread itself, though unleavened, was firm, crisp and delicious. We made a meal of it with cheese and tea and then we composed ourselves to sleep.

At sunset Sa'ad 'Ali sent Hamed to bring in the hobbled horse from its grazing. He intended our man to seek out Metwallah bu Jibrin, who he thought might be with his people at one of the wells near Remteiat, and ask him to come and visit us. Hamed was instructed carefully where to go, who to see and what to say, and definitely ordered to be back within thirty-six hours. Having repeated his instructions, he rode off in the gathering darkness.

We spent the next day, Sa'ad and I, sleeping and talking. The following morning Hamed had not returned, nor did he appear during the day, so we slept and talked again. The only living creature apart from ourselves was an owl that we saw flitting from tree to tree. The Jebel, with its green trees and abundant undergrowth, it strikingly empty of wild life. The reason is that there is no open water for the creatures to drink from. This owl, however, managed to make a living and in the general quiet we heard its dismal cries at intervals by day and by night.

Buma is the local name for an owl, and Sa'ad, who was getting impatient at Hamed's delay, addressed the bird: "Oh Buma, as you see we are still here in Wadi Buma near Qasr (castle) Buma, drinking from Bir (well) Buma. We have come out to fight the armies of the enemy and all we have found is a Buma. In our old days, the major and I, if we can still talk like men and do not hoot like you, Buma, we shall sit drinking tea and recall our brave deeds at the Battle of the Buma." The bird gave a few hoots and Sa'ad took up: "Oh Buma, don't mock poor old Sa'ad. He trusted Hamed, the fool who broke the glasses, with his last horse, he trusted him and now he has got lost, and the horse has broken a leg. When we go back to Egypt, if ever we do, our friends will ask: How many Christians have you slain, oh warriors?' and we shall answer: 'Of the Christians we killed not one, but we sat and listened to a Buma.'"

I guessed what was on Sa'ad's mind. He wanted to go himself and fetch Metwallah bu Jibrin or some other

trusty friend but he feared that if he left me alone I might
think he had deserted me. On the other hand we couldn't
both go together on account of our stores, which it would
have been inconvenient to abandon, but mainly because
the first approach is a matter in which great care must be
taken to compromise nobody, and I was too obviously a
British officer and my Arabic was too poor to risk a
meeting with the wrong person. So I said to Sa'ad: "Don't
abuse the Buma, she is good company and I will be very
happy with her."

He pulled a comical face at me but all he said was: "We
shall see tomorrow morning."

The next morning, the third since our arrival in Wadi
Buma, Hamed had not returned. Sa'ad packed a small
haversack and departed. His advice to me was to lie
low—if any Arab discovered me I was to say that my
camel had strayed and my guide, my "khabir," had gone
after it. Of my destination I had better say nothing except
that I was traveling north. If after two days Sa'ad wasn't
back, I was to make my way back southwest to the
Shegran as best I could.

I was left alone with the Buma and I sat down under the
bank to read Philip Guedalla's *Life of Wellington*. Next
morning I was still under the bank, alone in a silent
landscape and utterly happy. I had done everything that
had to be done, nothing remained but to wait for my plans
to mature and during the interval I was free, without
worry and at peace with myself. Such periods of waiting
were the only rests I took during the war; they offered so
complete a relaxation that I never felt the strain of
action.

Toward evening I saw movement under the trees at the
far corner of the clearing and a moment later peace was
shattered as a waving rider came galloping across the
meadow and pulled up in front of me with a hint of a
flourish. Sa'ad 'Ali leapt down, greeted me briefly and
inquired after the Buma.

"I have brought Metwallah bu Jibrin. He is in the woods
with his friends. In the saddle, Major, in the saddle, we are
moving on." Sa'ad was a hustler, strangely for an Arab; he
made me climb on to his mare to make a dignified
appearance before his friends, but the short Arab stirrups,
adjusted to Sa'ad's diminutive legs, dangled just below my
knees and rather spoiled the nobleness of my bearing.

However Metwallah, standing under the trees with two of his friends, gave me a grave welcome when I hoisted myself out of the saddle, and after the formal introduction and compliments, he asked me to accept his hospitality for that night.

In the background stood the horses and three of Metwallah's camels with their attendants. These Sa'ad took with him to load our stores and on his return he wouldn't let us tarry over our courtesies but, still in his hustling mood, he said: "Tonight we shall talk. Now we want to get away from the Buma," and turning to me he gave a low derisive owlish hoot.

3

COUNTRY LIFE

NIGHT had fallen when we dismounted amongst dim trees and rocks. Dogs were barking in the distance. Metwallah pushed on to his tent to make sure that the coast was clear, found all safe and came back to lead us in. I stopped low on entering as the roof reached to four feet from the ground and I found myself in the reception half of Metwallah's home—on one side a flimsy canvas partition cut off the domestic half where women and children lived; on the three other sides the low outer curtains were rolled up to let in the breeze. Wooden sofas covered with carpets and a few hard pillows were all the furniture, and on them we squatted down, our legs folded under us, in the light of two oil lamps of the old-fashioned type with glass chimneys.

A wooden bowl, the size of a large wash basin, filled with sour milk, was handed round and we drank deeply in turns, holding up the heavy bowl with both hands. Sour milk, from goats and ewes mixed, called leban locally, was to be my standard food as long as I stayed with the Arabs, and I thrived on it; it is not considered as a real meal by the Arabs but more as a refreshment offered to the thirsty and hungry traveler the moment he arrives.

An hour later, in preparation for the dinner, a boy came round with a metal hand basin bearing a cake of soap on its raised middle. He poured water over our soaped hands from a long-spouted pitcher and then handed us a towel. We all squatted on the ground round a low table which was then brought in and on which was placed a bowl of steaming 'esh. This is a meal of barley flour flakes, boiled in water and soaked in melted butter. On festive occasions it is sometimes sprinkled with sugar. We turned up the sleeve on our right arm, said: "In the name of God the merciful, the compassionate"—by way of Grace—and dipped into the bowl in silence. As soon as we had had our fill, it was removed to be finished off by the minor guests and attendants, squatting outside the tent, and in came a boiled kid on a brass tray. Metwallah, our host, tore the joint to pieces with his hands, handed me the choice shoulder piece on a flat loaf of hobs, bread similar to that baked by Sa'ad 'Ali in the Wadi Buma, by way of plate; the others helped themselves (the host always last—and he eats hurriedly after he has made sure that the guests are well looked after) and we all fell to, still in silence.

Melted butter had been poured over the kid's meat, making it a rather messy dish, and it required more skill than I then possessed to eat it off a limp loaf held in my left hand, without staining my clothes, and seated on the ground. Noticing my awkwardness, my host spread a hand towel over my knees and regretted he could not provide a Roman (meaning European) board and proper cutlery, but, he added laughing, "Now that you have come to live with the Arabs you will have to learn to eat as we do." To which I agreed and indeed I soon became skillful at eating in the natural way, with the fingers. When I had finished Metwallah offered me a piece of meat torn off the bone he was holding, which I accepted, but when I refused a further helping no more food was pressed on me, for such is the etiquette amongst the Senussis. Not so in Egypt, where good manners require the guest to be stuffed beyond his will.

As soon as we had finished, Metwallah called for his servants: the tray with the reduced carcass was removed and soap and water went round once more. We washed our hands and lips, rubbed our teeth with a soapy forefinger, rinsed our mouths and then lay back on the pillows. Glasses of water were handed round and a little later tea was brought in. Hardly a word had been spoken during the meal but now the gates were opened and talk flowed.

Metwallah's position was unique among the Senussi Arabs who helped the British during the enemy occupation of their country: cattle owner and tradesman, he led, in peacetime, a dual life; in his town house in Derna, he was a wealthy trader with connections overseas, in Europe and in Egypt—in the Jebel with his flocks, a traditional nomad Arab. Though very wealthy, he was not a sheik and had no political ambitions. What the nature of his participation had been in the long struggle against the Italian invader

from 1912 to 1929, I have not been able to find out with
certainty. I don't think he fought in person; I have always
thought of him as a banker with a great devotion to the
cause, helping to finance the poor Senussi Army—at no
loss to himself. In the present crisis he had taken a definite
stand on our side and, remaining always carefully in the
background, he preferred cautious help. What I wanted
from him on that first night were his views on the leading
men of his Obeidi tribe, the cynical opinions of a man
through whom passed the main threads of intrigue, but
who, determined to remain behind the scenes, took no
sides in tribal rivalries.

Through the night we gossiped: from sheik to sheik, and
to meaner men too, our talk followed a zigzag course.
Who was a reliable friend and who was halfhearted, who
was vainglorious, who ambitious, who mercenary? To
these Arabs, a closed community, gossip and intrigue are
the very breath of life: Metwallah and Sa'ad 'Ali threw
themselves into the game with passion; and all I did was to
put a question now and then and listen. Sa'ad of course
had been out of the country for many years and his
interests tended to concentrate on events of the old Italian
wars. About two in the morning they were hard at it,
recalling battles long gone by and I let myself go to sleep
on my bench. Later in the night Sa'ad shook me awake,
offered tea, and, much refreshed, I brought my friends
down from the ecstasies of reminiscence to concrete plans
for the morrow: they had talked themselves out and were
ready for action.

While listening to the gossip I had decided that my best
course would be to visit personally as many as possible of
the leading men. My presence in the Jebel, thus openly
advertised, would give them confidence in the ultimate
success of British arms. I would explain my plans, ask for
their co-operation and make them feel that we were all
working together on an important scheme, simple, clear
and perfectly understood. Of course I ran the risk of being
betrayed to the enemy, but I banked on confidence breed-
ing confidence: I thought that, though a man might easily
be tempted to give away a British officer by whom he has
been stealthily summoned to an anxious midnight interview in the woods, he would hesitate to betray a guest who
had walked openly up to his tent and had accepted his
hospitality as a due. Dispensing favors not begging for

them, boldness, not timidity, was, I hoped, the way to acquire prestige and authority. Anyhow, I had much at stake and I could not afford to worry overmuch about risks.

We made a list of the men I would see and worked out a route. With nomads, ever on the move from well to well, visiting is a problem, but Metwallah, wise and encyclopaedic, knew or guessed where everyone was likely to be found. When dawn broke we went out and walked some distance into the woods: I didn't want yet to be seen in the village of tents by a chance visitor. We needed mounts for our trip and Metwallah arranged for a choice to be offered for sale. No good mares were available; we finally picked on two stallions, the best, we thought, of a very sorry lot. Though horsemen all, the Senussi Arabs were very careless of their animals: perhaps the difficulty of feeding them on barley, which, in wartime, was badly needed for human consumption, was the reason, or the fact that the Italians had taken away the best long ago, but I did not see a single horse in good condition. We bargained at leisure and when finally a price was agreed on—so many glasses of tea leaves, so many of sugar and so many cubits of cloth—we had the job to count out our strange money. Sa'ad kept a very small glass for this purpose but piled it conscientiously as high as it would hold. A cubit is the length from the finger tips to the elbow: with a man of Sa'ad's diminutive stature it is a very short measure indeed but, to my surprise, we never had a complaint on that account.

The horses paid for, we hid the bulk of our supplies, which we did not intend to carry with us on our tour, in a dry water cistern. An Arab shepherd was made responsible for the treasure which was all measured out before being stored; a boulder was pushed over the mouth of the cistern and the shepherd undertook to pasture his flock of sheep and goats in the neighborhood and keep an eye on possible looters. Nothing was missing on our return. As Hamed was still abroad, Metwallah provided us with two retainers on horseback.

Hamed returned to me weeks later, footsore, with a long and sad story. He had failed, being indeed a timid fool, to find Metwallah and had gone instead to visit his mother in a distant pasture. Rumor having reached him at last of our whereabouts he had left our horse with his mother and walked back to us. When he was brought to me, crestfallen

and apologetic, I sent him back, tired as he was, to recover
the horse and he finally returned just in time to be
evacuated to Egypt. Such was his inglorious share in our
campaign.

Toward evening we set out, myself, Sa'ad 'Ali Rahuma
and the two boys lent by Metwallah, on the first lap of our
visiting tour. We were very careful, in those early days, to
travel only in the darkness so as not to be seen by casual
travelers who might spread rumors. Later, when my presence in the country was known, officially so to speak, to
thousands and my status as a friend of the Obeidi sheiks
well established, I took to daylight traveling without running into much trouble. We rode across country and as the
enemy always kept to the very few tracks, the risk was
small of meeting him unawares.

I can't remember exactly how long my tour lasted
because I got no regular sleep but only a few hours here
and there, by day or by night, and after a while the
distinction between one day and the next became slightly
blurred. I rode usually most of the night, timing my arrival
at my new host's for the very early morning. Stopping at
some distance from his village of tents I would send in
Sa'ad and one of Metwallah's men to announce my visit.
While they were away I wrapped myself up in a jerd and
slept for an hour or so. Then I would go over to my host's
tent, exchange civilities, drink sour milk and talk while the
meal was being prepared. Generally some of my host's
friends came and shared our dinner. This, by the way, was
invariably similar to the one we had on the first night with
Metwallah. Sour milk, boiled 'esh with melted butter,
followed by boiled kid and barley bread. There was no
other food in the Jebel in those days, and from year end to
year end the daily fare was identical, with the exception, of
course, that meat was only served on festive occasions and
then only if there was time enough to kill a kid, clean it,
and cook it. I found this food satisfying and never tired of
it, though after some months I developed a craving for
fresh vegetables and fruit. But I kept extremely fit and so
did the Arabs, among whom I found practically no disease.

During the afternoon there was more talk in the tent,
with intervals of sleep, and after dark we rode away once
more. On the fifth or the sixth day of this tour of country
houses, having visited several minor characters, I made for

Kaf Herwa to meet Sheik 'Ali bu Hamed el Obeidi. I had got to like him four months previously in Derna when I had judged him to be the most powerful man among the Obeidat. A tall lean man of fifty, with flowing gestures and a soft voice with tender tones covering passionate fires; a subtle brain, a sharp wit, a natural assumption of authority, a knowledge of the Western world, master of intrigue and of the devious route, he led in fact the Obeidi tribe whose nominal head was 'Abdel Qader bu Bridan, an old sheik of over eighty years of age. Before the war (our war), having made his peace with the Italian conqueror, he lived in some splendor, with a house in Derna and another in Alexandria in Egypt where he spent several months each year.

Since the beginning of the present war, although his son was openly with the British in Egypt, a young officer in the Libyan Arab Force, he had, with dextrous duplicity, kept on good terms with the Italians, having led them to believe that his influence alone prevented a general armed rising, not only of the Obeidat but also of the other Jebel tribes. The Italians were very ignorant and with the memory of nineteen years of humiliating rough handling at the hands of the Senussis they easily fell a prey to the Arab bogy. With their German masters keeping in their hands the control of military operations but relying on their despised ally to keep the peace along the lines of communication, the Italians were very nervous; their policy toward their uneasy Arab subjects was a mixture of appeasement and bullying.

'Ali bu Hamed played on their fears and succeeded in maintaining a precarious balance; his advantage was that, with his spies in every place, he was in fact all the time at the heart of the enemy's councils, whereas the Italians, ill-informed and lazy, were double-crossed even by their miserable paid informers. 'Ali bu Hamed had fought the Italians all his life and he hated them; he had no particular love of the British but he wanted us to liberate his country—after the liberation, when it came, he wanted to be in a position of influence with the new masters and he foresaw that their goodwill might help him to succeed 'Abdel Qader bu Bridan as Sheik of the Obeidat, when the old man died. For the Germans he had no particular feeling, though, like many of the Arabs, he gave them the esteem which is due from warrior to warrior. The common saying was: "The Italians are dogs, the Germans are men."

'Ali bu Hamed had to be careful not to give any hold to Italian suspicions: he lived at that time with his family and retainers, not in tents, but in caves called Kaf Herwa in a wadi, wild, to be sure, and difficult of access, but not more than three miles from Acqua Viva, an Italian military post on the main road. I offered to meet him safely, far from his home, but he sent word that, for this first interview he wanted me to be his guest and he would send for me at Qaret Um Alfein the following night. The message added that, as he could speak the Egyptian dialect, there would be no need for a third person to interpret while we talked. This, I knew, was no reflection on my knowledge of Libyan Arabic, poor enough at that time in truth, but a hint that he had no wish to have Sa'ad 'Ali Rahuma as a partner to our discussions, for he disliked and despised my lieutenant whom he considered a mountebank—a brave soldier indeed but too much given to boasting—and of too obscure a tribe to be allowed to patronize an Obeidi sheik.

At midnight 'Ali bu Hamed's messenger arrived at my host's tent, draped in a black jerd and mounted on a black horse. Off we rode into the dark windy night like a couple of ghosts. After an hour's blind riding over broken and rocky country we stopped in a craggy defile where my guide made me dismount, threw his dark jerd over me, asked me to wait and vanished into the night. Later a tall shadow came noiselessly out of the darkness, a hand pressed mine and I heard the well-remembered low melodious voice greet me with anxious solicitude. His arm affectionately pressing mine, 'Ali bu Hamed guided me up the wadi, helped me up a slope, through an unseen crack in the cliff, and lifting a curtain he led me out of the black night into a vast, bright cavern, lit by four dazzling pressure lamps, and all hung with carpets. Carpets underfoot, carpets on the walls and in the center two sprung sofas piled with soft pillows. 'Ali turned to me, disentangled me from my jerd, and putting his hands on my shoulders smiled at me with joy. The stage management was superb and my amazement unfeigned. 'Ali laughed, cut short the usual formal greetings, helped me take off my shoes, made me comfortable on the pillows and clapped his hands. A servant appeared from an inner recess of the cave carrying teapot and glasses. The meal—sour milk, 'esh, boiled kid—followed immediately; we washed, drank more tea and time being short, we talked.

I said: "Sheik 'Ali, my friend, the British Government and your Amir, Sayed Idris el Senussi, knowing the friendship that is between you and me, have sent me to you so that, with your assistance, I may guide, advise and help your people and all the faithful Senussis in the Jebel Akhdar, in their struggle against the common enemy. My Government wants also to be informed of the enemy's intentions, dispositions and strength. Not rumors of a thousand tanks in El Abiar which turn out to be nothing more than a water truck and two motorcycles in Lamluda —we want facts. To get them we want spies in enemy headquarters, in the airfields, in the dumps and the stores. We want eyes watching every road and every harbor, day and night.

"Lastly," I said, "the British Government may at a future date request me to bring in raiding parties to blow up dumps. This will only happen when our armies will be marching forward and the work will be done in such a way that no Arabs can possibly be implicated." I said no more on this subject but reverted quickly to my first point: "As to advising the Arabs on their best course of action," I said, "I have noticed during the last few days that some of our friends are hotheaded and want arms to fight the enemy. I must tell you that such action is precisely what we don't want. Pinpricks against the Italians will not help our army, they will bring disastrous reprisals against the Arabs, which we will not be able to prevent, and my Government will lose its eyes and its ears. We don't want direct action yet, later perhaps—not now." 'Ali bu Hamed said: " 'Abdel Qader bu Bridan is very old but his blood is still hot. He wants to fight. He believes the war is nearly won and that if we don't move now we will miss our chance—then the English will think we did nothing to help. He has many friends."

I saw his difficulty and I told him I intended calling a conference of all the Obeidi sheiks under 'Abdel Qader and I would find means of damping their ardor without shaking their faith in the British victory. "You and I can persuade them," I said. "But nobody need know that we have made our plans together beforehand." 'Ali bu Hamed nodded dreamily: "It is better that way. Now what infor-

mation will you want about the enemy?" I told him—in
great detail—and he undertook to expand his network of
spies to meet my requirements. His main source of information were Italian-speaking Arabs employed as servants
in headquarters and messes. The Italian officers spoke
quite freely in their presence and left documents lying on
desks, never suspecting that their ragged servants understood and even read their language. At night the servants
met friends in the street or under the tents of neighboring
shepherds—words were exchanged and later a rider disappeared into the night with a well-memorized message.

'Ali bu Hamed promised to arrange for messages to be
transmitted to my headquarters when it would be established. "They won't come from me,"—I nodded acquiescence—"Sheik 'Abdel Jelil bu Tayeb will see to it."
"He is a man of honor," I said. "You and I need not meet
again in private. It is better so." There was no need to
dissemble with 'Ali bu Hamed: we understood one another
perfectly. He gave me the names of the men he wanted to
be invited to my conference of sheiks and we parted with
few words, the night being nearly spent.

I reached Qaret Um Alfein before dawn, roused Sa'ad
'Ali Rahuma and set out to call on 'Abdel Aziz bu Yunes
whose tents were pitched five miles away in a dreary steep
wadi of black shingle near Bir el Dei. I had picked on this
vain and very stupid young man, thickset with a broad
black moustache, because he was a nephew to old Sheik
'Abdel Qader bu Bridan. He entertained the foolish hope
of succeeding his uncle as Sheik of the Obeidat, instead of
which he came to an untimely end a few months later for
his betrayal of me to General Piatti, the Italian Governor
of Cyrenaica. But when Sa'ad 'Ali walked into his tent that
morning and announced my visit, he was delighted and
relieved because he had feared I might call on 'Ali bu
Hamed, the rival claimant to the succession, and not on
him.

We were given a princely reception; Sa'ad 'Ali, cheered,
I suppose at having avoided a snubbing interview with his
old enemy, was in an uproarious mood. He cracked jokes
with our many fellow guests at the dinner party and called
to the old lady (our host's mother) behind the canvas
partition, claiming that he had been a suitor of hers thirty
years ago. The old crone even came crouching from under
the curtain and shyly shook hands with me; she took heart

under the playful banter and with a mischievous twinkle in her old eyes protested that she had never as much as looked at that wizened little monkey. She then retired to her side of the partition and we started talking business. She, and the other women of the household, could of course hear every word that was spoken but neither then, nor in any tent nor on any occasion did a secret leak out through women's gossip.

The business of the day of course was the sheiks' conference and it pleased everyone. Here at last was official recognition of the Arab cause: not dark midnight confabulations between an unknown British agent and an obscure shepherd, underhand meetings behind bushes that led seemingly to nothing, but a full dress gathering of all the stars in the Senussi world called by a British officer in uniform, specially sent for the purpose by his Government, and the Senussi spiritual leader, Sayed Idris el Senussi. Kaf el Qsur was chosen as a suitably central and sufficiently concealed spot for the meeting and the date fixed at twelve days hence to give time for the most distant sheiks to arrive.

Sheik 'Abdel Qader bu Bridan's only surviving son (the others had all been killed in the Italian wars), a delicate youth of seventeen, was with us that day, staying with our host, his cousin. He was dispatched to summon his father from Mekhili, fifty miles to the south. Such was the enthusiasm that the boy did not wait for the end of our council: he learned his message word for word, mounted his mare and departed. An Arab does not prepare for a journey: he wraps his jerd around him and is gone. Food and water will be got from Arab tents on the way.

By midnight all the messengers had left to deliver the invitations—in my name and that of 'Abdel Qader bu Bridan. Overcome with weariness from much talking I curled up on the wooden couch and slept till dawn. At daybreak Sa'ad 'Ali rode away, bound for Metwallah's tent at Er Rteim. They were to be responsible for the commissariat: we reckoned that between our guests and their retainers, eighty men at least would have to be fed for three days at Kaf el Qsur and I relied on Metwallah to provide food and servants in a style suitable to a historic occasion.

Meanwhile with 'Abdel Aziz and two of his men, I went down to have a look at the enemy traffic on the road, two

miles away. It was not the tarmac but a very good
motorable track, which we called the Martuba by-pass: I
suspected that it took most of the traffic going westward to
the enemy main forces at Gazala, avoiding the tiresome
descent from the escarpment to Derna and up again to El
Ftaiah, and I planned to establish a permanent watch on
the track. On this occasion 'Abdel Aziz showed sense and
took me to a spot from which a good long stretch of the
road was visible in both directions. Cover was not too
good but sufficient for my purposes. We left our mounts
behind a sheik's tomb called Sidi Shaher Ruha and proceeded over a broken plain rather sparsely grown with
scrub till I stopped and made myself comfortable under a
bush forty yards from the track. Three men on foot are
not very conspicuous and anyway army drivers never take
their eyes off the road, so the chances of being noticed
were slender and the lack of shade made it unlikely that a
convoy would stop here for the midday rest.

It was a busy day on the track that morning: a steady
stream of vehicles went by in both directions and from
where I sat I could see the faces of the soldiers as they
drove by. There is something deeply satisfying in watching
the enemy war machine from the wrong side of the fence
and this, my first opportunity, gave me much pleasure. A
snooper's enjoyment, no doubt, but marred by no guilty
conscience; with, indeed, a sense of virtuous achievement
and a happy knowledge of having outwitted the enemy. I
had never seen so many Germany soldiers in all my life as
I did that morning; watching them I thought: "Smug-faced
fools, you think the enemy is ninety miles away! If you
only knew! He is a stone's throw away, sitting under a
bloody bush and writing down in his book every bloody
vehicle of yours." I had ruled several pages of a notebook
in columns with headings: Mark III tanks, Mark II tanks
—five-ton trucks with troops—ditto with supplies—staff
cars, motorcycles and so on. The right-hand page for
westward traffic, left-hand for eastward traffic. The density
of traffic was about two hundred vehicles an hour, which
kept me pretty busy and I filled up the pages, with
considerable satisfaction.

By noon traffic became scarcer and I had periods during
which no vehicles were in sight. Then the periods length-
ened and by two o'clock the road seemed permanently
deserted. The sun was overhead, the heat was consider-

Pz. Kpfw. III

able, I felt drowsy. A lonely truck roared in the distance, appeared round the bend, loaded with German troops, was entered in my book and passed on. I lay back and stretched my legs: my two companions were asleep, their head cloths drawn over their eyes. Then I realized something was wrong: I had not heard the last truck grind up the next rise after it had passed us. I lifted my head and I saw it halted on the track, five hundred yards away. Through my glasses, in the shimmering heat, I saw the men out of the truck, gathered in a bunch. Brewing up, I thought. I touched my companions on the shoulder, they woke up without a start and turned their eyes as I pointed. I lay back and 'Abdel Aziz kept watch. Ten minutes later he touched me: I turned on to my stomach and looked through the glasses at two mirage-distorted figures: they came nearer and resolved themselves into two German soldiers. The glasses lowered, I judged the distance to be still quite safe and I said to 'Abdel Aziz and his companion: "Go back to the sheik's tomb—I shall meet you there later," and I cocked my tommy gun. 'Abdel Aziz got up and walked away—he was just an Arab in the landscape, no one would notice him. His companion grunted: "I am staying," and we both crawled behind our bush and kept our heads down.

The two Germans, a private and a *feldwebel*, had a rifle

and a pistol between them. They were now quite near and seemed to be making for our bush: as they had not unslung their weapons it was likely that they were not suspicious, but still they were making straight for us. Very carefully I shouldered my tommy gun. Between us and the two Germans was a rather conspicuous small tree, about twenty yards away from our bush. I slid the catch to single shot, brought the foresight to bear on the *feldwebel* and decided to fire when he reached the tree. If I succeeded in bringing both men down with no more than three or four shots, I hoped that the others, at the truck, would not notice and I would have time to withdraw unperceived in spite of my (as I thought) conspicuous uniform. The *feldwebel* advanced with a glassy stare. I drew breath, aimed at the pit of his stomach and started squeezing the trigger.

As he reached the tree, however, he stopped, turned away from me, and his companion did the same. I released the trigger hoping that I would not, after all, have to kill these two men that I didn't know. They undid their belts, slid down their slacks and squatted in the shade of the tree. I let my weapon rest on a stone and looked at my companion: he was quite unmoved but he turned his head toward me and his face cracked into a tiny smile.

For a quarter of an hour these two squatted chatting at the top of their voices, then they hurried back to their truck and drove away. My Arab said: "You might have killed the two Christians." "Yes, but there are many Germans besides them. May God let them live till the end of the war." The Senussis used the word *Nasrani* (Nazarene) so commonly for *enemy* that they forgot that the original meaning of the word, which is of course *Christian*, would apply equally to myself and to most of the British Army.

I told my companion: "You should have gone with 'Abdel Aziz."

"Oh no," he laughed, "I am your khabir. If you die, I die."

Strictly speaking, not he but his master 'Abdel Aziz was my khabir, but I thought better not to argue and simply said: "God bless you," and let the matter drop.

A khabir is the guide, the sponsor, to whom a stranger is entrusted and as long as he hasn't brought his charge back to safety it is understood that the khabir is responsible in every way for his comfort and his life. The relationship is easily and casually entered into. Once undertaken, the duties are binding unto death. But death is of small moment to a good Senussi compared to a breach of good form; the return of a khabir having lost his charge would be very shocking indeed.

I resumed my watch of the road till an hour later when 'Abdel Aziz and his second henchman, who had been left at the tomb, appeared in the distance with plates of food carried in handkerchiefs. We left the newcomer to keep an eye on the traffic and retired to the shade of a watercourse for our meal.

A few more vehicles passed till sunset, and then, just before dark, I made the snooper's scoop: fifteen German Mark III tanks going up to the line, with their attendant vehicles. German tanks in those days were the bogy of our headquarters (with very good reason) and the main object of a road watch was to detect and report any tanks coming up. Two hours after dark, having confirmed that, as I thought, the enemy didn't travel by night, we all returned to 'Abdel Aziz's tent. I was well pleased with the day's work: the Martuba by-pass was, as I had guessed, used extensively by the enemy and it would be easy to set a watch on it. Moreover I had, with my own eyes, seen German tanks and made a note of their markings, and with childish eagerness I wanted to pass the information back to army headquarters without delay.

The only means I had of getting in touch with headquarters was Chapman's radio set in the canyon near Wadi Shegran, and Sa'ad 'Ali was the only man who could direct a messenger to it. So back to Er Rteim I rode, leaving about midnight and arriving shortly after dawn. I found Metwallah and Sa'ad 'Ali already (or was it *still*) up and told them what I wanted. They discussed the matter and decided that Mohammed bul Qassem was the man to take my very important message down to the radio—if he could be induced to go—and the man was sent for. He was a grizzled warrior of a surly disposition, dark-featured and scowling. Sa'ad told him that a message of the utmost urgency had to be carried—Mohammed said he wouldn't go—Metwallah insisted—Mohammed didn't know the wadi with the radio—I asked him as a personal favor: he said he would take orders from nobody. I said, never mind, I would go myself.

Mohammed bul Qassem asked: "Where is the message?"

I gave it to him and we all got up. Sa'ad took Mohammed apart and standing with his head to one side, tense and absorbed, gave him directions in a whispered singsong chant. He told him the landmarks of the thirty-mile route: a bush, then a hill, a bush again, a ridge, a rise, a wadi, a hummock . . . then at last a kharruba tree, over a rocky ridge and down into the canyon. Mohammed bul Qassem listened with averted head and vacant eyes. When Sa'ad 'Ali stopped talking he grunted and walked away. At three o'clock the next morning, as I lay asleep in Metwallah's tent, he shook me by the arm, and handed me a message form: Chapman's acknowledgment. He had walked, over unfamiliar mountains, sixty miles in seventeen hours.

I left Sa'ad 'Ali and Metwallah busy counting sheep and collecting pots for our party and I went and stayed near Qasr Wertij with Sheik 'Abdel Jelil bu Tayeb. He was the kinsman whom Sheik 'Ali bu Hamed had mentioned to me in his Arabian-Night cave, who was to work out the details of my intelligence service. Here was the perfect follower of a great man: middle-aged, level-minded, efficient, hard-working and kindly. He had received his orders and had carried them out diligently. His relationship to me was strangely paternal: he considered it his duty to guide me. With unusual insight he realized that, in spite of deceptive appearances, I was really a stranger to the Arab world—his world—and he undertook to coach me.

We settled the practical side of my business: where I would place my radio sets, who would be my regular messengers and how much they should be paid. He gave much attention to the kind of information I considered useful and to the means of getting it.

For the road watch he produced an elderly man called Jibrin with three grown sons, whose tent at that time was pitched near Sidret Haraij, only two miles off the Martuba by-pass. I spent a day with him watching the traffic to show him how I wanted the work done and to make sure he could identify the different types of vehicles. When I left I arranged that he would start work as soon as I came back with the radio. His sons would take turns as daily runners to my headquarters. Later, trained by Chapman, he became head of an important firm of road watchers.

The next few days before the sheiks' conference at Kaf El Qsur were spent in leisurely talks with Sheik 'Abdel Jelil bu Tayeb.

4

OBEIDI CONFERENCE

FROM the well-wooded mountain tops we rode south-ward, winding down Wadi Qsur. At Kaf el Qsur, the landscape is desert suburb: clumps of trees and a little grass along the wadi banks; the bed is of boulders and gravel for, dry now in May, in winter it runs a full spate of torrential yellow water and carries torn-up trees whose black skeletons line the banks like the remains of a forest fire. The hills on both sides are crumbling and barren, shapeless and desolate. At a sharp bend of the wadi, however, a high yellow cliff is exposed in which are many caves, walled in by the Romans for some purpose of their own. The Arabs don't build; and wherever hewn stones are found together they say the Romans put them up. Eleven hundred years ago the armies of Islam took this province from the decaying Roman Empire, but so uneventful has been the pasturing of flocks ever since that to the inhabitants it seems that living memories nearly take them back to the greatness of Rome.

The caves that give their name to the spot, empty now, were used to store grain in more prosperous times, and the higher ones, which had not been fouled by cattle, were clean and free of ticks. I found myself a home high up the cliff side: it was reached by a pleasant climb up a crack in the rock and had two windows overlooking the northern mountains.

Sa'ad 'Ali and Metwallah, with the food and the ser-vants, had already settled in the wadi when I arrived, and so had some of our guests. The others came riding in during the next day. Sheik 'Ali bu Hamed arrived early and retired to a cave. I had posted watchers on a hilltop, some distance down Wadi Qsur and when, toward sunset, they reported the approach of Sheik 'Abdel Qader bu

Bridan I rode out to greet him. A robust, thickset man of over eighty with a white moustache and pointed beard, the hoodless burnoose he wore under his ample white jerd made him look far too bulky for his small prancing mare, whose trappings and black and scarlet tassels hung to the ground. He boomed out in a deep gruff voice and we shook hands repeatedly without dismounting. Riding to camp together we exchanged the customary formal greetings.

There is no more meaning put by the Arabs in these words than by us when we say and reply: "How do you do?"—"How do you do?"—and a little later, perhaps "Well, how are you?"—"Thanks. And how are you?"—and later again over a drink "All the best!" "Your very good health"—"God bless."

As befits a leisurely and dignified mode of life, the Arab greetings are more in number than ours and are exchanged a great many times, usually in a toneless clipped voice, and replied to alike, with a slight inclination of the head and a lifting of the hand toward the heart. It was, however, a recognized peculiarity of the well-bred among the Obeidat that they put in their greetings those soft lingering tones of tender concern which 'Ali bu Hamed used to the point of affectation. Not so 'Abdel Qader bu Bridan whose affectations lay, in the opposite direction, toward blunt manliness and a rough humor.

Later in the evening we squatted down to a meal, about sixty of us; some of the sheiks being still on their way, the formal proceedings did not start till the next morning.

During the night the remainder of our guests rode in with their attendants and spread themselves up and down the wadi, horses and camels hobbled and put to graze; fires were lit and tea boiled. I left Sa'ad 'Ali to entertain our friends and retired to my Roman home up the cliff for a reasonable night's rest: the morrow was to be a day of many words and I would need a fresh mind and clear wits.

At sunrise 'Abdel Qader bu Bridan led the prayers, tea was handed round and then I called the sheiks into the shade of an overhanging rock at the foot of the cliff. They squatted down in a many-rowed circle and I faced them with 'Abdel Qader bu Bridan on my right, and 'Ali bu

Hamed on my left; Sa'ad 'Ali, behind me, was ready, when necessary, to interpret abstruse turns of speech and to tell me the names of the speakers, many of whom were of course unknown to me. I stood up and said, picking my words:

"In the name of God the merciful, the compassionate! Sheik 'Abdel Qader bu Bridan, Sheik 'Ali bu Hamed, Sheiks of the Obeidi clans and families, Arabs of the Jebel Akhdar, faithful Senussis, brothers! It grieves me that on this solemn day I should be unable to address you in the proper way and with adequate words. My tongue is black for I am not a scholar but a soldier, a man, not of knowledge, but of war, who comes to you from his foreign land, ignorant of your language but yet a brother to you, a brother in arms, to fight with you the war against our common enemy, the oppressor of your land, the murderer of your kinsmen, the robber of your flocks, the enemy of the faithful."

I stopped to take breath, while 'Abdel Qader nodding in polite approval repeated in his rumbling bass: "The murderer of your kinsmen, the robber of your flocks, the enemy of the faithful!" and a murmur went round the assembled listeners. I looked round to Sa'ad 'Ali, who winked and whispered: "Excellent, carry on. Don't mention your black tongue any more, it is a word of Egypt." I went on:

"Your spiritual leader, your Amir, the venerable Sheik Sayed Idris el Senussi, God bless him, has offered his help and that of his people to my king, who is the King of England. At the present moment the Arab battalions of exiles are fighting side by side with their English brethren, and also with the faithful from India, with the men from Australia, New Zealand and South Africa, in fact," I added lamely, "with soldiers from the whole world.

"The black-and-white standard of Sayed Idris, the crescent and star of the Senussi, flies alongside the flag of the King of England. But this is not enough: the British Government knows that they have no more faithful friends, no allies more eager to join in the battle than you, the Senussi Arabs of the Jebel, than you assembled here today, the Arabs of the Obeidi tribe, oppressed, invaded, massacred but undaunted, expelled from the pastures of your fathers by vile 'Sicilian' settlers, poor, hungry, but still and evermore, men and fighters—my Government know you and they want your help."

'Abdel Qader bu Bridan rumbled the chorus: "Oppressed, invaded, massacred but undaunted, expelled from the pastures of your fathers by vile 'Sicilians,' " and an appreciative murmur came once more from the assembly. I had by now completely run out of big words and the remainder of my speech had to be said in vernacular—in the vilest pidgin.

"My Government want your help and they want to help you. Because of this wish, I am here with you and I am going to stay with you. I command the Allied forces in the Jebel. I want your sheiks, I want all of you to tell me what you need and if it is possible, it will be provided. I want you to know that you can come to me when you are in trouble. I want you all to help such of my people as I will bring here—to guide and to shelter them. Above all I want you to bring to me all the information you can get about the enemy. I want you to be the eyes and the ears of the British Army."

Rather exhausted and very pleased with my eloquence I was going to sit down when I caught an anxious look from 'Ali bu Hamed, and I remembered that the essential had not yet been said. So I started once more:

"We are strong and confident of success but God alone knows the hour of victory. In the meanwhile we need every man who can fire a rifle and you also will be called upon. You are all warriors—many of you have considerably more experience of war than I have—so it is not for me to remind you that in war you must strike at the right moment. If you strike at the wrong moment, neither you nor your brothers survive to regret the mistake—and the enemy rejoices. What I don't tell you, you can guess; what I will tell you now, is that today is not the right moment for you to strike. I also tell you that the moment will come, and I shall be there to give you your orders and provide you with weapons to fight your enemy."

I stopped and stood, as if uncertain and debating with myself the advisability of saying more. Then, tossing my head, and addressing 'Abdel Qader bu Bridan, in a lowered voice:

"I shall tell you something that will make you understand why I want you to wait. We are preparing a surprise for the enemy, a surprise that is coming from over the sea and out of the sky. Over the sea—out of the sky. Do you understand?"

'Abdel Qader stared out of rather protuberant eyes and said uncertainly: "I understand."

I turned to 'Ali bu Hamed who said softly and clearly: "I understand perfectly, Excellency the Major: birds, eagles."

I turned to Sa'ad 'Ali as if to ask him also if he understood but what I said in a very low voice was: "The old man opposite, with the gray beard and the camel stick—is he important?"

"Yes, Major," said Sa'ad 'Ali quite loud, "I know what you mean," and he whispered the name "Tayeb bu Jibrin."

I walked across to the old sheik: "Do *you* understand Tayeb?" He nodded gravely.

I went round the circle of my listeners saying: "You have understood, 'Abdel Jelil bu Tayeb? And you, Metwallah? And you, 'Abdel Aziz? And you? And you?"

The chorus came all round: "We understand."

Back in my place I resumed:

"When the surprise is ready, your hour will be very near. You have heard Sheik 'Ali bu Hamed. 'Eagles,' he said. Our eagles will want nests to lay their eggs in. You, all of you, are going to find nests for our eagles' eggs. That is going to be your work now. And the nests will be surprised!"

A subdued decorous chuckle came from the ranks.

"With you be the peace and the mercy of God and his blessings," I said suddenly and sat down.

Sheik 'Abdel Qader bu Bridan now started talking. The ceremonial opening to his oration was altogether beyond me: I only caught a word now and then in the sonorous flow of his eloquence. Illiterate as befitted a gentleman of his generation, he was an artist in words and expressed himself in classical Arabic. The seventh-century dialect of the Koreish, which the Prophet's immediate successors used in the compilation of the Koran, is used all over the Arabic-speaking world from Oman to Morocco for ceremonial speeches and also—in theory—for all written literature, even newspapers. It differs from the various vernaculars as much as classical Latin from French, Spanish or Italian, and I had little knowledge of it. I waited to hear my name mentioned and acknowledged the unintelligible compliment with polite bows, then I let my mind wander, relying on Sa'ad 'Ali to recall me when necessary.

I looked at the crowd around me: nearly every petty sheik from Tobruk in the east to Lamluda in the west and as far south as Mekhili had left his tents and was now squatting in the Wadi Qsur listening to seditious speeches. Out of sight over the mountains, but only seven or eight miles away, German convoys followed each other over the dusty track to Martuba and the east: it seemed hardly possible that the enemy should be unaware of my games and miss an opportunity of putting an end to British subversive activities. The Italians had held the coast of Cyrenaica for over twenty-five years—since 1929 they controlled the whole of the interior; they had large settlements dotted over the fertile parts of the Jebel, in Giovanni Berta, Luigi di Savoia, Beda Littoria, Maddalena, D'Annunzio and Barce, luxury hotels in Derna and Cirene. They should know what was going on in this, virtually, their own country. Surely at any moment now, armored cars would appear over the hills and wipe out our gathering. But nothing happened—a tribute to the loyalty and the craftiness of the Senussi Arabs and the complacency of their Italian masters.

The old sheik had lapsed into colloquial and was saying: "In the days of *our* war when the call came to raid the enemy you remember how it was: only those of us who had less than *three* rounds of ammunition were excused from the fight. And where did the rounds come from, and the weapons themselves? Captured from the enemy. Cut off from the outer world, alone, penniless, we fought for twenty years. Now, we can have English help, a wealthy nation in the world—not three rounds a head but perhaps a hundred. Shall we sit back and watch our English friends from over the sea chase *our* enemy from *our* country? The major has asked us what he can do to help us; we want weapons and ammunition—nothing else."

Thus 'Abdel Qader bu Bridan ended his speech in the first round of the argument. The call to arms was taken up by one speaker after another and grave murmurs of appreciation from the audience rewarded the eloquent. The day wore on. I grew restless, and when a camel boy, a mere lad of seventeen, got up in the back row and started on a fiery but halting speech, I said to 'Abdel Qader: "Are we not wasting time?"

"Let him have his say," replied the old man. "He is a freeman and entitled to speak. He is young and drivels but he will learn." The solemn old men of the tribe nodded approval and the youth was allowed to bring his maiden speech to a repetitive and lame conclusion.

In the early afternoon, 'Ali bu Hamed stood up with dramatic suddenness and spoke for the opposition:

"The Dursa, our brothers the Dursa, are fighting the Italians now." The Dursa, a warlike Senussi tribe, lived on a strip of land between the northern road and the sea coast from Appollonia to Tolmeta. From the rich uplands where the Italians had settled, they had been evicted, but the precipitous wooded gorges where the escarpment plunges three thousand feet down to the narrow coastal plain were theirs—strongholds and hide-outs from which they had recently been raiding Maddelena, a large Italian settlement. Little more really than the pilfering expeditions of men made desperate by starvation, their operations were cunningly described by 'Ali bu Hamed as a military campaign.

"The Dursa," he went on, "are hard pressed. Planes have been brought against them and Italian troops. Alpini, are being gathered now to attack them in their wadis. The Dursa must be helped—their need is greater than ours, they have first call for help. Brethren, we must ask the major to bring arms and ammunition and we shall get them over to the Dursa. I say: overlook our own straits and help the Dursa or they will be wiped out."

The crafty fox carried the assembly. Speeches were made in support of immediate assistance to the Dursa and the risk of a premature rising of the Obeidat seemed averted. I was well pleased and in the final speech for that day I said I would undertake to bring into the Jebel on my next trip weapons and ammunition for the Dursa. Later, I said, we would build up dumps of arms for the Obeidat. There was no immediate hurry and I would see that they were issued in time. Other forms of material help remained to be discussed: I suggested we might deal with the matter on the morrow and we adjourned for dinner.

One problem, however, suffered no delay: while the meal was being brought in I went into a private conference with 'Ali bu Hamed and arranged with him that he would send immediately messengers to the four main Dursa sheiks to ask them to meet me six days later at Sidi Ahmet bu Rweiq.

The dinner was very happy, we were pleased with the day's work. 'Abdel Qader and 'Ali bu Hamed, the rivals, both felt they had scored off the other, the tribe was united, everyone rejoiced in the planning of great deeds and we all knew we had scored off the Italians.

After the final pacification in 1929 when half the Arab population of Cyrenaica had been massacred by General Graziani, the Italians had tried conciliation. 'Abdel Qader had been made a knight, a Cavaliere, of some Order and was given a large jeweled star worn on a broad blue ribbon. Then, at the beginning of the war, he had been summoned before the Military Governor, General Piatti, he told us, and warned that unless Arab aid to escaping British prisoners of war ceased, his Order would be taken away from him. He removed the star and ribbon, put them in his pocket and asked: "Am I no more a Knight?"

"Certainly not," said Piatti, furious.

"But I am still 'Abdel Qader bu Bridan, am I?"

The old man roared with laughter as he told the story, hugging himself, showed me the Star and repeated: "Am I still 'Abdel Qader bu Bridan?"

He then called on 'Ali bu As to give us his poem on Graziani. This was a ballad of many stanzas, each line in a stanza ending in the same rhyme; the delivery slow and clear, impressive and very strongly stressed. The last line or two of each stanza were taken up as a chorus by 'Abdel Qader and others. The ballad told of Graziani's cruelties, of the rebel sheiks he had contrived to be thrown alive out of a plane over their own tents, of the mass deportation of all the Jebel Arabs, their families and their cattle to Mersa Brega, of his treacheries and his bullying. It then went on in a triumphant mood to tell of his utter defeat at the hands of the English and ended scurrilously with an imagined interview between Graziani and Mussolini.

Several other poets came forward with their compositions referring to incidents in the history of the tribe, some of them going back to pre-Italian days of intertribal warfare and celebrating the defeat of the Barasi at Lamluda. But the bulk of the poems were about the struggle against the Italians, which had been the background of these people for two generations.

Sheik 'Ali bu As, a grizzled old warrior with only one eye, a noted poet in the tribe, had meanwhile retired within himself and I could see him by the firelight, muttering and beating the measure with his hand. When he started to declaim, all talk stopped, for he was admired. He told of the events of these very days, of the stirring summons reaching the Arabs in their lonely pastures, of the mounted travelers converging by day and by night on to Wadi Qsur, of the English major and his outlandish speech, of the words of the great sheiks, of the stammering camel boy, of the dinner and the feast and the reciting of poetry. He drew great laughter with a description of Piatti, insolent and fooled, writing to Mussolini that all was well in the Jebel. He concluded with a prophetic description of the final rout and massacre of the enemy and the glory of the English Army, the Amir Sayed Idris, the Arabs in general and the Obeidat in particular.

One after another my guests fell asleep. Sheik 'Abdel Qader bu Bridan wrapped himself head and all in a black jerd and lay himself down by the fire. 'Ali bu Hamed retired to a cave and I climbed up to my eyrie by the flickering light of the dying fires.

The next morning early we went into committees to discuss practical arrangements. I knew what was expected and said I would bring tea, sugar, flour and cloth, as much as our trucks would carry above the arms and ammunition. I then took each of the sheiks in private and asked them what gift would be most acceptable to them.

At midday I addressed once more the whole assembly. I told them that my government had solemnly undertaken never to let their country come again under Italian rule after the victorious conclusion of the war. They took my word for it and expressed decorous gratefulness. There was another claim that they wanted me to settle: the "Sicilians" (the Italian settlers) must be prevented from coming back to their farms after the war. I had discussed the matter in private and had tried to avoid raising the question, but as 'Abdel Qader bu Bridan was determined to bring up the matter in public if I didn't, I said:

"As for the 'Sicilians,' when our armies occupy the Jebel Akhdar, those of them who have been left behind by the Italian Army will be deported to Tripoli. My government will take over the farms and dispose of them to the best of the common interest."

My audience was pleased enough by my assurance that the hated "Sicilians" would no more be seen; they would also have liked a promise that the Arabs would be allowed to pasture their flocks over the land which had been put under plow—but they didn't press me for it.

I proceeded to thank them, wish them good luck and concluded with a promise of stirring deeds.

'Abdel Qader handed me two written addresses, one for the British commander-in-chief, the other for Sayed Idris. The wording had been discussed interminably and finally put down in pencil by Sheik 'Abdel Jelil on leaves torn out from my pocket book.

Dark, lean and mysterious, 'Ali bu Hamed slipped away in a hurry lest the Italian command grow suspicious of his long absence, but 'Abdel Qader departed at leisure for his southern pastures.

I rode away to Er Rteim with Sa'ad 'Ali and Metwallah. With much entertaining our stocks had run low, we were completely out of cigarettes and Sa'ad 'Ali's temper suffered accordingly. He became so irritable that we had to stop chaffing him and he rode in sullen silence. Toward evening we stopped at a well to water the horses, in spite of his abusive protests, for he wanted desperately to get back to our cache and his store of tobacco. So distracted was he, that when we started again he mounted from the right-hand side and found himself in the saddle facing the tail of his horse. We burst out laughing, he glowered at us and nearly lost his temper; then only he realized his predicament and joined us in mirth.

I took a strong line with the Dursa sheiks when they turned up on the appointed day. I told them their action was ill timed and badly conceived and could only cause embarrassment. In the future they should take care to undertake no such operations without my order. The poor creatures were rather harassed, having been through anxious times, on top of which had come a dangerous ride through the Italian settlements to meet me, and they were like children who have got out of hand, landed themselves in trouble and welcome the comforting scolding of their elders. I told them I would give them what help I could in the way of weapons, but it would take time, and advised them in the meanwhile to break off operations straight away, retire to their mountain fastnesses where the Italians had no troops to pursue them, and start negotiation with

the enemy, who, I assured them, would be glad to give
them good terms. I was counting (and rightly) on the
Italian fear of the Germans and their desire not to appear
unable to control their own Arabs. Any of their tribesmen
whom the Italians might insist on having handed over, I
told them to send to Abiar bu Sfaia in the south of the
Obeidi country, where I would eventually arrange to have
them picked up by an L.R.D.G. patrol and removed to
Egypt. I also undertook to arrange with the Obeidat to
give them asylum. I was glad to be able to send them back
home, comforted, and I made my own way to Er Rteim,
Metwallah's tents and my temporary headquarters.

During the four more days I had before catching the
return L.R.D.G. patrol at Wadi Shegran I went to look for
a suitable backdoor entry to the Jebel in the south where I
could come in from the desert on my next trip and I also
made arrangements for the transport and the storage of
the immense amount of supplies I intended to bring in.

I was faced with a problem that was rather worrying:
how was I to induce the staff in Cairo to supply me
without delay with all the stuff I had promised? I decided
that the fancy branch of Middle East Headquarters under
whose direct command I came were too bewildered to take
any notice of my requests and I resolved instead to put my
faith in the Eighth Army. I was quite certain that they
would appreciate my policy of arming the Arabs so that
they shouldn't fight. My first job was to make them sweet,
and to this end that very same night I sent Mohammed bul
Qassem on a second trip to the radio set in the canyon,
with two memoranda: one for Eighth Army Intelligence
with a summary of the military information I had picked
up during my trip, including some pretty good bombing
targets, the other for the Western Desert Liaison Officer,
with the political gossip. I hoped thus to find army headquarters already well disposed when I arrived in the flesh.
It was a gamble because if I came back to the Jebel
without being able to show the Arabs tangible proofs of
my self-assumed greatness, I might as well stay at home.

On our way south we nearly ran into an adventure. To
save time, and grown careless, Sa'ad 'Ali Rahuma and
myself on horseback and one of Metwallah's Arabs riding
a camel, had chosen to ride along the motor track leading
to Mekhili, in daylight. Sa'ad 'Ali, his uniform covered by
a jerd, would not have been too conspicuous if he had not

had a tommy gun slung across his shoulders; I was wearing as usual a very dirty khaki drill shirt and slacks, with a pistol in a holster on my army belt, and a broad-brimmed New Zealand hat. We heard a car coming up behind us and had just time to move off the track when it came in sight with two Italian officers and a driver. They drove past slowly, looked at us, laughed—at our grotesque appearance I presume—and, unobservant fools, passed on. We avoided motorable tracks after that encounter.

I visited several dry wells and caves suitable to store my treasures if ever I brought them in, and I renewed my acquaintance with an old friend of Sa'ad 'Ali's, who had been up at the sheiks conference. This kindly old man called Musa had large flocks pasturing at that time north of the Baltet ez Zala'q; he promised to provide me with camels to carry my stores on my return trip.

We rode on, and, one day ahead of schedule, I scrambled down into the canyon to meet Chapman and Chevalier and get the news from the outer world.

Both these officers were very unwilling to return to Egypt the next day with the L.R.D.G. patrol as they had so far achieved nothing and felt frustrated. I invited them to stay on in the Jebel and operate with me: they accepted and I undertook to square things with headquarters. It was arranged that during my absence they would move up with the radio set and their two operators to the Obeidi country with Sa'ad 'Ali Rahuma and organize the road watch.

Olivey and his patrol turned up the next day punctually, having completed a task farther west, and I drove off with them, on our way back to Siwa. When I entered the private world which they carried with them like a ship at sea, the character I had acquired while I lived with the Arabs dropped off, and I reverted to my usual self.

5

WAYS OF LIFE

I HAD never tried to impersonate an Arab and I couldn't have done it if I had wanted to, for I am a desperately incompetent actor. Awkward in fancy dress, incapable of imitating a foreign accent, unable to assume a character, self-conscious in front of a camera, I can only be myself. Thus the ease with which I adapted myself to Arab ways was due to no histrionic gift nor was I accepted by the Senussis because they mistook me for one of their own. To them I remained always a stranger—a very friendly one—and I never tried to make them forget that I belonged neither to their race nor to their religion. Yet, as soon as I was among them, slipping without conscious effort into a new personality, I adopted their manners and their prejudices. I liked them and admired them so well that I had no difficulty in sharing their outlook; although I never really behaved like an Arab, in a way I thought and felt like one. I find a deep satisfaction in such a change of character, which I have experienced also with other people: Italian partisans and Russian soldiers during the war, and others again after it.

Although in our mutual understanding we forgot easily our differences, they were so great that it would seem that there should be an unscalable barrier between a Senussi Arab and an urbanized Westerner. The Senussis, through the accident of their history and the barrenness of their land, were, at the time I was living with them, a small isolated group whose mode of life had remained little changed since the Arab conquest, eleven hundred years previously; an anachronistic, self-contained community, nearly completely cut off, not only from the Western but even from the Moslem world. Their pilgrimage was seldom to Mecca but commonly to the oasis of Jaghbub where lies the tomb of Sayed Mohammed bu 'Ali el Senussi, founder of the Senussi sect and grandfather to the present spiritual leader, Sayed Idris el Senussi.

Until 1912 they had been under the sleepy suzerainty of the Turks who bothered little about their internal arrangements, but offered no encouragement to foreign visitors. Then came the Italians who, after defeating the Turks, became the nominal masters of the land. But they occupied effectively only the coastal towns; the dogged resistance of the tribes prevented them from spreading inland. During this long-drawn-out conflict the Arabs had little access even to their own towns and were cut off from Egypt. Thus they came to remain in a sense true Arabs, while the rest of the Moslem lands from Egypt to Morocco were being westernized.

In the days before the Italian conquest they had grown barley and even wheat: but the arable lands in the fertile plain round the town of Barce and on the uplands near Beda Littoria had been taken away from them and Italians (mostly Sicilians) settled in their stead. When I knew them they did indeed cultivate a few acres here and there in the wadis running southward, miserable crops of stunted barley, sown after the winter rains, but their economy was pastoral. Their flocks were of sheep and goats and a few camels, and their food mainly of milk and butter. The increase of their flocks they sold in the coastal towns Benghazi and Derna (and, before the war, in Sollum for export to Egypt), where they bought flour, tea, sugar, clothes and the few implements required for their austere households. Of industries they had none, with the exception of the weaving of the roofs of their tents, which was done by the women on the very primitive looms, with yarn spun by the men from the wool of their animals. the low walls of the tents were made of sacking and not of their own weaving.

Outside the coastal towns there was not a single Arab house made of stone but they all lived in villages of tents, ten to fifty tents to a village. Their only furniture were the low wooden benches on which they slept and a few small chests, nor could they own anything more cumbersome, for all their possessions had to be loaded on camels each time they moved camp, which happened not when the grazing was exhausted but when the cisterns from which they drank and watered their animals came to be empty.

The men looked after their flocks and traded their animals, but otherwise worked not at all: not because they were lazy but because work, an occupation fit only for slaves, was despised and considered a degradation; in the activity which befitted a free tribesman, in war, they exerted themselves ceaselessly and took infinite pains. Untaught and illiterate, their lives were ruled by a rigid code of behavior; to preserve it they were at all times prepared to lay down their lives.

Bred to despise trade, abhor violence and revere laboriousness and the activities of the mind, I could, it seemed, have no link with these ignorant warriors: yet the pure austerity of their behavior fired me with an enthusiasm which overrode our differences. Thus it was that I shed the sophistication of my Western ways and shared joyfully the clean pattern of their simple lives.

Traveling with the L.R.D.G. our lives also followed a well-planned pattern; familiar duties left us delightful leisure. On the march, the patrol commander's truck went first, picking the route; then the navigator, then the radio; the other trucks followed—the mechanic came last, his job was to help whoever fell out with mechanical trouble. In the open desert, where there was little risk of detection, we avoided the hazards of traveling in the dark, and journeyed from sunrise to sunset, stopping for an hour or two in the middle of the day for lunch and to allow the radio operators to get in touch with headquarters. In single file, a quarter of a mile or so apart, was our usual formation, but we spread out considerably right and left in the areas where we thought enemy planes might be roving. When a plane was reported we stopped in our tracks to lay our wakes of cloudy dust which made us conspicuous from the air.

Before starting in the early morning we ate our breakfast of tea, porridge, bacon, biscuits and jam. Each man's water bottle was filled for the day and we drove off. Later in the day, when the patrol leader put out a colored flag, the trucks pulled up and we went to collect our lunch of biscuits, cheese, tinned fish and pickles. Then until the signalers, having completed their job, took down their aerial, we sat on the ground in the shade of our truck and read books, for the heat of the day did not induce talk. At dusk the trucks came to rest close together and we all went with our mugs for our daily ration of rum and lime-powder. On a fire of dry desert bushes, dinner of bully-beef stew and spices was cooked, to be followed by a slice and a half of tinned peach or apricot, and tea. Round the fire we talked and joked till, night drawing on, one after the other we went up to our trucks and laid ourselves to sleep on the ground. The signalers went on hammering at their keys long after everyone else was asleep.

Five men composed the crew of a truck and five or six trucks made a patrol.

We made a peaceful passage back to Siwa, and three days later I sat in Lieutenant Colonel Prendergast's office on the top of a hill, while he rang up Eighth Army headquarters to arrange my visit to them. Prendergast had been a member of Bagnold's early expeditions in the desert before the war and he had now succeeded him in command of L.R.D.G. I overheard him mentioning on the phone somebody called Popski and when he had done he turned to me, and, somewhat embarrassed, he said, "As you heard we call you Popski. Nobody can understand Peniakoff on the phone. Do you mind?" I assured him I was delighted with my nickname and remembered that my namesake was the comical, hairy little bolshy in—was it *the Daily Mirror?*—comic strip. Whether I liked it or not, Popski I had become and Popski I have remained to this day.

Army headquarters at Qambut, east of Tobruk, was a number of heavily camouflaged tents and caravans widely dispersed in a dusty plain. Nobody knew where anybody was, and having left my car at the military police tent I wandered around till I hit the Operations caravan.

With my head full of my own schemes I hadn't lately had much time to consider the general situation; it was a shock to realize that no one at army headquarters had confidence in our ability to resist a German attack. The prevailing view was that when Rommel chose to advance there was nothing to stop him reaching Egypt. In a sense the morale of our forces was low; there was little confidence in our own strength and no faith whatever in our High Command. And yet everyone was cheerful. The Eighth Army staff in particular, already at that early period and before Montgomery's reforms, were shining models of friendliness and helpfulness. They trusted me and assumed that my requests were reasonable and justified. Much to my relief (for I had been anxious about their

response to my demands), they granted everything I asked
for and took steps to provide me with the odd assortment
of supplies I wanted to take back with me to the Jebel. I
was pressed to return urgently to the theater of my
operations and to prepare myself to spread "alarm and
despondency" (an expression that was just then coming
into fashion) as soon as I would be given the sign.
Destruction of gasoline had the highest priority, which
suited me well enough. For my political schemes with the
Arabs I received a free hand, and I was given a tactfully
non-committal written reply to the sheiks' address. I had a
session with Intelligence, told them what I had found out,
then I was asked questions that the German quartermaster
general alone could have answered. However, I undertook
to do my best and left headquarters with the pleasant
delusion that the fate of the Eighth Army was in my
keeping.

I drove back to Siwa the same night, nonstop, and
ransacked the market for my warlike stores. What couldn't
be purchased locally was flown to me from Cairo. Some
items on my bill of lading were as follows:

Calico, white	yards	1600
" red	yards	900
Pots, tea	dozen	9
Nails, horseshoe	lb.	20
Sweets, boiled	lb.	100
Leather, shoe	sq. feet	200
Scarves, head	dozen	2
Girdles, embroidered	pieces	12
" gold thread	pieces	4
Slippers, colored	pairs	12
Thread, cotton reels	gross	12
Caps, skull (with tassel)	dozen	2
Chocolate	lb.	40
Bloomers, red (ladies')	pairs	6

Apart from a month's army rations for my party of
twelve, the L.R.D.G. quartermaster supplied me with
(among other items):

Tea	lb.	600
Sugar	lb.	600
Flour	lb.	2400
Cigarettes, tins	dozen	50

Strangely the British Army in the Middle East was unable to provide me with a saddle and I finally purchased a looted Italian one in the Jebel from an Arab.

L.R.D.G. supplied me also with the weapons which I meant to show to the Arabs as a token of our intention to make them fight when the time came. (That in my opinion the time would *never* come was no business of theirs and

Boyes Anti-Tank Rifle

only Sheik 'Ali bu Hamed knew the secret of my duplicity.) These arms came from a store of obsolete weapons discarded by the L.R.D.G.: Boyes anti-tank rifles, two-inch mortars, captured heavy Italian machine guns and others: an impressive array well suited to my purpose. I also got a .45 Colt automatic for Sheik 'Abdel Qader bu Bridan, and a small pocket pistol inlaid with mother of pearl for Sheik 'Ali bu Hamed.

My own weapons, ammunition and explosives made up the load. I took twelve Arab privates with me from the twenty-two I had left behind at Jaghbub—the remainder I transferred to Siwa with their British sergeant, to be looked after by the L.R.D.G., till such time as I might require their services. I also took with me a new British recruit, a very young subaltern whom I had known as a schoolboy in Cairo. A nice red-headed lad, eager, level-headed beyond his age, he had just completed his course at the Officers Cadet Training Unit; he had taken a special course in explosives, he could talk Arabic, and he had not been spoiled by service with a base unit. I hoped to train him in my ways and get some help from him. His name was Shorten.

6

SPREAD OF ALARM

THE patrol that took us out was commanded by David Lloyd Owen, then a captain.

The rendezvous with Musa had been fixed Arab fashion, rather vaguely, "North of the Baltet ez Zala'q." A balat (or baltet) is a shallow lake in the plains south of the mountains; it fills up with muddy rain water, pouring down the wadis during the winter, then dries up; by August it is a dry mud pan with a hard surface perfectly level and without a ripple, over which our trucks could race in any direction. In May, as we were then, the Baltet ez Zala'q, twenty-five miles south of the foothills, was still a sheet of water roughly five miles square and a few feet deep. The Arabs bring their flocks south from the mountains at this season, water them from the lakes and let them crop the desert bushes, a more wholesome food, they say, than the more abundant mountain vegetation.

With cumbrous stores weighing nearly seven tons I was anxious to reach my rendezvous early in the day: thus I hoped to have time to inquire of Musa's whereabouts and reach his tents before dark. It turned out differently. We reached the southern shores of the balat in the early morning; the rippling water was tempting. We all bathed, then had a late breakfast. We lingered so long that, when we were ready to move on, it was nearly time for the midday radio transmission, and we delayed our departure to allow the signalers to exchange messages with headquarters in Siwa. Rounding the lake on the western shore we came across recent car tracks and a camp site.

Our Arabs got to work, tested the moisture of the remains of food attached to opened tins, found the sand under the dead embers of the camp fire still lukewarm, analyzed footprints and car tracks, and after a leisurely whispered consultation, decided unanimously that an

Italian patrol of five light trucks carrying not less than twenty-one men had stopped for a meal in this spot about noon on the previous day, and had driven off in the direction of Mekhili. The knowledge that the enemy was patrolling this remote and usually deserted area increased my determination not to be dumped before I had reached a spot where I could get transport; it had the opposite effect on Lloyd Owen who wanted to get rid of me and my heavy junk as early as possible and be free to regain, undetected by the enemy, the open desert farther south where he had to relieve another L.R.D.G. patrol. Their work at that time was to lie off the Triq el 'Abd, and watch enemy traffic using the short cut from Benghazi to the east.

The going along the lake shore was in soft sand and very slow. We tried the high slopes on our left and found them covered in sharp-edged boulders which slowed us down even more and ripped open two tires. Furthermore they were barren and uninhabited. Most of the afternoon had gone before we came across our first Arab and he had no knowledge of Musa, who didn't belong to his tribe. We made once more for the low ground near the lake in the hope of meeting someone who could help me. We got bogged—tempers grew short—I had to use charm to avoid being dumped among the migrating water fowl who seemed to be the only inhabitants of the lake shore. We pushed on, however, and just before sunset I caught up with an Obeidi Arab who undertook to guide us to Musa's tent.

Unfortunately my guide believed that where a man could walk, an overloaded truck could follow; in the growing darkness we found ourselves engaged in a confusion of large boulders over which our trucks lurched and rolled. Then one of the trucks blew a tire and Lloyd Owen's patience snapped. He came over to me with an awful scowl on his usually humorous countenance and declared his conviction that my guide had no idea where he was leading us to. I had to agree with him and I gave up the struggle. Orders were given to unload and ten minutes later the retreating trucks rolled out of sight in the dusk. Cases of tea and rolls of calico lay in confusion among a wilderness of rocks. My only link with my friends in the Jebel was a very old and very shaken Arab with a gray pointed beard, who seemed completely lost and bewildered. In fact he was only sick as a result of the first motor ride in his life.

My twelve Arabs were undismayed. They might feel lost in a town but never in the desert. We drank tea and cooked a meal; then two of my men set out with the guide to fetch Musa. Shorten was enjoying his first taste of adventure; he would, I am sure, have been disappointed if everything had gone without a hitch. I felt, as I often do, unhappy in the dark—a remnant of childish terrors—but I comforted myself with the thought that no Italian trucks could possibly reach us over the rough ground we had just covered with the L.R.D.G.

At ten minutes past three that morning I was awakened to greet Musa, who had just been brought in. Tea was made and we exchanged gossip. After my departure from the Jebel, ten days ago, he had been visited by Sa'ad 'Ali Rahuma and they had picked on a natural cave in a small wadi running into Wadi Gherna, forty miles away, as the best hiding place for our stores. Sa'ad 'Ali had then left him to visit sheiks round Barce farther west, Chapman and Chevalier and the radio operators were established in a wadi at Er Rteim, in the neighborhood of Metwallah's tents.

Musa said he had camels ready to carry our loads but when, at dawn, he saw the amount of junk we had brought he was troubled and he feared he would not be able to lift everything in one journey. He then walked back to his tents and returned later with twenty-eight camels of various ages and sizes, having collected every animal capable of carrying a load. Two of the camels had riding saddles for myself and Shorten, three or four had pack saddles— the remainder were bare and the loads had to be tied on to their backs with ropes. A host of youths and children had driven the camels in with shrill cries; in great apparent confusion we started loading up. The first stage was to ferry everything across to Musa's tents. When this was done I sorted out what I would take with me and two of my men were left behind to look after the flour, tea and sugar which I had to leave in Musa's keeping. At five o'clock that afternoon we set out on a forty-mile trip to Wadi Gherna with twenty-six camels (two of the original lot had proved unmanageable) and twenty-one men. The waning moon rose about midnight and lit our ghostly plodding. Camels and Arabs, vociferous at the loading, are dead silent on the march and though the untrained animals gave trouble and the brittle, homemade ropes that held up the loads kept breaking, not a sound was heard. Senussi Arabs don't get flustered when they are in their natural surroundings; bolting camels were recaptured quickly and efficiently, shedded loads tied up again, and not a word uttered louder than a whisper. At dawn we were in the foothills, winding up the rocky Wadi Gherna. At nine o'clock, hidden in boulders and trees, an opening showed in the cliff that towered on the right bank. In we went, in single file, up a steep and deep tributary of the main wadi. The unwieldy beasts climbed with unexpected agility over the tumbled rocks. At ten our guide called a halt, the first since we had left the day before, the camels were unloaded, hobbled and left to graze, and while tea was being boiled everyone joined in carrying the stores into a deep natural cave high up the side of the ravine.

At that moment a three-engined German plane came over the mountain top and flew exactly overhead, so slowly, it seemed to me, that I thought it had stopped in mid-air to look at us. We all froze in our tracks till it finally dragged away, then we sprang to camouflage the

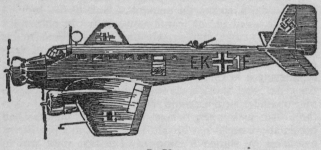

Ju 52

more conspicuous weapons with branches. The plane came over a second time a few minutes later, even lower and slower than at first. It must have decided that we were just another lot of Arabs because nothing more happened. We kept stores in that cave for over a month without ever being bothered.

When all our gear had been stowed away in the darkness of the cave I had a meal and slept for an hour. I then left Shorten in charge of the party (with instructions to do nothing without the advice of my Arab sergeant), sent Musa's camels back home and rode away towards Er Rteim. Walking alongside my camel was my guide, an elderly, white-bearded Arab. He had a concave profile, like the man in the moon in my book of nursery rhymes, and was quite witless.

My mount was tired and hungry and kept lowering its long neck to snatch at tufts of scrub as we went, pulling the rough camel's-hair headrope painfully through my fingers. We had to climb over two thousand feet on rough ground—our pace became progressively slower: we took twelve hours to cover twenty-five miles: when we arrived at Metwallah's tent the sun had risen a long time ago.

I had slept for seven hours only out of the last eighty and had been twenty-nine hours in the saddle. I was pleasantly weary but by no means exhausted. With Metwallah was Sa'ad 'Ali, who had just arrived back from his visits of prestige to the sheiks in the west. While we ate they gave me the gossip of the Jebel and we then rode down to my new headquarters in a discreet and well-wooded wadi, about an hour's ride away.

I found the two radio operators in good spirits, though their life was hard; they spoke no Arabic and knew nothing of what was going on around them. At a later date they got to be irritated by one another to the point that, to avoid quarreling, they had to put up their quarters under separate trees a quarter of a mile apart. Chapman and Chevalier were away establishing the road watch on the Martuba by-pass; they turned up the next morning.

On that day, the fourth since my return to the Jebel, we got ourselves organized. I left Chapman, with Chevalier to help him, in charge of the roadwatch, the radio station and the intelligence service generally. One of them would always be present at our headquarters to interrogate the Arab informants as they came in, check on their information, and make out the messages to the army. In this matter we set ourselves a high standard of accuracy and we refused to give in to the temptation of transmitting information which we couldn't vouch for. Even so, we soon found we had to compromise and we graded our reports as follows:

Plain, unqualified, statements were about facts we
vouched for personally.

Confirmed report meant that several independent informants had brought in first-hand information that
tallied.

Reliable report referred to information brought in by
one only of our trusted and proved Arab informants. It had to be first-hand and we submitted
the man to a long and searching interrogation to
find out what exactly he had seen or heard.

Rumors, even widespread rumors, we absolutely refused
to mention in our messages, though of course we had to
take them into account for future investigations, for they
were generally founded on fact—often a very small fact. I
missed thus what might have been the greatest scoop of
all: the presence of Mussolini himself, incognito in the
Jebel, as I shall relate in due course.

We soon had a number of regular informants working
full time for us; we trained them in our ways and sent
them out on special investigations. The curse of our trade
was the amateur sleuth who brought in elaborate and
detailed information of which not a word was true. We got
caught in that way on an occasion when we had left young
Shorten in charge of headquarters for twenty-four hours. I
found him beaming the next morning when he handed me
the message file:

"GERMAN TANKS," it read, "FIFTY-TWO MARK III,
FORTY-SEVEN MARK II STOP LORRIES SIXTY-THREE STOP
MOTORCYCLES TWO STOP LEAGUERED JUNE IST NORTH
OF SLONTA ROAD STOP MAP REFERENCE BENGHAZI
0.532 376 STOP STAYING SEVERAL DAYS STOP BOMBING
TARGET A I STOP INFORM R.A.F."

This fairy tale had been brought in the night before by a
notorious busybody, a very plausible liar by whom poor
Shorten had been taken in. I signaled:

"MY MESSAGE SEVEN OF TWO REFER STOP TAKE NO
ACTION STOP INFORMATION INACCURATE TRANSMITTED
BY MISTAKE STOP PLEASE APOLOGIZE R.A.F. STOP WHAT
ARE THEY DOING ANYWAY?"

The last words referred to the fact that none of the bombing targets I had given so far had received attention. The fact was that our very small air force was hard pressed at that time bombing Benghazi and Tripoli daily, trying to stop the flow of supplies coming in at these ports and thus delay the impending German offensive; it had no machines available for casual targets.

I told Shorten unkindly that he was a gullible fool and disconcerted him by refusing to check up on his sensational scoop. "There might be twenty tanks," he said. "Perhaps no more than ten—but even then . . ." But *I* thought there were none at all.

I had now a small dump down at Musa's tents north of Baltet ez Zala'q sixty-five miles away—another in the cave of Wadi Gherna twenty miles away—another at headquarters. I wanted to keep some food and ammunition at the two first places as a reserve in case of disaster, with men to guard them, but the bulk of the supplies were to come up to headquarters at Er Rteim with the main party of men. The weapons would be displayed there for the fiery Obeidi sheiks to see, and to judge me a man of my word. Some of the arms, however, would have to be carried over to the Dursa, who, to be sure, had followed my instructions and made a truce with the Italians, but were still in a state of smoldering rebellion.

I made Sa'ad 'Ali my quartermaster and put him in charge of these complicated movements. He also had the job of delivering the gifts I had brought for my friends.

The next problem was of remounts. Of the three horses I had purchased originally, one was still away with Hamed, one had been ridden to death by Sa'ad 'Ali, leaving us with only one poor creature. I bought eight camels and four horses, which would make us in a sense self-supporting in the way of transport. In an emergency I could now move my little force and its essential supplies without calling for help. For my own use I got myself a white mare with the brand of the Italian Army. Christened Birdybird, she was no flyer but did me good service till the end of my stay in the Jebel. She had brittle hooves and kept on casting shoes but she was reasonably fast and had much more stamina than most horses in the Jebel. The problem of finding enough barley to keep the horses in good trim was a permanent worry and I often thought I had better discard horses altogether and rely only on camels: they were slow but they fed themselves. All these purchases were paid for in what was then the normal currency in the Jebel: tea.

I had now completed my domestic arrangements; I next turned my mind to finding the means of spreading "alarm and despondency" as had been suggested by the Eighth Army. I couldn't help feeling that the size of my force was too small to be able to cause any serious material damage to the enemy war machine and I treated the matter somewhat as a joke. However, it would be fun to have a crack at the enemy and to let off loud bangs in earnest. It would also help us to overcome the boredom resulting from the monotonous routine of intelligence work. Both Chevalier and Shorten had asked to be allowed to take a hand in any fun that may be going—more serious-minded, Chapman turned down our boyish enthusiasms and declared his intention of carrying on with the work while we played our pranks.

Already on the first day of my arrival I had sent word to all my Arab helpers asking them to find me large (if possible unguarded) gasoline dumps, and the same instructions were given to every informant when he came into my camp with his piece of news. I dispatched such of my own men as I could spare to various parts of the Jebel on a similar quest. To prevent heart-searchings, which the prospect of reprisals might cause, I let everybody believe that the gasoline dumps when found, would be bombed from the air. As soon as I could free myself of administrative duties I went and called on 'Abdel Jelil bu Tayeb, my spiritual adviser, and impressed on him the urgency of my quest. He thought he knew a man who would be able to help me and promised to send him along as soon as he could be found.

Two days later, at my headquarters, a short, lean, rather ragged Arab was brought up to me. He dispensed with any but the barest civilities and in a low and singularly deliberate voice he said that his name was Mohammed el Obeidi, that he had been sent by Sheik 'Abdel Jelil bu Tayeb, that he knew of an Italian gasoline dump in the neighborhood of a place called El Qubba (or as the Italians called it: Giovanni Berta), that his tent was not far from the dump and he knew the area well. Having said that much he stood silent, waiting.

His countenance was pensive, he seemed to be following an intricate pattern of inner thought. A grave, somber man, of few words, when he was pleased, which was seldom, no more than a ghost of a smile lighted his features. An old soldier, he had spent a lifetime fighting the Italians, he knew equally the virtues of long patience and of swift action. I liked him from the first moment.

The interrogation followed its course:

"You know the dump?"

"Yes."

"You have seen it yourself?"

"I have been in it."

"How do you know it is gas?"

"I have seen the black drums."

"How many drums are there?"

"I don't know."

"Are there a thousand?"

He made a mental calculation: "More."

"Are there two thousand?"

"I don't know."

"When was the dump made?"

"In winter, soon after the Italians came back after the British troops left."

"Has it been used since?"

"No."

"Where is the dump?"

"Near the houses of El Qubba to the east. South of the road."

"How far from the houses?"

"I don't know. Near."

"Can you see the houses from the dump?"

"You can see the fort."

"Is there a guard?"

"No. There is a wire fence on posts."

"Are there any troops in the neighborhood?"

"There is the camp of tents north of the road. In the village there are the workshops where the Italians repair the trucks, and the stores where they issue the rations. At night the trucks that travel on the road go into the car park." (El Qubba at that time was a staging post on the main German line of communication.)

"Can the dump be seen from the air?"

"I don't know."

"Are the gas drums covered?"

"No. But there are trees and the whole place is overgrown with thistles."

"Can you take me to the dump?"

"I can take you inside the wire at night. There is no difficulty."

"Even if I am in uniform?"

"Even in uniform."

I liked Mohammed el Obeidi more and more. His information was accurate and to the point. I was sure he was not romancing. And if there were really more than a thousand forty-gallon drums of gasoline in the dump and I succeeded in blowing it up at the right moment, there might be a small amount of "alarm and despondency" in the enemy camp after all.

I told Chapman that I would be leaving for El Qubba the next afternoon, taking Chevalier with me, and one of my Arabs, and asked him to get a demolition party of three Arabs under Shorten to stand by till I sent instructions. Shorten was down at the dump in the Wadi Gherna but due back two days later.

That night a message came on the radio for me. It said: "SPREAD ALARM AND DESPONDENCY." So the time had come, I thought, Eighth Army was taking the offensive. The date was, I think, May 18, 1942. On the nineteenth in the late afternoon, with Chevalier, Mohammed el Obeidi and one of my Arabs, I rode off from Er Rteim. The trip was timed to take us across the Martuba by-pass about two in the morning and to reach Sidi bu Halfaya before daylight. When we got there Mohammed el Obeidi took us to a huge, dry Roman water cistern hewn out of the rock on the top of a spur. The horses were put to graze and we made ourselves comfortable and drank tea in the three-roomed cistern which was to be our home for the next week.

At dawn I made my way cautiously to the western edge of the spur. A few yards from the opening of our cistern a vertical cliff fell three hundred feet to the wadi below. On my left, half a mile away on the opposite side of the wadi, I could see an Italian ammunition dump with trucks loading and, further to the left, a stretch of the Martuba by-pass on which the daily convoys were beginning to raise dust. To the right a wide panorama opened with, on the skyline six miles away, the ambitious Italian monument that stands up on the hills beyond El Qubba. We took turns during the day, Chevalier and I, alternately to sleep and to watch through our glasses the Italian ammunition dump.

This dump might provide a useful alternative target, if the gasoline dump at El Qubba could not, for some reason, be attempted, and I asked Chevalier to reconnoiter it at close quarters in the dark hours of the next night, taking with him our Libyan soldier, while I went to El Qubba with Mohammed el Obeidi.

I started immediately after dark—too early really—for we were much vexed with the barking of dogs and were compelled to make repeated detours to avoid Arab tents where the inhabitants were not yet asleep. I didn't care to be seen by anybody so close to an important enemy center. Yet it could hardly be avoided and when a rider appeared coming directly toward us we had to stop and greet him, for any other course would have made us suspect. While Mohammed el Obeidi, quite changed from his ordinary taciturn demeanor, engaged the rider (an Arab returning to his tents after a day spent at El Qubba) in voluble talk, I grunted a few non-committal noises and drifted along out of sight in the dark.

I heard Mohammed el Obeidi explain away my churlish behavior by saying that I was a rich merchant from Jalo Oasis traveling to Derna and very cross and hungry because Mohammed, my guide, had blundered and lost his way. I thought the story would not have taken in a mouse but the other man tactfully accepted it and commiserated with Mohammed el Obeidi on the troubles of a guide. He offered to take us both to his tent and give us a meal but my guide managed to disentangle himself politely and rejoined me, chuckling grimly. It must be realized that not I but *Mohammed el Obeidi* was the man who risked his life in this adventure: if the worst happened I would become an honorable prisoner-of-war, but my friend had a good chance of ending his life strung up by an iron hook through the jaw. For such was the kindly Italian method of dealing with disaffected Arabs.

A little later we alighted at the tent of Mohammed el Obeidi's brother, where we left our horses and ten minutes' walk took us to the dump.

Enclosed with a rustic three-wire fence it covered about ten acres of scrubby ground, dotted with trees and overgrown with tall dry thistles. The gasoline was laid in lots of twenty-five to thirty drums lying close together on the ground. The lots were irregularly dispersed in the undergrowth but were not too difficult to discern, even on this moonless night. For two hours I walked up and down within the wire, counting the lots and making mental notes of landmarks. I found ninety-six lots: at an average of twenty-seven drums to the lot that dump held over one hundred thousand gallons of gasoline. It seemed good—I wondered what snag there might be; with one or two exceptions all the drums I had lifted were heavy and apparently full. With a tool I had brought with me I unscrewed a few stoppers and verified that the contents were indeed gasoline. Mohammed el Obeidi had served me well.

On one side the dump abutted on to a track leading to the main road, about five hundred yards away. Crossing the wire on my way out I saw a glow coming from the lights of El Qubba, but the little town itself was hidden by a low rise.

We arrived back in the cistern at Sidi bu Halfaya before daylight. Chevalier and his Libyan soldier were in: they had been unable to find the ammunition dump in the dark, and had returned having achieved nothing. I was annoyed because it was an easy task—the distance was no more than half a mile. Chevalier couldn't be blamed as he had no experience, but the Libyan, I knew, could have had no difficulty in reaching the dump and reconnoitering the approaches. He had had the whole day to map out a route of which every yard was visible from the top of our cliff. I said nothing but marked down our soldier as being a fool and faint of heart and resolved never to employ him any more on a job of this kind. His failure didn't matter much to me anyhow because, having decided to attempt the destruction of the gasoline dump at El Qubba, I concentrated exclusively on this project.

I wrote a message to Chapman asking him to send up the demolition party with the explosives and gadgets required. I told him the size and the layout of the gasoline dump and the manner in which I intended laying the charges. He would then have no difficulty in sending up the right stuff. We understood one another perfectly in these matters.

I had to wait till dark before dispatching the Libyan soldier with the message. I then told him that, in spite of

the fact that he had been unable to find the ammunition
dump half a mile away, I knew he was quite capable of
riding in the dark sixteen miles to Er Rteim. If he got
there safely before dawn, delivered the message and guided back to us the men that Chapman would eventually
entrust to his care, no more would be said about the
matter of his unsuccessful reconnaissance. He gathered my
meaning, nodded (with relief I thought) and went off. I
hoped I had made the best possible use of a very imperfect
instrument.

From that moment till the arrival of the demolition
party there was absolutely nothing for me to do and I fell
into a delightful inactivity. I slept sixteen hours a day, ate
and the remainder of the time I lay in the sun and watched
the kite hawks wheel in the sky. Chevalier fretted and was
bored and wanted to play paper games. I knew he was
worrying, for he was cursed with a premonitory imagination; my duty was to soothe him and take his mind off the
coming ordeal, but I couldn't do it, I was too lazy. I was
out of the world of strife and wouldn't be recalled. If I
failed him then I hope he has forgiven me.

On the second day of waiting Mohammed el Obeidi
brought me back to our schemes. He came to me where I
lay on a rock and asked permission to speak.

"When you asked to be taken to see the gasoline," he
said, "I thought you had in mind, after making sure of the
target, to send on your radio a message to your airplanes,
and they would come to bomb the dump. I realize now
that such is not the case. You have seen the dump, you
have sent a letter with that simpleton to your friend the
tall major, but yet you are still waiting here. I assume then
that you intend blowing up the dump yourself and that you
are waiting for your men to come up and help you to do it.
I must tell you, Major, that I don't like it, because, if it is
done in that way, the Italians will think that the *Arabs* set
fire to the gas and there will be reprisals. My family, my
friends, all have their tents around El Qubba. They may
have to pay the penalty: some of them will be hanged, the
others will be deported—their cattle will be taken from
them, and they will starve. They are my people, Major: I
don't like it." He said these words in his deliberate way
and paused as if listening to an inner voice. I knew only
too well that the success of my scheme was in his hands. If
his intention was to betray me and I couldn't talk him out

of it, it seemed I would have to kill him. I had a pistol down in the cistern, but I liked the man. In a few minutes I would have to make up my mind.

Mohammed resumed:

"Why don't you trust me, Major? Why don't you open your mind to me? Tell me your plan. You are in command, you know best. If the airplanes can't do the destruction *you* know why and *you* know what has to be done. This is war and not the time to think of families. If you know that the gas has to be burned and that it can't be done in any other way than by walking and setting it on fire—so be it. I don't like it but I am a soldier, Major. What has to be, has to be. You must tell me your plan; I can help you." He waited. I had to decide at once one way or the other, there was no middle course. I believed he was sincere. If he turned out to be a liar, I would be proved unable to judge men, unfit to command, unsuited for the tasks I had chosen for myself, bound anyhow to fail sooner or later. I was on test, not he. I made up my mind and I told him what arrangements I had made.

"When will your men arrive?" he asked.

"Late tomorrow night or the night after."

"Mounted?"

"Yes."

"How many will you be altogether?"

"Eleven."

"How many men on the job?"

"Nine."

"After you have been in the dump and laid your gadgets, how long will it be before the fire starts?"

"Three hours."

He nodded, wrapped his jerd round him and walked away toward El Qubba. I had twenty-four hours—till his return the next evening—to wonder if I had been a fool.

He then came up briskly, sat down and spoke as follows:

"There is hurry. Soldiers have begun yesterday to load gasoline from the dump. I hope your men arrive tonight. When they arrive they will be tired: they will rest here in the cistern till the next evening. Then, starting at ten, the nine of you and myself, we shall walk, carrying the explosives, to a dry cistern near my brother's tent at El Qubba, where we shall arrive before light. In the cistern there will be food and water. No one, under any excuse, will leave it during daylight—not even to relieve nature. On the slope outside there will be a little boy with his sheep and goats. If he sees anything alarming, such as armed soldiers making for the cistern, he will whistle in this way to warn you.

"At sunset more food will be brought. At eight-thirty you will be ready to go over to the dump, carrying only what is indispensable: explosives, one weapon I should say for every three men, and a few rounds of ammunition. The remainder of your kit will remain in the cistern. I will take you to the dump where you will arrive at nine. I will leave you there and you will do what you have to do. Not later than ten forty-five you will make your own way back to the cistern, where I shall be waiting for you. You will collect your kit and we shall walk away to Kaf el Kefra.

"In the meantime your two surplus men will drive the mounts, carrying your rations and any kit left behind, to Kaf el Kefra where we shall find them when we arrive. There is water in a pool under some rocks and we can rest at the Kaf until the evening. We shall then ride back in the dark to Er Rteim."

I said: "It is good. We shall do as you say. I am grateful to you." Mohammed el Obeidi grunted and went down into the cistern to boil himself some tea. He was my master in the art of war, and since that day every plan I have made has had his perfect "operation order" as a model.

I couldn't find Kaf el Kefra on my map and the landmarks leading to it mentioned by Mohammed el Obeidi were all unknown to me; I had to be contented with the knowledge that it was "not far to the west of El Qubba and south of the main road."

I wanted to leave the enemy with the impression that the gasoline dump had been raided by a motorized party and not by local Arabs. I remembered being told that after the unfortunate raid on Rommel's headquarters the parties waiting on the coast to be picked up by submarine had been lost because someone had carelessly dropped a map marked with the rendezvous. I wanted to do deliberately what had then been the result of an incredible folly, and I spent the next hours in marking a small-scale map with an imagined route, leading in to El Qubba from the west and leaving it toward the east, then curving down to the south in the direction of the open desert. The route I remarked in yellow pencil, the halting points in green; a red circle surrounded the approximate position of the gasoline dump, with a brown question mark. When I had drawn fasces in black for the Italian troops in El Qubba and a purple swastika for the Germans in Derna I thought that my map looked pretty convincing. I scribbled a few sums in the margins (gas consumption for five vehicles doing eight miles to the gallon and suchlike calculations), then an address, Mademoiselle Laura Vanetti, 9 Rue Morpurgo, Alexandria. Next I folded the map backward and forward several times till the creases looked worn, then I spread it out and crumpled it up and spread it out again, laid it on a flat rock and wiped my shoes on it, smeared it with fat from a tin of bully beef, burned two cigarette holes in the righthand edge and carefully tore it half down the middle. I then folded it up and put it in my pocket, ready for use.

Shorten with the demolition party arrived that night in high spirits. They rested, then they passed the time preparing the explosives. We used a device christened the daisy chain, made from gun-cotton primers threaded on a five-foot length of primacord, an instantaneous fuse that looks like a thick blind-cord. Gun-cotton primers, the explosive on which we relied to set the gasoline on fire, are in the shape of a truncated cone, the size of a large pipe bowl and have a longitudinal hole through their centers. Five primers went to each daisy china, spaced out and held in place by knots in the cord. At one end of the cord a detonator was fixed with adhesive tape: into the detonator we crimped a time-igniter, an automatic device that was meant to set off the detonator at a fixed time after the safety-pin had been withdrawn. On this occasion we used three-hour igniters. For our own safety daisy chains and detonators were carried separately and assembled at the last moment only, after the chains had been laid under the gasoline drums.

We adhered strictly to Mohammed el Obeidi's schedule. About one in the morning, after three hours' stumbling walk, we arrived in the outskirts of El Qubba. Late as it was the little settlement still showed a few lights; a screeching radio played Italian jazz in the army brothel on the hill, where I had once been billeted at a time when the place was ours. An electric welding plant in the workshops threw fitful flashes of cold, violet light. After our fearful march in the dark the mean lights and the thin noise coming from the well-known piddling Italian settlement of less than sixty hours were magnified by contrast and filled the landscape. I fell into a dreamlike fancy: the trees showing against the glow were a city park; beyond it were wide streets full of lights. Trams clanked, cars slid by, well-dressed people walked the pavements and sat in crowded cafés, where bands played soft music. Over the cinema neon lights flickered. I didn't click back into reality till long after we had slipped into our cavelike cistern.

The food provided by Mohammed el Obeidi's brother was good and plentiful. Our bellies well filled we all slept late into the next day. Our little watchman outside had no occasion to whistle. I was told later that two Italian soldiers had crossed the foot of our slope, but the child seeing them unarmed and their purpose but an idle wandering had wisely refrained from giving the alarm. The last hours of waiting wore heavily on my two British companions; Chevalier was gloomy and irritable. Shorten, excited, talkative and restless, laid down the law about the fine points of the art of demolition, and I had to interfere tactfully to prevent a quarrel. The Arabs, fortunately, were self-possessed and chatted drowsily together.

At seven-thirty that evening a small boy slipped in, carrying on his head a tray with a hot meal. At eight-thirty we hung our daisy chains round our necks, put the detonators and time-igniters in our pockets, and walked over to the gasoline dump. We crossed the wire, and collected round a small, white rock, where I gave my instructions: I had divided my force into three parties of one British officer and two Arabs each. To each party I allotted a sector of the dump which I described to them as well as I could by the landmarks—trees, rocks and bushes —that I had noted on my previous visit. Starting from where we stood they were to work their diverging ways into the dump, laying one daisy chain under each of the cluster of drums they could find in the dark. Each party had twenty daisy chains and they were to lay as many of them as they could, bearing in mind that we were all to collect again at the white rock at ten-fifteen. On no account were they to be late at the rendezvous for, I said, I wouldn't wait one minute beyond the appointed time.

Unused daisy chains were to be brought back. I repeated my discourse in Arabic, asked each man if he had perfectly understood where he was to go, what he had to do and where and at what time was the rendezvous. Our watches had been synchronized beforehand and off we went.

There was no moon but the sky was clear and, though the stars gave us enough light to work by, the darkness was sufficiently thick to make us feel safely invisible. Across the dump, in the distance, shone the headlights of three Italian trucks which were being loaded with gasoline drums. I welcomed this activity for, I thought with pleasure, the enemy would find his dump gone up in flames at the precise time when he had planned to use it. It seemed unlikely that he would be able to replace this large amount of gasoline so quickly that the course of the battle would not be affected.

We worked methodically and unhurriedly. My two Arabs lifted a drum and I laid a daisy chain underneath— then, while I fitted detonator and igniter (which has to be done with some care), one of them kept watch by me; the other walked ahead and prospected for the next lot of drums. In this way, and helped of course by my previous knowledge of the topography of the dump, we wasted no time.

It was too easy—I felt like a sneak, trespassing in the dark and, what is more, plotting to damage somebody's property. Wasn't I taking unfair advantage of the good-natured confidence of the owners of the dump who hadn't even thought it necessary to put a guard on it? Soon, however, the pleasure induced by our smooth teamwork dispelled my initial distaste, for I was no more a cowardly burglar but an honest workman doing efficiently a good job of work.

From lot to lot our broken way took us closer to the Italian trucks. Their lights were a comfort to me, they dispelled the anxiety I often feel in the dark and anyway, by day or by night, the sight of the enemy is always exhilarating. Soon I could hear the men talking in Italian, as they handled the heavy drums. With many blasphemous repetitions, they cursed the officer who had caused them to be detailed for this unwelcome nightwork. We worked up as close to them as I thought reasonable, then made our way back. We were well ahead of time and we disposed of our three remaining daisy chains on lots we had skipped on our way up.

At eight minutes to ten with twenty-three minutes to go, we squatted near the white rock. Two minutes later Chevalier and his two men loomed out of the darkness and joined us. They had used all but two of their daisy chains. We waited in self-satisfied peace. At ten past ten I posted one of the Arabs two hundred yards ahead in Shorten's sector to guide him in, in case he had trouble in finding the white rock. At twenty-five past the Arab returned, having neither seen nor heard anybody. I waited till a quarter to eleven: Shorten's party was then half an hour overdue. They must have come to grief in some unexplained silent manner, for they couldn't have lost their way; I took the decision (awful to me) to abandon them and withdraw the remainder of my men. We walked away in single file, and had gone perhaps thirty paces when the man behind me touched my arm and dropped to the ground. I did the same, and looking back toward the rock I discerned shadowy shapes moving. Our last man got up and made carefully back toward them. A moment later he brought up Shorten and his two men. I whispered weakly: "You are late." I was so shaken with relief that for a few seconds I couldn't think. He started talking and brought me back to my senses. "We shall talk presently," I said. "Follow Chevalier."

Back in the cistern, while the others gathered their kit, I had him up; he stood to attention, with a foolish grin of satisfaction on his pink face and started his report.

"Sir. I laid sixteen daisy chains in sixteen different lots of gasoline drums—" I cut him short.

"Why were you half an hour late?"

"Was I, Sir? I didn't think I was that late. Surely?"

"Why were you late?"

"Well, Sir, after we had laid our sixteen daisy chains I noticed that the primers were immobilized by a single knot on the cord. Now, Sir, on the demolition course, we were advised to tie a double knot to make sure of the explosive wave propagating itself from the cord to the primer. So I went back to all the lots and tied a second knot in the sixteen daisy chains. Ahmed and Sayed have been most helpful, Sir."

"Christ Almighty," I whispered, "What do you think we

are doing here? Running a bloody demolition course? I'll
propagate an explosive wave up your f———arse. You
are sacked. Dismiss."

I felt better—Shorten grinned in the light of my torch—
he appreciated my language and was too pleased with
himself even to feel guilty. I looked round:

"All set? Out we go," and, Mohammed el Obeidi leading, out we went.

Time was running short. The first charges had been laid
shortly after nine, two hours ago. If the delayed igniters
worked properly the dump would start blowing up in an
hour—or less—illuminating the countryside. We had to
get away before this happened and the alarm was given—
and I had still a job to do. I had arranged with Mohammed
el Obeidi that he would take us along the side of the dump
on to the main road. When we reached it I got everybody
across, took the marked map out of my pocket and fixed it
in a bush by the roadside, hoping it would look as if it had
blown out of the back of a truck. The six remaining daisy
chains and a few igniters I laid neatly in the ditch, together
with a packet of cigarettes and a field dressing, as if they
had been forgotten and left behind in a hasty departure. I
then rejoined the rest of my party across the road. We
skirted tents—a reinforcement camp that held up to two
thousand troops—dispersed on the north side of the road.
There were dim lights in some of the tents but we saw
nobody about. When we had cleared the last tents I called
to Mohammed el Obeidi to slacken the pace a little. With
the camp and the road between us and the dump I thought
we were safe for the time being; it was unlikely, if the
alarm were given, that the enemy would search for us at
first in his own territory, he would rather assume that we
had escaped to the south, toward the desert or to the east,
toward our own lines—not to the northwest where there
was no cover and every village held troops and Italian
settlers. We had, however, to get out of this area before
dawn and we were taken by Mohammed el Obeidi in a
wide curve to avoid El Qubba, then across the road once
more and on to the mysterious Kaf el Kefra.

We had hardly dipped into a gully beyond the camp
when a dull boom came from the dump, a dark red flame
rose in the sky and fell again, leaving a glow behind it.
Chevalier, who was walking with me, turned around without stopping and muttered softly: "Oh Lord!" With a

timid disposition he was a man of courage and persistently involved himself in improbable adventures. Pigheadedly he fought his natural inclination to take things easy; hardly out of one breath-taking scrape and still panting, he searched for some new way of getting himself scared. He was generally successful in his enterprises and, surprisingly, survived the war to return to cotton-broking in Alexandria.

We stumbled on in the dark led by Mohammed el Obeidi at the swift, tireless Arab pace. The glow in the dump behind us had died out. I was worried about it: that first explosion had been premature and had probably been caused by one only of our charges, but I thought it would have been sufficient to keep the fire going till the others went off.

We walked on. By one o'clock nothing had happened though all the charges should already have gone up if the time-igniters had functioned properly. With a sinking heart I felt the despair of failure overcome me. Weary and dispirited I walked on, suddenly so tired that, had I been alone, I would have lain down to sleep. Time dragged on; in my mind I kept going over the sequence of charge-laying: primers, fuses, detonators, igniters. How could they *all* have failed? We had laid fifty-four daisy chains and one only had exploded—without much effect apparently. I decided to keep up hoping till one-thirty. The half-hour came and nothing happened. Cursing the makers of our gadgets I admitted failure. As nothing could be done about it my spirits immediately began to revive and I started working out in my mind a plan to blow up a bridge on the railway line between Benghazi and Barce. I looked at my watch; my despair had lasted half an hour.

At five minutes to two the skyline behind us exploded. A broad curtain of yellow flames lifted to the sky and stayed there, lighting the bare landscape around us. Rumbling thunderous explosions followed one another throwing up more flames. Drums of gasoline, projected upward, burst in mid-air, blazing globes of fire that floated slowly down. A moment later a rolling wall of heavy, billowing smoke, lit to a fierce red by the fires burning on the ground, had taken possession of half the horizon and reached to the sky. It seemed incredible that the petty manipulations we had done so quietly in the dark could result in such a glorious catastrophe. It was more than we expected; our

reward was ten times what had been promised, such a
munificence made us wonder; we felt slightly awed and
very powerful.

For a whole hour the blaze increased in intensity. Our
men kept falling out to gaze back at the wonder and then
caught up again at a trot. The glare of the burning dump
lit our way and made the going easier. Then, as we
increased our distance and intervening lulls threw longer
shadows, I found myself once more stumbling in the dark
and hard put to it to keep up with our indefatigable guide.
On we walked. Overcome with exhaustion, I renounced
my self-respect and asked Mohammed el Obeidi how far
we were now from Kaf el Kefra. "Not far," he replied
laconically and we plodded on.

The first light of dawn came. The fire behind us shone
with undiminished fierceness. We plodded on. The sun
rose; we were in a barren wilderness of sandy hills and
scrub. My head swam with fatigue; to keep awake I tried
working out a sum: *The Germans have two hundred
tanks—they do five miles to the gallon—in battle they run
fifty miles a day. How many days' supply are one hundred
thousand gallons of gasoline?* I kept losing the threads of
my argument and starting again from the beginning—then
I got a surprising answer: *sixty-two days.* This was too
good, it couldn't be correct. Patiently I began again. This
time the answer came: *a third of a day, eight hours.* As a
period as short as that was rather disappointing back I
went to my premises. Mohammed el Obeidi came up to me
and said: "Kaf el Kefra is now near." We were all well
tired out by now but we went on under the warmer sun. I
worked once more on my problem and got as an answer:
twelve days. It seemed satisfactory and I lost interest. We
walked ... Our guide said: "Beyond that hill is Kaf el
Kefra." I laughed out loud because of a joke of ours:
When you start on a trip the guide says the objective is
far—after four hours' walk he says it is *not far*—four
hours later he says it is *near*—four hours' walk again and
he says it is *beyond that hill*—then you walk another four
hours before getting there. With dragging feet and an aching
body I tramped along for another eternity, then I looked
up again; the sun was hardly higher in the sky, which
was surprising. Someone said in Arabic: "There comes
Musa riding a camel." And indeed I saw a rider approaching across the yellow plain—one of our men, mounted on

one of our camels. We had arrived. Musa slid off his camel and shook my hand with fervor—he patted me on the shoulder and pointed to the eastern horizon where a solid black cloud of smoke stretched from north to south.

We scrambled down into a semicircle of low cliffs below the level of the plateau, dotted with caves: Kaf el Kafra. If was only half-past seven.

Musa and Yunes, the two men who had brought our kit and the animals from Sidi bu Halfaya, boiled tea for us and cooked breakfast. Squatting in the soft sand, quite revived, I looked at Mohammed el Obeidi; to my amazement his usual dark composure had gone; he was grinning and chuckling to himself.

"What is it, Mohammed?"

"Those Italian soldiers who were working last night in the dump. They are now under close arrest. The charge is "Smoking while handling gasoline and thus causing grievous damage to Mussolini's property,'" and, for the only time in my experience, he burst out laughing. We all laughed, we shook with uncontrolled mirth, we rolled in the sand, sobered down and then sputtered out again. We thought his remark infinitely funny, it summed up beautifully for us the events of the last week.

I took guard duty for the first hour, before turning in to sleep. I climbed up to the plateau and looked down; our men were all invisible, asleep in the caves—the campfire had been carefully covered with sand, the empty food tins buried. Our camels and horses were out of sight, grazing up and down the wadi. It was well. On the horizon the black wall of smoke billowed lazily.

The Arabs around El Qubba, including Mohammed el Obeidi's brother and his family, were all rounded up by the Italians and closely interrogated. They were released after a few days. Eventually a copy of the official Italian report on the incident came into my hands. It attributed the fire to the action of a *British motorized Commando*. I couldn't say whether this was the result of my attempts at deception or should be attributed to the desire of the local Italian commander to put the blame on a mysterious raiding party entirely beyond his control. After all he *might* have put a guard on the dump!

Tactfully no mention was made in the report of the amount of gasoline destroyed but I was amused to learn that a dump of small arms ammunition which, entirely

unknown to me, lay on the far side of the gasoline dump,
had been caught in the conflagration and had also blown
up. Apparently the thistles and the dry undergrowth had
spread the fire and even several of the tents in the camp on
the far side of the road had been burned.

A few days after our return to Er Rteim one of our
amateur spies came in bursting with important news:
British planes had bombed El Qubba and completely
destroyed an immense gasoline dump!

7

SETTLEMENT IN THE JEBEL

AS it was followed by no reprisals against the Arabs, our success at El Qubba established our prestige right through the Jebel. I received congratulations even from the cautious 'Ali bu Hamed. Sheiks from distant tribes, whom I had never seen before, came to visit me and proffered their services. This enabled me to extend our network of intelligence as far as Benghazi, where many supplies were landed, about which I was very glad to have regular information.

A drawback to our popularity was that sheiks now came to me with their problems, asked me to settle their differences about water points and tried to make me take a hand in tribal politics. I did my best but I had neither the time nor the staff to carry out properly the duties of Governor of Cyrenaica.

Chapman in the meanwhile had got his road watch functioning with an astonishing degree of efficiency. Every night, for nearly five months he radioed to the Eighth Army a detailed account of the enemy movements on the main line of communication during the preceding twenty-four hours. His show was run as a business. He had watchers on the road, relays of runners, supervisors, everyone paid a monthly salary, with premiums for regularity and fines in case of inaccuracy or slackness. Every few days he would go and watch the road himself from morning till night and check the result against the report of his Arab watchers further up the road. In this way he kept them on their mettle and made sure that they wouldn't concoct their lists of vehicles in their tents, far from the tiresomeness of road watching. He succeeded in firing his helpers with enthusiasm for this tedious work and gave them a love of accuracy which is very foreign to the Jebel Arab's nature.

Chapman gave me a black report on Sa'ad 'Ali Rahuma's activities as a quartermaster; an investigation revealed the disastrous extent of his lavishness. I relieved him of his administrative duties and sent him to reconnoiter the railway line running from Benghazi to El Abiar and Barce. As I was particularly ill-fitted to be my own quartermaster I sent an urgent request to Middle East to send out Grandguillot, a Frenchman from Alexandria, now a captain in the British service, of whose administrative abilities I had good reason to have a high opinion. I knew that he was looking for a job and would be willing to quartermaster for us.

In the meanwhile, putting aside more congenial tasks, I set out to visit our dumps. I was climbing out of our deep wadi at Er Rteim when I saw, coming toward me, an Arab leading a horse on which two men were riding. I soon recognized the man, an Arab called Sayed el Barasi whom I had employed casually to collect information, a good man and of a pleasant disposition, but the riders puzzled me. They were unshaven and in tatters, yet there was something indefinable about them that put me in mind of the R.A.F. Sayed el Barasi told me he had brought those to me, would I see what they were? I had a sudden notion that they might be Italians, disguised, sent out to spy on me and addressed them abruptly in what I thought might be their language. They looked up languidly and replied in halting but unmistakable cockney. They were, as it turned out, two of a crew of eight who had bailed out of a bomber near Benghazi six weeks earlier.

They had wandered a long while in the inhospitable desert south of the Jebel, had been picked up by friendly Arabs in a state of considerable exhaustion and passed on from tent to tent till they had fallen into the hands of Sayed el Barasi, who, being familiar with our camp, had brought them in to me for inspection. When they realized that they were talking to a British officer, their countenances lit up a little, but thinking that I was only a fellow sufferer (in slightly better condition than themselves) and being tired and bewildered, they disbelieved my account of my position, or they assumed that my mind was wandering. It was only when I brought them to my camp and poured them each half a mugful of whisky that they realized, with an expression of angelic delight on their poor tired faces, that they were indeed saved and had found someone who could look after them. I handed them to our radio operators, recommending that they should be fed very sparingly, wrapped in blankets and left to sleep. That night their names went out on the air to the R.A.F.—and their families.

Sayed el Barasi, in the meanwhile, having talked to some of our men, came up to me and, after I had thanked him and given him a reward, asked if I would employ him as one of my regular staff. I replied that, as he well knew, I was always willing to give him work but as he had his family and flocks to look after and couldn't give me all his time, I couldn't take him on my staff. "Never mind my family and my flocks," he said, "I want to work for you permanently. Will you take me? I have also got a horse." I agreed to this and told him he would be attested and enrolled as a private in the Libyan Arab Force. He would then receive the same treatment as the men I had brought with me from Egypt. I was puzzled, however, and inquired from my men about his motives. I learned then that his journeys on my account having become known to men in his tribe—the Barasa—among whom was an informer in Italian pay (I remembered Sa'ad 'Ali Rahuma's dictum: "The Barasa are all traitors"), he had been betrayed and, in his absence, a party of Italian police had raided his village, burned his tent, killed his cattle and taken his wife away as a hostage. His children were looked after by relatives—having lost everything he had come to me for employment. A lesser man might have flaunted his sacrifices and the losses he had suffered; not so this simple Senussi who only asked *as a favor*, to be allowed to join us in fighting the Italians. He didn't think it seemly for a man and a warrior to try and make capital out of his losses or to importune a friend with the tale of his misfortunes.

I sent Sayed el Barasi to investigate the prisoner-of-war cages near Benghazi. I thought I might find it possible to organize escapes and bring some of our prisoners back to Egypt. His instructions were to find the location of the camps, how many they held, of what troops (British or Indian) and to find out about the guards, the wire and the state of the defenses generally. A tall order, but he rode away contented enough (I had bought his horse from him but let him ride it).

The plan had been suggested by the arrival in my camp of three escaped prisoners, brought in independently by

Arabs a few days after the two air force lads. They had escaped from a camp—somewhere south of Benghazi, they thought, but couldn't say where it was—and had had the good sense to keep to the southern foothills of the Jebel where they met many Arabs who fed them and sped them on. In this way they reached me quite rapidly and in good condition, though they had walked about one hundred and forty miles. It seemed to me that with a little organization in the prison camps and among the Arabs on the way it would be possible to keep a steady trickle—or even a flow—of escaping prisoners making their way back in comfort to our lines.

I signaled the L.R.D.G. asking them to divert a patrol to collect the five men I had now in my camp. Their reply came the next night: R1 Patrol (New Zealand) would call three days later at Haqfet Gelgaf in the southern foothills, arriving about four o'clock at the usual rendezvous. So we put our five escapees on camels and sent them down with an escort of our soldiers. They reached the rendezvous in an easy two days' ride, were picked up as arranged and arrived in Egypt in due course.

Poor Shorten went with them: sacked. He was a lovable lad and extremely brave but as yet too young and irresponsible for my jobs. I couldn't employ him with Arabs who were much better at the game than he was. I gave him a glowing testimonial and he joined the S.A.S. Regiment shortly after his return to Egypt. Later I was sad to learn that he had got killed when his jeep overturned during the chase that followed the battle of El Alamein.

I was getting a little worried about the number of visitors who came daily to our camp at Er Rteim. We were getting *too* well known and inevitably sooner or later the wrong kind of person would be calling on us. I moved my headquarters to a wadi near Khaulan, closer to the Martuba by-pass where Chapman had his road watch and thus a more suitable location for the radio set. There was water nearby, and there were friendly tents in the neighborhood from which we could get milk and occasionally a kid or a lamb. I left two men at Er Rteim, to screen the visitors and send on to our new camp only those they could vouch for. The radio operators welcomed the change in the very dull routine of their lives.

My investigation into the state of our stores had resulted in a long list of requirements sent out on the air to

L.R.D.G. In reply a few days later I got a signal which said:

R2 PATROL WILL CALL BIR BELATER JUNE 4 TWENTY-ONE HUNDRED HOURS CARRYING SUPPLIES AS REQUESTED STOP GRANDGUILLOT AND TWO ARABS WITH SUPPLIES TRAVELING WITH R2 STOP MIDDLE EAST REQUEST YOU GIVE HIM EVERY ASSISTANCE MESSAGE ENDS.

Grandguillot was the officer I had just asked for—to be my quartermaster. Such expedition in complying with my demand was astounding; I felt I had never given Middle East Headquarters their due. The last sentence in the message puzzled me—wouldn't I naturally give every assistance to an officer joining me at my request?—but I dismissed the matter lightly as being beyond my comprehension.

Chapman, Chevalier and myself rode down in great spirits to Bir Belater to meet Grandguillot. Dick Croucher and his patrol of New Zealanders rolled in on time and we had a party. New Zealanders are pleasant and Croucher, unaffected and humorous, was an old friend of mine; for an hour we discarded the Arab way of life and the intricacies of tribal politics, we forgot the road watch and our plans to damage enemy property, we chatted and laughed and drank beer and rum-and-lime. Then they departed again, leaving us to load our camels with the treasures they had brought.

Grandguillot, a French international tennis player from Alexandria, liked to play the part of a stage Frenchman. He shouted and got excited and, though he didn't actually kiss us, he made me feel that he might do so at any moment. He had two Libyan Arab soldiers with him and a large number of mysterious, heavy, sausage-shaped bags. On our leisurely ride back to camp I gave him an outline of our position and our activities and told him what I expected him to do.

"I would love to help you," he said, "but I shall have my own work to see to."

"What is your work?"

"I can't tell you."

"How come," I said, "don't you know?"

"I do—in a way," he replied, somewhat embarrassed. "I am not allowed to tell you."

"Why?"

"It is secret and I have been specially instructed not to tell you."

"Haven't you been sent here at my request?"

"Did you ask for me? I was never told."

The situation was ludicrous and we both laughed. I pointed out that if I didn't know what his job was, I couldn't help him, and without my active support he would not be able to achieve much in the eastern part of the Jebel which, in a sense, I controlled: he might *perhaps* succeed in doing *a little*—but, whatever he did, I would be informed of it automatically day by day, and his awful secret would be out of the bag. So hadn't he better be sensible and tell me *now* what it was about? I might be able to help him.

Grandguillot was no fool, and he understood well the position we were in in the Jebel; he was also a well-trained soldier and the orders of his commanding officer were to be obeyed—up to a point. He meditated a moment then leaned from the saddle and said in French:

"Ce sont des cons"—referring to our masters in Cairo— "mon vieux Popski, mais nous allons être plus malins qu'eux." Then he told me that a new organization had come out from England to the Middle East, with the object of helping our prisoners-of-war to escape from enemy cages and to make their way back to our lines. He had joined this organization and had been sent to the Jebel with orders to establish a chain of food depots along the routes which the escaping POW's might take and to induce or bribe the local Arabs to guide them from depot to depot till they could be collected at a suitable spot and picked up by the L.R.D.G. The mystery bags, he said, contained special, scientifically prepared rations, and he had with him forty thousand lire to bribe the Arabs.

I said the scheme seemed sound enough, and could be made to work,—with some alterations to suit existing conditions. In fact I had had a similar plan in mind for some time and would be glad to help him.

We came to a friendly agreement: we would work together the schemes to recover escaping prisoners and Grandguillot would get the credit for as many as we brought back. In return he would take over my administration and share our fortunes. I was well pleased with the arrangement; hard-working, methodical and efficient, he was an asset to my party and furthermore he was a pleasant companion, full of fun and of unexpected knowledge. As to the escaping prisoners, as long as the poor blighters were brought out safely, I didn't care to whose account they were chalked up.

8

VINDICATION OF SA'AD 'ALI

WHEN I received the message inciting me to spread alarm and despondency, I assumed that the Eighth Army was about to take the offensive: ever since, we had been watching the behavior of the enemy for signs of how the battle was developing. Army received our information but gave us none in return, the B.B.C. news was deliberately out of date; we had to rely on our guesses.

Enemy road traffic increased considerably, the shallow port of Derna was put to use by coastal craft and sailing boats, and every day large flights of German transport planes landed their cargoes at El Ftaiah, on the escarpment above Derna. At night the eastern sky was aglow with fires and flares—which I took to be caused by the R.A.F. bombing enemy landing grounds and dumps. There could be no doubt that the battle had started but we looked in vain for signs of an impending German withdrawal. On the contrary, stores and troops were going up and none coming down, we even spotted a convoy carrying bridging equipment for which no use could be imagined before the German Army reached the canals of Egypt. The gossip reaching us from Italian officers' messes spoke of the varying fortunes of a developing German offensive. Grandguillot, though fresh from Siwa, knew only that a big battle was on and that it was thought it was going well for us. In fact Rommel had forestalled our offensive by attacking us on May 27, 1942, with armored forces south of Bir Hakeim and with infantry (mostly Italian) at Gazala. For three weeks the battle was fierce but fairly static with alternations of successes and reverses. For us in the Jebel it was a period of intense activity and we undertook several demolition operations with some success. We were confident that a British victory was near, the Italians, on the whole, shared our views, and the Arabs, in the presence of such an unanimity, couldn't help but feel that the battle had already been won. As a consequence, conditions were easy for us and, although we had never been so active, we took few precautions to remain concealed.

Then the nightly illuminations which had heartened us receded, decreased and finally ceased altogether; the road traffic fell back to normal and the big dumps around El Qubba were found empty, completely transferred forward. Sheik 'Abdel Jelil bu Tayeb rode in one morning to tell me he had heard a rumor that Tobruk had fallen, and during the day and the following night more and more reports came in confirming, with an increasing accuracy of detail, that this had indeed happened, on June 20, with the capture of over twenty thousand of our men.

Some fool invented a spurious ancient prophecy to the effect that "whoever holds Tobruk holds Cyrenaica." The Arabs went repeating it, scaring each other: in twenty-four hours a full-sized scare had developed. "The Italians had won the war, they would remain in Cyrenaica for ever. Reprisals against the Arabs would soon start." Everyone suspected his neighbor of being a basas—an informer—and I was asked when I would remove my compromising headquarters to a more remote area. I thought it was a sensible suggestion but I didn't think it wise to increase the panic by running away in a hurry; also I had been caught on the wrong foot: several of my men were away on distant jobs, some of the camels were grazing at some distance, and our camel gear, ropes and containers were in a shocking state of disrepair. I prepared to move to a more discreet and less populated area (my present headquarters were only five miles from the main road), planning to leave in three days' time. Very early on the morning of the second day Metwallah arrived with the information that an Italian party led by a basas (unnamed) would leave Lamluda at dawn to come and round us up. He advised me to move out at once. I knew only too well that if we were discovered by an Italian patrol, even if it failed to capture us, all the Arabs in the neighborhood—and included in this number were all our most faithful friends—would be made to pay the penalty for harboring us; I had no choice but to decamp.

Dawn found us on the move, our stores precariously tied on to our camels with pieces of decayed rope, the men themselves heavily loaded. Thanks to Sa'ad 'Ali Rahuma's hustling, we had managed to lift everything we had, but frayed ropes kept snapping and loads falling off; we hadn't been going for two hours before we had to stop and slink into a shallow gully where we thought we would not be too conspicuous. I heard some riders coming, and peeping through the bushes over the bank of the gully I recognized Metwallah and three of his friends galloping along. He pulled up when he saw me, said hurriedly he was going to Derna to get the news and show himself to the authorities, and galloped away. Having to hide behind hedges was humiliating enough—the realization that my friends and supporters were running away from me put me in a fine state of dejection. In complete misery I sat down in the gully, at a loss what to do next. My companions sat in gloomy silence, waiting for a lead, but I had been caught in the confusion and couldn't find a word to cheer them. I was beaten.

Sa'ad 'Ali Rahuma came and squatted next to me, very quiet, very self-possessed. He said: "The heavy weapons we have got and their ammunition were meant only to impress the sheiks. They will not be needed till better news comes. Our explosives too are heavy and can be spared for a few days. Perhaps, Major, you will think fit to dump them here. If we do that we shall be able to carry the remainder of our stores: the radio sets and small arms and the food. I believe there is a disused well near here, where we could hide our equipment. Let us ride over and look for it, you and I, and see if it is fit for our purposes."

I agreed languidly. Sa'ad 'Ali sprang on to his horse and made it scramble noisily over the bank of the gully. "A fig for the basasin," he said and waved his hand, the middle finger crooked, a rude gesture he must have learned in Egypt. Interpreted it means: "My finger up his backside." We rode in silence till he reined in on the edge of a smooth meadow and cast a glance at me as I slumped sadly in the saddle. "I shall race you to that tree," he said. "One, two, three—go!" Off we clattered, he on his scraggy bay and I on Birdybird, my white mare. (For once she had four shoes on!) At the tree he was leading by two lengths. "Not fair," he said. "You are twice as heavy as I am. I shall give you now a start." Back we galloped; he won again, easily. "Wait," I said, "I shall beat you yet," and I unbuckled and threw down on the grass my heavy belt with the pistol in its holster and the ammunition pouch. "Three lengths start I'll take and good-by to you." I won the third lap by a head.

We walked our panting horses back to where I had dropped my belt, Sa'ad 'Ali chattering away: "When I was a young man we had horses, real horses. We prided ourselves in our horsemanship. I was a good rider: I could have galloped round this meadow with a silver dollar poised on the toe cap of my boot and never dropped it. I wonder, Major, have you got a silver dollar?" I hadn't, but I found a flat stone which I balanced on his foot. He cantered away carefully but the stone soon fell off. "What can you expect with a horse like mine?" he grumbled. "Now you try, with your comely 'Berdberd.'" I lost the stone even quicker than he had and came back laughing. Sa'ad 'Ali Rahuma's face crinkled up in an impudent grin:

"I believe the major is happier now."

"A thousand thanks to you. Now where is that cistern?"

We found its concealed entrance amongst tumbled rocks near the top of a hill. I complimented Sa'ad 'Ali on remembering the existence of this well after all those years. "There are over ten thousand disused cisterns in the Jebel and I know them all," he boasted.

This particular one was well suited to receive our dump: dark, dry and deep, its bottom could be reached only with a rope or a ladder, enough to keep the casual pilferer away. We rode back to the gully where my party was still crouching moodily. Sa'ad 'Ali was in his most hustling mood; he dispatched a party to the cistern with a first installment, and leaving one man to keep an eye on animals and stores, he led us all to a bank overgrown with the long stalks of alfalfa grass.

"Now boys, to it. Cut the grass. The long stalks are the best. Come on boys. Have you been idle so long, you pampered soldiers, that you have forgotten how to make ropes?" He set to with an incredible energy till he got every one of us cutting frantically. He sat himself by the mounting pile and with quick, deft movements rolled and twisted the coarse stalks into strands and then into ropes. Whatever this remarkable man set his hand to—kneading dough, shoeing a horse or rope-making—he did with the economy of gestures and the quick aptness of action of a

practiced professional. In this respect he was unique
among his people who despise manual labor and, when
compelled by necessity to put their hands to some work,
are found to be all thumbs. Three of our older men joined
Sa'ad 'Ali at his labors and emulated his deftness, clumsily.

His hands engaged, Sa'ad 'Ali Rahuma kept up a stream
of bantering abuse and would allow his helpers not a
moment of relaxation. I rode over to the well. The work
there completed, I returned to find yards of coarse rope
stretched on the ground. The men were tired and happy,
and when an Arab we knew came slinking in to warn us
with awe that he had just seen a basas hot on our trail he
was greeted with general laughter. Sa'ad 'Ali had restored
our morale.

By mid-afternoon one hundred and seventeen yards of
rope had been made and we started loading up. Sheik
'Abdel Jelil bu Tayeb, whom I had sent for, arrived,
urbane and cool. I discussed the situation with him and
decided to move camp that same night to Bir Semander in
Wadi Ramla twenty miles to the southeast.

With our loads well secured and our minds at ease we
covered the stage during the night. In the early morning
we settled under acacia trees on the banks of the dry wadi.
I shared a tree with Grandguillot; Chapman and Chevalier
took another two hundred yards away; the remainder of
our men spread themselves further downstream. That
evening our radio opened up and we put our usual intelligence report on the air. We didn't mention our changed
fortunes to the Eighth Army: they had, we thought,
enough worries of their own, and we felt quite capable of
looking after ourselves.

Every other night a party went to Bir Semander to draw
water. Relays of runners kept up communications with the
road watch. The scare died down very rapidly in the Jebel
and our informants found once more their way to our new
camp. There was, however, no disguising the fact that we
had less and less to do. As the battle moved eastwards and
reached the Egyptian border two hundred miles away the
Jebel became a backwater, a military void. My immediate
problem was to keep up the faith of my Arab friends in
the ultimate victory of our side. In their eyes I was the
British Government; so long as they saw me among them,

plotting my schemes with their help, they wouldn't take much notice of the confusing rumors that filtered through from radio Derna, and they would believe that, as I told them, the withdrawal of the British Army was a cunning trap laid to catch Rommel with an extended line of communication and deal him a crushing blow on our own ground. I should have been much surprised had I been told then that my medacious prophecy was to come true.

To show the Arabs that I was still active—and also in the hope of being able to arrange mass escapes—I sent reconnaissance parties to several points from Tobruk to Benghazi to find out in what manner the twenty-thousand-odd prisoners captured at Tobruk were disposed of.

In our changed circumstances, however, I had no more use for a large party and I decided to send back to Egypt the bulk of my men with Grandguillot and Chevalier. Chapman thought he would like to stay on with me; we decided to come to a final decision on the matter when we had received fresh news from the outer world. I sent a message to L.R.D.G. asking them to pick up a large party and fixing a rendezvous at some distance from our present camp. They promised to send a patrol about the middle of July.

My party was growing daily. The Italians, believing they were once more the masters of Cyrenaica, had started reprisals against the Arabs they suspected of having helped the British, and as a consequence refugees came trickling in to our camp hoping we would evacuate them to Egypt. Then one morning a little South African was brought in. He had escaped from a prison camp near Benghazi ninety-two days previously and for over two and a half months he had wandered by himself in the inhospitable southern desert where in the dry season no Arabs go. He had lived on a little water he found now and then in the radiators of abandoned vehicles and scraps of food left in opened tins, making his way slowly eastward through the endless desert. At times his mind had wandered and he had been unconscious for several days. Yet such was the greatness of heart of this little clerk who had spent his life in an office in Johannesburg that, after he had been only a day with us he asked to be allowed to remain in the desert and help us with our work, rather than being evacuated to Egypt by the next convoy. I granted him his wish for a while till I had to give in to pressure from South African Headquarters who insisted in sending him home to the Union.

It was Dick Croucher who turned up with his New Zealand patrol. He told a strange tale: the Eighth Army, weakened but by no means crushed, was standing up to the Germans, still in Cyrenaica but falling back steadily on to the Egyptian border. Headquarters in Cairo, on the other hand, thoroughly upset were preparing to remove themselves elsewhere—Palestine or the Sudan, he thought. The diplomats also were packing and he had seen bonfires of burning archives in the Embassy gardens. Civilians, European and Levantines, were scrambling away to the Congo, South Africa, India and Australia—wherever they could find a plane or a ship to take them. Among the troops in Egypt, he said, all was confusion; everyone was running around, either pestering harassed staff officers or issuing impossible orders to bewildered underlings.

At first I had listened with amusement to Dick Croucher's humorous account of what he had seen in Cairo a few days ago but when he came to say that his orders were to withdraw the whole of my party (including myself) and to take us to Cairo, to the very center of this unsavory mess, a wave of panic came over me. I didn't mind fighting a losing battle against the enemy (I had learned to take military reverses without fuss) but I was terrified at the prospect of having to fight our own General Staff as a jobless officer in a panic-stricken rabble far in the rear. Rather than submit to this indignity I would remain in the desert, carry on with such jobs as I could find to do behind the enemy lines and take the risk of being left stranded in Cyrenaica till the end of the war if things went wrong with the Eighth Army and Egypt fell to the enemy. I hate panic and mass hysteria so much that the possibility of becoming, perhaps for years, a fugitive in enemy land seemed a better lot than becoming involved in the confusion Dick Croucher described so well. I didn't then fear capture much because I was confident that if I was surprised and taken I would escape again soon. Later I lost some of my cocksureness and I came to dread the prospect of spending years behind barbed wire: of all the hazards of war, captivity is the one against which I am the least well armed.

I found many arguments to reinforce my determination not to go back to Cairo: I couldn't let down my Arab friends—I had still the possibility of collecting information which might be useful to the Eighth Army, and my scheme to liberate some of our prisoners-of-war was taking shape. My real motive of course was that behind the enemy lines I was free and my own master.

Chapman also was disposed to stay on, though he didn't tell me what his motives were. He just said that he didn't feel like going to Cairo. Worried as he was about his family in Cairo, this decision required great courage. Though we lived for months in the closest intimacy of purpose we never revealed our inner thoughts to one another: a confidential talk would have embarrassed us both. Chapman asked our two British radio operators if they would volunteer to stay with us and they agreed readily to do so, without apparently giving much thought to the matter. Neither did I, for I had used up all my cunning in handling the Arabs and I tended to take for granted the co-operation of our British soldiers. I was embarrassed when I had to deal with the very few problems they presented and I let Chapman tackle them, which he did very skilfully. I had yet to learn the handling of British troops.

In a radio message to L.R.D.G. headquarters I explained my scheme for the liberation of prisoners-of-war and asked them to send a patrol in a month's time to collect such of our men as I would have been able to get out of the cage. The next morning their reply arrived: they agreed to my request but made it quite clear that the general position was so uncertain that no one could tell for sure if in a month's time there would be any patrols at all operating in the Jebel. I thanked them and said I would take the risk.

9

ESCAPE FROM PANIC IN CAIRO

DICK CROUCHER drove away in the early afternoon, taking with him Chevalier and Grandguillot, the escaped prisoners, Sa'ad 'Ali Rahuma, the Libyan soldiers (save two) and the Arab refugees—about thirty men all told. His parting words, unexpectedly emotional, were: "Good-by, Popski. I shall never see you again." Chapman, myself, two radio operators and two Libyan soldiers remained, with one month's supplies. All over the sandy wadi, and particularly where dry desert bushes had been crushed down, the trucks had left unmistakable track marks which I was puzzled how to obliterate. The problem was solved by driving a flock of sheep and goats up and down the wadi; by sunset the tiny hooves had churned up the soft surface so completely that no trace remained of the passage of our vehicles. We dumped some weapons under rocks, against an emergency, and we walked back in the dark to our camp in Wadi Saratel.

We decided, Chapman and I, to share out the work in the following way; I would liberate prisoners and he would organize hide-outs in case the Germans occupied Egypt and the L.R.D.G. failed to relieve us at the end of August. We thought that in the wooded crags and the cliffs on the northern coast, where the inland plateau drops three thousand feet to the sea, we would be able to hide indefinitely if the local Arabs gave us food: these Arabs were the Dursa, to whom I had given a scolding at the time of their rebellion. Accordingly Chapman left for Dursaland the very next night, with his Libyan, who knew the country well. They were both riding camels. The return trip would be about one hundred and fifty miles.

I stayed alone with the radio operators and my Libyan in the Wadi Saratel, waiting for my emissaries to come back from various places on the coast where I supposed prisoners might be collected. Till they arrived I had absolutely nothing to do, and for some days my physical activity was limited to the pulling of my rug round the tree under which I camped, following the shade as it moved from west to east. I had only one book left: *The Canterbury Tales,* and it didn't matter at all that I had read it several times. At first I had guessed my way through; at each reading I understood a little more, thus the book was ever new.

Rumors were brought to me that Mussolini himself was in Qubba. I disbelieved them. Then a man I trusted well enough came with a tale of having seen him disguised as a sergeant in the market at Qubba, not once but on several occasions. He had seen Mussolini before the war at public functions and swore he recognized him. The story seemed too circumstantial and the fact so incredible that I decided to take no action till I had confirmation. I didn't even mention the rumor in my daily message to the army, for I didn't want to lower my standard of accuracy, and moreover, I was not much interested. Unprovided with vehicles I had no means of kidnapping the fat blusterer, and I drew the line at assassination. Eventually I got confirmation of his presence in Cyrenaica: as the matter might have had some political significance I informed the Eighth Army after all.

Then I heard that the Germans had two large transit camps in Derna where our prisoners, captured at Tobruk, were kept for a few days on their way to Benghazi. Here was my chance; with a thousand or more prisoners coming in, and going out again, every week, the nominal rolls could not be kept very tidily, nor would the guard be very strict. It might be easy for prisoners to escape from the camps; and they might have a chance to get clear before the hue and cry started. So I set off immediately, to examine the camps and make arrangements for escapes.

As I didn't know the country round Derna well enough to travel alone by night I rode up to the tent of a Sheik Mukhtar, ten miles up Wadi Saratel, and asked him for a guide—a khabir. He promised to do his best at once and sure enough I had hardly got back to my tree when a decrepit old Arab rode up on a very tall camel. "I am Omar bu Qasem," he said. "We are going to Derna together to see 'Ali el Barasi. Have you got a mount or will you ride my camel?" "I shall ride my mare," I replied.

"Let us go." I folded my jerd, picked up a haversack, called to my Libyan soldier to saddle Birdybird, told him I was going to Derna for a week leaving him in charge of the radio operators, mounted and rode away with Omar.

Darkness fell as we scrambled out of the wadi. Omar struck a course over a slightly rolling, stony plain and we rode in silence. The night was very dark, the sky was overcast as one of the rare summer storms was brewing. Birdybird kept stumbling and our progress was slow. I looked at my compass now and then: Omar kept us on a steady course, slightly north of northeast. How he did it I don't know, for no stars were visible nor could I notice any landmarks on the ground except a few low bushes and patches of soft sand now and then in shallow dips of the hard gravel plain. Even by daylight the landscape would have appeared featureless. We had ridden three hours when he pulled up and asked me if I could see the white superstructure of a well somewhere ahead of us.

I peered very carefully through the woolly darkness and saw nothing. "Can you see it?" I asked. Omar said in a querulous voice: "How could I? My right eye is quite blind and the left one is not much better. You can't expect me to see a thing; this is a dark night." My heart sank, like a fool I had entrusted myself to a blind guide on a black night, and I was lost. Derna, forty miles away, suddenly appeared unattainable. Quietly Omar said, "We ride on." He pulled up again after ten minutes: "Please dismount and put your head near the ground. I think you will now see the well against the skyline." I did so and sure enough a small rectangular shape showed up, dark against the faintly lighter sky: the well, about one hundred yards ahead of us.

Omar gave no sign of relief, for he had never had the faintest anxiety. "This is Bir bu Hataja. We won't go any nearer because it is much in use and our tracks in the soft sand might be seen tomorrow morning. All the Arabs know the tracks of your mare. We go on to Bir Qashqash which is on stony ground, to water the animals." Our track now lay up a narrowing rocky wadi with sides rising steeply it seemed to at least a hundred feet: there was no doubt about the way and an hour later we climbed up on to the plateau at the head of the wadi where stood the well. Omar took from his saddle bag a coil of rope and an empty gasoline can and we watered Birdybird and also the camel. While we were drawing water I tried to get Omar to explain how he found his way: I had no more success with him than with other Arabs on many previous occasions. As usual I got the puzzling reply: "I know the way."

It was a perpetual disappointment to me that though I had been walking and riding backwards and forwards over the Jebel for months I had still got no nearer to acquiring a sense of direction in any way comparable to that of the dumbest Arab. At night without a compass, even over familiar ground, I inevitably strayed from the direct route when there were no conspicuous landmarks; any Arab child could have given me lessons. In fact it is quite common to meet a toddler of eight or ten all by himself two or three days' walk from anywhere, gravely following the tracks of a stray camel. There is of course no magic and no sixth sense in their ability in finding their way: landmarks, so minute as to escape our notice altogether, remain fixed in their memory, not only visual landmarks but also the feel of the ground underfoot. Moreover they have in their mind a picture of the general structure of the country: on a featureless plain, they can distinguish watersheds and slopes. Dry, sandy watercourses faintly marked with poor bushes seem to us distributed haphazardly; the Arab recognizes them as part of the general drainage system, flowing ultimately to one of the big wadis: Ramla, or El Fej, or Belater. In a similar way, walking in a side street in London, though I have never seen it before, I may know that following its general direction I shall ultimately arrive in Oxford Street. The desert Arab is hopelessly lost in a town.

We rode away from Bir Qashqash and had been going some time when we heard dogs barking faintly. Omar asked me if I had any food with me. "Only a tin of bully," I said, "which I would like to keep for an emergency. And anyhow it is Christian food and not suitable for you." He asked me to stay where I was and made off in the direction of the dogs, returning after a while with four loaves of bread and a small lump of cheese. "There were seven tents," he said. "An old woman in one of them called to me when she heard me coming. I lifted the flap and told her I was a traveler and hungry, she gave me the food. It should last us till we get to Derna." It was then about three in the morning.

Shortly after dawn we stopped in sight of the German road (the Martuba by-pass) somewhere west of Karmusa, intending to cross it during the afternoon lull in the traffic, and in the meanwhile we made ourselves comfortable in the shade of an acacia tree and ate our meal.

About eleven o'clock we saw a lonely camel rider crossing our tree-dotted wadi a hundred yards away. As he had seen us I sent Omar to call him to our hospitality. He turned out to be an Arab of an obscure western tribe of low reputation, which accounted, I supposed, for his extraordinary bad manners; indeed, against all courtesy, he kept asking questions: who we were and where we intended going and what was our business. Omar went and lit a fire in a hollow some distance away, taking teapot and glasses with him; he called to me after a while; I walked over, leaving our guest. "This Arab may well be a spy. We must shake him off somehow or he will follow us to Derna." "Go and talk to him," I said. "I shall make the tea. Be careful you don't touch his glass for there will be *special* tea in it."

Left alone I slipped five tablets of morphia into one of the glasses. I had been told that seven tablets were a fatal dose, so I hoped that five would induce a nice long sleep but leave no unexplained corpse behind. I contrived that our guest should take the doctored glass—I had made the tea particularly strong and sweet so as to cover the taste of morphia—and I went on listening for over an hour to the idiotic stream of questions of our bumpkin friend. At last he grew drowsy and finally fell asleep. We made him comfortable in the shade of a bush, covered him up with his jerd and when the traffic on the road died down we rode over. It had been pleasant to hear once more the rumbling trucks on the road and to catch a glimpse of the enemy through the trees where the road crossed the wadi: it stilled a secret feeling of futility which I had been suppressing, not quite successfully, ever since our withdrawal to Bir Semander.

Two hours before dawn we arrived, Omar and I, at the edge of El Ftaiah plateau on the escarpment above Derna and we dipped into one of the precipitous gullies that run nearly vertically down to the coastal plain, six hundred feet lower down. We climbed down as far as our mounts could go and stopped in a hollow among rocks and boulders, thick with trees and bushes, grass and even moss, for a small trickle of water seeped out of the rocks, ran a few yards across the hollow and fell out of sight in a sheer drop, a tiny waterfall. Omar unloaded the camel and advised me to take some rest while he went to make contact with 'Ali el Barasi and some other of our friends in Derna. He would be back, he said, about midday, and rode away on Birdybird. I lay back in my bower, glad to sleep, having been up for two days and two nights.

The sun was just up when I woke in my enchanted retreat. After months in the desert where all water is in cisterns or in stagnant pools, there is a magic in running water, even if it is no more than would come from a dripping tap. I fancied glades of mossy banks, dragonflies and fish rising. I washed and made myself tea and lay back again, very happy, waiting lazily for Omar to return. Then I remembered the camel. Omar had said that he would leave it unhobbled as it wouldn't stray, if I wanted it all I had to do was to whistle. The brute, however, had strayed and never answered. After a while I got vaguely worried and strolled to the head of the gully. No camel. I ventured on to the plateau, whistling at intervals. It was silly, losing a camel and going about at dawn, whistling for it; I wanted to get back in the hollow and watch my little stream, and the bushes growing out of the rocks. In the desert nothing grows on rocks, the vegetation is all in the hollows and the dry watercourses. I rounded a hill and came across an Arab with a flock of goats and sheep. I realized at once that I would have some difficulty in explaining my presence but he had already seen me and anyhow I wanted to get my camel back, hobble it tight and lie once more on the damp moss. I walked up to the Arab, a young man of no particular brightness, dressed in an assortment of castoff army clothes, and asked him if he had seen my camel. "It has strayed, and I am looking for it," I added rather self-consciously and, I am sorry to say, with a suppressed giggle. It was a well-worn joke with us in the Jebel that we kept meeting improbable people in unlikely places and all they had to say to account for themselves was: "I am looking for my camel." How likely would it seem to this Arab shepherd that a strange, middle-aged European officer in uniform, should indeed be looking for his camel on the outskirts of Derna town in the early hours of the morning? What business had I got with a camel at all? The situation was preposterous and I laughed outright, ruining my very slender chance of having my story believed. The Arab, however, was an Obeidi and well-mannered; he answered my greetings politely and regretted that he had seen no stray camel at all that morning. Which was a lie, as it appeared later; the camel at that very time was sitting, tightly hobbled down, outside his tent half a mile away.

"Come along," I said, "and have some tea." He followed me, leaving his flock at the head of the gully. He drank tea, looking curiously at my few possessions, obviously trying to draw conclusions as to my identity.

Finally he brought himself to ask: "You are not Arab?"

"Of course not, I am English."

"In that case where is your khabir?"

I explained that my khabir had gone to collect some of my Arab friends and would be back at any moment.

He laughed: "You are not English, you are German."

This was an unexpected development and I launched into long explanations, trying to convince him that I was indeed English: I spoke to him of the sheiks of his tribe, I showed him an Egyptian pound note, a portrait of Sayed Idris, English cigarettes. He wanted to know who my friends were in Derna, but that of course I wouldn't tell him. After all *he* might be in German pay.

He let me talk and talk and finally gave his verdict: "You are a German posturing as an Englishman and trying to catch out the Arabs. You want to find out who is helping the British. I am going now to report to the German post on the road that I have found an English officer."

"Stop, wait a moment, you will be sorry to have done such a thing. Do you want to be called a basas by all the Obeidat? I am really English you know."

He was shaken, thought a moment, then said: "No Englishman would be such a fool as to come here without a khabir. I am off to the military post."

"Sit down," I told him very gently. "You will understand that I can't let you go and give me away to my enemies. You will stay with me until my friends arrive. If you try to go I shall have to shoot," and I showed him my weapon.

"That is fair," he said. "You are quite right—you can't let me go," and he sat down once more, much relieved in his mind to have dispensed with the need of making a decision.

We chatted amicably for quite a long while, till he got worried about his flock. "Look," he said, "I can't lose my sheep because I have had the privilege of meeting you. Would you mind coming with me to gather them? We can then keep them near this gully of yours and we shall not miss your friends when they arrive."

I thought the arrangement was fair and for the second time that morning I found myself walking up and down the plateau whistling. We got the wretched little beasts together and spent another hour very pleasantly talking of the marvels of the great cities. Then there was a scramble and a rush and Omar bu Qasem arrived with 'Ali el Barasi and two more friends from Derna, all mounted. I gravely introduced my prisoner (who knew 'Ali well enough), and we all sat down to our greetings. I told Omar I was very sorry, I had lost his camel. "Not at all, don't worry," he replied. "The camel has been found. It is being looked after by this man's people." There was something farcical in the air at El Ftaiah that morning—as there was to be right through my stay in Derna—and we all laughed and chattered.

From where we sat on the plateau the main Derna-Tobruk road was just in sight in the east, and I had a good view all round. I drew my companions' attention to a group approaching us from the south: "That's our breakfast," they said. And so it was, carried on the head in metal dishes by members of the household of my former prisoner whose tents were just out of sight in a dip of the ground. A most colossal breakfast and a very merry one.

I was the only one to keep a lookout and later I reported two figures coming over from the road. Through my glasses I could see they were armed but my companions would not be alarmed and went on eating the boiled kid, till two Italian soldiers appeared quite close and making straight for our breakfast party. I was whisked away back into my gully while a screen of Arabs advanced toward the soldiers and masked my undignified retreat. The dishes had come down with me and I was in no danger of starving. Ten minutes later Omar appeared grinning: "False alarm; they were soldiers from the road post, who wanted to buy eggs and had lost their way to the tents. They are out of the way now—come back and finish breakfast."

'Ali, my new friend, was a wealthy Arab of the Barasi tribe who had settled as a merchant in Derna: he was very eager to help me. When I had explained my intention of arranging escapes he was full of suggestions and tried to give me a very detailed description of the two camps in which the prisoners were kept, but though I knew the town well enough he couldn't make me visualize the topography to my satisfaction. I wanted to present the prisoners who might be willing to escape with a detailed plan: where to cross the wire and a route to follow after getting out, and I couldn't do this without seeing the ground myself. We decided then that I would spend the next day in the Turkish fort on the escarpment overlooking the town and observe the POW camps through my glasses. In that way, he thought, I would be able not only to see the lie of the land, but to observe the disposition of the camp guards and their movements. "From the fort," said 'Ali, "you can see Derna as on the palm of your hand."

'Ali was devoted to our common cause; he was also, I soon noticed, very ambitious, and his enthusiasm for my plan derived largely from the hope that the operation, if successful, would put him in the limelight and allow him to steal a march on the Obeidi sheiks who were already well known to the British authorities. He, on the other hand, through lack of opportunity, had remained so far in the background. He wanted official recognition and I gave it him in the shape of a document I wrote out appointing him *Chief Controller of British Agents in Derna, Wadi Derna and El Ftaiah*, with the *honorary rank of captain and a monthly salary of fifteen hundred lire payable in advance in the sixth of each month*. As a token that I was entitled to make such appointments I paid him six months' salary in advance.

When I had finished with him I moved to a high knoll and spent the rest of the day watching the German landing ground which was in full view below me on the far side of the road. I saw forty-two transport planes take off empty for Crete all in one flight at ten o'clock and return loaded with gasoline and troops at four o'clock. It was apparently a daily routine; a rash one as it appeared a few days later when a squadron of our Beau-fighters shot down in the sea

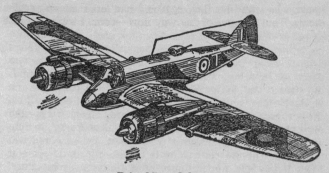

Bristol Beaufighter

thirty-eight of these planes on their return trip. One of the last messages transmitted from my radio before it broke down had given the R.A.F. the tip. I tried to account for one of these planes myself, with what success I don't know.

After dark that same day, I walked over with my former prisoner to the landing ground, which was poorly guarded, and deposited in the tail of one of the Junkers all the explosives I had with me, four pounds of gelignite with a twelve-hour delay ignite, in the hope that it would go off and split the fuselage while the plane was in the air on its outward trip the next morning. No more than a nasty practical joke, (for the loss of one plane would not worry the Luftwaffe), yet it might annoy the Wehrmacht who would feel compelled to employ more troops to guard the airfields at night. My guide, who had the job of waking the guard at the entrance to the airfield every morning when he brought them milk for their breakfast, was delighted at the prospect of meeting his clients with the private knowledge that *he* had put a tiny seed of destruction in one of their formidable machines.

Back from the airfield I slept till moonrise, about two in the morning, when 'Ali el Barasi came to take me to the fort where he wanted to arrive before dawn. A long steep scramble over rocks and screes took us down nearly to sea level where we turned left into the canyon of Wadi Derna. A footpath wound its narrow way up the wadi between low garden walls, orange and pomegranate groves, and vineyards passing many mud-built houses, all asleep at this hour except for the furious barking of dogs which reverberated and thundered from the high cliffs. A swift stream of sweet rippling water runs down the wadi, widening into pools, or enclosed within secret banks, spanned by wooden bridges, clear and bubbling. On each side, sometimes two yards apart, sometimes leaving only room for the bounding stream and the path here cut out of the rock, rise the vertical rocky walls of the wadi. Brightly red and yellow, they stretch upwards for six hundred feet, crags and pinnacles and great slabs of stone. According to the winding of the watercourse pink moonlight now reached the bottom of the cleft, now left us in the darkness and lighted only the upper floors of a fantastic architecture. There wasn't a sigh of wind; the moist air was thick with smells of flowers and trees; the heat oppressive. My companions walked fast, apprehensive less somebody be awakened by the dogs and question our wanderings: the settled Arabs were by no means as united against the Italians as the tribal nomads inland; my friends called them contemptuously Derna Arabs—Arabs without a tribe—and suspected every one of them.

We walked thus an hour, I think, then started climbing out of the wadi, up a tributary gully. In a moment I was out of my dream world, back amongst the familiar dry boulders and dusty screes of the desert scenery. I reached the fort panting and far behind my companions.

The town and harbor can indeed be seen from the old Turkish fort but not by any means as on the palm of the hand. As the distance to the furthest prisoner-of-war camp was over two miles I realized at once that I should have to look at it from much closer if my visit was to be of any practical use. I asked 'Ali to find some means of taking me to the outskirts of the town two hours before sunset: I would then find my own way to the camps. He grumbled and argued: the streets, he said, would be full of troops in the later afternoon. That was precisely what I counted on: the Germans would take me for an Italian, the Italians for a German, and I would pass unnoticed in the crowd. He agreed that if I *had* to walk the streets the crowded hour was probably the best, but couldn't he go in my stead? I declined his offer. Giving up the argument, he called to his three friends and discussed the matter with them at great length in low whispers while I kept my glasses on the white town lying on the plain below me.

For eight hours I kept my watch and saw much of interest: coasters unloading in the small harbor, convoys of trucks running into the barracks inside the Benghazi Gate where we had had a supply point at the time when Derna was ours (it was obviously used for the same purpose by the Germans), tents stretched along the coast west of the town: rest and reinforcement camps, I guessed, some Italian, some German. Intricate calculations, mainly guesswork, led me to the figure of twelve to fifteen thousand as the number of troops in and around Derna. About one o'clock, in the growing heat of the day, the bustle slowed down everywhere. At two, not a soul was astir. I got into the shade of a wall and curled up to sleep.

At four o'clock 'Ali woke me up. I mounted a donkey that had been driven up to the fort while I slept, wrapped myself head, face and all in my jerd, leaving only my bared feet showing, and rode away hunched up and head rolling, supported on each side by an Arab: a patient taken to the doctor *in extremis*, a dying man about whom—we hoped —nobody would bother. I was led down to the town and into the courtyard of a friendly house of ill repute where I cast off my jerd, pulled on my shoes, and, taking the plunge, strolled out, trying to behave like a soldier coming out of a brothel, frightfully self-conscious, very scared and remembering my feelings when, as a small child as yet unable to swim, I was made to jump into a deep pool.

Round the first bend in the narrow alley the sight of a police *feldwebel* walking towards me sent me into a wild panic: the district might have been put out of bounds and my being in it, instead of a safeguard, as it was intended, might be the occasion to be taken directly to a police post. My discomposure must have been apparent, but attributed to another cause than fear, for the German as he passed gave me a dirty grin and cracked an obscene joke *in broken Italian* about games unsuitable for my age. His unkind remark revived my courage; if the *German feldwebel* had judged me to be *Italian* my deception was working as I expected and all was well. When I reached the end of the alley my knees were still wobbly, but my mind was at rest, and I launched myself quickly into the main street. It was full of soldiers, Afrika Korps, Luftwaffe, Italians, all dressed in drill like myself—uniforms originally of many shades of khaki but now bleached and discolored to a nondescript sandy yellow, among which my own dirty British shirt and slacks did not particularly stand out. There were hundreds of soldiers strolling in that street, every one of them an enemy: not one bothered to notice that my dress was different and alone of its kind.

I started along the houses, ready to bolt up a side lane, then realized that the more comfortable I felt the less I would be noticed: if only I could manage to forget altogether the singularity of my position it wouldn't matter even if I wore red and green and feathers in my hat, nobody would think of questioning my right to be in Derna on August 6, 1942.

This knowledge gave me the assurance to go and jostle my way at a good pace down the middle of the street, bumping occasionally into one of my enemies. But I hardly looked at them now: I was turning over in my mind the problems of escape for my prisoner friends, and I hurried toward the first camp I wanted to examine. I had a job to do—and over four miles to walk before dark: I wasn't going to let anyone delay me. I even came to have a feeling of fellowship toward these other lads, soldiers like myself, with duties not dissimilar to mine; in a confused way I felt that we were all on the same job. I worked up to a state of bliss, awareness of my unusual position nearly dismissed from my conscious mind; not completely though, for I had to be on the lookout for officers and be ready with an Italian salute for a German officer and vice versa.

Apart from the officers I looked no one in the eye, for nothing discourages overtures, friendly or hostile, better than a vague abstracted stare: one doesn't go up to a stranger walking purposefully who, by the look on his face, is absorbed in his own thoughts and is only just aware of his surroundings.

I walked out of town through the Benghazi Gate: a few hundred yards further on in the open plain on my left and just off the road stood my camp; tents closely packed within a perimeter of barbed wire, with elevated wooden platforms at intervals, on which stood the guard. Poles carrying electric lamps showed that the camp would be lit up at night in the usual way: they were far apart and I judged that they would leave useful areas of semi-darkness. I made for the far side of the camp, skirting the wire at a distance of fifty yards, looking curiously at the prisoners and making no pretence of being there for any other purpose: I just kept walking, neither hurrying nor loitering and observing the ground as I went. One-third of the way along this side, which faced inland away from the road towards the escarpment, a narrow dry runnel about three feet deep ran at right angles into the camp; the untidy wire barrier had not been stretched quite to the bottom, and I decided it would be fairly easy for a man to crawl unseen along the runnel, under the wire and away. The nearest watch tower was a hundred yards away and the only light in the neighborhood seemed to be a small searchlight on the tower. Inland, away from the camp, I made a note of landmarks which might help a man to find his way in the dark toward the mouth of the nearest wadi running down from the escarpment, twelve hundred yards to the south.

I had just jumped over the runnel when in the very still evening air I heard a faint commotion in the camp. I looked round, expecting a challenge from the guard or a burst of fire, but I saw only that some South African prisoners—I could tell them by the red tabs on their shoulder straps—were crowding up to the wire and I imagined they were discussing my appearance. I took a few more steps, stopped, lit a cigarette, to give any inquisitive member of the guard a token of the ease of my conscience, then walked away at an angle, increasing slowly the distance between me and the camp. No one, however, took any more interest in me, and having completed the circuit I approached the road once more near the end of the camp furthest from the town.

With the information I had collected alternative plans of escape were taking shape in my mind; I liked the way things had turned out, the guard was not too fierce, the wire haphazard and the deserted plain would offer a fairly safe getaway toward the escarpment. With several hundred prisoners in the cage the chances were that a few adventurous spirits would be found among them to attempt an escape.

I had now to make for the other camp, a mile and a half away at the opposite end of the town. As I got on the road and began to retrace my steps towards the Benghazi Gate a longing overcame me to scrap this part of my program and to fade away quietly towards the friendly safety of the escarpment wadis. I suddenly was desperately weary and repelled by the prospect of a long walk through the town and back, along that terrible, crowded street. Hadn't I achieved enough for my purpose? The conditions of escape from the other camp, which was in the buildings of the old hospital beyond the Tobruk road, would be rather unfavorable and the getaway difficult, as it would have to be through the town.

I dragged my feet along the road as I turned these matters in my mind, fighting my weariness of heart, and with my interest in the whole scheme completely dead. I finally decided to cancel my visit to the hospital.

About three-quarters of the distance along the road from the camp to the city gate I had noticed a small track turning to the right off the road and leading to a clump of tall bushes. This track I now made for, intending to make my way from the bushes to the escarpment, and I stepped along the road, much fresher for having made up my mind.

A few yards before reaching my turning-off point I looked up and saw, just beyond the Benghazi Gate, a group of twenty to thirty Italian soldiers come out of the quartermaster's stores and walk away towards the town. The unwelcome sight of so many enemies made me realize in a flash that my decision, however sensible, had been inspired by fear; if I didn't face the dangers of the crowd now I knew I would never stand up to any danger in the future. Running away today was as good as running away once and for all. So I walked on, past the track, past the Gate, into the town and trod my way once more among the crowd, gingerly and with a quaking heart, convinced of the utter futility of my quest but determined to see it through.

I thought a shock would help me to recover my nerve and a moment later, peering fearfully up a side alley, I saw an Italian youth running toward me. He had a fatuous grin on his thick lips, a misshapen nose and flapping ears, a perfect booby. As he was about to reach the main street I took a step into the alley so that he crashed into me with some violence. I was braced and escaped being knocked over, but the lad was winded and startled: I held him up by the shoulder and shook him soundly, hissing out angry meaningless German noises: "Strum strum heidelpferd—strum knöbelstein—strumbelneck—strum strum strangverneckerst niegerloos." (I was back in the nursery, talking

German "Pingo" with my sisters.) The lad gasped and
gaped, when I let him go he ran back up the alley and out
of sight. Two pleasant-faced German N.C.O.'s grinned at
me from the other side of the street; I gave them a little
wave of the hand and plunged away in the crowd.

The rest of the trip was quite pleasant. I made up a
story for myself: All the men about me were prisoners, my
prisoners—I was their camp commander and I pretended
not to see them so that the poor wretches shouldn't have to
salute all the time. Thus grave and detached I wandered at
last up to the hospital building. It stood on a low cliff
overlooking the sea, the compound was full of tents nearly
to the cliff edge. I walked up and down the beach,
apparently wrapped in contemplation of a very picturesque sunset, but casting an eye now and then at the red
rocks above me. I soon found what I was looking for: in
three different places easy chimneys led down to the
beach, the wire on top was perfunctory. The camp must
have been designed in a hurry and it had obviously been
assumed that the cliff was unscalable.

The sun dipped into the sea behind Ras bu 'Aza. I
waited a little longer, then, in the gathering dusk, I made
my way once more along Derna's main street, a happy
man. I had done what I had set out to do and I was now
quietly going home, looking back on the day's work. The
tremulous plunge I had taken three hours earlier really
belonged to my distant youth, when my apprenticeship had
been served, and I had now become a master of my craft.
My former fears appeared to me pathetically immature; in
fact I saw now that I had nothing to fear at all; for,
supposing I was recognized and apprehended, I would only
be taken to one of *my* camps (for my captors would
assume I was just an escaped prisoner) and all I would
have then to do would be to apply to myself one of my
own escape plans and get away the next night.

Thus I built up a newly found courage. The apprehension of personal danger can easily be mastered once the
lesson has been learned that nothing worse than death can
be expected—and the prospect of death, though it can be a
bother, is not particularly terrifying to most of us. Thus
the stage is reached where danger loses its awesome
horror, and it becomes easy to overcome the urge to run
away. Each time a man has *not run away* he becomes less
liable to be afraid in the future; he can now enter a bout of

fear and come out again without surrender; fear is no
worse than a fit of the colic—damned unpleasant while it
lasts but the easier to withstand the less fuss is made. But
if a man run away but once he may never recover his
nerve.

Some men of course are too stupid and unimaginative
even to experience fear at all—many such heroes find their
way into the army—and there are also others, who enjoy
wallowing in terror: for them there is no remedy but to
send them home.

There is another fear, the fear of failure, which to me is
a much more formidable enemy. Insidious, it takes the
shape of an irrational conviction that if I were to fail in
one enterprise I could never be successful again in any
other; that is why I have to take infinite trouble in the
preparation of each of my undertakings, and why, once
engaged and things going wrong, I can hardly bring myself
to listen to reason and pull out in time.

This day in Derna however had been a success all
round, and I made for home with a light heart. Passing
German headquarters I caught sight of 'Ali, who, it
seemed, had been shadowing me most of the time; after I
had given him a discreet sign of recognition he walked on
ahead and led me into a dark, narrow lane; a moment later
an urgent whisper called me under an obscure archway.
'Ali with his friends were there with the old donkey; I
mounted, a jerd was thrown over me and without more
ado we rode away. My fate, for the time being, was out of
my hands, and as I jogged along I composed in my mind
the instructions I wanted to write for the prisoners in the
cages.

On top of the escarpment I was taken to the tent of one
of 'Ali's friends, where I found all a bustle for my
reception. Two smiling girls, whose firm, high breasts
showed through their wide sleeves when they lifted an
arm, hurried with friendly laughter in and out of the tent,
with rugs and cushions, soap and water, and then a long
drink of leban. We were all happy and talkative, slightly
excited and glad to be together: I have never had a
friendlier, merrier homecoming. To be sure, having slept
no more than six hours in the last four days, I was a little
drowsy, but it didn't matter, I enjoyed the party and the
pleasant prospect of a long night was ahead of me. The
solicitude of my friends went to my heart: they had had an

anxious time watching my movements from afar, and now, happy with relief, they wanted to show, with their homely celebration, how glad they were of my safe return. With the exception of Omar, who was an Obeidi, all the others were of the Barasi tribe, none of them had I met before our meeting at El Ftaiah, the day before. These Barasi gave more freedom to their womenfolk than any Arabs I have known, which may account for their lively cheerfulness, remarkable even among the sociable Senussis. The Egyptians, on the other hand, who live entirely apart from their women, are very glum and would not deign to lower themselves by laughter.

I fell asleep on my bench, expecting to sleep late next morning, but I was awaked two hours before dawn to be taken away as some suspicious characters had been seen lurking about. The two daughters of my host came to shake hands, an unusual courtesy among the Arabs with whom leave-taking is the occasion of only the shortest, shame-faced compliments. One hour's walk took us to another tent in a hollow of the escarpment plateau, and here I was left alone to sleep out the remainder of the night.

When I woke I found 'Ali waiting for me with paper and envelopes which I had asked him to buy in Derna, and I set about writing out five copies of instructions for each of the two camps. I wrote to the prisoners that they had friends outside the camps who were ready to help any of them who attempted to escape; I suggested places, means and times for crossing the wire and indicated a route to follow when clear of the camp. I added a rough sketch of the camps and a hand-drawn map of Derna and the area inland as far as the escarpment to each copy of the instruction.

My plan was that the escapers should get out of the camps early on a dark night (the easiest part of the undertaking) and find their own way to the escarpment, trying to make for one of the wild gullies that I indicated on the map. There they would be met by my Arab helpers, into whose hands they were to put themselves entirely. The Arabs would collect them in suitable spots, feed them, and eventually bring them to my camp, somewhere in the neighborhood. I ended with a recommendation to wear the strongest footwear they could lay their hands on. I had seen too many escapers attempting a three-hundred-mile walk in dilapidated gym shoes. As a token of a bona fides I enclosed in each envelope one Spring bok (South African) cigarette.

I couldn't give them more details as the documents could easily fall into the wrong hands, and I wanted to compromise my Arabs as little as possible. While I gave the escapers the impression that my camp was quite near (they all assumed eventually that it was just on top of the escarpment) I told 'Ali that I would be found in the lower reaches of one of the wadis: Saratel, Ramla, El Fej or Belwetat, roughly in an area extending from Amur el Jill to Zumlet en Nawamis, some forty-five miles from Derna. To deliver my messages to the prisoners I counted on the fact that the Italians in charge authorized a few local Arab boys to enter the camps with eggs they sold to the prisoners. 'Ali had a few friends amongst the petty tribesmen and undertook to bring them up for my inspection and to receive my instructions. As writing the instructions and drawing sketches and maps would take me a whole day, before setting to work I settled with 'Ali and his friends the other major points of our scheme: numbers which would be needed for the screen of men waiting for the escapers at the foot of the escarpment and the provision of food. He then left me to my labors.

When I had finished I took a clean sheet of paper, sharpened my pencil and wrote out the following document:

To: Generale Piatti, Commando Superiore, Barce.
From: O.C. British Advanced Headquarters in Cyrenaica, Libya.

It has been brought to the notice of this H.Q. that a certain number of Senussi Arabs resident within the area of my command have been apprehended by your orders and put to death without trial. The only crime of these men is that, following the dictates of humanity, they have given, at various times, asylum to unarmed members of H.M. Forces who have escaped from prisoner-of-war camps. The execution without trial of the above-mentioned Senussi Arabs no less than the cowardly and barbarous method employed in carrying it out are in direct contravention of international law and the usages of war as recognized by civilized nations. This H.Q. has forwarded to H.M.

Government the names of the Senussi Arabs thus tortured to death by your orders, together with the particulars, dates and places of their execution. H.M. Government will take every step in their power, as well during the present hostilities as after the conclusion of the war, to bring to judgment any person responsible for the commission of such crimes. In the meanwhile, so as to ensure that such acts of barbarity shall not recur, I have ordered my commanders in the field to take measures of retaliation in the eventuality of any new executions of Senussi Arabs coming to their knowledge. These measures of retaliation will consist in the shooting of one officer of the Royal Italian Army for every Senussi Arab executed. These Italian officers will be selected among the members of your staff. The shooting of the a/m Italian officers will be carried out by members of H.M. Forces operating in Cyrenaica.

POPSKI, MAJOR
O.C.B. Ad H.Q.C.

August 7, 1942.
   Appendix (A)—Nominal roll of Senussi Arabs executed from January 21, 1942, to August 1, 1942, inclusive.

Appendix (A) included the names of several of my local helpers who had fallen into Italian hands when the fall of Tobruk and our retreat to the Egyptian border had given heart to the Italian bullies who administered Cyrenaica. The method they employed to put to death Arabs suspected of giving help to the British was to hang them by a steel hook inserted in the jaw and leave them to die of shock.
This letter was eventually slipped into the mail box at German H.Q. by an Arab sweeper. I received no acknowledgment from General Piatti but, coincidence or otherwise, until I left Cyrenaica I heard of no more executions.
I moved that night to a cave in a wooded hillside overlooking the sea and I worked there the whole of the next day with 'Ali. Two egg merchants were produced (one for each camp) and briefed. I advised them to give my messages to N.C.O.'s rather than to privates and to make sure that the recipients were quick-witted. The lads (they were no more than twelve years old and pretty sharp)

eventually acquitted themselves of their task with great success.

I then interviewed the men whose job would be to intercept the fugitives on their way to the hills. They were to be careful not to alarm the prisoners by springing suddenly on them in the dark, but shadow them for a while, then send *one* man alone to make contact. I gave them each a document stating that they were in my employ and I left money with 'Ali to reward them according to their deserts.

I moved again that evening, to one of 'Ali's stone houses in the upper reaches of Wadi Derna, above the waterfall, where we ate a farewell dinner for about twenty guests. There was an alarm when a neighbor (of dubious allegiance) came to inquire what the fun was about, and I was bundled indecorously behind a sofa. But the unwelcome guest stayed only a short while and we resumed our mirth. It was remarkable how merry we all were, surrounded by enemies and with the threat over my hosts' heads of finding themselves the next morning hanging from the gallows with a steel hook through the jaw. I of course ran a considerably lighter risk.

I was relieved to depart about eleven o'clock that night, for I felt my presence among them added unnecessary danger to the already precarious position of my hosts, and there was nothing more I could do to further my plans. In fact, not only did they take the larger share of risks, but they did all the work, and the credit for our final success, such as it was, should go to them. Birdybird and the camel, which I hadn't seen for four days, materialized at 'Ali's back door; we took our leave, Omar and I, and rode off in the night. We crossed the Martuba by-pass before dawn, pushed on right through the following day, and arrived on the site where I had left my camp in Wadi Saratel in the early afternoon.

The camp was gone. In case somebody was lying in wait for us we rode straight on, without stopping, pretending we had no local interest whatever, then took a wide circuit out of the wadi, found the neighborhood deserted, rode back to the spot where the camp had been and dismounted to investigate. Everything had been tidied up—not a match stick had been left lying. Omar was puzzled by the tracks of two camels that he couldn't account for but I decided they were those of Chapman's mount and his Libyan's.

Omar wanted to follow the tracks which moved westward; I knew however that if Chapman had been in charge of the move we should find the tracks doubling and redoubling on themselves in a knotted intricacy (for he was very cunning); so, to save time, I decided to call on Mukhtar as he would know where my party had moved to. Mukhtar, however, had also moved house and we had to ride nearly up to Bir Belater before we found an Arab who could tell us that Chapman had come back from Dursaland two days before with a party of refugees and had thought it wise to move camp to Wadi el Fej somewhere north of Amur el Fej. We set out immediately on the fifteen-mile ride, watered our animals at Bir Semander in Wadi Ramla, lay down and slept till dawn in Wadi el Fej, picked up Chapman's tracks, and rode into his camp half an hour later.

I slept most of the next three days. On the evening of the fifth day after my return from Derna, an Obeidi, whose tents were a few miles away, walked up to me and, after greetings, said: "They have arrived." I called for Chapman and we rode over together to find fifteen or twenty men lying in the sand round a fire: the first batch of escaped prisoners. They were so exhausted that we couldn't find one who would take an interest in us, which rather hurt my feelings! Their indefatigable Arab guides had made them walk forty-five miles with only one break of an hour. They had never been trained to such feats of endurance, for the last six weeks they had sat inactive and underfed in prisoner-of-war camps, and furthermore, when they had started, they had been given to understand that their destination was "Quite near." Their guides, on the other hand, quite fit and wonderfully pleased with themselves, were looking forward to a fat reward (which they got).

We gave our new friends leban and tea—they were too tired to eat—and we left them where they were, to sleep it out till morning, when, footsore and stiff, they hobbled over to our camp.

Our new recruits were mostly South Africans with a few men from England. When they recovered, after two or three days, they forgave us what they had considered a deplorable practical joke. They turned out to be a cheerful lot, extremely resourceful and quite capable of looking after themselves.

One of them, a Londoner, had not come from the cage

at all. He had been wounded in the knee during our withdrawal six months previously; unable to keep up with his companions he had been picked up by an Arab, who had taken him to his house in Wadi Derna. His wound had been tended with dressings bought by his host, and had finally got well. As soon as he could be moved he had been carried to another house, then to a cave, then to another house and so on, never staying more than three or four days in the same spot. On the food provided by his hosts, far in excess of their own meager rations, he had grown fat, and they had provided him every single day with a ration of seven cigarettes bought from Italian and German soldiers. Knowing the scarcity of cigarettes in the Jebel at that time, this last touch seemed to me to belong to a fairy tale, but the lad, who was of a methodical disposition, had kept a diary in which he had entered day by day every item received from his kind hosts (with some idea at the back of his mind of repaying them some day), and sure enough the entry "Cigarettes, 7" appeared regularly.

We had now the responsibility of a growing family. The first lot of escaped prisoners was followed by others, Chapman had brought some Dursa refugees with him from his trip, and other Arabs came in, all of whom had to be fed and looked after till they could be evacuated to Egypt. Feeding was our greatest problem; having collected all my dumps I still had a sufficiency of flour but everything else was running very short; our meals were frugal and had to be very carefully planned. I bought a few kids and sheep from my neighbors (who were very short themselves) and I sent to Derna for fruit, fresh vegetables and German and Italian Army cigarettes. We never went really hungry but I had to give so much thought to food, with my party growing every day, that months later I still woke up in the night turning over supply problems in my mind.

I was running out of money also. I sold all our animals with the exception of Birdybird and two camels, then I issued I.O.U.'s. When I was finally relieved I owed over half a million lire—mostly for salaries and my debts were all settled in one fantastic orgy of paying out.

Chapman and I had early made a wise arrangement: we lived separately—he under his tree, I under mine, two or three hundred yards away. Thus we never got irritated with one another. Every two or three days his Libyan soldier would come over and say ceremoniously: "Will the major please come and dine with the major tonight at seven?" and I returned the compliment. At these meals we produced little titbits carefully saved: half a bar of chocolate, a small tin of dressed crab, half a dozen fresh grapes from Derna. Once we crowned a standard meal of bread and bully with two small raw onions, a treat indeed.

The various groups in our party were all camped separately: we had the South African camp, the radio operators', the Dursa, the Barasi, the Obeidat, all dotted along the wadi. We lived peacefully.

The last of our charging sets for the radio batteries broke down. We heard the B.B.C. news one night announcing the fall of Mersa Matruh, then no more. The last message we had received was from Cairo. It was so garbled that after three days working on the cipher all we could bring out was one sentence: "God bless you"— which didn't sound too optimistic. (We discovered later, back in Egypt, that this message was only a reply, composed by some emotional idiot, to our news of the arrival of the first batch of escaped POW's).

We were now quite cut off, and we decided with Chapman that the time had come to make arrangements for the future. Assuming Egypt to have fallen, we had two possibilities, either to go in hiding, perhaps for years, in the country of the Dursa—not promising, as Chapman had discovered on his last trip—or to make our way to Cufra, an oasis four hundred and twenty miles to the south from where we could reach the Sudan, which we hoped would still be in British hands. We resolved to attempt the trip if L.R.D.G. failed to relieve us at the appointed time. The journey, avoiding the regular caravan route which started from Jalo, now in Italian hands, would involve a stage of twelve days' camel riding without water. I got in touch with old Musa, my friend of Baltet ez Zala'q, who undertook to start training camels for this long waterless trip. In two months' time they would be ready, but he thought we should postpone our departure till the coolness of the winter.

Two of the South Africans, mechanically minded, undertook to improvise a charging set and get our radio to function once more. The gasoline engine part of one set was still in good order; it was the dynamo which was irretrievably burned out. Some one of us knew of a broken-down Italian motorcycle lying abandoned some-

where on the Karmusa-Mekhili track. We sent a party out
to find it; after four days they returned with a small
dynamo off the motorcycle, apparently in working order.
The South Africans now built a wooden frame and contrived somehow to clamp on to it the gasoline engine from
our charging set and the Italian dynamo. The two had now
to be connected by a belt cut out of leather straps which
had also been collected from abandoned Italian equipment.

One morning at last I heard the chug-chug of the engine
and I walked over to where the South Africans were
laughing over this success. The dynamo was running, and,
what is more, giving the required voltage. It had been a
gamble, for we had no idea at what speed it was meant to
run. There was, however, a snag: the dynamo, built to be
belt driven, was fitted with a pulley but the engine wasn't,
and the belt had to be run off the coupling; to keep the
belt on it had to be held between two guiding rods, and the
friction wore the soft leather across in little more than five
minutes. Our engineers were not to be beaten, they cut
dozens of belts ready for use and fitted on a new one as
the old one wore out. It remained, however, a slow process
because each new belt had to be sewn on; they considered
themselves very successful when the dynamo ran fifteen
minutes in the hour. They stuck to it day and night and on
the third day our exhausted batteries began to revive, but
we dared not switch on the radio yet. At this stage our
engineers' labors were interrupted.

10

HIDE AND SEEK

SHEIK 'ALI BU HAMED came riding down our wadi, stopped his mare opposite the tree under which I was sitting, alighted and put his arms round me. I hadn't seen him since the sheiks' conference at Kaf el Qsur—a lifetime ago it seemed. In view of his cautiousness, he was the last man I expected to visit me (by daylight too) at a time when all hope of a prompt liberation of Cyrenaica had vanished.

He came directly to the point: " 'Abdel Aziz bu Yunes, Sheik 'Abdel Qader bu Bridan's nephew, whom you have long since ceased to employ (and for very sound reasons, as I well know) has been mortally vexed by the withdrawal of your confidence. In his anger the fool decided some time back to turn basas—informer; he wrote to General Piatti, then went to see him insistently several times with the information that British officers with a radio set were operating in the Jebel. Piatti laughed at him and dismissed him with hard words. The general was well informed of what was going on within his command. The English were *all* back in Egypt—in fact they would very shortly be pushed out of Egypt—and he did not approve of petty sheiks wasting his time with cock-and-bull stories. These sheiks had better mind their own business. So 'Abdel Aziz went home with more anger than ever in his heart.

"Then, ten days ago, I don't know why, Piatti sent for 'Abdel Aziz and asked him if he knew where the British officers were. 'Yes,' said 'Abdel Aziz, 'in the Wadi Ramla.'

"General Piatti," said 'Ali bu Hamed, "then called for me and for Sheik 'Abdel Jelil bu Tayeb, my kinsman, and other sheiks of the Obeidat, and told us that this 'Abdel Aziz bu Yunes knew of English officers in Wadi Ramla. We all swore that there was not a single British officer at large in the whole of the Jebel. In the past one or two may have come in and run out again, when the English lines were at Gazala, but, long since, we hadn't even heard rumors of any such things happening. Piatti said it was our business to know, not to peddle rumors, and he was determined to clear up the matter once and for all. So he is sending a motor patrol to comb your district, looking for you. Myself and 'Abdel Jelil and 'Abdel Aziz will be traveling with it, and we all leave from Mekhili tomorrow noon. If you are found, Abdel Jelil and I both hang—if not, something unpleasant might happen to Abdel Aziz."

"God bless you," I said. "Let it be 'Abdel Aziz. Where shall we move to now?"

We decided on the next hide-out. 'Ali bu Hamed promised to send me a runner every night with the news of the Italian patrol, and took his leave. We loaded our few belongings, obliterated our tracks and walked away. We had a watch of two Arabs stationed at Zumlet en Nawamis, a conspicuous hillock, which was our rendezvous with L.R.D.G. We sent them word to tell the L.R.D.G. patrol, if they turned up, to keep clear till the alarm had blown over.

During the next five days we played at hide and seek with the Italian patrol. Every night, as arranged, a runner arrived and told us what route was intended for the morrow, and we shifted accordingly. The dice were loaded in our favor to be sure, but it was still a sporting event: the Italians drove in trucks, whereas the fifty-odd of us walked, leaving a conspicuous trail, restricted in our roaming by the need to keep within a night's ride of one of the only four live wells available, as we couldn't carry more than one day's supply of water. The Italians, assuming in their innocence that we would be hiding in one of the main wadis where bushes and caves could give us a certain amount of cover, stuck to these watercourses, but we took to the open high plateau between the wadis. A gently undulating surface of stones and gravel, sparsely dotted with scrub, provided no hiding places and our camps were visible for miles. As the plateau was quite accessible to motor traffic, the Italians could have driven out of the wadis, if they had chosen, in which case they would have stood a good chance of making a catch. Through a combination of good management on the part of our Arab friends, who acted in fact as guides to the motor patrol, and of the ineptitude of the Italians, we

succeeded in eluding their inquisitiveness, though on the
third day they drove so near to us that we heard the roar
of their engines down in the wadi. On the fifth night Sheik
'Ali bu Hamed signaled that Wadi Ramla had been declared clear of enemy by the Italians, who were now
moving further west, and he advised me to move into it.
We found a deeply encased bushy stretch of the wadi,
where we made ourselves comfortable in the shade, rested
our poor feet, and got the South African engineers to
resume their work on the radio batteries.

The Italian patrol went home. 'Abdel Aziz bu Yunes
tried to take refuge with them, but General Piatti ordered
him back to his tents, and 'Ali bu Hamed saw to it that the
order was carried out. A month later he was found with
his throat cut, a suitable death for a basas.

On the third morning of our repose, as the sergeant was
reporting that he was about to test the radio set with the
revived battery, one of our Arabs who had been keeping a
lookout from the top of a hill came in with the news that
he had heard a noise as of vehicles in a southeasterly
direction; a little later another man reported having just
seen unidentified trucks winding up our wadi, about two
miles off. I sent word all along the line to get under cover
and walked over to Chapman's bower, where he lived
inside a particularly thick and high bush. I found him
shaving and told him the news. He looked at the unaccustomed tommy gun in my hands and said, completely
unmoved:

"Is there anything we can do?"

I thought of the fifty unarmed men in our care. "Nothing at all."

"Right," said Chapman. "I go on shaving," and smiled
through the lather.

I laid down my weapon and seated myself at the
entrance to Chapman's bower. Our men had all taken
cover and hardly breathed but enough fresh litter lay
about to open the eyes even of the most townbred Italian. I
could hear now approaching trucks grinding in low gear
through heavy sand. When, through the branches, I saw
the first one come slowly round the bend in the wadi—
suddenly quite close—I got up and stepped forward to
stop it: if there was to be a surrender, let it be decorous
and orderly, with no winkling out of reluctant bodies and
no shooting. As the truck drew nearer I recognized it: a

1½-ton Chevrolet carrying five bearded men, familiar, grinning L.R.D.G. faces. It pulled up and Hunter jumped down; I shook his hand, pretending I had known all the time who was coming. Chapman came out of his bower when he had finished shaving.

Hunter and his seven trucks were two days early, alarmed by our silence on the radio he had thought we might be in trouble and had hastened to the rendezvous at Zumlet en Nawamis, where he had found our two Arabs who guided him to our camp.

The news Hunter brought was good: the enemy had been stopped, exhausted, at El Alamein, our scare had died down and an offensive spirit had spread among our troops since the arrival of a new commander of the Eighth Army. Many plans were afoot, of which he knew only that the L.R.D.G. would be involved, and that somebody had said that, if he was still alive and free, Popski would be required for one of the operations.

Cheered by the prospect I dismissed from my mind any inclination to let Hunter go back to Egypt without me, and gladly renounced the throne of the Jebel. My Senussi subjects were not, I think, sorry to see me go, and looked forward to a pause in the constant anxiety which our safety had lately been to them. I assured them that their country would be liberated, and that I would be back before the winter; strangely enough, they believed me and, stranger still, it turned out as I said.

Before I went however I wanted to tie up loose ends and leave everything in good order. We called in those of our creditors that could be reached in time, appointed representatives for the others, and, with funds brought by Hunter, paid out all our debts. Birdybird, my white mare, I sent to 'Ali bu Hamed, my dearest friend among the Senussis, to whose secret and powerful support I really owed what success I had had.

An old Dursa sheik, Chapman's protégé, being a scholar, was appointed head clerk and chief accountant. We worked with him for thirty-six hours, at the accounts first, then writing testimonials and instructions. I left a little food, and fixed another rendezvous in case more prisoners were got out of the cages.

On the second evening we all piled on to Hunter's trucks and drove off towards Siwa. On the way, however, we were instructed to go to Cufra instead, as Siwa was being evacuated by our troops; so we called at Hatiet el Hetla, a patch of scrub and bushes northwest of Jaghbub, where the L.R.D.G. had a secret dump. We filled up with gasoline and food and drove off across the sand sea on the four-hundred-mile trip to Cufra.

I remember little of that trip: I had been for over five months continuously behind the enemy lines, and my mind was affected by "Jebel fever." The problems and the responsibilities of the last months kept buzzing round in my head—nothing else in the world mattered to me. I spent an impatient day in Cufra, then boarded a plane for the six-hundred-and-seventy-mile flight to Cairo. I landed at Almaza in the evening, got a taxi and reported directly to Middle East Headquarters, leaving my kit at the gate. I was hurt to find that everyone had gone home at eight o'clock without waiting for me, and the duty officer, though courteous and kind, didn't think my business urgent enough to justify ringing up his brigadier at the Turf Club. Indeed he urged me to go home and have a bath and a drink and a good night's rest, and come back the next morning. I gave in, feeling confusedly that by my weakness I was compromising the whole issue of the war.

PART II

JAKE
EASONSMITH

11

BUFFALO BILL

THE next day I received a lesson in humility. The fancy headquarters that were supposed to be responsible for me had been completely renewed since I had visited them six months previously. Furthermore, they had moved to Palestine, then back to Cairo, mislaying their records in the process. As a result, when I called, nobody knew me, nobody had even heard of me, nor was anybody interested in me in the least.

An orphan, unacknowledged and unwanted, I wandered about Middle East Headquarters in search of a sponsor. I finally drifted into a newly formed branch which, I was told, co-ordinated all military activities behind the enemy lines. Shan Hackett, a very young colonel, was in command, a witty, active, short cavalryman, who had heard of me and greeted me as a friend. I was too stupidly embittered to respond to his bantering, instead I poured out my grievances:

"Five months on operations . . . back to Cairo to find my unit disbanded, myself without a posting and my pay stopped for the last four months."

Shan Hackett moved his short legs, sat back in his chair and burst out laughing.

"Now, Popski, for your private reasons you fade out into the desert. You go and fight a private war with your private army for your private convenience, taking orders from no one, and when you choose to come back you expect H.M. Government to pay you for your fun!" My surly self-righteousness dissolved, the last fumes of Jebel fever blew away, and I was ready once more to behave sensibly.

Shan Hackett was a man after my own heart; he set things going with a touch of light fantasy and treated nobody too seriously, an attitude which, in my heavy-

129

footed earnestness, I ever vainly tried to achieve. He suggested I should take part in one of the raids that were being planned at the moment. Then on my return he thought I should raise a force of my own to operate on the lines developed by me in a report I had sent back from the Jebel some time ago. I was surprised that he should have read it.

I was introduced to a turmoil of planning activity. In that late August of 1942 Rommel was expected to attack the Eighth Army at El Alamein; the operations I was getting involved in aimed at interfering with his line of communication from Benghazi to Tobruk and upsetting his supplies at the time of the battle. Three simultaneous raids by light forces were finally decided upon to take place on the night of September 13, 1942. One on Tobruk, one on Barce and one on Benghazi by David Stirling's Regiment, the S.A.S.*

I was appointed to the raid on Barce which was an L.R.D.G. responsibility. I was glad to be on the move once more after little over a week in Egypt. It did not occur to me that I might be in need of a longer rest after five months behind the enemy lines.

The expedition I was now on was really a holiday to me: my responsibilities were limited to providing local information when we arrived near Barce, and I was under the command of an officer when I admired and loved. Jake Easonsmith, a wine merchant of Bristol, at the time I am writing about was a major commanding a squadron of L.R.D.G. Simple and upright, he had a directness that gave confidence to troubled minds. His deliberate speech, warmed by a slow smile, reflected an inner sureness, a perfect balance, and a mature consideration of life and death; it had, as no other man's, the power to put me at peace with the world and myself. If he ever had doubts, he never showed any, with him all was secure. Unflustered, undaunted, he raised our lives above strife into a limpid world of spiritual values where our duties were clear and pleasant. Under him we all did our best and worried not about the success; he led us without using any of the tricks of leadership, for it was a privilege to do his bidding, a means of joining him in a superior adventure as if he had some hidden knowledge which made worldly success of

*For the exciting story of the Special Air Service read "Stirling's Desert Raiders" another volume in the Bantam War Book Series.

little moment, but gave immense value to our striving. What mattered was to follow him in his rectitude. He talked but little and never gossiped: his life was his own, and when he wasn't at work he followed his inner thoughts. I served him with a devotion which I have given to no other man.

We left Faiyum on our way to Barce on September 2, 1943, with twenty-two vehicles in three patrols, New Zealand, Rhodesian, and one of Guardsmen, bound for the Egyptian Sand Sea, a route of extreme difficulty which had been selected because no one in his senses would have expected us to take it.

We struck the sands at Ain Dalla, and for the next three hundred miles we coaxed our trucks and our jeeps across the loveliness of the great sand dunes. The long successive ranges of tangled sand hills, five hundred feet high or more from trough to crest, had bold, sharp curves and deep shadows on the soft slopes. Valleys of sand, sometimes three miles wide, ran roughly north and south between the ranges, completely lifeless but for, every two or three days, a rounded bush of vivid green, its fleshly leaves swollen with sap, fresh, shiny and alone. The wind-fashioned landscape recalled the beauty of mountain snows: the shapes were alike, and, as off an Alpine peak, blown plumes streamed from the tops of the dunes, but not a stone broke the purity of the sand, whereas in the mountains rocks stick up incongruous through the clean lines of swept snow. The upper ridges of the dunes were white with yellow depths—not the blue-white of snow; the lower slopes and the valley bottoms had color: from butter yellow to pale purple, rippled or infinitely smooth, they stood out boldly in the morning, then dimmed to a common gray under the midday sun. From the higher dunes a wide tangle of ranges showed, razor-edged ridges, crescent-shaped circuses, nearly vertical slopes, drawn with acute precision. In nature there is nothing tidier than blown sand.

Our route lay at right angles to the successive ranges: up and down we drove our trucks, with much labor. The flat bottoms of the valleys were treacherous: sailing across a table-smooth plain I would feel my wheels go sluggish, and see the featureless sand drifting past me slow down and stop. Looking round I would find the other vehicles, dispersed right and left, also bogged. Alone in the distance

Jake's little jeep crawled on. He had finer perceptions than most of us and could spot bad patches of sand where we could discern no difference. On the flat each truck would extricate itself by the unaided efforts of its own crew. With steel channels six feet long laid under the wheels, one man driving with care, the others pushing, a few yards at a time, the vehicle reached a firmer surface. Driving up the slopes and over the ridges called for infinitely more skill, and at times all the men available from the three patrols had to help in getting one vehicle at a time over a tricky stretch. Lines of steel channels were laid to make a kind of railroad: further ahead men waited with channels ready to be thrown under the wheels as soon as they were seen to start a spin in the sand. The art of channel throwing was difficult; the few who had mastered it were in constant demand.

Much depended on the selection of the route; on approaching a new range Jake Easonsmith drove ahead in his jeep and tried here and there till he found a route to the ridge. Hard slopes are generally steep, and moderate ones soft and boggy, it was a question of striking a happy mean. Moreover sand slopes moderate enough to be climbed by a loaded truck generally fall off nearly vertically on the far side of the ridge. Our method was to rush the slope and deliberately bog the truck on the top. A team waiting on the ridge would then manhandle it gently on to the downward slope; if you bogged too early you couldn't be pulled over, if too late you took a flying leap of forty of fifty feet. It was slow work and strenuous, but in no way heartbreaking because we knew the difficulties and did not expect quick progress. Nobody grumbled on a day when we covered only eight miles. We were I think well pleased with our skill in getting all our vehicles as far as we had over a very difficult range of dunes.

I was crossing the sands for the second time only, and I suspect that allowance was made by my companions for my comparative inexperience, and also for my age: I was nicknamed on the trip "The Old Major" (as opposed to Easonsmith, "The Young Major"). I think I was made to do less than my share of digging and shoving and carrying channels. I certainly was not exhausted at the end of the day and had enough vitality left to enjoy the pure splendor of this land.

The officer commanding the Guards patrol had not

fallen under the spell of Easonsmith. One morning, as we were halted at the foot of a high dune, with the New Zealanders ahead under Nick Wilder breaking the trail, he said to me in a peevish mood: "All this waiting doesn't make sense. Jake thinks he is the only man who knows the sands. I shall find my own route."

Off he drove in his jeep, leading his patrol. Retribution came terribly quickly: half an hour later Very lights came over a dune two or three miles along the valley, signals of distress. He had rushed up an unreconnoitered slope and reaching the razor-back top with speed to spare had dashed down the opposite slope, his overturned jeep rolling over him and his gunner. The officer suffered from a squeezed skull, the gunner had a spinal lesion and was paralyzed from the waist downward. He died many months later in hospital. The officer recovered without much damage; his face longer and narrower than ever. Jake said nothing and waited for the medical officer we were carrying on this trip to attend to the casualties and make his report. He then made arrangements by radio for the two men to be evacuated by air from Big Cairn.

Big Cairn, six feet high, was built by a very early L.R.D.G. patrol on the west side of the Egyptian Sand Sea in a featureless plain. It was a regular landmark for L.R.D.G. patrols, and on this occasion a dump of gasoline, water, and rations had been laid for our use, from Cufra. From Cufra also, two hundred and fifty miles to the southwest, came a plane for our casualties. The first time it missed Big Cairn, but made it the second day, and we proceeded on our way with only a few hours to spare if we wanted to be outside Barce on September 13.

On the twelfth, having had no further delays, we were driving westward along the southern foothills of the Jebel Akhdar somewhere south of Marawa, when we came across fresh tank tracks. I assured Jake Easonsmith that there had certainly been no enemy tanks in this area the last time my men visited it about a month earlier. Nor was there, in the normal course of things, any reason why the enemy should bring tanks into this backwater, five hundred and fifty miles from the front line.

Jake gave me a quizzical smile and said nothing. It seemed that we had wasted our trouble in taking the arduous route through the Sand Sea. The enemy had other sources of information.

The next morning, September 13, Jake called a halt in a sparsely wooded wadi five miles from Benia and fifteen miles southeast of Barce. The Rhodesian patrol had left us the day before to join with Stirling's party farther west. They were to raid Benina airdrome. Our remaining fifteen vehicles were dispersed in the wadi and camouflaged.

Our original plan had been to arrive two days earlier; two Libyan Arabs whom I had brought with me were to walk into Barce, make contact with their fellow tribesmen, get the information about the enemy, and return to our camp before we went in to attack on the night of the thirteenth. Owing to the accident in the Sand Sea we had arrived much too late to carry out this program. Our discovery of the presence of tanks made it now even more necessary than we had foreseen to get information of what was going on in Barce; Jake decided to drive my two Arabs as near Barce as he could reasonably go by daylight, drop them and come back to our camp. I instructed the Arabs to collect hurriedly what information they could and to meet me again at Sidi Selim, a sheik's tomb about six miles from Barce, that afternoon at five o'clock. I gave them money—perhaps too much. The short time available hardly left them time to achieve anything useful; it was the best we could do.

I stayed in our camp and put out scouts with instructions to stop any Arabs seen wandering in our neighborhood and bring them to me, with the double object of getting information and of preventing the news of our arrival from leaking out and reaching the Italians. By the early afternoon I had collected a dozen Arabs, who put up with their temporary confinement with good grace. One of them had been in Barce the day before and confirmed the recent arrival of a few tanks; he also had a rumor of twenty thousand troops collected in the big rest camp at El Abiar thirty miles to the west.

During the morning the two patrols had been lazily busy cleaning the guns and tidying the loads, then the men had gone to sleep in the shade of their trucks. At three o'clock Easonsmith collected everybody under a tree and gave his orders.

The enemy, mainly Italians, had a landing ground on the outskirts of the small town of Barce, fifteen-odd miles away. On this landing ground they had aircraft. Headquarters were in the main street, in a hotel. The garrison, such as it was, lived in barracks outside the town on the road leading to El Abiar. There was a possibility of the enemy's disposing of several light tanks. They also had light A.A. defenses.

We had two L.R.D.G. patrols. A British raiding force was on the outskirts of Benghazi, seventy miles to the southwest. The main British forces were at El Alamein, five hundred and fifty miles to the east.

His intention was to destroy the enemy aircraft on the landing ground at Barce on the coming night, and simultaneously to create a diversion by attacking the enemy headquarters and the garrison.

To this effect Popski would drive in a jeep to Sidi Selim, leaving at four o'clock. He would wait there for his Arabs to arrive. When they came he would sort out their information and have it ready for the main party when it arrived.

After a meal at six-fifteen, as night fell, the two patrols led by Easonsmith would drive off to Sidi Selim, arriving at seven. T patrol's radio truck would remain there and make contact on the air with Stirling's S.A.S. force outside Benghazi. Our medical officer, Dick Lawson, was to remain with that truck and wait for any casualties that we might bring back from Barce later during the night.

At nine the whole raiding party would leave Sidi Selim for Barce. On reaching the outskirts the New Zealand patrol would make for the landing ground, the Guards for the barracks, Popski with one Guards' truck would hold the road leading out of the town.

Rendezvous were fixed for stragglers.

When Jake had done, with maps and air-photos and a postcard I described the town and the buildings which I knew well. I hoped it would thus be easier for the parties to find their way in the dark. Barce has two Italian-built streets forming a T, with a square and the railway station where the two strokes meet. Off these two streets are a maze of alleys with small Arab stone and mud-brick hovels. We should come in along the left-hand top stroke of the T. Italian headquarters were halfway down the vertical stroke, the landing ground at the bottom of it. The right-hand top stroke led to the barracks.

At four o'clock, with the sun still high, I went off in my jeep with a driver. A quarter of a mile down our wadi we hit the Benia track and turned right: the country was hilly and wooded and the track followed a sinuous course. Rounding a corner, my driver said: "Let them have it, Major."

Taken by surprise (for that was the kind of soldier I was then) I fumbled with the twin Vickers machine guns as I watched a motorcycle come toward us ridden by two Italian officers. Before I was ready to fire they were passing us, and, instead of killing them, I waved and smiled and shouted a cheerful "Ciao." They replied and their cycle gave a wide lurch as they both turned their heads to look at their unrecognized friend. Then they passed out of sight round the bend. I had of course played the right move, but I thought I must pull myself together and be quicker on the trigger: the days of snooping and hiding in ditches were over. With two L.R.D.G. patrols at my back I felt I ought to open fire on a German armored division—if I met one. I looked at my driver; he didn't seem to mind.

Farther down the track, at Sidi Rawi, I saw on the right-hand side a rough shelter which looked like a road post; it was not manned, or the men were asleep inside. Just off the road I saw long low huts and I stopped a moment to watch; horses were being led to water by what I took to be Tripolitanian soldiers: it was all very sleepy and peaceful. I pushed on along the track through a shallow rocky gorge and arrived at Sidi Selim, a white sheik's tomb just off the track. We parked the jeep and camouflaged it, then looked for my Arabs: I gave three times the hoot of the Buma, then again and again, but they had not yet arrived. Well concealed, we waited.

At dusk just after six o'clock, a plane flew low, coming from Barce and following the track. I wondered if it would catch our patrols on the move, but they hadn't started yet. They waited till complete darkness, which would be about forty minutes after sunset, about a quarter to seven. At half-past seven I heard a few shots in the distance. Then silence. We cut the telephone wires that ran on poles along the track to prevent the alarm being given in Barce, then, after waiting twenty minutes, we drove back along the track in the dark. I was nearing the last bend in the gorge before reaching the post at Sidi Rawi, when a hullabaloo broke out: tracer went flying over the hill and a rattle of several machine guns. We pulled the jeep off the road and up the bank as best we could to avoid misunderstandings when our trucks arrived: when I saw them coming round the bend, I signaled with a torch and was hailed by Jake. All was well and we went on together to Sidi Selim. At the post which I had found deserted Jake had been challenged by a Tripolitanian sentry called Hamed, whom he had promptly disarmed and captured. An Italian officer had turned up and been killed, then Jake had chased out the occupants of the huts and destroyed the telephones. I found out from Hamed that there was also a radio set somewhere in the camp, but Jake had not seen it. Two trucks had collided at Sidi Rawi, and had to be abandoned, leaving us with thirteen vehicles.

I suggested to Jake Easonsmith that the presence of an Italian-Tripolitanian camp on our line of retreat called for a change of plan. I knew a track leading away from Barce from a turning on the El Abiar road, which would take us back to Benia, avoiding the Tripolitanians. He considered the plan but decided against altering his arrangements.

"A night operation must have a very simple plan. We may fall into some confusion in Barce; we shall be more likely to get our men out if they come back along a route they already know." I know now that he was right in being more concerned about withdrawal than attack. After a night raid loss of control comes easy; try then getting your men together if they don't know the way to the meeting point!

We stayed at Sidi Selim in complete darkness till ten. I spent the time whistling like a wretched owl; no answer came to the call of the Buma, my Arabs never turned up and I don't know what happened to them.

At ten we drove off, Jake Easonsmith leading in a 1½-ton truck, I second, then the remaining trucks and the jeeps of the Guards' patrol, then the N.Z. patrol with four trucks and a jeep. The N.Z. radio truck with the doctor had been left near the tomb at Sidi Selim. Our route lay along the track coming from Jerdes el Abid which runs into the southern tarmac road from Derna to Barce on top of the escarpment six miles from Barce. In the darkness Jake ran off the track and we got involved in some difficult going. When he flashed on his headlights I had a vision of his truck crashing through a wooden gate into somebody's back garden, of a concrete one-story house and of frightened silent people, Italian civilians, slipping out of a window on the ground floor. Then all was darkness again: we all drove over vegetable beds like stampeding cattle, followed Jake sharp left and back on to the track.

On the main road we turned on our lights, pretending we were an enemy convoy but feeling more like tourists in the unaccustomed glare. We wound down the escarpment; on the straight, in the plain, where the road runs on a low embankment, our lights picked out two light tanks with Italian markings, hull down, one on each side of the road. My heart gave a leap. Jake Easonsmith opened up with two guns: I saw his tracer bounce off the closed turrets. We did the same as we came within range: I expected to be blown up, for I fancied that the tanks' guns were swinging on to me, but they drifted past without giving a flash. A racket arose behind us as our trucks opened fire in turns, then silence: we drove on to Barce in the cool of the night.

When we stopped just outside the town only a few lights showed here and there, with the sleepy noises of a small town at midnight. Nick Wilder and his New Zealanders drove off towards the landing ground, avoiding the town, Sergeant Dennis took the Guards' trucks past the main square along the El Abiar road, Jake and his driver drove away in a jeep on a job of his own, I remained on the road with one 1½-ton truck and five Guardsmen. They had got hold of a jar of rum and were already far gone; to my vexation they took no notice when I tried to stop their drinking. They drove their truck off the road and went on boozing, talking in hushed whispers. Their speech was rudimentary, propped up by an expletive every three or four words, such as: "If a f—— tank comes f—— along the f—— road; f—— me if we can stop it with our f—— guns."

I stood on the road, expecting the tanks to come after us. There was a distant clatter of tracks, which came to nothing. Across the road, fifty yards away, a low hum came from a tall building. I walked over and peeped in at the door into a well-lighted workshop: several Italians in overalls were at work on lathes; their faces were white, their talk in whispers; their hands were sluggish as if fighting an overpowering sleepiness. I returned to the road and sat down on a stone like an old man taking the cool of the evening on his doorstep.

A chatter of guns came from the far side of the town, a

glow lit the sky, and suddenly the show started. Tracer flew, fires sprang up on the landing ground: the dispersed planes were being set alight one after the other, and, by the columns of red smoke that arose, I followed Nick Wilder's slow progress round the airfield. More distant bursts came from my left, where Sergeant Dennis had driven off, and, close at hand in the main street, I heard the small thuds of hand grenades. The lights snapped off in the workshop, the Guardsmen went on whispering in their foul gibberish. Elated, I made a note of the fires as they appeared on the airfield: I thought Nick Wilder would like to know how many planes he had set alight.

A vehicle approached from the main square, stopped, signaled with a torch and drove up. It was Jake, back from his games in the town; he had had a good time and chuckled contentedly, relieved of the burden of leadership. He was not sure he had spotted headquarters, and he asked me to go back with him. We drove along the still deserted main street and pulled up outside the well-remembered hotel: H.Q. offices were on the ground floor and billets upstairs. We wanted to alarm the staff and make them look after their own skins instead of organizing a defense of the airfield, but we forgot a little our military purpose in a boyish enjoyment of a wild-West stunt. We banged on the door; as nobody came we blew it open, went in and ran round till we found the signal office with a lonely signaler on duty at the telephone exchange. He went and sat down in a corner of the room while we put two hand grenades inside the standard: he beat a retreat with us, saluted on the doorstep and walked away down the street; having gone twenty yards he suddenly bolted.

We then lobbed hand grenades through the first-floor windows and got a meager reward of muffled shouts and dark shufflings. You would think a couple of hand grenades exploding under the bed would stir them up. But neither the racket on the landing ground, nor our own efforts seemed to bring anybody out. Jake took me round to a little square behind the hotel where earlier he had found and damaged some parked trucks; we now set these on fire, and when the flames leaped up we went quietly to the far end of the long, straight main street and drove down again very noisily. We fired our machine guns into the houses, emptied our pistols into the doors and dropped hand grenades in our wake. On our second rush, nearing the main square, a small shell ruffled overhead, first response to our provocations. From the jeep parked in a dark alley, we peeped out and saw a tank lumber up from the El Abiar road and turn into the main street. This at last was what we had been working for, and with a little regret that our party should be over, we returned to our Guards' truck.

"Buffalo Bill," I said. Jake nodded and gave a low laugh.

Just over half an hour after Nick Wilder had driven off I counted twenty-eight fires blazing on the landing ground, and there was apparently quite a battle on. The Italians had got a machine gun going on the roof of a hangar and a mortar thudded at intervals. At ten minutes to one I counted thirty-two blazes on the landing ground, and the streams of tracer thinned out.

On arriving at the landing ground Nick Wilder had opened an unguarded iron gate and driven his trucks through: his first target, as luck had it, was a gasoline tanker, which went up in flames at once, and kindly lit up the scene. He then drove in single file from one parked plane to another as he discovered them, each truck in turn firing a few volleys as they went by. Their last truck carried incendiary bombs, one of which, if the plane was not yet on fire, was deposited by hand in the cockpit: the truck then caught up with the party. The landing ground was big and the planes widely dispersed: Nick led a leisurely procession round and round, meeting at first with no opposition. The Italians were in confusion, for, although they had been warned by their intelligence of our projected raid, they had not taken the threat seriously, and beyond posting perfunctorily on the road those two tanks we had fired at as we came in, had made no other arrangements to defend themselves. As I found out later, they had had too many scares passed on to them from headquarters to bother much any longer.

After nearly an hour on the field, having dealt with all the planes he could find, Nick Wilder decided to return to the rendezvous, which was for one o'clock at the Guards' truck. There was now plenty of wild fire coming at him from heavy machine guns on top of a hangar, and also a mortar or two were flopping bombs here and there, neither men nor trucks had been hit. Driving out of the airfield gate he mistook the road somehow (I think he turned left when it should have been right) and a moment later he realized that instead of skirting the town by the way he had come, he was leading his line of trucks down the narrow main street of Barce; in his headlights he picked out three light tanks staggered across the street: the

Italian M13

headquarters defense which had been called up as the result of Jake's and my boyish pranks. The two rear tanks, in a grotesque eagerness to come forward both together, crashed into each other and went dead; the third one, dazzled by the headlights, started firing high.

There was no room for the New Zealand trucks to turn round under fire, and they carried no weapon heavy enough to knock out the tank: they could thus neither withdraw nor fight it out with guns. Standing on the accelerator in the leading truck Nick Wilder gathered speed and deliberately rammed the tank head on. His 1½-ton truck rose and crashed down on top of the tank turret, converting both vehicles into a mess of mangled metal; the New Zealand crew jumped down unhurt, and piled into the following trucks, Nick Wilder taking the lead in the gunner's seat of the jeep. The way was now clear right down to the station, from which fire was coming: down they charged, firing as they drove. At the station square roundabout, the driver of the jeep, blinded by the tracer Wilder was firing, hit the curb and over-turned the jeep. The driver was thrown out, but Nick Wilder, pinned under and soaked in gasoline, passed out.

The crew of the following 1½-ton truck put the jeep back on its wheels, loaded poor Wilder—unconscious or dead—in the back, and a moment later I saw them arrive at the Guards' truck, in a jeep and two 1½-ton trucks. One truck had been wrecked on the tank and the other— the last in line—with Craw and a crew of four had been cut off and wasn't seen again.

As the gasoline evaporated off him Nick Wilder recovered in a remarkably short time, and he told me his story in his usual clipped speech while we waited for Sergeant Dennis' Guards' party to turn up. The New Zealanders sorted themselves out: one man, who had been wounded, suddenly collapsed and slid to the ground. As we stood in a bunch on the road round his body someone said:

"Poor Jimmy is dead."

"The hell I'm dead," said Jimmy's corpse. "I was only resting," and he scrambled to his feet, suddenly quite fit. We all laughed, feeling light and gay.

Dennis arrived a moment later. He had had a rowdy party in the barracks, driving round the huts, lobbing hand grenades and firing through the windows. He had been entirely successful in keeping the troops away from the main battle on the landing ground.

We had now done our job and we all drove back towards Sidi Selim where Lawson, the doctor, was waiting for us with the radio truck. I thought the two tanks might still be watching for us in the dark, and rode rather gingerly till we reached the top of the escarpment having seen no enemy. Then we turned off the main road along the track leading to Sidi Selim, Jake Easonsmith pushing ahead to the radio to exchange news with David Stirling's S.A.S. party in Benghazi. But the signalers had been vainly tapping their keys: we feared that things had gone wrong with our neighbors, as indeed they had.

While we waited in the dark at Sidi Selim for the tail of our party to arrive, Sergeant Dennis drove up at three o'clock with the news that the last Guards' truck had missed the track and turned over. They were drunk, I thought, and deserve what has befallen them. I would have written them off, but Jake Easonsmith, quite unmoved by moral indignation, drove back with me to the scene of the mishap.

He knew, as well as I did, that if he chose to leave the

careless crew to their fate and push on immediately with the rest of our party, we could in the remaining two hours of darkness be well away in the open desert to the south before the enemy got aircraft in the air (which would have to be called up from Benghazi to the ravaged airfield in Barce), and in the trackless expanses beyond the foothills, planes would be hard put to discover our few remaining trucks. An hour's delay in getting started meant the difference between a sound withdrawal and probably disaster. Jake Easonsmith deliberately accepted the delay: alone I believe among us, he would not have been content to save his best men at the cost of abandoning a weak crew after it had got itself in trouble through its own incompetence. He had achieved against the enemy everything he had set out to do, but this success was far from enough for him: he would have considered his enterprise a failure if he had refused to give succor to the most inexperienced and most helpless of his men. His standards were not altogether of this world, and I acknowledged his greater rectitude with a certain humility.

We found the Guardsmen sitting sullenly by their overturned truck, amongst the litter which had spilled out. With a truck towing a rope passed over its belly the fallen truck was hauled up to an upright position: it rocked back on to its wheels and settled on the road; equipment was piled in and back we drove to Sidi Selim, where we collected the main party and pushed on. The first gray light had already broken the deepness of the night when our column entered the rocky gorge near the Italian-Tripolitanian camp at Sidi Rawi which Jake had shot up earlier in the night. As we approached the rocks I saw flashes on both sides of the road and heard the rattle of many machine guns: a few streamers of tracer converging, as it seemed, on to me made me duck in my seat (I was riding in a 1½-ton with the driver on my right), but many more invisible bullets whined around me, which did not upset me at all. I was making a note in my mind of the psychological effect of tracer when I felt my left hand knocked off the side of the truck, where it was resting, as under a blow from a hard fist. A fraction of a second later a similar blow hit my left knee, and my driver gave a gasp. I looked at him: he seemed unmoved.

"Been hit?" I asked.

"Hit in the leg," he replied.

"Can you drive?"

"I'm O.K. for the present," and drove on with care.

I lifted my left hand: the little finger dangled, hanging by a piece of flesh, and there was some blood. For the first and only time during the war, anger seized me. I wanted to get even with the creature who had taken a liberty with my wholeness, who had broken off maliciously *my* finger. I seized the handle of the gun in front of me, swiveled it sideways and fired bursts and bursts in the direction of the flashes on my left. When I had emptied the pan a man sitting behind me fitted a fresh one for me and I went on firing with rage in my heart.

A little later I saw, in the feeble light, that the truck following us had stopped and we halted also, for it was our rule that if one vehicle stopped everyone did the same. There was trouble behind us and we waited, firing at the flashes, dim as they were in the growing daylight. Sergeant Dennis in his jeep appeared, left the track and drove in a wide curve to the left toward the enemy huts with both his guns spurting. The rhythmic buzzing of bullets slowed down, and we also held our fire to save ammunition. Jake drove up, stopped a moment to tell me that the radio truck had had a tire ripped open by a bullet. "Never," he said, "have I seen a quicker change of wheel," and he drove on smiling to himself. We followed in a straggled column, round a bend, which put us out of sight of the enemy ambush. By the side of the track two mounted Tripolitanians sat their horses, completely immobile, staring at me out of curiously gray faces.

I asked my neighbor: "What have they put on their faces? Dust? Powder?"

"I think they are scared," he replied. "See, they can't move."

Paralyzed with fear, they waited for death, but my anger had passed and I let the helpless men be. I would have been better advised to kill them.

Another quarter of an hour's drive took us to the rendezvous, where Easonsmith waited and guided us to our position under a tree.

I limped a hundred yards over to a tree under which Lawson, the doctor, was opening shop, and waited with the others to be attended to. Although (as we made out) thirty-six guns had fired at us at close range for nearly fifteen minutes, my driver and I were the only casualties in

the ambush: the others had been hit during the fighting at
Barce, none of them much hurt. My driver, a tall Guards-
man, had a neat bullet wound through the calf: his leg had
stiffened and he could hardly walk, but he was quite
unmoved, and we all sat on the rough ground smoking and
joking, enjoying ourselves quietly. Dick Lawson, a cheerful young M.O. with a chubby face, made a quick survey
of his patients: he took on first those who required least
attention: thus I came last. I have always had a fondness
for messing about with other people's wounds, and I
proffered perfectly unrequired assistance to the doctor and
his medical orderly. I realized that I was a bit of a
busybody, but the excitements of the night were still in me
and wouldn't let me remain inactive.

Bandaged up, the other men moved off, and my turn
came. Dick Lawson injected anaesthetic into my hand, and
said:

"I am going to amputate your finger. Don't look. It will
soon be over." Dutifully I turned my face away under the
unreasonable impression that he would feel abashed if I
watched him do something indelicate. I felt the bone
crunch under his tool, then looked round to see him stitch
the flesh over the little stump. It was done, without any
real pain. My knee had only a few small splinters em-
bedded in the flesh which he prized out with the point of a
scalpel. It wasn't even stiff.

Meanwhile the fitters were busy with the two trucks
which, damaged at Sidi Rawi the previous evening, had
been recovered and towed in after we had come out of the
ambush. Loads were sorted out and guns cleaned in a
cheerful activity: we all thought we had done with fighting
for this trip, and we prepared for the seven-hundred-mile
run to Cufra.

As we were widely dispersed over rolling scrubby
ground, where occasional trees grew, I could not see what
was happening at every truck. When I heard a few bursts
of one of our machine guns followed by several rifle shots,
I picked up a tommy gun and walked over to find out the
reason of this new disturbance. I was told that some
Tripolitanian horsemen had been seen galloping in the
distance and that Jake Easonsmith had driven off in a jeep
to chase them away; the bursts I had heard were his. I had
nothing to do and felt restless—I believe also that Lawson's injections combined with the fatigue of a sleepless

night had slightly affected my judgment. I fancied I saw someone moving behind bushes and off I went, crouching low, stalking the enemy on foot, alone with my tommy gun. I crashed, a very noisy Red Indian, through the undergrowth, and uncovered one of our New Zealand trucks and its crew. A wave of self-consciousness swept over me: I saw myself as in a mirror, a stoutish, awkward man, with hand and knee bandaged, preposterously stalking his own men. I had been seen too, and the tale of the "Old Major" chasing the enemy with his tommy gun entertained many simple souls for months to come.

12

THE ORYX

JAKE EASONSMITH returned after a while, having chased away the snoopers: as he thought that the horsemen's report of our position would be passed on to enemy aircraft he decided to move on. Repairs on the two damaged trucks were completed, we tidied up our camp and, as I was to travel once more in a jeep, I went over to collect my kit from the truck in which I had driven during the night. The men, busy and in a hurry to get on the move, had already piled some other stuff on top of the bedroll and rucksack which held all my belongings: they persuaded me to let things be for the present, and to collect my kit at the evening halt. Back at my jeep I took stock of what I had left: the rubber-soled shoes, socks, slacks, and shirt I stood in, a bandage and a sling on my left hand, a bandage on my left knee, an army belt with compass, revolver and ammunition, field glasses, a tommy gun, a copy of *Paradise Lost*, and a water bottle. Because one of the few rules I kept was never to let myself be separated from my kit, I worried over my weakness in giving in to the Guardsmen—with good cause, as it turned out, for their truck was burned out shortly afterwards.

Spread out over two miles of sparsely wooded hills so as to be less of a target to aircraft, our trucks and jeeps got underway, keeping parallel courses. The sun, well up by now, was kind to chilled limbs and weary bodies. Glad to be on our way home after the success of our battle, we rocked sleepily in our seats; now and then images of incidents of the previous night flickered through our minds, bringing a glow to sleepy eyes and raising self-centered chuckles: we were contented and at peace.

There is a satisfaction in being wounded and yet well enough to be no burden to anybody. My injuries were light enough to enable me to look after myself and to take a share of duties and I wouldn't have called myself a casualty; nevertheless I was well pleased with the bloodstained dressing on my hand, and I took an interest in the curious pain I felt in the finger which Lawson had clipped off. I had seen it dropped into an enamel basin, but I could still feel a sting under the nail which wasn't there. A dim childish pride in cutting a fine figure no doubt, but the main pleasure I got from my wounds was that they were tangible and visible evidence to the reality of my previous night's enjoyable experiences. I was a little dazed with lack of sleep, slight shock and anaesthetic, but I had only to look at my hand to be assured that I wasn't living a daydream.

We drove a few miles: at twenty-past ten we heard a noise of low-flying aircraft, and every one of our vehicles

CR-42

stopped in its tracks. Two C.R. 42's, old-fashioned Italian fighter biplanes, abreast and half a mile apart, flew over our vehicles dispersed in the low scrub, nearly disappeared over the hills, then banked and returned in line ahead. They flew directly over my jeep, disregarded it, but dived and clattered away with their guns at the Guards' radio truck—the one that carried my kit—which I could see behind me stuck on the top of a bare hill. After the third or the fourth dive I saw black smoke rise, thin at first, then a thick rolling column lit by the sharp reports of exploding ammunition and that was the end of the radio truck. The crew got away and walked over to another truck unmolested.

The Italian planes flew away to the north. When after a minute they had not returned we required no orders to thaw out and make for cover. There was not much of it: thin, isolated acacia trees, with little spread and transparent shadows, were our only comfort. Camouflage nets had been spread out when half an hour later the planes returned. They had landed at Barce, fifteen miles away, well contented with their success, but unfortunately for us, an angered commander, still smarting under last night's trouncing, had sent them up again to go and destroy every vehicle and kill every man of the English raiding party. They made for the beacon of smoke from our burning truck, now a couple of miles in our rear, and flew crisscross over the neighboring area, searching for our vehicles. They discovered another one of our trucks and machinegunned it till it went up in flames. After fifty minutes they left to refuel and reload the guns, returned after twenty minutes and kept up this regular rhythm during the remainder of the day.

During the intervals of peace we hurriedly moved our vehicles to a new pattern and cached some gasoline and some rations. Each time the planes returned we left the trucks and took cover. Wilder and I disagreed with Easonsmith about this, and suggested that we should man such antiaircraft guns as we had and fire at the aircraft. He had been in similar situations before and objected that the only result would be to give away to the enemy the position of our trucks and add human casualties to our losses of equipment.

Toward half-past one, I was sitting with my back against a tree trunk, reading Book Two of *Paradise Lost*. Ten yards away, on my left, Jake Easonsmith sat under another tree, also reading. From the hills around us rose five gigantic, spreading bushes of black rolling smoke, signs of our disintegrating military power. Overhead, now near, now far, the two Italian aircraft swerved and banked fussily, looking for fresh targets. The sound of their engines came in gusts, then died down to a faint purr.

Some change in the noise reached my mind through the baroque Latin verbosity of Milton's verse and made me look up: I saw two thin parallel horizontal lines and the

blurred propeller circle of a plane gliding down head on
directly at us. "In a few seconds," I thought, "I shall be
full of holes," and a mortal apprehension came over me.
Jake Easonsmith under his tree also lifted his eyes from his
book, watched the approaching plane for a while, then
turning toward me, his bearded face broke into a humorous smile of tender understanding: he nodded twice pen-
sively and resumed his reading. Thus, silently, he proclaimed the vanity of human fears and destroyed in me for
ever the seeds of dread.

Until that day I had had to rely on a carefully cultivated
enjoyment of risk to keep up my spirits: under the pleasant excitement of danger I succeeded in overlooking the
threat of bodily violence, but an underlying fear remained:
I was always happy in battle but often uncomfortable on
night patrols which provide no excitement. Jake enjoyed
danger as much as I did but he had a serenity which
carried a deeper strength; in his contemplative mind he
examined dispassionately the threat of disaster and found
it was of no moment, neither the prospect of death nor of
failure had the power to trouble him. The secret of his
strength became mine also the moment I saw him smile at
the gliding plane; it has remained with me ever since.

In wonderful peace I returned to my book. A few
moments later puffs of dust rose out of the sand around us
as the plane fired and missed. We went on reading,
expecting another assault which never came. Either the
Italian pilot had lost interest, or he was unable to find our
trees again in the featureless landscape.

On my right the scrubby stony desert rose slightly to a
small acacia tree a hundred yards away, then to another,
then to a larger one under which stood one of our trucks,
beyond that the ground dipped out of sight. The two
planes reappeared and made for the truck; one of our
men, unrecognizable at the distance, scrambled to his feet
from under it and ran towards the dip; the planes opened
fire, the man fell to the ground, out of sight, and didn't get
up again after the enemy had flown over. Easonsmith put
down his book and rose. I said: "Don't bother, I shall go."
He nodded and sat down again.

The sky being temporarily clear I walked briskly towards the first tree. Halfway over, a plane came, flying at
no more than a hundred feet: I saw the goggled face of the
pilot looking over the side of the open cockpit. He saw me

too, fired two bursts at me, then drifted away. I picked myself up and ran for the tree; I could see the other plane coming from the opposite direction. I reached the tree in time to crouch on the ground with my head pressed against the base of its trunk: it wasn't more than six inches thick and I felt as large as a house; my position was so undignified that I broke into a silly laugh; twisting my head to one side I caught sight of the plane as it dived and spat bullets at me. It missed, I got up, waved a hand at the pilot and dashed for the next tree, chased like a rabbit on the way by the first plane, which came up on my left. Its bullets also went wide, and I reached the second tree with no holes in me. I stayed here a good while because the two aircraft, taking steep turns, kept coming alternately from the right and from the left and hardly gave me time to squirm from one side of the trunk to the other. After each miss I waved an arm, a foolish thing to do, but the two big machines with their thundering engines and their guns chasing me around my puny acacia were too incongruous to be taken seriously.

Suddenly all was quiet, the planes had left, their ammunition all wasted, for none of the pieces of metal they had thrown had torn into me. I got up, somewhat out of breath, and looked around; the landscape, surprisingly, was unaltered; smoke was still coming up from the five burning trucks; Jake Easonsmith in the distance lifted an arm in greeting; in front of me I could see our truck under its tree, but the man I had come to help was nowhere visible. I picked up my tommy gun and walked over a ridge into a shallow dry wadi; under an overhanging rocky ledge where the waters had scooped out a recess two feet high, I found my man lying, eyes closed, white and very shaken. I sat down in the sand and spoke to him.

"Not hurt," he answered, "just upset. I'll be all right in a moment. This is a good shelter. Stay here with me." I did, because the planes, having rediscovered the truck on the bank above us, strafed it in endless rounds for nearly an hour. One behind the other they roared across the wadi, firing as they flew, then turned round and did it again. During each assault thousands of bullets buried themselves in the sand and clattered on the rocks of our cave. It was rather unnerving. Across the wadi, on the upward slope, thirty yards away a hobbled donkey hopped about grazing on the bushes, untroubled by the noise.

His master appeared from up the wadi, a ragged Arab as unconcerned as his ass, and squatted outside the narrow cave where we both huddled and engaged me in a polite conversation in which reference was made neither to our strange position, nor to the bloody bandage on my hand, nor to the burning trucks, nor to the planes overhead, nor to the general hullabaloo. This battle of ours, which of course he couldn't help noticing as he was in the very heart of it, was no concern of his and he studiously ignored it. What he wanted to know, as it appeared in the end, was whether we would like to exchange a few cigarettes for sour milk which he offered to go and fetch for us from his tent. He departed on this errand, riding his donkey among the whistling projectiles.

When the planes at last departed I was much surprised to find our truck on the wadi bank still sound, and drove it into the wadi a few hundred yards below our shelter against a rock from which the western sun now cast a shadow. The planes came back, failed to discover the truck in its new hiding place, and made for other targets. I stayed in the wadi, waiting for the planes to leave to join Easonsmith once more.

The afternoon wore on. A Tripolitanian horseman showed up on the skyline at the head of the wadi, then rode cautiously down. Crouched behind a bush I took a slow, careful aim with my tommy gun; slowly, slowly, dragging his feet it seemed, the rider came nearer. At twenty yards I fired one shot. The man started, turned his horse round and walked it away as slowly as he had come; when he had gone thirty yards, he tossed his head, rolled off the back of the horse and lay spread-eagle in the sand, his left foot twitching. When I got up to him I found him dead. The horse cantered away up the wadi.

Shortly before sunset I joined Easonsmith once more, and he gave me the news. Lawson, the doctor, had managed to drive away a truck with all the casualties and hide it in a deep wadi under a wooded hill two miles to the south. With the exception of two jeeps, all the other trucks, he said, were burned out. Nick Wilder had bullets through both his legs and a slight face wound; two other men had been hit, making with the men wounded the previous night six casualties in all, including myself. I told him about the truck I had concealed in the wadi, which he had counted as lost. As soon as the sun dipped below the horizon we collected a few men and set ourselves to load it with the rations, and the gasoline which had been cached. Dusk was thickening, we thought we had done with air attack; having still two 1½-ton Chevrolets, two jeeps, and plenty of supplies we could easily carry our thirty-three men to Cufra, only seven hundred miles away. Then came a setback: in the failing light a slow heavy three-engined transport aircraft lumbered overhead. We didn't bother, for generally transport aircraft are not interested in the ground, all their attention is for hostile fighter planes. Unexpectedly this plane gave us two bursts of its guns and went on its ponderous way, without looking round. It was as if a friend had suddenly slapped you hard in the face. Unfortunately their aim was good and after they had gone, smoke started pouring out of our truck. Hurriedly we pulled off what stores we could before the whole load was sheeted in flames. We then found that the jeep which had been standing by had a large hole through the top of the gasoline tank and a gashed tire.

Easonsmith gathered his men in the thickish wood on the hill above Lawson's truck, and took stock of the situation. He had thirty-three men, of whom six were casualties, two of them serious: Nick Wilder, wounded in both legs, and Parker, with a bullet through the stomach. One Chevrolet truck in good condition, a jeep in good order, another jeep with a punctured tank and a torn tire. Enough gasoline and water for two hundred miles, some rations. No radio, no spare tires.

Forty miles away to the southeast, near Bir Jerrari, he had left on his way up to Barce a truck with stores of water, gasoline, and rations. One hundred and forty miles further on was L.G. 125, a disused R.A.F. landing ground of the year before, used frequently by L.R.D.G. as a rallying point: this had been given as a common rendezvous to stragglers on the present operations. Five hundred miles again to the south, beyond the Sand Sea, was Cufra, with the headquarters of A Squadron L.R.D.G., and 216 Bomber Squadron R.A.F., and a garrison of the Sudan Defense Force.

Jake divided his force into a driving and a walking party. In the driving party were the six casualties, the doctor (Lawson) in command, driver (Wallbrook), a navigator (Davis), and a mechanic. They were to make first for Bir Jerrari for supplies, then for L.G. 125, where

they might meet an L.R.D.G patrol. If they didn't they
were to push on nonstop, skirting the Sand Sea, which was
impassable for a single truck with six cripples on board,
slip through the Jalo gap (avoiding enemy-held Jalo), and
on to Cufra, a trip of some seven hundred miles, which, all
being well, could be covered in seven to eight days.
Lawson doubted that Parker, with his stomach wound,
could survive that long. The jeep with the punctured tank
would travel with the truck.

The remaining twenty-three men under Easonsmith,
with the other jeep to carry supplies, would walk to Bir
Jerrari, collect the spare truck and push on to Cufra. I
wanted to be included in the walking party, but Easonsmith determinedly overruled me, saying that my wounded
knee, though it left me enough agility to dodge Italian
C.R. 42's, would not stand up to the forty-mile trek to Bir
Jerrari.

With the New Zealand sergeant, Easonsmith wrote out
a nominal roll of each party; the men were called one by
one and told to which party they belonged, everyone to
report to the sergeant in an hour's time at eight o'clock,
in the woods on the hill. We then got busy getting the
trucks and their loads ready. It was quite dark under the
trees; several Arabs from neighboring tents turned up and
provided us with milk, among them my friend the donkey
rider. Hamed, the Tripolitanian lad captured by Jake the
previous night, had now his first meal; we were in Rama-
dhan, and nothing I could say had induced him to eat
before sunset. The Moslem custom exempts the traveler
from the fast, but Hamed, about to set out on the longest
trip of his life, didn't consider himself a bona fide traveler.

At eight o'clock the sergeant called the roll and found
two men missing: Jake's driver, Gutteridge, and another,
both good men with a long experience in the L.R.D.G.
They had been seen only a few minutes previously and
somebody had heard them talk of going over to the Arab
tents in search of eggs. I walked over in the dark to the
Arab village and questioned the women; they had indeed
seen the two men, given them eggs and seen them wander
away in the opposite direction to our trucks. I called and
shouted and got no answer: the two blighters had gone for
a walk and could not be recovered. These two lads, eager
and competent both, would never have been found missing
from their patrol in the normal course of their journeys,

but tonight, when their very life depended on being with their companions—a situation which they could appreciate as well as anyone in the party (one of them was a navigator)—they chose to stroll away and enjoy the cool of the evening. I have experienced a similar mental derangement in other men, so often that, in later years, I made a rule on such occasions as this to allow no one out of sight. We left without them.

We drove off in the moonless night, Wallbrook driving the Chevrolet truck and I the damaged jeep, with Doctor Lawson in the passenger seat. David in the Chevrolet set the course. The going, up a rocky wadi, was abominable. We seemed to be going up steps, then hanging with two wheels on to a rocky ledge, then we got jammed between two large boulders. The front left-hand tire of the jeep was flat, which didn't make the steering easy, and, with the jolting, the gasoline splashed out of the torn tank and compelled me to add a gallon or so every ten minutes. My left knee was getting stiff and I found it increasingly difficult to press down the clutch for the perpetual changes of gears. After an hour's driving the walking party was still ahead of us. We caught up with them only when we came out of the wadi on to a plateau. At that moment the other jeep, which had been making no better progress, blew a tire. I decided to abandon my jeep and to give two of its wheels to the walking party, who would thus have a spare. We pushed the doomed jeep on to its side, removed two wheels which we gave to Jake, set a time incendiary bomb over the tank, climbed on to the Chevrolet and drove on.

For a while we could hear the voices of the men in Jake Easonsmith's party, but the going was better now and we left them behind.

Davis, our navigator, tried to keep a straight compass course and the driver did his best to follow his instructions, but the night was so dark that he could just see far enough ahead to avoid crashing into trees and boulders. Of the general lie of the land he could see nothing: he drove ahead in a straight line as long as he wasn't stopped by an impassable obstacle. We found ourselves, at one time, driving along the steep side of a hill at such an angle that we could hardly cling on to our seats and we expected the truck to topple over, but it righted itself; then, some time later, we stopped dead with our front wheels nearly over a cliff, a vertical drop of forty feet or so to a wadi below. We drove round, followed the curving cliff edge for a long time, found a way down, slid and skidded to the wadi bottom and started climbing up the opposite bank. Night was wearing out, there was no time to send a man on foot to reconnoiter ahead; if dawn found us anywhere near our starting point, the planes would soon be on us and our adventures at an end. The climb out of the wadi proved difficult: it was steep and of screes, which had to be rushed, and protruding rocks, which should be taken with care. The heavy truck rocked and swayed, the uphill wheels on rock, the downhill ones on shingle in which they spun, digging a hole which slowly brought the truck to a dangerous angle; suddenly the wheels gripped (having reached rock I suppose) and sent us lurching forward, over boulders and through high bushes with a loud crash.

We pulled up on a level keel, and while the fitter got down to inspect the damage, Lawson injected a dose of morphia to Parker, to whom the jolting was an agony. Surprisingly no damage had been suffered, and we continued on our wild, blind course, the driver muttering to himself over the wheel as he dodged and skirted. Later the going became better and finally at three-thirty that morning Lawson called a halt. He wanted to spare Parker, who was weakening. We had covered nearly fifteen miles; by stopping now and starting again at daybreak we could put at least twenty-five miles between us and our starting point before the planes got into the air: they would have to search an area of a thousand-odd square miles to find us.

Accordingly we stopped on a sandy patch, made tea, and went to sleep for a couple of hours. The sand was soft under the truck, but the early hours of the morning were very chilly and I had neither blanket nor coat. I woke up with the first signs of dawn and stretched painfully a very stiff knee. I saw Lawson on the truck, bending over the still body of Parker, his chubby face ruddy in spite of fatigue and two sleepless nights. I grunted, he nodded cheerfully; against all the rules Parker was still alive. We drove off straight away.

Wallbrook, our driver, was a half Maori, with a black beard and an indomitable cheerfulness. He denied that he had nearly overturned the truck once or twice during the night drive: he knew exactly where he was going and all

Maoris could see at night anyway. Davis, the navigator, was a short New Zealander, with a thoughtful disposition and a quick temper. Our lives were in his hands and he had a difficult problem: with a magnetic and a sun compass he had to navigate our truck by dead reckoning over seven hundred miles, making landfalls at Bir Jerrari and at L.G. 125 on the way. As he had neither theodolite nor radio he couldn't check his position from the stars. His starting point after the night drive was doubtful, but his first landfall, the truck near Bir Jerrari, should be fairly easy to make because it was in a wadi covered in thick scrub and bushes, quite conspicuous in the bare plain, and very familiar to many of us who had used it frequently as a lie-up for operations in the Jebel and on the Triq el 'Abd. Having found the truck, he would have a good start for his second lap, as its position had been determined by astrofix. Davis had not been able to save his theodolite but he had his log book and his maps.

We drove steadily the whole morning. When we halted at noon for dinner we had left the Jebel foothills and their trees behind us, and were in pleasant yellow hills of gravel and sand, the watercourses marked by heavy bushes. The sun was quite hot and we drove the truck in the shade of a particularly high bush. Parker was too ill to be moved—he was half stunned with morphia and not quite conscious—but his heart stood up well. Nick Wilder was taken off the truck and laid on blankets on the sand; when I went over to him he glared malevolently at me, as if I was the cause of his helplessness. He felt perfectly fit and resented not being allowed the use of his legs. His patched-up face gave him a comical appearance which caused half-concealed grins and increased his annoyance.

We pushed on and by four o'clock we were in Wadi Jerrari. Davis, receiving unsolicited advice, shook his head as if throwing off raindrops, said nothing, steered a sinuous course down the wadi and finally halted opposite a great tangle of matted bushes, inside which we found, well camouflaged, the truck we were making for. Within an hour we had taken our load of gasoline, water, and rations, collected a spare tire and left a note for Jake saying we had called at four o'clock on September 15, 1942, and left at five o'clock for L.G. 125.

We drove till dark and slept ten hours, our first real rest since the morning of the thirteenth.

Parker was still alive the next morning, September 16, but in great pain. Morphia seemed to have lost its power to put him at ease; he was conscious and apologized for the trouble he was giving, though I have not known a quieter patient. He could not eat nor was he allowed to drink: all we could do was to try and make him comfortable in the back of the truck, where Lawson gave him a shot of morphia every few hours. The bullet which had gone in at one side and out at the other had made a long serrated gash in his stomach. Fortunately the going was becoming better as we progressed to the south so that the jolting in the back of the Chevrolet was less desperately painful.

The weather was exceptional: very clear with sparkling sunshine. We were now in the desert, not yet quite barren, but too far from water for any human beings or their cattle. The northerly breeze had lost the aridity of the summer blasts, touched for the first time with the approach of winter. The horizon expanded and contracted as our lonely truck rose and sank with the long yellow rolling hills, still and quiet but not devoid of life: under a bush in the very early morning I saw a huge hyena turning round and round like a dog before settling down to sleep; then an hour later I saw a couple of oryx. The heavy beasts, the size of a large calf, their coats milky white, and with long curved horns, grazed on the sweet-smelling bushes. We stopped the truck for a while to look at them, for none of us had seen such animals in all our travels in the desert, nor did I see any again. We propped up Parker so that he too could have a look at the creatures; it seemed important that he should know about them before he died.

From first light until darkness we plodded along, slowly so as not to jolt too much, but steadily and with only short stops to ease the patients and for a very short meal at midday. We were trying to reach L.G. 125 as early as possible in the hope of catching there one of the patrols which we thought would visit the place periodically. They would not, however, we imagined remain more than a few hours each time in the neighborhood of the landing ground, for it was an occasional target for the Luftwaffe and it offered no cover whatever. If we met a patrol they could, with their radio, get a plane sent up from Cufra in a few hours to take Parker to hospital in Egypt; if we met no one we should have to drive on to Cufra ourselves, and

Oryx

Lawson was positive that Parker could not survive the five-hundred-mile trip, some of which was very rough going.

We covered over a hundred miles on that day and I reckoned that when we bedded down for the night we were not more than thirty miles from L.G. 125. I wasn't sure, however, because Davis was very jealous of his navigation and evaded my questions. L.G. 125 was not marked on my map and I had to go by memory.

The next morning, September 17, we traveled about two hours, then Davis, who had been watching the speedometer, told the driver to stop, climbed on to the back of his seat and looked slowly round the horizon; behind us stretched the tracks of our wheels like the wake of a ship—otherwise nothing was in sight but the smooth undulating surface of the desert, of flourlike dust strewn with hard shiny, gray stones. We had traveled one hundred and forty miles from Bir Jerrari on a general bearing of 140° and according to Davis's reckoning we *were* on L.G. 125. In fact we were not, nor did he expect us to be. But he knew he was only a few miles away. I looked round and, strangely enough, in spite of the emptiness of the barren landscape, I shared his confidence. Davis climbed down and said:

"We shall soon find it."

"What do we look for?" I asked, for I had never been to L.G. 125 before.

"The tail of a wrecked Hurricane standing on its nose."

Davis took us slowly two miles due west, two miles due south, two miles due east, two miles due north; when we completed the square we had seen no Hurricane. Davis then started us on a four mile square; halfway down the second side, I touched him on the head and pointed to the west where something showed which didn't seem to be desert.

"Would that be it?"

Davis looked and said: "Could be."

We didn't know whether there might not be some Germans about, so we crept up slowly to the thing. It was the Hurricane on its nose all right, and other wrecked and burned Blenheims and Hurricanes began to show up. As soon as we were sure, we took a wide detour and circled the landing ground out of sight, looking for fresh wheel tracks, but found none. We then drove boldly on to the far end of the landing ground, away from the wrecked aircraft, found some old covered dugouts and put the patients in one and converted another into a surgery for Lawson. Parker was very faint and the doctor wanted to look after him in peace.

We collected some water and food we found. The truck was then driven against the remains of a hut and camouflaged. Under the net, the fitter did his maintenance.

Just after sunset we heard the engines of several vehicles. We took cover and waited, while the unidentified visitors seemed to settle at the other end of the ground, out of sight. Later when darkness fell, we saw the glare of a fire they had lit. About half-past nine Davis crept away to reconnoiter. We waited, lying on the sand outside the dugouts, a long time. We waited an hour and more. Davis must have been captured we thought. Nick Wilder suggested that just before dawn I should take the men who could carry weapons and attack the enemy in their sleep. It seemed to me a sensible thing to do, and at half-past ten I set out with Wallbrook, in whom I had great confidence, to reconnoiter the enemy position; having got beyond the last dugout I saw a shadow walking towards me, swinging a torch. I challenged, the man shone the torch on his own face and revealed the features of David Lloyd Owen. It seemed that our troubles were over.

What had delayed Davis was that on approaching the camp he had heard the radio which someone had tuned into a German broadcast and he had naturally assumed that the visitors were German. Only when the radio was turned off did he hear and recognize the voices of his friends in Y Patrol.

Many signals passed between L.G. 125, the Faiyum and Cufra during that night, while I slept like a beast and Parker moaned and fretted. The next morning Lloyd Owen warned us that a plane was due from Cufra at one o'clock to pick us up. We knew enough of the difficulty for an air navigator to find our small landing ground at the end of a flight of four hundred and fifty miles over flat, absolutely featureless desert, to be sceptical about the time of arrival. It might be two or three days before the R.A.F. succeeded in finding the landing ground, we said, and went deliberately and unconcernedly about our business. At twelve-thirty we lighted a smoke generator as a wind indicator—just in case. At twelve-forty-five some credulous fool reported a noise of engines and was laughed down, but three minutes later a fat Bombay bomber circled the ground and landed; I walked up and arrived just as the door opened and Bill Coles, an old friend of mine, climbed out of the cockpit. He commanded 216 Bomber Squadron and had flown the plane over himself, which was natural enough, but to me the apparition at that moment of an unexpected friend seemed to be an act of personal gracefulness of the Fates.

That night we slept in Cufra like children without a care in the world. On the next morning, September 19, we were put on board a Hudson and flown nonstop to Cairo. It was a long trip and the sun was setting when our plane landed in Heliopolis; I was surprised to see two ambulances

Bristol Bombay

waiting for us. We had a long drive to the New Zealand General Hospital in Helwan; as I came out of my ambulance I saw Parker being wheeled away on a trolley. I followed, talking to him, as far as the door of the operating theater, where a surgeon and two sisters waited ready for action. He had traveled for six days with a gaping stomach but now he would be attended to without a minute's delay. That was the way with the New Zealanders.

Though I was not strictly entitled to it, I was admitted to the New Zealand hospital along with my companions and I felt I was receiving a great favor. I was taken upstairs, where an orderly undressed me, put me in a bath, scrubbed my back, poured me out a glass of beer, lit me a cigarette and then put me to bed. It seemed a lot of attention for a little finger shot off, but it was done so kindly and I was so tired that I made no effort to defend myself.

But when I woke up next morning I found on my locker a flowered toilet bag labeled: "With the compliments of the New Zealand Red Cross." In it were all the soaps and brushes a man can desire, two packs of cigarettes, a bag of sweets, writing paper, and chocolate. This was too much; abashed I packed everything back and when the sister came round I drew her attention to the mistake which had been made: I was not a New Zealander and not entitled to this bounty. She laughed and said the folks at home would be glad if they knew that their present had gone to a Tommy. Sister Simpson was gay and kind and lovely to look at; I unpacked my treasure once more and started on the happiest five weeks in my life.

Before I left hospital Parker was up and about, the pride of the staff, who maintained that by all medical standards he had no right to be alive. He rejoined the L.R.D.G. and I met him once more in Wilder's patrol a few months later.

Nick Wilder also recovered perfectly, and the last time I saw him toward the end of the war, he was a lieutenant-colonel commanding Div. Cav., the New Zealand armored regiment. He is now back in New Zealand, sheep farming as of old, and absorbed entirely in ewes and lambs, black faces and merinos.

Jake Easonsmith and his walking party were picked up by chance by Olivey's patrol. They spent some days in the Jebel collecting most of the stragglers, then returned to Cufra. A year later, on November 16, 1943, a lieutenant-colonel in command of L.R.D.G., he was killed in action on the island of Leros and we lost a great man.

Out of a comfortable civilian mediocrity he had joined the L.R.D.G. in 1940, aged thirty-four, as a sergeant. His active life lasted thus something under three years. In that short period of time he developed a new and powerful personality, as has happened to others in wartime, and he learned and perfected a type of warfare for which there was no precedent in military tradition. His most remarkable achievement was to create a standard of behavior which came to be followed as a matter of course by hundreds of men who came under his influence.

PART III

POPSKI'S PRIVATE ARMY

13

LOST

THE Barce raid was the last of my freelance ventures. From the time I left the New Zealand hospital till the end of the war I was in charge of a unit of my own and the new responsibility weighed at first heavily on me, till many mistakes taught me the difference between the duties of a commander and those of a lonely adventurer.

On October 14, 1942, though I had not yet been discharged from hospital, I thought I was well enough to discuss with Colonel Hackett his plans for my future employment. I called on him at Middle East Headquarters, where he told me, in veiled terms, that the battle of El Alamein was due to start shortly (in ten days as it turned out). During the battle itself, and even more so in the course of the pursuit which would follow, the enemy could be much hampered by shortage of gasoline, the supplies of which were carried by road partly from Benghazi, partly from Tripoli, respectively six hundred and twelve hundred miles away. On the strength of our success in burning the dump at El Qubba I was docketed at headquarters as a gasoline destroyer; my knowledge of the Jebel Akhdar and the help I could command from the Senussi Arabs enabled me to get information and to reach places denied to our other raiders; for these reasons Hackett wanted me, as soon as I left hospital, to raise and take command of a small motorized force with which I would raid the enemy gasoline line between Ajedabia and Tobruk.

I refused. We had already, I said, L.R.D.G., S.A.S., Adv. A. Force, G.(R.), and others unknown to me, all tripping over one another behind the enemy lines; it was bad policy to add to their numbers another small independent unit. Furthermore, to be able to carry out the task he wanted me to do I ought to be allowed to concentrate on the operational side and have my mind free from administrative duties. What I didn't tell him was that my ambition was to become a member of the L.R.D.G., the finest body of men in any army as I thought (and still do), and I was not going to miss my chance of getting in. I suggested that a new squadron be added to L.R.D.G., with special duties, under my command; in this manner, with the support of the best unit operating in the desert, I would achieve results far greater than if I was saddled with the responsibilities of a unit of my own.

To this Hackett finally agreed, subject to the consent of Lieutenant Colonel Prendergast, commanding officer L.R.D.G., and on the understanding that I would recruit my own men and make no call whatever on L.R.D.G. personnel. I left headquarters full of joy.

For seven days I remained a member of L.R.D.G. It appeared then that the war establishment of that unit did not allow for an extra squadron, and I was thrown back on my own. I grumbled and argued and threatened, but as I had no alternative to offer I found myself a few days later appointed commander to the smallest independent unit in the British Army. A war establishment, M.E. W.E. 866/1, was hastily drawn up: it allowed for twenty-three all ranks:

Five officers:	one major
	one captain
	three subalterns
Eighteen other ranks:	one sergeant
	two corporals
	fifteen privates
And six vehicles:	four armed jeeps
	two three-ton trucks.

We had no adjutant, no quartermaster, no tradesmen, no scale of equipment or weapons.

The provisional name of the unit was No. 1 Demolition Squadron.

My instructions were to recruit the men, draw vehicles, equipment and weapons, and be ready to move to my chosen theater of operations by November 15, in twenty days' time.

We all treated the affair as a joke: not because the unit was so small (it was in fact larger than I needed for my immediate purposes), but because it was an independent command. I decided that if I was to be a fool, I would be a glorious one and behave in the grand manner. I wanted a name for the unit that would be short, fanciful, easy to memorize, and, for security, such as would give no indication of its nature. Desert Raiders, Jebel Rats and many others failed to please. One morning in November, time getting short, Shan Hackett's patience failed:

"You had better find a name quick, or we shall call you Popski's Private Army," he said with feigned ferociousness. Why not? The name fitted well with the farcical aspect of the undertaking.

"I'll take it," I replied. "I would like to be known as that."

Hackett stared at me, undecided, then grinned, jumped up, and led me downstairs to the office of the Director of Military Operations, Brigadier Davy, with whom rested the decision. A man of imagination and of humor, he agreed immediately, and undertook to square it with the War Office. We laughed and I rushed out to an Indian tailor in town to order shoulder flashes of dark blue with the letters P.P.A. in red. (Later I altered the flashes to white letters on a black ground.)

I had used as a bookplate for several years a design of an astrolabe, several of my boats had been called by that name, and it seemed now a fitting symbol for a unit which would have to navigate its way by the stars; so I took my bookplate to a Jewish silversmith off the Shareh El Manakh and got him to cut in brass a reduced and simplified design of this astrolabe, which we would use as a hat badge. (Astrolabe is a name given to several astronomical instruments formerly used to measure the altitude of stars, before the adoption of the sextant at sea and the theodolite on land. My design is taken from a sixteenth-century Italian instrument.) The first badges were cut and engraved by hand; they turned out rather too exquisite for the roughness of our manners; later we had a die cut and made the badges of silver, which takes the stamp better than brass.

I took a specially worked specimen to Brigadier Davy for approval, with some trepidation, as it looked more like a jewel than a cap badge, but he sanctioned it, to be worn on a black tank corps beret which I had chosen as the unit's headdress.

We had now:

> A war establishment
> A name
> A headdress
> A badge
> A shoulder flash
> One man (myself).

I had two officers in mind, both from the Libyan Arab
Force. One of them, Captain Yunnie, from Aberdeen,
whom I have mentioned earlier, was released straightway
and joined me in Cairo. The other, Lieutenant Caneri, a
Frenchman, was not immediately available, but the commanding officer of the L.A.F. promised to send him on to
me as soon as he could be replaced.

I called on the commanding officer of the King's Dragoon Guards, the armored-car regiment with which I had
served for a short while a year previously, and asked him
to spare me the services of Regimental Sergeant Major
Waterson from Glasgow, which he kindly agreed to do.
Waterson, a regular soldier, was just out of hospital and
temporarily unemployed in his regiment. I had met him in
Abassieh Barracks, where I had set up my headquarters
(in the L.R.D.G. quartermaster's stores!). He had expressed a great eagerness to join my newly formed unit,
and I thought that his experience of fighting in armored
cars, his general resourcefulness, and his knowledge of the
ways of the army would make him a useful recruit.

I set Yunnie and Waterson to draw equipment, and
drove down to Ma'adi on a visit to the Director of Survey.
Among his personnel Sapper Petrie, a young Scottish
surveyor with considerable knowledge of practical astron-
omy and no battle experience whatever, volunteered to
join P.P.A. I drove him back to Cairo to select a theodolite
from the three instruments which were available in the
Middle East, and left him at Abassieh Barracks, the fourth
member of my squadron.

Two days later I flew down to Cufra via Wadi Halfa to
make several arrangements with L.R.D.G.: a two-thou-
sand-five-hundred-mile trip which brought me, among
other things, one recruit, Corporal Locke, who had been
on their waiting list for some time. Jake Easonsmith
thought I would find him useful and he was right.

On November 4 I had two officers and three other
ranks. The battle of El Alamein had been won and the

pursuit of the enemy started. As I wanted to catch the Germans on my own battlefield, I had to hurry or they would have been pushed out of the Jebel before I arrived. I went on a recruiting campaign in the Reinforcement Depots of the Suez Canal area. My determination to keep our aims and our methods secret didn't make appeals for an unknown unit very attractive. Mystery, and the promise of adventure, were my only assets: it produced nine volunteers, mostly R.A.S.C. drivers whose only experience of warfare had been the driving of trucks in convoys in the back areas, and none of them as solid and purposeful as I would have wished. Of these nine, Driver Davies, a Yorkshireman, was, with myself, the only original member of P.P.A. on the rolls when the unit was disbanded after the end of the war.

With two officers and twelve other ranks, nine of whom were quite raw, I had to be contented. I took with me also three of my Libyan Arabs, and by November 22 I informed Middle East Headquarters that I would move out the next day.

Our equipment had been drawn on the L.R.D.G. scale, with, in addition, such items as fancy or experience dictated and could be coaxed out of complaisant quartermasters. We had over a ton of explosives, but only eleven days' rations, gasoline for fifteen hundred miles, but very few spare parts for our vehicles, for they were nearly unobtainable. For the jeeps we had none at all, barring what Yunnie had succeeded in wheedling out of an American technical base.

Our vehicles were four jeeps armed with twin Vickers-K .303 machine guns (swivel mounted) and fitted with racks to carry twelve four-gallon cans of gasoline, giving a range of six to seven hundred miles. These jeeps carried a gunner and a driver each and constituted our fighting force. To carry our stores we had two three-ton trucks, armed with one Vickers-K gun each, and manned by two men. My plan was to conceal the two trucks in the Jebel foothills and use them as a base from which we would raid in our jeeps. I hoped to be self-supporting for two months.

On November 23, 1942, we left Cairo for Cufra Oasis, the first lap of wanderings which ended in Venice three years later. Our route lay first along the main road up the Nile Valley to Asyut, then one hundred and thirty miles to

Kharga Oasis, along a well-marked track. In Kharga began the desert trip of nearly six hundred miles to Cufra.

It had been arranged with L.R.D.G. that they would issue us a radio set (and an operator) when we arrived in Cufra: for the journey there we were out of touch and I hoped we would not get into trouble. The day before we left Cairo I had received from L.R.D.G. a signal giving me the route I should follow from Kharga: it was a number of astronomical positions such as 24° 16′N., 29° 32′E. and so on; between these points we were to make our way as nearly in a straight line as the ground permitted.

At Kharga we had filled up with gasoline from an L.R.D.G. dump and we left at midday. Minding the limited experience of my drivers, who were driving jeeps for the first time in their lives, I led at a cautious pace. The going was good and by nightfall we had covered sixty miles. Bob Yunnie was in exuberant good spirits, so was Sergeant Waterson, and the men caught the infection. I was more subdued; the only one in the party who had ever traveled over the open desert, I felt the weight of my companions' inexperience and tended to expect disaster at every moment. Petrie did his first astrofix with assurance; I was relieved to find that it tallied with my dead reckoning. For his own satisfaction, for he was that kind of man, Petrie did another astrofix later that night, by a slower and more accurate method which kept him up till the early morning, when he was satisfied that he knew our position within a mile.

On the first day out I started worrying everyone into a meticulous routine and I went on doing this—with other men and in other places—till the end of the war. From now on the matter was never out of my mind: an endless conflict between my companions' longing for carefree adventure and my own determination to avoid disaster. Successful adventures, in our line of business, depended on a rigorous attention to detail, as seamen know well enough, but soldiers will not readily admit. I wanted my adventurers to be tidy and thrifty, proper misers chained to a perpetual repetition of tedious duties and piddling cares; they had to have minds like ants, stamp collectors, watch makers, and accountants: orderly, precise, unhurried—at the same time I expected them to risk cheerfully the sudden loss of everything they had, to take chances, to make quick decisions, to keep their heart when fortune changed, and to carry out unexpected orders vigorously. I required of them to be both cautious and extravagant, matter-of-fact and imaginative, to plan carefully their enterprises and also to act on sudden inspiration: conflicting qualities seldom found in the same man. In my selection of men and in their training I put more stress on the plodding virtues than on dash, assuming (often rightly) that each one who had volunteered to join our parties cherished in his heart a boyish desire to take a hand in some fun (an understatement which described our more extravagant performances), and would, when the time came, rise to the occasion. My job was to see to it that on that occasion, often a very sudden one, my prospective hero's gun, having been kept clean and well oiled, fired freely, that his vehicle, well maintained, was fit for pursuit or for flight, that he could, without hesitation, lay his hands in the back of his jeep and bring out what he needed: a belt of ammunition or a hand grenade or a torch. I wanted him also to have made sure that gasoline had not leaked out of faulty cans, that his emergency rations were at hand, and that his map case had not been torn off his truck when he had last forced his way through bushes. In action, untroubled with mechanical difficulties, my ideally trained soldier would be free to apply his mind to the fundamental problems of his trade, and be ready with an answer to the ever recurring questions: "Where am I?"—"Where is the enemy?"—"Where are my friends?"

On that first evening halt I imposed only the most elementary duties, for my men were raw and could easily have been overwhelmed with instructions. I put first every one of the drivers, man or officer, to maintain his vehicle, and the gunners to clean their weapons. Only when these tasks were completed was the evening dinner cooked, after I had supervised the issue of rations and water. We all messed together and took an equal share of fatigues. The Arabs, however, cooked their own food from their own rations.

Petrie, the navigator, who was also gunner on his truck, then set up his theodolite and picked out his stars. Welsh, the fitter, went round the vehicles asking for a job. Sergeant Waterson checked the stocks of gasoline and water, of which he brought me a daily statement. Dry desert bushes were collected for the morning fire. When all was done, we sat in the sand round the fire, and drank the Arab tea of our Senussis. Then one by one the men dropped out to roll themselves in their blankets alongside their trucks. Silence fell, the fire flickered out, and, as I fell asleep, I heard the pervading hum of the constellations overhead as they pivoted round the low-lying pole.

With the first lighting of the eastern horizon, I rose, folded my bedding and stowed it in my jeep. Chilled in my shirt and slacks I wrapped myself in a coat and waited for the flash of flames when the cook threw a live match on gasoline-soaked branches. The dancing light showed up the yellow sands, the trucks, and the still sleeping men. I wanted to make an early start, for I have an irrational belief that an hour gained in the morning is somehow worth three extra hours' driving before sunset, and everyone was so eager that we were on our way as the sun cleared the horizon. I set the sun compass for the first lap of the day's course, adjusted its dial for the time of sunrise, read the speedometer, set my watch for local time (another watch kept Greenwich Mean Time received on a small civilian radio set) and led off through hilly country. Petrie, following in his jeep, noted down the course followed: bearing (read on the sun compass), distance on the speedometer; then in line ahead, the two three-tonners, the third jeep, and finally Yunnie in his jeep brought up the rear. To avoid the risk of vehicles going astray the rule was: if one stops everyone stops. On each truck the gunner was responsible for keeping a watch on the following vehicle, but he seldom did, and every hour or so I stopped the column and drove back to the tail to see that no one was missing.

The going was on softish sand between hills of crumbling rock, a desolate landscape. The trucks bogged many times, practice for us in the use of the steel sand-channels. I noted that all my men worked willingly: they might be inexperienced but they were keen and took their duties to heart. Nearly all Scotch or north country men, they had a natural stubbornness and quiet tempers; they struggled cheerfully to keep the trucks on the move, and delays did not make them lose patience. Yunnie and Waterson cracked jokes and gave to our desperate enterprise an atmosphere of a Sunday picnic.

On the second day out from Kharga at about three o'clock, Davies' three-tonner stopped, its fan belt having snapped. Welsh the fitter drove up, and started fitting a new one. I waited, waited, went round to investigate, and found that our spare fan belts were of a wrong type, too short and too thin to fit our Chevrolet trucks: the passing incident had turned into a minor disaster.

I had to send Yunnie and Petrie back to Kharga in their two jeeps with instructions to signal Cairo from the Egyptian post asking for the spare belts and ten days' rations for eighteen men to be flown to Kharga. I reckoned they could be back in three days. Petrie was confident that he would not get lost, and what I had seen of his navigation made me trust him.

While we were waiting for Yunnie to come back, Waterson and I got down to train our men in the elementary tricks of our trade. Few of them had ever fired a gun, and none of them could handle our Vickers-K machine guns. There was nothing for it but to go at the old rounds from morning till night: strip, put together, strip, and once more put together. For variety we threw a few hand grenades and, as a reward for those who could strip and put together blindfolded, we, staged a mock jeep battle which was designed to amuse them and no more, for battlecraft can only be acquired by surviving your first battles.

Corporal Locke stood out among our men. He was of a ferocious appearance, with a piratical black patch over an empty eyesocket, his face and indeed most of his body crisscrossed with scars and multicolored grafts. We had nothing to teach him about weapons or the driving of cars, and he seemed to have been through the most excruciating adventures. I say seemed for I never got to know what his past history had been. Locke was imaginative; the tales he told were rich in detail and of a glorious inconsistency. When I first interviewed him he told me that he was of French birth—his name, he said, was really Loques, which he had altered to an English spelling when he joined the British Army—that he had studied chemistry for one year at London University, which accounted for his elegant, slightly bookish English, that he had an unquenchable thirst for German blood, that he had already killed several of the enemy with his own hands, and that he hoped, if I took him in my unit, to kill many more with a dagger he carried in his battle-dress blouse. He had served in tanks, but had come by his wounds in the course of hand-to-hand encounters with the enemy. Another version, which came out later, was that he was of British birth with parents in Leeds, and that he had studied chemistry for one year at the Sorbonne, which accounted for his very colloquial French. He had lost his eye on an occasion when he had jumped down the turret of a German tank and killed the crew with a wrench.

His French and his English were faultless—I could never catch him out in either language—and not only was he perfectly bilingual but he could behave like an Englishman or a Frenchman according to his company. He was very popular with our men, who never doubted that he was as British as they were themselves; on the other hand I have heard him exchange slangy obscenities in a greasy Parisian accent with French soldiers in Algeria, by whom he was accepted without hesitation as one of their own. His written English was terse with some literary elegancies, his French spelling was sometimes shaky, a contrast which after two years led me to believe that Leeds was more likely to be his birthplace than Reims, Villefranche or Paris.

Bombastic and bloodthirsty, he showed at times a disarming modesty as if asking that his tall stories, a failing which he could not help, should not be held against him. In action he was sensible and composed; although he tended to look for trouble when he was on his own, he took care when he had men in his charge, not to expose them to unnecessary risks. He liked to adorn himself with daggers and bludgeons and secondhand articles of clothing of enemy origin; he stated in refined tones his determination to bring back the ears (or the head, or the privy parts) of the German he would kill, but in fact he never carried out his beastly threats. Locke was a braggart, but a very unusual one, for he was not a coward, but a sensible, brave man.

Yunnie arrived back with the supplies a day later than I had expected because he had found the Egyptian radio operator at Kharga willing but in fact incapable of sending his message to Cairo, and consequently he had had to drive all the way back to Asyut in the Nile Valley, where an R.A.F. camp helped him out.

We pursued our cautious way on a southwesterly course, our drivers learning a little more desert craft each time they got bogged till we reached a point 23° 11′N. and 26° 32′E., where my instructions showed that we should set a course due west. We had been traveling for the last twenty-four hours across a level plain, but now, barring our new route, a continuous escarpment stretched north and south along the western horizon. The maps of this part of the desert show few features, but even so, our new course would it seem lead us directly against the eastern cliffs of the Gilf el Kebir. This is a triangular plateau which rises vertically fifteen hundred feet above the surrounding desert plain, like a large island from the sea. From its base, one hundred miles long, somewhere in latitude 24°N., where it emerges from the Egyptian Sand Sea, it runs south to its apex in latitude 22° 42′, presenting all along its odd ninety miles an unscalable obstacle to vehicles bound for Cufra from the Nile Valley. The only practicable route is round its southern tip and then northwest to Cufra; not quite round the tip though, for there is a kind of Magellan's Straits, narrow, tortuous and precipitous, but quite accessible to vehicles, which cuts off the mass of the Gilf el Kebir from its outlying southern extremity. These details didn't appear clearly on the maps; in fact, the main use of the map in these parts was that of a conveniently scaled sheet of paper on which we plotted the course we had followed, and the isolated features of which we had determined the geographical positions with sufficient accuracy.

So west we drove and got immediately entangled in a maze of valleys half filled with soft blown sand, among rocky crags which rose higher as we proceeded. The three-tonners were soon hopelessly bogged; pushing forward with two jeeps, then climbing on foot to the top of a scarp, I discovered a wild landscape through which the route I was intended to follow with my heavy vehicles could not possibly lie. I returned to the trucks and we spent the rest of the day in getting them back to the plain.

My instructions had gone wrong—corrupted in transmission—and I cursed once more those who had not delivered me a radio set for the trip. I then sat down in the headlights of my jeep, with the maps, and tried to think of the right thing to do. Up to this point my job had been to take a party of vehicles on a routine trip from Cairo to Cufra. I found myself now unexpectedly in the position of an explorer in an uncharted country: all the information I had was that I had to get round the barrier of the Gilf el Kebir where it petered out somewhere in the south, how far to the south I had no means of telling. I decided to move roughly southward over the plains where the going was good, keeping the cliffs of the Gilf el Kebir in sight if possible; and to stop every twenty miles and push a reconnaissance westward to find what was happening to the escarpment.

I felt very acutely that overloaded three-tonners, clumsily driven, were not suitable for the work of exploration: the next morning at dawn, having lightened my jeep of everything it carried except some gasoline, water, and food, I set off to reconnoiter the route ahead, leaving Yunnie in charge, with instructions to take advantage of the delay and pump a little more weapon training into our men.

I set my gunner, a man called Hough, to log the route. With a bewildered look on his face he took up notebook and pencil and set himself to write down bearings and distances; as he was one of those men in whom the points of the compass arouse an uncomprehending hostility, the task made him very sad, and I am afraid his career in P.P.A. was doomed from that day. In contrast with his misery I enjoyed myself thoroughly. I liked the meticulous work of breaking a new route through unexplored country; gone were my haste and my impatience and I even forgot the war as I became immersed in delightful details. After two miles of sandy hummocks I came upon a dead level plain of yellow sand, a dry lake bed; its shimmering flatness reaching to the southern horizon invited speed: so smooth that, with the accelerator quite down, the jeep skimmed over its surface without a tremor. To the east white sand dunes, lifted above the ground by mirage, floated in the air like sharp clouds; on the opposite side the broken towers of the Gilf el Kebir, lit by the rising sun, rose in formidable black and white solidity.

After nine miles of dreamlike gliding came the shore of boulders and sand, with outcrops of decayed rock, through which the going soon became heavy. When I judged I had gone twenty miles from my camp I turned westward toward the Gilf, now out of sight behind some hills. Five miles onward I topped a rise and discovered once more the line of the escarpment, a dull gray now under the higher sun and blunted by the midday haze. It fell off to the west, but, just visible, the line of cliffs turned south again in the distance: the passage was not yet here.

Instead of retracing my steps I drove down into a broad valley where the going seemed fair. I found I could make good progress on a bearing of 243° which slowly converged on to the distant line of the escarpment. After ten miles I merged on to another level pan; just as I was slowing down for the far shore I cut across the tracks of a vehicle. I stopped, examined and came to the conclusion that not more than four of five days ago an L.R.D.G. type of 1½-ton truck had gone this way, traveling slightly north of east. As it did not take me much out of my way I followed the tracks, going in the direction from which the unknown vehicle had come, on a general bearing of 260°.

Less than a mile away two more tracks joined up with the first one, then two more, and a mile ahead the five tracks hopelessly intermingled where a defile between two rocky hills had compelled the trucks to travel in line ahead. Beyond the defile the tracks separated again, but kept roughly parallel courses on a bearing of 245°. At this point I told Hough we would have a meal, and after he had got the gasoline cooker to burn and I had drunk my tea, I lay down on the sand to think. If the tracks had indeed been made by L.R.D.G. vehicles, it was likely that they were not a surveying party—which had little reason to operate in this area—but just an ordinary patrol on its way from Culfra to Kharga and Cairo. If such was the case I could stop playing the explorer: all I had to do was to follow the tracks all the way to Cufra.

I made my way back to camp by another route than I had taken going out, shorter and, as it turned out, easier. We reached the lake bed which I had crossed in the early morning: in the whole of its flat seventy-odd square miles there was one rock, in shape like a plowshare buried upright in the sand with its nose sticking out no more than three inches; I hit it at fifty miles an hour with my right-hand wheels, destroyed both tires and buckled a wheel. Hough, who had become more and more despondent over his grubby notebook, jumped out and set about the jack and the spare wheels with an ostentatious heartiness which meant all too clearly: If I had been *driving* and not made to do bloody *sums* like a schoolboy, we would have saved two of the precious tires you keep preaching about. In which he was probably right. I would have liked to appear like a demigod to my men, but I had been conspicuously unsuccessful so far: I had bungled the navigation, as far as they knew, with all my pretenses at scientific accuracy, I had got them all lost in the mountains the day before and had found my way again only when I had got on to a track (which any fool could do), and now with my reckless driving I had lost two new tires when no other driver had yet even had a puncture.

While Hough was driving me back to camp at a sensible pace I made two resolutions which I believe I have kept ever since: one was that I would preach no more, the other that I would publish my blunders widely and use them as demonstrations of the way things should not be done.

I saw so much gear unnecessarily unloaded, lying around in camp when I arrived that, although there was scarcely an hour's daylight left, I ordered an immediate move as a lesson in mobility. We camped again on the far shore of the lake bed.

The next day, the second of December, following the tracks we reached the entrance of the defile at the southern tip of the Gilf el Kebir. In the distance I saw some vehicles and, I moved up to attack with four jeeps, Sergeant Waterson, much more of an expert than I was, leading. At closer range the vehicles were seen to be, not an enemy patrol, but part of a heavy supply column of the Sudan Defense Force on its way from Wadi Halfa to Cufra, where they had a garrison; we covered our guns and lashed them down before driving up. The cheerful black Sudanese led us to their British officers, with whom we exchanged the gossip of the desert.

On December 4, eleven days out from Cairo, winding our way among decaying hills, we caught sight of the palm groves of Cufra, a low, dark line stretching across the horizon. When I reported to Lieutenant Colonel Prendergast, under whose command I now came, I submitted meekly to his banter about achieving the slowest journey on record from Cairo to Cufra and thus missing my last chance of fighting in the Jebel. Blundering commander of a half-baked unit, I had no wish to put on airs.

14

PROOF OF YUNES

ON November 23, the day we left Cairo, the Eighth Army in Jedabya, south of Benghazi, completed the third (and last) liberation of Cyrenaica. When we reached Cufra the advanced units of the army were sitting opposite Rommel's entrenchments at El Agheila between the coast and the salt marshes, building up for the next assault. No more a battlefield, the Jebel had become the playground of Occupied Enemy Territory Administration, and the purpose for which P.P.A. had been formed had ceased to exist.

An attractive objective for us now lay six hundred miles farther to the west, beyond Tripoli and well inside Tunisia, in the area where the Germans were preparing a rather formidable defensive line btween Jebel Tebaqa and the sea coast. This Mareth Line, as we called it, had originally been fortified by the French in Tunisia against a possible Italian invasion from Tripolitania. After the fall of France and the Allied landings in North Africa, the Italians, who now occupied Tunisia, had turned the Mareth Line inside out to make it face northward instead of to the south, so as to protect Tripoli from an eventual Allied thrust. When Rommel suffered defeat at El Alamein, realizing that he might have to abandon Tripoli and be pushed back into Tunisia, he ordered the Mareth defenses to be switched back to their original quarter, in the hope that he might contain there the advance of the Eighth Army and thus preserve Tunisia as an Axis bridgehead in Africa. About the Mareth Line, the Eighth Army knew little and counted on the L.R.D.G. to discover more.

For me this change of objectives brought up a ticklish problem. I had been well contented to take my gimcrack unit, raw as it was, into the Jebel when all I required of it was to provide me with transport, supplies, radio communication and eventually an escort. With Yunnie, Waterson, Lock—three good men—a few proved Arabs, and the help of the whole population of my Libyan kingdom, I should have had a force quite large enough to blow up and destroy all the gasoline dumps I could locate. The sneaking tactics successfully used on my previous expeditions would do the trick again. Operating in Tunisia, over unknown ground amongst the possibly hostile local population, was a different kettle of fish. Moreover my targets in Tunisia would have to be completely altered: to the enemy, with his line of communication measured no more in thousands but in hundreds of miles, gasoline supplies would cease to be a vital problem; the topographical investigations so urgently required by the Eighth Army would be done entirely by L.R.D.G. They had the numbers and the experience, and I hadn't. I set my mind on harassing enemy convoys and on raiding headquarters and landing grounds; I would, I decided, employ my unit in spreading "alarm and despondency," a much derided policy which I would turn into a grim reality. For this purpose I knew I had enough cunning and the ability to make use of local circumstances; I lacked a striking force and I set about forging myself one.

From Cufra, where we now sat, the nearest point at which the enemy line of communication on the coast could be reached was over seven hundred miles away, and a desert journey of about eleven hundred miles was required to get to the Mareth Line. I did not want to undertake operations at such a distance from my base as, if I did, I should have, on reaching my destination, barely enough supplies for the return journey. What I wanted was to establish a forward base where I could be self-supporting for two months and have leisure, first to investigate local conditions and then to carry out a succession of raids. I had consequently to remain with the L.R.D.G. until forward dumps had been established. This suited me well enough because I had made up my mind the best means of training my men was to attach them to L.R.D.G. patrols and make them share their experiences.

Prendergast ran his unit with a businesslike efficiency. Ignoring deliberately the glamor of his enterprises, he hated improvisation and organized his fantastic patrols on the solid basis of a railway service. The patrols ran to a

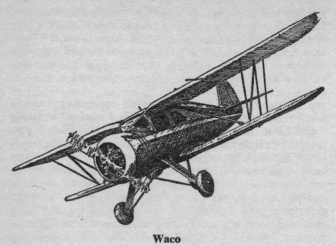

Waco

timetable, and, however great the distance, reported twice a day on their radio their position to headquarters. Quiet and matter-of-fact, when his presence was required Prendergast flew his own plane, a civilian Waco, to a pin point in the desert, and returned to headquarters to take up the burden of routine administration. He spoke little and kept somewhat aloof from us all: yet he inspired us with enthusiasm—an improbable enthusiasm which had for its object punctuality, not adventure.

I foresaw some difficulty in persuading him to train my men as I thought he would (very rightly) be reluctant to burden his patrols with "passengers." There were, however, precedents: L.R.D.G. had in their time trained the Middle East Commandos and the S.A.S., and they had given courses in desert navigation to many armored units of the Eighth Army, not to mention the innumerable lifts given to myself, to Advance A Force, to G.(R). S.O.E.* and others on the Jebel bus line. I bided my time doing chores and running errands. On December 16 L.R.D.G. headquarters moved up leisurely five hundred miles to

*Special Operations Executive. This was the organization in charge of British undercover operations throughout the axis occupied territories.

Zella Oasis in the Fezzan, which had been partly evacuated by the Italians. Four days before Christmas I took a convoy of the Heavy Section up to El Agheila on the coast road for supplies. The enemy had been pushed out eight days earlier on December 13, and the Eighth Army had already established there a supply point and a NAAFI dump.

Back in Zella I found everyone recovering from a colossal Christmas party. The next day I resolved to tackle Prendergast. Instead, it was he who tackled me; I possessed four little treasures which he coveted, four precious jeeps with which, at that time, he was but sparsely provided. These vehicles had more agility than the standard L.R.D.G. 1½-ton trucks: for reconnaissance on mountainous country they had no rival. As a result of our arrangements Corporal Locke with two jeeps was attached to Hunter's Yeomanry patrol, which drove out from Zella on January 3 bound for the Jebel Nefuza, the semicircular range which covers the approaches to Tripoli from the desert, with the object of discovering an unguarded motorable pass leading from the Fezzan to Tripoli.

I left Zella on January 8 with my two other jeeps, accompanying Lazarus and his Rhodesian patrol, with the mission of reconnoitering passes across Jebel Nefuza farther west than Hunter, in Tunisian territory. I took with me Petrie, our navigator, of those abilities I had formed good hopes, the Arab Yunes, Sergeant Waterson, my mentor in many things, and an untried cockney. I left Bob Yunnie in Zella, sore and nearly mutinous, to repair one of our trucks and complete our equipment from L.R.D.G. stores. Our trip which was to be topographical, turned out differently from what we had planned.

Whereas Hunter was searching for a pass through which the Eighth Army could send an armored force to outflank Tripoli and thus make easier the capture of this port by the main forces moving up along the coast, our objective was in a sense the opposite. When the army had taken Tripoli the next obstacle on their line of advance would be the Mareth Line, with its main defenses lined up between Matmata on the Jebel Nefuza and the sea. West of Matmata very weak defenses stopped the twenty-mile gap between the Nefuza range and Jebel Tebaqa. Montgomery's intention was to threaten this gap with a very strong diversionary force, thus outflanking the Mareth Line proper and doubling the length of defenses Rommel would have to hold. To achieve this left hook it would be necessary to find a pass through which the diversionary force, issuing from Tripoli, would cross over to the west of Jebel Nefuza and then move northward to outflank the Mareth Line. The discovery of such a pass was our objective. On January 8, the day we left Zella, the attack on the Mareth Line was still ten weeks in the future, the enemy main forces were at Bucrat on the Gulf of Sidra; Tripoli, the whole of its plain within the semicircle of the Nefuza range, the range itself, and most of the Fezzan including Mizda, Shweref and Hon were still in enemy hands. In the southern Fezzan General Leclerc was moving up with his French force from French Equatorial Africa and had just captured Murzuk.

Captain Lazarus, a young New Zealand surveyor, had worked in Rhodesia before the war; for this reason he had been taken from his survey section and put in command of one of the two L.R.D.G. Rhodesian patrols during the absence on leave of Captain Olivey. The other one was commanded by Lieutenant Henry, whom I was to meet surprisingly in the lavatory of the Hotel Transatlantique at Tozeur five weeks later. With Lazarus, his patrol of five 1-½-ton trucks and twenty-five men, and my own little group of five men, we spent the night of January 12 in the upper reaches of Wadi Zemzem. We had met some friendly Fezzan Arabs who entertained us in the tent of their sheik.

With the help of Yunes, more at home than I was in the Fezzan dialect, I gave them a political speech. We were the first British troops they had seen, a momentous break in the monotonous round of their pastoral lives; the party went well and they told us that there had been considerable enemy traffic moving northward on the Shweref-Mizda road, twenty-two miles to the west. I issued goodwill gifts and bought from them a couple of lambs for our consumption. The next morning we drove cautiously up Wadi Zemzem toward the road; the going was good but very tortuous between twenty-foot sandy hummocks covered in scrub, which gave no visibility. Toward ten o'clock, when by our reckoning we were getting very close to the road, Yunes told me he heard a noise of vehicles *behind* us. I laughed and said:

"You are wrong for once, Yunes. The road is *up* the wadi and the noise you heard surely comes from the road." We stopped our vehicles; I climbed a hummock; and, sure enough, there was the road a mile away crossing the wadi at right angles, and with a good stream of traffic flowing along it: elements of the Italian garrisons of the southern Fezzan withdrawing to Tripoli covered by an Auto-Saharon company with armored cars. As our route was across the road and to the westward we had to wait for a pause in the traffic to slip across. Knowing the Italian custom of a long midday halt and siesta, we thought our opportunity would come in two or three hours' time.

Lazarus moved his trucks quietly one at a time to dispersed positions, from which, well-camouflaged amongst the hummocks and quite invisible from the road, they could fire on the enemy vehicles if the need arose. We would engage only if we were discovered: at the start of a long trip it didn't suit us to risk casualties in men or vehicles, and an eventual pursuit by aircraft, for the sake of destroying a few ramshackle Italian trucks. The successful issue of the reconnaissance we were to do for the Eighth Army was much more important than the infliction of minor damage on the enemy.

Having posted the trucks to our satisfaction, we drove forward three hundred yards in my two jeeps, Lazarus and I with Yunes, Petrie, and one Rhodesian, to the foot of a specially high hummock, from the top of which we had a close view of the enemy. We took out our notebooks and set ourselves to take down the particulars of the vehicles as they streamed past us. We were well hidden under bushes, seated on comfortable sand, and commanded a long stretch of road; of our own vehicles behind us we could only catch a glimpse of one.

We had been at work about half an hour when we heard close at hand the slow thudding bursts of an Italian twenty-millimeter gun. We carried one of these weapons, but so presumably did the enemy. In the maze of hummocks, sound was so broken up that it was impossible to decide from which direction the gun had been fired. A column of black smoke arose behind us from, it seemed, one of our trucks; a moment later came the rattle of several machine guns. We could see puffs of dust raised on and near the road as our men fired at trucks, making them spurt along, but of the enemy which presumably had attacked us and, by a happy hit, set fire to one of our trucks, we could see nothing, though the noise of the battle increased and seemed to come from all sides. We decided that Italian armored cars, unperceived by us, must have left the road, and, driving down the wadi, which was here half a mile wide between rounded rocky banks some a hundred and fifty feet high, were firing at our men from the cover of some of the hummocks which filled the wadi bed.

Leaving Yunes on watch on top of our hummock, and our two men manning the guns of the jeeps at its foot, I walked back with Lazarus toward our burning truck. To our bewilderment we found it exactly as we had left it, unharmed but quite deserted, and another unaccountable vehicle burning fiercely sixty yards farther downstream. There was no sign of a struggle around the Rhodesian truck, no gear lying around, no paper, no clothing: our men had just walked quietly away. The firing died down, and all sound, excepting the low roar of the burning truck. We stood scratching our heads, thinking of the stories we had read of the *Marie Celeste* found abandoned at sea with her sails set and all in good order. On closer examination we thought that perhaps a halfhearted attempt had been made to drive the truck away, and that it had got bogged as the wheels were somewhat low down in the sand. Another of our trucks, which should have been visible from where we stood, had vanished.

After a while I walked toward the mysterious burning wreck. Halfway across, a wail of bullets around my head sent me flat on the ground, I crept along to take cover behind a hummock. Somebody was invisibly watching me, someone who wanted to kill. I made a cautious way forward, cleared some bushes and uncovered the source of the fire: a small armored car with a black German cross on its side.

Going back to the deserted truck by a roundabout route, I found Lazarus still figuratively scratching his head. I told him the identity of our blazing visitor and we concluded that Yunes had rightly heard a noise of vehicles *behind us,* that a German armored-car patrol had been following on our tracks up Wadi Zemzem, the twenty-millimeter gunfire we had heard was ours and it had knocked out one of the enemy cars. Why, with such a nice initial success, our men had chosen to walk away, abandoning their truck undestroyed, we could not account for. It was a rule with us that a vehicle which had to be abandoned in a place where the enemy could possibly get at it should be set on fire, and an incendiary bomb fitted with a short time fuse was always carried under the driver's seat for this purpose.

The remainder of the Rhodesian patrol and the Germans, we thought, were probably now playing a silent game of hide and seek among the hummocks, and as there was nothing useful we could do before we got more information, we ran back to our jeeps, half expecting to find them vanished. Petrie and the Rhodesian, however, were as we had left them; Yunes, they told me, was still on top of the hummock, firing his rifle they knew not at what. I climbed up and found the Arab enjoying himself hugely: in his high tower, from a glimpse here, a flutter in a bush there, a puff of faint smoke, the echo of a shout, the whirr of an engine, he had pieced together a plausible account of our little battle. Remembering no doubt my earlier snub, as soon as he saw me scrambling into his nestlike retreat he said:

"Let me tell you first, Major, what I have understood. A party of five or six German armored cars and two small trucks, *which I heard this morning,* have driven up Wadi Zemzem, following our tracks. The leading car came unexpectedly upon that one of our trucks which carries in the back the big Italian gun. Our gunner was quick on the mark, he fired first and knocked out the German. That is his smoke there. Our men then tried to get their trucks together, but they were unlucky, three of them got stuck in the sand and were abandoned by their crews who walked over to the remaining two trucks. One of these I can't account for—the last one, with many men on board, is at this moment trying to get out of the wadi up the far bank. The German cars have spread out and are searching the hummocks: they have found one of our bogged trucks and are trying to drive it away. There, that is its engine racing. The German commander has parked his armored car in that hollow, behind those bushes, and has climbed that hummock; he is now looking round with his glasses." Yunes shouldered his rifle and fired carefully.

"A near one," he remarked. "He will now keep low for

a little while. I don't want him to see that truck of ours on the far bank."

With my own glasses I managed to pick out some of the details of Yune's picture. One of our trucks with at least twenty men was struggling among the rocks halfway up the south bank of the wadi half a mile away. I could also pick out the German commander's armored car, about four hundred yards away, and I caught a glimpse of the man himself before another shot from Yunes made him duck.

I slid down the hummock to confer with Lazarus. Our two jeeps with their light machine guns could not engage the armored cars; our only hope was in deception. We drove back to the Rhodesian truck, set the time incendiary bomb on the tank, and fired several bursts of our guns in the direction of the German commander to give him something to think about. We then drove a distance up the north bank where there was some cover of trees and scrub, poured gasoline over dry branches and set it on fire, hoping to distract the attention of the enemy scouts from our truck and men on the opposite side of the wadi. Finally we returned to Yune's perch and I called to him to come down. He refused.

"I have hit a man in the car," he shouted, "and with my next shot I shall get the commander on his hummock. He is now looking at your fires."

"Come down, Yunes," I cried. "We are going." I heard two more shots, then a muffled:

"Missed! I am going to get him though."

Yunes's head appeared over the top:

"Just a moment, Major. I am going to get him now."

Three more shots of the rifle but still no Yunes. I got very angry and started climbing up, when in a cloud of dust Yunes came slithering down.

"Got him. They are carrying him down this very moment. Let us go and get some more."

His long, sinuous lips were twisted into a smile of austere enjoyment, his eyes sparkled, the whole of his dark scowling face was lit with satisfaction. He dusted himself, and, perching his long bony self on the back of my jeep, he said ecstatically:

"Major, this is war!" He was older than any of us, but as happy as a child. We were not enjoying ourselves at all: Lazarus had lost his patrol, temporarily he hoped, but the

chances of being able to carry out his mission were
slender. I was blaming myself for having left our men to
themselves—we should not have gone forward together,
Lazarus and I: two officers to the patrol and neither of
them with the men in their trouble! Petrie, under fire for
the first time in his life, was puzzled and missed the
comfort of experienced companions on whom he could
model his behavior.

Seizing the opportunity of a gap in the stream of traffic,
I led our two jeeps onto the road, turned right and drove
leisurely northward for a mile or so, as if we were part of
the straggling convoy; then I left the road and drove
parallel with it for another half mile—then half a mile
once more along the road—then off again on the far side
on a slanting course that took us gradually away from the
road and finally out of sight behind a hill. From this point
I doubled back in a wide circle that brought us to a spot
opposite the south bank of the wadi where we had last
seen our truck. I intended by this maneuver to lead anyone
following our tracks to believe that we had driven along
the road on to Mizda.

I left the jeeps under cover, told Petrie to clean our twin
guns (to keep him occupied), and with Yunes climbed a
low hill. At our feet a bare fifty yards away ran the road,
now quite deserted; beyond it the hummocks of Wadi
Zemzem, and up the hillside, four hundred yards away,
our truck stuck at a crazy angle and apparently abandoned. I hoped I had turned the tables on our enemies—
we were now on their flank, and if we engaged them we
would be firing from the wrong, the unexpected quarter. I
watched a long time through my glasses, Yunes beside me
fingering his rifle. A few Germans appeared from the wadi
bottom clambering on foot over the rocks toward the
truck; a burst of small arms fire from somewhere above
sent them to cover, but they soon renewed their advance.
We brought the jeeps round the corner of the hill, from
where we opened up with our four guns, then pulled back
under cover. The Germans, however, never suspecting that
a new enemy had joined in the battle, fired steadily uphill
from behind their rocks, and never looked at us on their
right flank. We repeated the game many times and kept
the Germans moving so slowly that they were nearly two
hours in reaching the truck. They brought two of their

armored cars to the foot of the bank to fire uphill with their guns.

The Germans finally reached the truck, bringing two machine guns with which, from under cover, they opened up on a position near the crest of the bank. A moment later I saw our men running out one at a time from a sort of cave, up the hillside and out of sight over the rim. In spite of the heavy fire none seemed to be hit. I counted twenty men, more or less, out of twenty-five to be accounted for. We kept up an intermittent fire to prevent the pursuit till we thought our men had enough advance to escape capture. It seemed incredible that the Germans never suspected that they were fired on from across the road. After our men's escape they must have realized that the fire was not coming from above. Obsessed with the notion that we were all in the wadi on their side of the road, they searched the hummocks with their armored cars and never even looked westward, where they could not have failed to spot us, for we had become rather rash and also the part of the wadi west of the road, where we were, was flat and offered only the inadequate cover of bare rounded dunes; the bushy hummocks all stopped at the road.

The sun was now setting. Guessing that the Germans would leave before dark, we took a wide circle, and a few miles north of the wadi hit the road again, in which we hurriedly dug holes for all the mines we had, covered them up with gravel, and gingerly rolled a spare wheel over them to obliterate the signs of our work. We then retired under cover, four hundred yards up the road, and waited. Dusk was gathering when the German column appeared: Five armed cars, two trucks and three L.R.D.G. trucks on tow, a heartbreaking sight. They passed slowly in front of us. Lazarus looked at me and said in a choked voice:

"I know."

Then the leading armored car hit one of our mines, lost a wheel, and the convoy stopped. We drove up immediately, opened up with our four guns and dashed away madly, zigzagging down the road. It was over in thirty seconds— when the rear armored car started firing we were already out of range.

The battle was over—we had now to tidy up. There was enough of a moon to light us among the hummocks. We drove across the wadi, calling for our men in case some

Sd. kfz. 222

had remained concealed or wounded in the wadi: but none answered. We then went up to the truck on the hillside which the Germans had failed to remove and set it on fire. Before starting homeward we crept along the road to where the armored car stood at a drunken angle, abandoned. We put an incendiary bomb in its belly and we departed.

Our rule was that when a patrol got dispersed the rendezvous for the next twenty-four hours would be at a point fifteen miles back on its tracks. Shortly after midnight we started back with two jeeps, following our tracks as best we could in the dark, Lazarus leading. About three o'clock having covered twelve miles, we saw a faint glimmer of fire among rocks on our right: we hailed—Sergeant Waterson came out to us, genial as ever:

"All nice and snug, sir. Come in and have a look."

In a natural cave nineteen men were asleep, comfortable on beds of twigs and leaves, around a smoldering fire. Waterson told us how, shortly after Lazarus and I had gone forward, the gunner of the twenty-millimeter Breda

gun was foraging in the back of his truck looking for a
book, when some noise made him look up, and he stared
at a German armored car sixty yards away. He cocked his
gun and got the armored car with his first burst. They tried
then to get their truck out, thinking of joining the others,
but got bogged. The situation didn't seem serious, so they
walked over to the next truck, never thinking that they
would never see their truck again. Confused fighting followed, their position rapidly grew worse, with the enemy
all around them and invisible: they all got into one of the
trucks which they drove up the hillside, thinking of hiding
it in safety and then coming down for the others. Their
truck got jammed against a rock, the Germans had seen
them, and they were under heavy fire.

Carrying their small arms (Waterson had a tommy
gun), they made their way to a cave under the hilltop,
Henderson the navigator being hit in the stomach on the
way. There they lay for several hours, potting at the
Germans who were trying to make their way uphill. When
the Germans reached the truck Waterson decided with the
Rhodesian sergeant that the time had come to get away.
They had to abandon Henderson, who was in great pain
and couldn't move; Binney, our cheerful cockney, usually
full of banter and brave words, lost his nerve and refused
to face the dash in the open to the hilltop under the
German bullets. Waterson tried hard but didn't succeed in
putting heart in him, so he let him stay with Henderson to
become a prisoner-of-war. Waterson took the trouble to go
through his pockets to make sure he had no document on
him that would reveal the existence of P.P.A., then dashed
out after the others and over the crest. No one was hit but
three Rhodesians got separated as the party made its
roundabout way over the hills back into the wadi and up
our tracks.

The balance of the day's scrap was:

Two enemy armored cars burned out.
Enemy casualties (if any) unknown. (Yunes claimed
two.)

and

Two of our men captured (one of whom was danger-
ously wounded).
Three men missing.

Tommy Gun

Five trucks lost, of which three had been captured.
Our trip to Tunisia canceled.

The next day I arranged with our Arab friends of the
day before that they would search the hills for the three
missing Rhodesians; and surely enough they found them
and sent them back on camels to Hon a week later. We
proceeded to Shweref, fifty miles away, where an emergency rendezvous had been previously arranged.

Henderson died on his way to hospital in Tripoli.

Binney, though in perfect health, had also found his way
into a hospital, where he was found when our forces
occupied Tripoli. He asked to be allowed to rejoin P.P.A.
but I wouldn't take him.

15

STRAFING OF BOB YUNNIE

WE slunk into the wadi at Shweref with our tails between
our legs to find a kind of general assembly of L.R.D.G.,
which mercifully took little notice of us. Never had I seen
so many patrols together in one place, some going out,
some coming home to Hon, where headquarters had
moved from Zella.

Prendergast flew his Waco over on the second day. He
listened to our reports and commented: "It was rather
unfortunate, wasn't it?"—a very strong rebuke from him.
We had no time to cry over spilled milk for the war was
moving on. The Eighth Army was attacking Rommel at
Buerat that very day, expected to be in Tripoli a fortnight
later, and urgently wanted information about the Mareth
Line. Nick Wilder, now on his way back, had signaled that
he had found a pass through the Nefuza range suitable for
Montgomery's left hook, some forty miles north of Dehibat,
and now the ground leading north from Wilder's Gap to the
Mareth Line had to be reconnoitered and a route found,
not just as an agile L.R.D.G. patrol, but such as could be
negotiated by an armored division. The defenses between
Matmata and Jebel Tebaqa also had to be investigated, no
time could be lost because in a few weeks, with Rommel's
forces established in that desolate area, it would be awkward for us to move around.

Dumps of gasoline had been established near the Tuni-
sian border and also at Tozeur, an oasis in southern
Tunisia, in the hands of the French troops of North
Africa, who were now fighting halfheartedly on our side.

With these dumps at hand we could now reach Tunisia
with supplies to spare for operations: on Janauary 18,
P.P.A., complete and all there was of it, set out in
company with Lieutenant Tinker's New Zealand patrol. My
orders were to proceed with Tinker to Ksar Rhilane, three

hundred miles away, in Tunisia, to reconnoiter with him the going leading up to the Mareth Line; then to get information concerning the defenses of the line itself between Matmata and El Hamma. When these reconnaissances had been carried out, my intelligence role would come to an end and I should have a free hand to operate in any area *behind* the Mareth Line and do what harm I could to the enemy according to the information I could collect locally.

Yunnie had brought up from Zella the tail of P.P.A., and Hunter had also joined the assembly in Shweref, bringing back with him our Locke and his companions. In this way, by a succession of coincidences, my little band was reunited. I moved forward from Shweref, leaving no one behind.

We had lost Binney, captured in Wadi Zemzem, but we had received a powerful reinforcement which increased our officer strength by fifty per cent: Jean Caneri, a Frenchman, had turned up in Zella. At the time we left Cairo he was with Chapman, my former companion in the Jebel, engaged in sinking ships in Benghazi harbor. The method they used was to swim at night across the harbor carrying special mines (nicknamed Limpets) strapped to their chest. Having reached a ship, they unstrapped the mine and fixed it to the hull under the water line. The mine was fitted with magnets by means of which it adhered to the steel plates of the ship's hull. They then set the time fuse, swam back to shore, recovered their clothes, and walked through the town and on to their hide-out ten miles out in the hills. In due course the mine blew a hole ten feet square out of the hull and the ship went to the bottom.

The liberation of Benghazi had put an end to these exhausting exercises.

I had now two officers according to my heart: experienced and determined men tied closely together by deep friendship, mutual understanding, and a common purpose. Our outlooks differed and were in a way complementary: Yunnie, matter-of-fact as he was, had a romantic side with a touch of flamboyant bravery which gave color to our undertakings and inspired our men; Caneri, hard and somewhat cynical, had a cold-blooded courage together with a disarming ingenuity: he was both liked and feared—and obeyed. He had a passionate love of tidy details which put order in our affairs where my haphazard negligence produced an incredible confusion. I had imagination, a broad view of our problems, and a certain flair for picking out men suitable for our purposes, but without this persevering pair to implement them, most of my plans would have petered out. We had all three of us an obstinate continuity of purpose which urged us on unceasingly and never allowed us to relax.

I could open my heart to them both and yet lose none of my authority: I was thus spared the loneliness which induced a dangerous autocratic pig-headedness in so many commanders incapable of choosing outspoken confidants. With them I was by no means "always right"; I could not take their acquiescence for granted and I had to consider my decisions more carefully than if my orders had invariably been law.

We set our course through the Hamada el Homra (the red stony desert), about ten thousand square miles of blank on the map, as yet uncrossed by any of our patrols, which we expected to find very difficult going as it had somehow got a reputation for frightfulness. We were agreeably disappointed: the going was quite good over a rolling plain of firm sand strewn with stones. Coming after the black basalt boulders of the Kharug surrounding Hon, where trucks had to travel snakewise, and, however, carefully driven, had their tires shaved off by the razorlike edges of rock, the Hamada el Homra gave us a holiday drive. The reputation for frightfulness came from the complete absence of vegetation; it is a very empty stretch of desert, without a single bush for a hundred miles, but very lovely, the sand a pearly gray, with red stones about the size of a hand, set in it vertically on edge. When the sun is low on the horizon each slope according to the incidence of light comes out in a different color, shifting, as the traveler proceeeds, from pale coral pink to dark crimson.

One morning I noticed along the top of a slope to my left a multitude of small serrations bobbing up and down. Puzzled, as I thought, by a peculiar form of mirage, I drove idly up the slope: my serrations were the heads, just visible above the skyline, of a herd of gazelle bounding along in the same direction as we were going and keeping pretty well the same speed. There were, we estimated, more than two thousand of them, in one compact mass bound on some migration across the inhospitable Hamada.

Suddenly the whole herd took a right turn and joined the path of our trucks; in a moment the beasts were among us, so close that I had to brake sharply to avoid running one over. On every vehicle rifles came out, but such was the amazement of our men (to whom hitherto a dozen gazelle seen at one time had been a wonder) at the number and the fearlessness of the lovely animals that not a shot was fired. They ran with our moving trucks for a while, then another turn took the herd out of our path over the northern skyline.

Out of the Hamada we drove into rocky hills looking for the gasoline dump. With the "chart and the instructions" we discovered our treasure: cans spread out under rocks and covered with stones. While we were loading, the trucks of T2 Patrol, with Nick Wilder, came lurching down the wadi, like small ships in a choppy sea with the wind astern. They struck their sails and we exchanged the news. Wilder had found the gap in the range which several other patrols had searched for before him, and was now on his way back to Hon to report, refit, and set out again. Much of his reconnaissance had been done wearily on foot, but driving, he told us, had been even more exhausting than walking. The going in the corridor thirty-five miles wide between Jebel Nafuza and the Grand Erg sand dunes was the most exasperating he had ever been over, and he sardonically wished us better luck than he had had, for we were bound for the same unattractive parts. We parted the next morning in our opposite directions.

In uncharted country, each patrol endeavored to break a new route and to cover fresh ground on each voyage: the information brought back was the material from which surveyors built up maps on which layers of colors denoted the nature of the going. These maps were used by army headquarters to plan their movements over the desert and were also issued to the units concerned. Thus it happened that the next day we were running along the edge of an unknown escarpment, searching for a gully down which we could drive our trucks into the plain three hundred feet below. The gullies were all found to end in vertical drops; in desperation we chose to build ourselves a ramp at a spot where the cliff face itself had crumbled down somewhat. For five hours we rolled boulders and carried stones, then drove the jeeps down, then the ton-and-a-halves, and finally my heavy, overloaded, three-tonners slithered, lurched and bumped their way down. All the time Italian traffic was running up and down the Sinawen-Nalut track, two miles across the plain. We had a meal and after dark crept across the track and away to the west to rest under cover of very meager bushes.

The next day we crossed the Tunisian border and immediately encountered the exasperating country Wilder had promised us. Our course lay to the west of his, skirting ocher-colored dunes, outliers of the Grand Erg Sand Sea, over choppy, closely packed, sandy hillocks twelve to twenty feet high, overgrown with repulsive bushes. The whole of Tunisia seems to be covered with the decaying carcasses of monstrous, dead animals. In the north, straight, broken-edged mountain ranges sticking out of the plains are sharp backbones from which the flesh has rotted away and flowed down in streams of pus to fill the cesspools of the shotts (a shott is a salt marsh); in the south we traveled as on dubious pelts, firm on top but supported underneath only by sagging putrid entrails. In the tracks of our bumping trucks I expected to see oozing viscous purple projections. In my childhood I had one day slithered down a high bank and landed smartly on my bottom on a very dead sheep covered in grass and leaves: the horrible long-forgotten memory never left me as long as I stayed in Tunisia.

We struggled on a few miles a day. The long three-tonners alternately bellied on the crests and wedged in the troughs of the sand waves; when we struck easier patches of more undulating ground the brush, thick, dry and brittle, collected under the bellies of the jeeps, jammed the steering, and caught fire over the exhaust pipes.

On January 24 we met human beings for the first time, a band of twelve Arabs with two camels, ragged, starved and diseased, sulky and suspicious creatures who accepted our hospitality but kept their shifty eyes averted. I took one of them, Abdel Kerim ben 'Ali el Bendiri, with us, nominally as a guide, in fact as a hostage. I had less difficulty in understanding their speech than I had expected, and our Senussis conversed with them quite easily.

The next morning I decided with Tinker to leave behind all our heavy vehicles and to carry out the reconnaissance northward with jeeps only. We drive westward under a hill called Qaret Ali, intending to establish our base a few miles inside the sand dunes of the Grand Erg, where it

SHOTT EL RHARSA

Gafsa

JEBEL MORRA JEBEL EL ASKER

Krïz

Eff

Nefta

Tozeur

SHOTT JERID

SHOTT EL FEJAJ

Udref

El Hamma

GULF OF GABES

Gabes

Katena

MARETH LINE

JEBEL TEBAGA

Kebili

Bir el Haj Amor

Jemna

Chemiali

Matmata

Medenin

Duz

PICKED UP BY TINKER'S JEEPS

Bir el Hajila

Bir Zawha

Ain bu Rdaf

Bir Jabeur

Bir Soltano

Ksar Tarcine

WALKING PARTY

Bir bu Krabla

Bir el Jebel

Bir Tawil el Adara

Bir el Haj Brahim

Ksar Rhilane

Fum Tatahum

Bir el Maatij

Bir Zenigra

Tembaine

Dekamis el Kebir

Qaret Ali
Qaret jesseb

Wilder's Gap

TUNISIA
ALGERIA

GRAND EASTERN ERG

SOUTHERN TUNISIA

Miles

0 10 20 30 40 50

—— Roads
----- Motorable Tracks
Mountains

Sand
Mud
Wadis

would be safe against surprise by enemy land forces. At our first attempt we realized that the technique which had taken us over the Libyan Sand Sea would not serve us here; the dunes here were made of dirty brown, powdery, siltlike sand, into which our steel channels sank as in water. We gave up the attempt and established our base on a long patch of hard ground, surrounded on three sides by high dunes, a position easy enough to defend as it could only be reached along a narrow neck. Vehicles trying to force an entry would have to negotiate this difficult gap under the fire of our trucks, well covered themselves by low hummocks. To make things more difficult we laid a few mines in the gap, leaving only a passage for our own use. We filled with water from brackish wells under Qaret el Jesseb, three miles to the south. I put Yunnie in charge of the party, handed him our hostage, wished him good luck, and left, to be back in four or five days.

Our reconnaissance party was made up of Tinker, his navigator, and two of his New Zealanders in two jeeps, myself, Caneri, Petrie, Yunes, and one man in two other jeeps: a nice party to handle, small enough to keep easily under control. As each one of us knew exactly what we were doing I had no worry about a tail that might go astray. Our low vehicles were practically invisible: the only enemy we had to be aware of were armored cars, and as long as we kept off the tracks, which they couldn't leave in this difficult country, we were quite safe. The local Arabs had reluctantly told us that the only German and Italian posts in the neighborhood were at Duz, Jemna and Kebili. Ksar Rhilane, an old Roman fort twenty miles north of Qaret Ali, was empty by their account. We first made sure of this, and found the only inhabitant within its crumbling walls an elderly Arab called 'Ali, a former sergeant major in the French colonial troops, who spoke French, and preserved in his raggedness remains of military swagger. He told us that a number of vehicles similar to ours had been at the fort a few days previously and had driven off northward (an S.A.S. detachment we concluded), and that two of these men, their jeep broken down and mislaid, had been living at the fort ever since—but they could not be found before we left.

Separated in two groups to cover more ground, we made, as nearly in a straight line as we could, for Matmata, two miles short of which we arranged to meet again in the evening. Up, down and round we switchbacked over the hillocks, stopping only to clear the brushwood from under the chassis. In the early afternoon we reached higher ground and better going. Two unknown jeeps came dashing up a slope behind us: I turned to face them and put out a yellow flag, the agreed recognition signal for all our troops operating in Tunisia, but they took no notice, and stopped only when I fired a burst over their heads. They were six hearty paratroopers of the French section of the S.A.S., who had had originally three jeeps (but had smashed one), and now in their eagerness they were rushing off to Kebili for some vague purpose of their own, and wouldn't listen to my warnings of enemy trooops, but drove off at an unreasonable speed, waving and shouting excited farewells.

At four o'clock of the afternoon we pulled up in a discreet wadi within sight of Matmata, a small stone-built town perched on one of the last spurs of the Nefuza range. Less than ten minutes later Yunes, posted as a lookout on top of a hill, waved Tinker in. He and I immediately walked toward Matmata over rocks and grassy slopes— this corner of Tunisia was like a real country—and before nightfall we had seen as much as we needed to make a fair sketch of the western approaches to the town. We had even been near enough to look into the sleepy streets, where, apart from a few Arabs, we had only seen two fat German officers, a very different picture from what I had expected of the fortress which guarded the western end of the formidable Mareth Line.

The main defenses of the original Mareth Line extended westward from the coast to Matmata. The gap through which Montgomery intended to launch his left hook extended from this town to the Jebel Tebaqa range: it was the main object of our reconaissance. We had that day examined the approaches and found a possible route for an armored division; it remained now to reconnoiter the actual battle ground. We knew that the planners at Eighth Army headquarters were waiting for the results of our investigation and we made all the haste we could.

During our absence Yunes had been gossiping with some Arab shepherds, to whom he had given out that we were German officers concerned with the building of the new defenses, and had given them hopes of employment. He had heard that some of our supposed colleagues were indeed engaged in building strong points along a line extending from Matmata to the eastern tip of Jebel Tebaqa. This was precisely what we had come to investigate; during the next day, roaming gingerly in the twenty-mile gap between the two ranges, we saw I believe most of the work being done by the Germans at the time, which was not very much. They were not taking too seriously the possibility of an attack in force west of the Nefuza range. We knew better and felt very powerful in our four little jeeps.

Tinker had a gravity well beyond his years—I believe he was only twenty-two—but a great big, black, bushy beard gave him an elderly appearance. I treated him as a man of my own age, and such was the assurance of his manner that I tended to take his advice in many matters. Several months later I called on the L.R.D.G. in Egypt, where they had gone to refit, and saw most of my friends. Left alone in the mess I went over in my mind the names of those I had wanted to see and found that Tinker had not put in an appearance. An unknown, slim, clean-shaven youth came in, whom I had noticed previously keeping shyly in the background as if he was a new recruit. I asked him:

"Do you know if Lieutenant Tinker is in camp? I particularly want to see him."

Surprised, he laughed.

"I am Tinker. I wondered why you wouldn't speak to me, Popski."

At the end of the fourth day of our reconnaissance we considered that we had the answers to the main problems set by the Eighth Army: we had found a route—of terribly bad going, but just practicable—from Wilder's Gap up to the western end of the main Mareth Line; behind the line and as far as El Hamma we had found, with the exception of one wadi, the ground free of major obstacles, either topographical or man-made, and we knew the location of the defense works that were built at that time.

Six weeks later the New Zealand Corps, comprising the Second New Zealand Division, the Eighth Armored Brigrade, and General Leclerc's force, reinforced later by the First Armored Division, was to advance along the route we had reconnoitered and to attack Rommel's right wing on the ground over which we had just been wandering. They forced their way as far as El Hamma, outflanked

Rommel, compelled him to withdraw his forces to Wadi
Akarit and won the battle of the Mareth Line.

Our share in the coming events was now to pass on our
knowledge to the Eighth Army, and accordingly we made
for our radio at Qaret Ali.

We separated once more: I took an easterly route along
the Nefuza foothills, Tinker went zigzagging toward Kebili
and promised to join us at our base the next day, calling at
Ksar Rhilane on the way. With Caneri we struggled on for
hours in a maze of hillocks till we emerged on the
Kebili—Fum Tatahuin road: it was lovely and smooth, the
temptation great—we fell, and, ignoring the risk, whizzed
along the road. I pulled up to ask a young shepherd how
far to the water.

"Quite near," he said, and went on to gossip of other
things. As we were leaving he said: "The two cars of your
friends are at the well now," and pointed to two Italian
scout cars which—unnoticed by us—were drawing water
from Bir Soltan a quarter of a mile to the right of the
road. I had a hurried conference with Caneri: we were in
great spirits, our reconnaissance had been more successful
than we had dared to hope, only forty miles away the
comfort of our big trucks would be ours this very night,
and we could now afford to enjoy a little fun. I decided to
shoot up the Italian cars and investigate the wells. Water
supplies, I speciously argued to myself, were a matter of
vital importance to a large force moving in the desert: the
Eighth Army would want to know all about Bir Soltan,
and my mission would be incomplete without a report on
this water.

We cocked our guns and I led slowly along the road,
looking for the turning which led to the wells. The plan
was to drive our two jeeps abreast and thirty yards apart,
straight at the wells, and open fire at a hundred yards
range. Carefully—round a bend—and uphill. My gunner
tapped my arm, pointed ahead and said: "Do you see what
I see?"

What I saw was the turret of a whacking big tank, hull
down by the roadside a hundred yards away. I stuck out
my arm for Caneri, turned sharp left off the road, put my
foot down and went bouncing along the hillside out of
sight. Caneri, who had seen nothing, had the sense to
follow me and caught up when I had gone in a wide circle
and crossed the road again three miles below the wells.

The laugh was on us even more than we knew: I heard later that what I had seen of the turret was all there was—it had no tank underneath! Set up at some past time as a machine-gun post to guard the wells, it was not manned.

At another well five miles from Ksar Rhilane where we stopped for water, an ancient, toothless Arab, nearly unintelligible, made desperate efforts to warn us of some urgent danger. All we could gather was that something had been burned and that the enemy was about. The poor creature could not know which of us was fighting whom. I thought there might have been a scrap between the French madmen and an Italian patrol from Duz. Anyway, it seemed reasonable not to drive into Ksar Rhilane without first making sure that the enemy wasn't in it: so two miles short of the Roman fort we concealed our two jeeps in thick bushes, and while we waited quietly for the night to fall I told Caneri of plans I was making.

Night came. Caneri and Yunes walked away toward Ksar Rhilane. Busy in my mind with the details of my plans, I lay down on the ground to wait for their return. An hour and a half later the lights of a car showed below the skyline. We brought the guns of the jeeps to bear on the track and waited: I thought Caneri had been captured and that the enemy were now searching for us. Two headlights that might have been those of a jeep appeared over a rise. I made up my mind and flashed R—R—R on my flashlight. The headlights blinked T—T—T, an agreed reply, and we uncocked the guns. A jeep pulled up, Caneri climbed out, with him was the French lieutenant parachutist. I said:

"I am glad to see you are still alive and free."

He laughed. "I know. But we never got to Kebili. We smashed another jeep, piled the six of us onto the last remaining one, and came back to Ksar Rhilane. Now it seems that the enemy has been active. I have heard rumors that three Messerschmidts strafed your camp at Qaret Ali yesterday morning and that some of your vehicles have been burned out."

We drove to the Roman tower. 'Ali, the friendly old sergeant major, late of the French Army, confirmed the rumor. Two of the Arabs we had met at Qaret Ali had ridden to the Italian post at Duz with the information of our camp.

I left Caneri and the six Frenchmen concealed outside
Ksar Rhilane to intercept Tinker on his return and prevent
him from falling into a trap, for if, as I expected, an
Italian armored patrol came down from Duz or Kebili to
deal with the survivors of the Luftwaffe raid, the only
track they could use ran through Ksar Rhilane. I drove off
in the night, with 'Ali to guide me to Qaret Ali.

The jeep crashed through the malevolent, man-high
Tunisian weeds with a continuous crackle. The glare of
the headlights gave them repellent, unnatural hues of
metallic green and white as they sprang at us out of the
night and vanished under the car. 'Ali understood his job;
after an hour and a half we turned right into the defile
leading to our camp; as I drove through, my lights suddenly picked out the skeleton of a three-ton truck standing
gauntly burned out among flung litter; I drove round the
camp, counting the wrecks: every one of my trucks and
those of the New Zealanders stood burned to the ribs.
There was a deadly hush and no sign of our men.

16

LIKE NEW ZEALANDERS

IN the sand at the far end of the camp we picked up footprints of many men, a trail leading into the highest dunes. I left the jeep and followed the trail on foot with a flashlight: up and up I trudged for a quarter of an hour, shouting my name, reached a crest, sank into a hollow, climbed another slope. I was challenged and shone my flashlight on a figure muffled in a blanket. Bob Yunnie led me to a hollow where his men were sleeping; they were all there, but two New Zealanders had limb wounds and couldn't walk.

He had saved a few pistols and tommy guns, some rations and a few blankets. Thirty cans of gasoline which he had buried had been dug up by the Arabs during the night and stolen. All the rest was lost. The Arabs, including our hostage, had vanished.

The extent of my disaster filled me with somber joy. My mind was swept clean of all the plans and the hopes with which I had been busy day and night during the last three months, and I had not even a flicker of regret for the strenuous preparations and the long efforts now suddenly wasted at the very moment they were about to bear fruit. From my long-cherished plans for defeating the enemy singlehanded, my mind switched over in a moment to consider the new and desperate problems which I had now to solve. Exhilarated by the urgency and the difficulty of the task, my brain functioned with a delightful, effortless lucidity, which I had never experienced before, for I am usually a slow and muddled thinker, full of questionings and doubts.

Woefully cheerful, Yunnie told me that early the previous morning three Messerschmidts had dived from just over the high dunes which surrounded the camp. The rattle of their machine guns was the first warning he had

209

had. Backward and forward they dived and machine-gunned, and flew away after five minutes, leaving his nine trucks ablaze and exploding. He had tried to save our radio jeep, which had not been hit, but a burning gasoline can, projected from one of the three-tonners, landed on the truck and put an end to it. Two New Zealanders had bullet wounds and several other men, including Waterson, had suffered superficial burns while they were attempting salvage from the blaze. Expecting an Italian motor patrol, he had withdrawn with his men into the dunes, where they could only be attacked on foot.

We sat talking in low voices, the men asleep around us. A fire had been kindled by our Senussis and they brewed us some tea, for they had salvaged, together with their weapons, their teapots and glasses. While I questioned Yunnie and listened to his replies, a picture of our situation formed itself in my mind with a clarity of detail that owed nothing to any conscious effort of mine. This picture in outline was as follows: the nearest spot at which I could expect to find help was Tozeur, the French oasis on the other side of Shott Jerid. The distance from Qaret Ali to Tozeur was roughly one hundred and ninety miles over unknown desert—probably very rough. The enemy, mostly Italian, had known posts along our route at Duz, Kebili, and Sabria. They knew of our presence in the area. The nomad Arabs were miserable but actively hostile: they might fight us themselves, and they would certainly attempt to ingratiate themselves with their Italian masters by reporting our movements. Though they were few in numbers we couldn't hope to move through their areas without their knowledge, and we should have to rely on them to show us the wells, and probably for food. We had no radio.

Our vehicles were five jeeps, with no more than fifty gallons of gasoline among them: probably enough to take three jeeps as far as Tozeur.

Counting the Frenchmen and the two S.A.S. men stranded in Ksar Rhilane, our party numbered fifty-one men, two of whom were wounded and unable to walk. The others were ill shod (most of us wore open sandals or gym shoes on our bare feet) and untrained for long marches.

The food available was sufficient for five or six days, on very short rations.

My immediate tasks, in order of urgency, were:

Communicate the results of our reconnaissance to the Eighth Army.

Get medical attention for the wounded.

Get our men out of the dunes at Qaret Ali, before dawn if possible, to avoid the risk of their being trapped by an Italian land force, and then march them to Tozeur to safety.

Warn Henry, who was coming up behind us with his Rhodesian patrol, of the danger he was in of being betrayed to the Luftwaffe by the local Arabs.

By the time Yunnie had finished his report I knew how I was going to set about my business. It was fascinating, I thought, to find all the answers without having to rack my brains; I hoped this unexpected power of decision would remain with me forever, and I looked forward to the next few days with pleasure. I had all the men awakened and sitting around me; with fresh wood on the fire I kindled a bright blaze so as to light their faces for me while I spoke to them; and to give them time to collect their spirits I made the Arabs draw extravagantly on our meager supplies of tea and prepare a powerful brew of Arab tea for everyone. I myself woke the two wounded New Zealanders and helped them to the fire; they had had a shot of morphia and slumbered heavily.

When I saw that I had everyone's attention I said:

"You may think that something has happened to Tinker that he is not here with me. Tinker is all right. He will be back tomorrow. While you were being strafed here we made quite a scoop, Tinker and I, and we want to get the news back to Army quick. We have now got no radio so we shall go over to the First Army to find one.

"Our mishap here was brought about by the local Arabs who betrayed us. I know the two who did it. The Arabs here are not like the Senussis; they are paid by the Italians and the Germans.

"The nearest place where we can get in touch with the First Army is Tozeur, held by the French. We are going to walk one hundred and ninety miles to get there. We shan't all walk: Tinker and Caneri are going to drive in three jeeps carrying twelve men, including our two casualties. The rest of us will walk. If possible when the driving party reaches Tozeur they will raise transport and come back to collect the walking party. But we mustn't count on it. I

reckon we can walk to Tozeur in eight days and we are
going to start in two hours' time so as to get out of this
place, which I don't like, before daylight. Also we haven't
got much food and we don't want to waste it sitting on our
bottoms.

"I shall drive the two casualties to Ksar Rhilane right
now and drive back here in the early morning to collect
the food and kit which the Arabs haven't looted. Sergeant
Waterson will be in charge of the walking party from here
to Ksar Rhilane, and Yunes will guide you by the shortest
route, which does *not* follow the tracks of my jeep.

"Bob Yunnie, Sergeant Garven, and Sergeant Moham-
med will remain here for no more than seven days, in case
Henry and S Patrol call here on their way to Tozeur. He is
to warn them of the danger of betrayal by the Arabs. If
Henry does not call they will make their own way to
Tozeur.

"With a little luck we shall get out of this jam without
any worse trouble than very sore feet. I want you all to
keep close together and allow no one to stray. This is not
the Jebel. A lonely man will not have a chance among
hostile Arabs.

"That is all. Thank you very much. Waterson will now
call the roll."

Yunnie, at that time thirty-three years old, was fundamentally a civilian. He held the methods and the discipline
of the army in some contempt and preferred—pas-
sionately—to go his own way. He claimed now, as a
privilege, to be allowed to remain behind on this risky
mission: I thought it would compensate him, in a way, for
his cruel disappointment at the loss of our equipment, for
he, more than anybody else, had had the trouble of getting
it together, and now it was all gone while he was still
waiting for his first chance to use it.

He thought that, assisted by the craftiness of Mohammed, they would be able to survive in spite of the treachery of the local Arabs. Mohammed had been with him on
the two-hundred-mile trek behind the lines, when his
Libyan battalion had walked from Jedabya to Tobruk
nearly a year previously; and from that time he had put
great faith in his ability.

The two wounded New Zealanders were carried to my
jeep, and I drove immediately to Ksar Rhilane, where I
left them with Caneri; then back again to Qaret Ali to

rummage for food by daylight. Waterson and the walking party had left at four guided by 'Ali, on whom Yunes kept an eye.

Bob Yunnie, Mohammed, and two men of P.P.A. were collecting tins when I arrived. Fortunately the Arabs had no use for tinned food, and had overlooked it in their very thorough looting, which had even included the theodolite, after it had been salvaged and hidden under a bush.

On my way back for the second time to Ksar Rhilane with our small stock of supplies and my two men, I followed the tracks of the walking party and overtook them about midday as they were resting and waiting for their dinner to be boiled: a large kid which Yunes had bought from some Arabs. They seemed all in good spirits and Waterson particularly ebullient. I believe that, like me, he enjoyed disaster.

At Ksar Rhilane Tinker was very impatient to get our reports sent over to the Eighth Army. We decided that he would leave the same evening for Tozeur and the First Army, and that my walking party would follow in the tracks of his jeeps. After sending off our messages to the Eighth Army, he would try to raise transport and come back along his tracks to meet us and give us a lift. We found that we had enough gasoline to send three jeeps to Tozeur, with a few gallons left over for my jeep and the French one which would carry supplies for the walking party and give us the protection of their guns, as long as the gasoline lasted.

My walking party consisted of thirty-seven men: seventeen New Zealanders, twelve British, six French, and two Arabs. As we were practically unarmed, our chances of avoiding being killed on our two-hundred-mile march were slender. On our right, and no more than five miles distant from our route, stood the Italian posts in Duz and Sabria. On our left the sands of the Grand Erg prevented us from giving the enemy a wider berth. All along the first hundred miles of our route any Arab who decided to betray us would not have to ride his camel more than a few hours before reaching an Italian post where a reward would be paid for his information.

I had no fear of a motorized column, as the Italians possessed no vehicles that could travel over the difficult country we would be crossing, nor could their aircraft hurt us much beyond compelling us to waste time under cover;

but they had mounted native troops against which we would be quite powerless once they got on our tracks. And the nomad Arabs themselves with their antique muskets could well snipe us out of existence if ever they discovered how few weapons we carried. In the latter part of our march we ran the risk of encountering patrols of French Goums, who had a reputation for shooting first and asking questions afterward, and for being rather indiscriminate in their choice of enemies.

My only chance of getting my men through alive lay in bluffing our enemies, Italians and Arabs, and playing them off, one against the other. This I proceeded to attempt without delay. The Italians first. Though three days had now elapsed since the air attack, they had shown no signs of sending out a patrol to investigate. I assumed that the reports they must have received of vehicles moving around Ksar Rhilane made them shy of risking a scrap with an unknown number of heavily armed and highly mobile jeeps. I decided to give them a fantastic idea of our numbers. I got 'Ali to invite a few of the neighboring shepherds to have tea with me at the fort: then, while we were sipping, Caneri drove smartly into the courtyard with two jeeps, came up to me, saluted, pocketed a document I handed to him, and departed with a great noisy revving of engines. A moment later Tinker repeated the ceremony with three jeeps, then the French lieutenant with two vehicles, and so on till, in the course of an hour, every one of the fifteen men we had with us at the moment had come up before me and our five jeeps had been displayed nine times over. Hurried alterations were made to the jeep loads between each scene, although I felt sure that to my untrained guests one jeep was as good as another. I knew that in the early hours of next morning an alarmed Italian commander in Duz would be pulled out of bed to listen to reports of fifty jeeps mounting six guns each, all passing through Ksar Rhilane in one afternoon. It would, I hoped, put him on the defensive, clamoring on the telephone for reinforcements from Kebili. A warning no doubt would also reach Sabria, further on our course.

The show over, I went into a huddle with Yunes and 'Abdel Salam to concoct a program of deception for the use of the Arabs we would meet on our march.

Waterson and his party walked in from Qaret Ali later in the afternoon and that evening Tinker and Caneri, with the two casualties and eight men, drove off to Tozeur, taking with them by mistake two of the gasoline cans which had been put aside for my use.

The next morning I called my motley party together, gave them my instructions successively in English, French, and Arabic, and we walked off in good order for a well, Bir el Haj Brahim, twenty-five miles away, where I wanted to spend the first night. Two hours later we were a straggling column stretched over a mile: Waterson and a group of enthusiasts led the pace at a rate that I found hard to keep up. Now and then I got into my jeep and counted the men as they went by, then drove up again, carrying the last stragglers to march with Waterson for a while. In this disorder we were lucky to gather all our men to the well at nightfall. The six Frenchmen insisted on riding in their jeep, and nothing I said could shame them into taking turns at walking and giving lifts to the more footsore of their companions. They were quite unconscious of the precariousness of our position and talked wildly of pushing ahead and clearing away the Arabs for us.

We found some shepherds watering their cattle at the well and tried on them the story we had prepared. Their acceptance gave us hopes that we would also succeed in deceiving warriors less obtuse than these simple-minded lads. The next day we kept better order, stopping every hour and collecting the stragglers each time, but we covered only fifteen miles. We saw no Arabs at all the whole of that day.

On the third day we again did fifteen miles. Some of the men were now going barefooted rather than in open sandals which collect sand between foot and sole and make walking very painful. But their feet were tender and they made slow progress. We camped for the night seven miles from Sabria in sand dunes. The night was so cold that I burned a hole in my leather jerkin sleeping on the fire; another man burned his socks off his feet. These comical mishaps considerably helped our morale.

We had seen no Arabs during the whole day, but two men came up to our fire after dark. It seems there was a feud between the tribe which pastured its flocks near Duz and that which kept near Ksar Rhilane and to avoid daily clashes they left an empty no-man's-land to divide their grazings. Thus it was our good fortune that gossip seeped through slowly, and rumors of our identity had not reached them.

Like all the tribesmen in southern Tunisia these men were destitute and lived miserably off their thin cattle for which they had no decent grazing. The French, the Italians, and also some of their Arab brethren settling on the land farther north had slowly squeezed them out of the rich pastures on which their forefathers had lived in plenty. Hence a surly resentment against all the people in the north, dull grievances which I intended to exploit for our own ends. 'Ali of the Roman castle, who was glib and politically minded as befitted a man who counted himself well traveled and enlightened, had provided me with a knowledge of local politics, sufficient, I hope, for my dealings with the half-savage tribesmen.

I entertained my visitors as nobly as my means allowed and asked them to inform their sheik, whose tents were pitched some twenty-five miles to the southwest, of my visit on the following evening. For their pains I gave them a present of money, generous indeed but not so extravagant (I had inquired from 'Ali the Italian rates of pay) as to excite their cupidity. I gave them to understand that I had matters of importance and secrecy to disclose to their sheik, counting on the Arabs' love of intrigue to keep their mouths shut.

My big bluff had to be made on the next day or never, because after that time I would be out of gasoline, and, without the prestige of a car, I couldn't hope to impress the intended victims of my deceptions with my secret importance. My visitors no doubt could not have helped noticing the scarcity of our weapons: so I hinted broadly that with us all was not as it seemed, as our common enemies, the French, would in due course find out to their grief. With this suggestion of secret weapons I sent them home.

On the fourth day we made an early start and walked over twenty miles following the tracks of Tinker's jeeps, to come to rest in the early afternoon two miles from a spring. Ain bu Rdaf. The going over choppy hillocks overgrown with bushes was tiring for the walkers and alarmingly heavy on gasoline for the jeeps. We had all suddenly become extremely ragged; every semblance of military smartness discarded, our appearance was that of a band of refugees. The raggedness, however, was not in our heart: shadowed the whole day by Arab horsemen, we moved in a close group, ready to fight at any moment, the few of us who possessed a weapon disposed at the head and at the tail of our column. My jeep drove a few hundred yards ahead, the Frenchmen in the rear, driving and stopping alternately so as not to outstrip the men on foot. During the afternoon more and more horsemen showed up on both flanks. With old French Chassepot rifles or long Arab muskets slung on their backs, they became bolder as their numbers increased and I thought that it was only out of respect for the twin guns on our jeeps that they refrained from falling on us.

At the evening halt I found that no more than a few pints of muddy gasoline were left in the tanks. We drained and strained the last drops from the French jeep and poured it into mine, hoping it would last long enough to enable it to perform its last task. I got ready for a ceremonial call: as I had carried my kit with me in the jeep all the time I had not suffered to the same extent as the others from the disaster at Qaret Ali; I managed to dress with some appearance of decency and strapped on to me a .45 pistol, field glasses, compass, and empty pouches. Yunes and 'Abdel Salam had salvaged some of their kit together with their rifles, and we made them look spruce enough. They were the only ones in our crowd who wore army boots. I took Locke with me as my gunner and covered his nakedness—for he wore only a pair of khaki shorts—with my sheepskin coat and gave him my spare pair of desert boots, three sizes too big. I armed him with a tommy gun and an automatic—he had also saved his dagger—and briefed him in his new role. Thus arrayed, the four of us drove off to Ain bu Rdaf, the spring of water at which I had arranged to meet my visitors of the previous night. An Arab, impressed from the crowd of onlookers, guided us. At the spring, to my immense relief, I found both my messengers waiting for me: perched on the back of my jeep they escorted us to the tents of their sheik.

A man of mean appearance with clever shifty eyes, he was sitting under a patched tent with the flaps up. As he rose to greet me I saw that he too had made an effort to smarten himself up: his threadbare burnoose was white and fairly clean, but his followers were clad in the usual ragged brown homespun. Assuming my best party man-

Colt 1911 Al

ners, I drew out as long as I could the exchange of courtesies, noticing hopefully some preparation for a meal. My host and his followers being unarmed, I unbuckled my belt and threw it in the jeep: my Senussis required no telling and had already placed their rifles under Locke's care. He remained sitting behind his guns and refused mutely invitations to alight.

We sat down under the tent on camel saddles covered with sheepskins: our host, a poor man, owned neither wooden sofas nor rugs. As we had arranged, Yunes sat next to me to help me in my conversation and interpret when the local dialect became too obscure for my understanding; 'Abdel Salam, a wizened old man of great cunning and sagacity, sat among the followers to spread calculated indiscretions.

I wanted to impress my host with the importance of my own person, as well as with the greatness of my condescension in visiting him. My aim was to make him feel flattered and eager to learn the object of my visit; never to suspect that I wanted favors from him. For this reason I dragged out the conversation interminably in polite courtesies and general gossip until the meal was brought in. Yunes, with whom I had rehearsed the proceedings, seconded me admirably, while 'Abdel Salam carried on the good work in the background. We talked and talked, on a multitude of subjects, but never mentioned our purpose. Beyond the fact that I was a high-ranking German officer, and my two friends Tripolitanian sheiks of high standing. I told him nothing of our intentions and aloofly ignored his pointed questions.

The meal of boiled goat and kuskus was silent as good manners required. When water had been poured over our hands, I asked my host to let down the flaps of his tent and admit inside only his trusted confidants.

I started then on the evening's business. The German command, I said, had become equally distrustful of the Italians and of the town Arabs in the north. As things were going the only consequence of us Germans winning the war in Tunisia would be to replace greedy Frenchmen by even greedier Italians in the possession of the land. What we wanted was a Tunisia controlled by warlike nomads under German supervision, a military base for us in which contented tribesmen would recover the fat pastures which had been filched from them by the French and their scheming town-Arab friends. Truly these town Arabs had now turned against the French and started a Free Tunisia movement: but all they wanted was plunder.

Our business was not to fight a painful war to the end that fat, deceitful, town dwellers should grow fatter and richer and finally turn us out of the land. Our friends were the faithful nomads, brave soldiers like ourselves; we intended that they should have a share of the rich loot of Gabes, Sfax, Sousse, and Tunis, and then pasture their flocks in peace and amity on rich grass lands—no more on God-forsaken parched and barren sand dunes.

In this vein I talked for hours, I never knew I could say the same things in so many different ways. When I tired, Yunes took up the thread and described the fabulous wealth of Tunis (which he had never seen). In the gloom of the far end of the tent 'Abdel Salam murmured to a close circle of enthralled listeners.

What we wanted from the tribesmen, I told my host, was their help to evict all the settlers, French, Italian and Arab alike—when the time came, which was not yet. I had taken the opportunity of my present mission to call on him, a man of influence as I knew, to prepare him for the call. He would understand that the matter must be kept secret from our weak Italian allies. They had still their uses for us at the present time and should not be made suspicious.

Loot, intrigue, treachery, fat pastures, glory—I had

exhausted the temptations I could offer my debased Arab host. Under his native composure I felt him excited; cupidity shone in his eyes. I thought he was ripe for further disclosures: I quietly kicked Yune's leg to draw his attention to the change of subject and said, quite casually:

"I might as well tell you the truth about the occasion which has brought us here. The French in Tozeur have three companies of Tunisian Goum. We heard that the men are much disaffected to their French officers. We have got together the German soldiers I have with me, all picked men, and dressed them up as escaped British prisoners-of-war. In this guise we intend to drift into Tozeur, where the French, unsuspecting, will receive us well and quarter us in the barracks with the Goum. We will get to work among the men and one night the three companies will rise, cut their French officers' throats, and seize the town. They will be led by men, every one of whom carries a powerful German automatic pistol concealed under his clothes."

I had done it! I watched Yunes anxiously out of the tail of my eye. He expanded my speech and added a few details. Our host leaned over and in a low voice asked Yunes some questions which I failed to understand. Then Yunes very deliberately lit a cigarette for the host—not from his lighter, but with an ember picked out of the fire. We had arranged this to be a sign that, in Yunes's opinion, the bait had been swallowed.

I went on: "For the sake of likelihood we cannot take our cars into Tozeur. I would like to leave them here if you would care to look after them till I send someone back to collect."

The sheik agreed and I thanked him casually. Standing up to stretch my legs I heard Yunes whisper to our host:

"These Germans are generous."

We talked of other matters, but I felt that he had something on his mind.

"Will Your Excellency walk with the men? I am very poor but I could provide you with a riding camel, not a good one, but still, one that would go."

I looked at him dreamily, as if I was turning over in my mind vast problems of strategy:

"I leave such matters to be settled by Yunes," I said, and strode out of the tent into the cold night.

When Yunes joined me later it appeared that we were to be provided with two camels, one intended for my personal use, the other to carry our stores. He had also obtained four sheep, one of which was being slaughtered at that very moment to provide supper for our hungry men. The three others would be carried on the camels. It was just as well that he had succeeded in refilling our larder, otherwise the next day would have seen the last of our rations.

Better still than transport and food, he had induced the sheik to provide a khabir to go with us, a guide who would vouch for us and smooth out unpleasantness which might arise with Arabs of other tribes along our route.

I gave Yunes a gold coin for our deluded host, and I drove back to camp extremely weary and fighting down an unexpected urge to giggle. I said to Yunes:

"We have told many lies tonight. Please God we may be able to tell the truth sometimes after this."

"God be praised," he said piously. "These Arabs are extremely credulous," and he chuckled softly. I shook with uncontrollable laughter.

The next day, fifth out of Ksar Rhilane, we started late. We made camp for the six Frenchmen, who had long ago expressed their determination not to walk and who now asked to remain behind to guard the paralyzed jeeps. Failing to convince them of the unwiseness of their choice, I arranged with the sheik for food and warned them not to forget that they were supposed to be Germans. They laughed: "Anything rather than walk!" They couldn't speak a word of intelligible Arabic so perhaps they couldn't give us away.

The khabir turned up with two camels and the three sheep, we loaded our blankets and few remaining rations, and walked away. We covered twenty miles before nightfall, one hundred and fifteen from Qaret Ali. The sixth day I estimated also at twenty miles. Waterson was like a bird, hopping about and cheerful. He had taken special charge of Petrie, who tended to brood but always kept in the van. Most of the New Zealanders walked with these two. They showed no signs of being upset. Some of my English lads dragged behind and required encouragement now and then. Locke, completely unperturbed, walked generally by himself, flapping his feet in my large desert boots. The Arabs were quite at home on the march and somehow their clothes suffered less than ours. The cold, sharp during the night, became unbearable toward morning, and as we couldn't sleep we walked away before dawn.

On the seventh day we saw several horsemen hovering about. The khabir grew nervous and talked of going home. During the afternoon we heard a distant noise of aircraft and we went to ground, dispersed amongst the hillocks. The noise grew and grew and suddenly one of my men stood on top of a hillock waving and cheering, and the next moment we were all doing the same: two hundred feet overhead, fifty R.A.F. bombers in close formation thundered over us on their way to Tripolitania.

We still had our noses in the air when I noticed, on the ground this time, coming toward us, a school of jeeps wheeling up and down over the hillocks like porpoise in a choppy sea. Tinker, in a hurry as usual, drove up to me. He had four borrowed jeeps with him. Caneri with another four jeeps was searching for us along a shorter route, in case we had lost the original track.

I sent Yunes to guide Tinker to the two jeeps we had left with the Frenchmen, and we all sat down and rubbed our feet; we had walked one hundred and fifty miles. In an incredibly short time he was back with our vehicles from the spring from which we had walked in three days.

We piled in, six and seven to a jeep, and drove off. That night we slept on the shore of Shott Jerid. The next morning we drove like birds over the mud flats at the western tail of the Shott, fearful of hitting a quagmire and of being engulfed. At eleven o'clock we hit the tarmac road which runs from Touggourt to Tozeur, and a little after twelve we sat down to lunch in the gaudy dining room of the Hotel Transatlantique in Tozeur. We looked very incongruous, sitting in fours at our tables, with white linen, an array of cutlery, and three glasses to each of us.

The hotel had been built just before the war for tourists who wanted to experience in luxury the thrill of visiting a Saharan oasis. At this time we were the only guests, but a large staff was at hand who tried hard to treat us "comme des millionnaires américains."

After lunch I was shown up to my room: I opened the door and closed it again with an apology, for there was already a bearded old gentleman standing in the room in the gloom of the dawn blinds. I told the servant:

"There seems to be a mistake, the room is occupied. It belongs to an old man with a gray beard."

The servant looked queerly at me, stepped forward and opened the door once more. I followed him in and gazed at my own unaccustomed reflection in a wardrobe mirror that faced the door. The unseen beard which I had grown during the last three months had turned me into a mournful replica of Great-Great-Uncle Henry, whose repulsive features appeared on one of the first pages of the family album. In our childhood, my elder sister and I had often praised our luck in being born long after the foul old man's death: and now had had come to life again with his dismal expression, his spaniel eyes, his untrimmed black beard with the white strip down the chin, his horrible stodginess.

I sat down in the darkened room and ordered the servant to fetch me a barber.

"Please tell my friends not to come and see me till I have been visited by the barber."

What with the shock of discovering in myself the image of my loathsome great-great-uncle, and with the aftermath of my orgy of lying, I lived for three days in a daze. I slept, I ate, I joked with Augustine the housekeeper, I took short convalescent walks in the palm groves and the walled-in fruit gardens of the oasis where limpid green sunlight filtered through the leaves and brooklets chattered between overgrown banks.

Caneri came back and left again for a place called Tebessa in Algeria, to return the jeeps he and Tinker had borrowed from kindly Americans for the rescue of our walking party. One day in the hotel lavatory, a noble room of silver and pink, "un pissing palace" according to our French parachutist, I lifted my eyes to see that the occupant of the slab next to mine was Henry, Lieutenant Henry who commanded the L.R.D.G. Rhodesian patrol, for whose benefit I had left Yunnie marooned in Qaret Ali. We greeted one another over our unbuttoned flaps. Yunnie, Garven, and Mohammed had come up with him: their warnings against the treachery of the Arabs had not been in vain for they had been sniped at all the way from Ksar

Rhilane and had suffered some casualties. Knowing we had gone the same way on foot and unarmed, he had hardly expected to find any of us alive.

Yunnie treated his performance as a joke; he had enjoyed himself, for this kind of activity suited him better than the wheedling of equipment out of unwilling quartermasters. He had, in fact, done extremely well and I was very proud of him. Henry had not called at Qaret Ali but had driven straight on. Yunnie saw his trucks in the distance and decided to take a short cut across the dunes of the Grand Erg to catch him around the corner. He had previously provided himself with three camels against this very eventuality. With Mohammed and Garven he had then ridden nonstop in a straight line fifty miles from Qaret Ali to Bir Jabeur, south of Duz, where they had caught up early one morning with the Rhodesians, who, having taken a longer route to avoid the Sand Sea and traveling only by day, had reached the same well only the night before.

I had arrived in Tozeur on February 8, 1943. Five days later we were all gathered there together and I decided, as everyone was well rested, that we would move to Tebessa in Algeria to refit. Tinker and his New Zealanders were about to fly back to the Middle East, and before they left they gave us at the Transatlantique a farewell dinner, memorable as much for the grandiose exquisiteness of the food and the abundance of the wines, as for the appropriateness of the speeches and the tactful art with which thanks were suggested and praise conveyed in matters so delicate that a direct statement would have been bombastic and brought embarrassment to all. New Zealanders are New Zealanders and there is no one like them.

17

ADMINISTRATION

In Tebessa we were refitted by the kindly staff of the U.S. Second Corps, our first contact with the fabulous American Army. Colonel Myers and Captain Montgomery were our godfathers; and, thanks to their efforts, nine days after arriving destitute in Tebessa we were able to operate once more. We worked for the American corps until the Eighth Army, having forced the Mareth Line came upon our right and we joined up once more with our old masters. Then Tunis fell and the war was over in Africa.

It appeared eventually that Italy would be our next theater and we prepared ourselves accordingly. We sent back to Cairo all our men except four and set about recruiting volunteers from various units. When we left Tunisia in September our numbers reached forty enlisted men and four officers.

I wanted to take behind the lines in Italy patrols of five jeeps, mounting between them ten heavy machine guns—the firepower of a battalion—and with enough gasoline for a range of six hundred miles. For this purpose I got P.P.A. attached to our airborne division and we started training in the use of American Waco gliders, which were designed to take jeeps.

At the same time we equipped our jeeps in a manner which, with some later minor improvements, we maintained till the end of the war. Our vehicles were uncovered and carried no windshield. On swivels fore and aft, they mounted two Browning belt-fed machine guns, one of .30 the other .50 inch caliber, firing in succession tracer, armor-piercing, and incendiary ammunition. In racks outside the jeep we carried seven four-gallon jerrycans of gasoline, which, with the tank, gave us an approximate range of six hundred miles. Ammunition, spare parts, tools for the truck, for digging and for felling trees, two boxes of compo rations, towing cable, two spare wheels, a cooker (altogether over two hundred items) made up the standard jeep load of approximately one ton. For the personal use of the crew (two or three men to each jeep) we carried a .45 automatic pistol each, plus a carbine (U.S.) or a tommy gun. Each patrol of five jeeps (later the number was brought up to six) carried two radio sets, a three-inch mortar, a hand winch, a Bren gun with an infantry mounting, land mines, and explosives.

I encouraged a certain diversity of clothing with the reservation, strictly enforced, that every garment outwardly worn should be a British Army issue. As a special exception Sergeant Curtis was allowed to wear a U.S. knitted peaked cap. Civilian and enemy clothing was banned, with the exception of dull silk scarfs worn *under*

the shirt collar, which could, if they so fancied, be worn by men who had taken part in at least one operational patrol. At that particular moment a camouflaged jumping jacket over K.D. slacks and shirt was much fancied by most of us: with its many pockets it was a handy garment, but being neither waterproof nor warm it came to be less favored in the rigorous Italian winter. Headdress was the black beret, worn without a badge on operations, or more commonly the nondescript knitted headdress. Sergeant Waterson still wore a stiff Kiwi hat. When I got my glider-pilot wings, I started wearing a red beret, but later, feeling it made my head rather conspicuous, I discarded it. Beards were still unregulated: eventually they became the privilege of the old hands with at least five operations to their credit, and were subject to my approval as to density of growth: no tufted fungus growth could be passed off as a beard!

On the whole we were still quite tidy—it was our first Italian winter that turned us into a band of scarecrows (and also the wider range of army issues of clothing).

Our bedding was of quilted sleeping bags and a ground sheet. Later we got issued with arctic eiderdown hooded sleeping bags, so warm that we slept in comfort in the snow.

Caneri loved order: mainly under his pressure I had now given some shape to our originally amorphous unit. We had two patrols (later the number was brought up to four) of fifteen men each, R and B, of which I commanded one and Bob Yunnie the other. In each patrol a commander, a sergeant, a corporal, a radio operator, and a fitter had their appointed duties. Caneri was in charge of headquarters with a radio section and an M/T section. He had acquired a wonderful knowledge of army administration, and from that time we put in all the returns required of a regular unit. In later years I could boast that our administration was tidier than in most regiments. He started at this time keeping a war diary and all the proper records.

Much of our time was taken up by flying in gliders, mostly at night, and trying, generally unsuccessfully, to check up on the route we followed while we were towed.

We went on in this way until the first days of September, 1943, when a decision of the Allied High Command, made known to us, altered our plans.

PART IV

ITALIAN PARTISANS

18

COGNAC FOR MAJOR SCHULZ

THE occupation of the whole of Sicily concluded, the Eighth Army crossed the Strait of Messina on September 3, unopposed (or nearly), and advanced into Calabria. Meanwhile negotiations with Badoglio came to a head, and the Italian armistice was signed but not yet published.

Ignorant as yet of these developments, the airborne division was, on September 1, put on a week's notice to embark at Bizerte. I was told that P.P.A. would provide five jeeps and their crews to land (wherever it was) with the first wave of troops—the remainder of the unit to follow later. The operation was to be sea borne, then land borne, and we put gliders out of our plans—as it turned out—once and for all.

McGillavray, a young officer who had been seconded to us from the Derbyshire Yeomanry through the friendliness of its commander, rushed away to Algiers to collect six new jeeps and came back having traveled over a thousand miles nonstop in his eagerness not to miss the embarkation. By the time he came back we were at twelve hours' notice. Without troubling to get any sleep he prepared his jeep for action with his gunner, Gaskell, and drove away with us at sunset in a long, slow convoy which was carrying the first elements of the airborne division to Bizerte. When we arrived at the port at dawn he was not with us. We got on board the U.S. cruiser *Boise*, and watched our vehicles as they were swung on deck. McGillavray appeared on the quay, riding a motor bicycle: the engine of his jeep had passed out halfway between Msaken and Bizerte. In the middle of the night he had stolen a motor bicycle, found and woke up an American workshop and had so well succeeded in convincing them of his urgency that they were at this moment putting a new engine into his truck. He rode away to collect it, promising to embark on our cruiser, if he came back in time—if not, on one of the other ships of the convoy.

We sailed without him, but when we had been at sea a few hours, I got a signal from H.M.S. *Abdiel* saying that he and Gaskell were on board that minelayer with their jeep.

We sailed on September 7. The next day the Italian armistice was announced to us and our destination given: Taranto, the naval base under the "heel" of Italy. According to the terms of the armistice our landing should be unopposed, but we were warned not to place too much reliance on this promise. On the afternoon of the ninth we caught sight of the Italian coast; then we saw the low shapes of naval vessels steaming out of port: the Italian fleet on its way to surrender at Malta. We entered the outer harbor and stopped. A launch flying Italian colors came alongside the *Boise*—and the commander of the naval base, an Italian admiral, in white uniform, gold braid and medals, came up the gangway and stepped on deck; an Italian officer, yet neither an active enemy nor a prisoner-of-war, which seemed strange. Night had nearly fallen when we moored at the quayside: to starboard stood a row of gaunt, bombed houses, silent and dead; to port, under the glare of our ship's searchlights, a company of our red-bereted troops formed up on the quay and marched off to the harbor gates.

The winches lifted our five jeeps ashore, we got in, and, leading our small company, I drove out of the harbor, past the guard, through the deserted rubble-covered streets of Taranto into the sleeping countryside, alone with my nine men in the dark, hostile continent of Europe.

Though it was not later than nine o'clock when we started, the whole population seemed to be already in bed. We saw no one in Taranto, then drove through San Giorgio Ionico and saw no one still. Halfway to Grottaglie a flickering light zigzagged across the road: a cyclist, too drunk to understand my questions—my first contact with the Italian civilian population. Before entering Grottaglie we stopped a good while because of a convoy we heard driving somewhere beyond a railway embankment. When they had driven away along a side road, we pushed on without meeting a soul. In Francavilla I discovered, with difficulty, a military office: a sentry seated on the steps outside the door slept with his rifle between his knees.

After he was woke up and disarmed, I put him next to me in the jeep, while Cameron, my gunner, kept him covered, and under his guidance we drove to divisional headquarters. Bob Yunnie having placed the jeeps to cover the approaches, I drove up to the door of a villa where the general lived, and bravely entered the lion's den. I stated my business to a sleepy corporal, and ten minutes later a captain walked in and said in English:

"Good evening, Major. I *am* sorry I kept you waiting while I shaved, but this *is* a pleasure *indeed*. Won't you sit down and have a drink? I have warned the general, who is now getting up and won't be a moment: he *is* looking forward to meeting you, I know.

"I do hope you have had a pleasant trip. What kind of sea did you have for the crossing? The weather at this time of the year is generally good, though perhaps a bit hot."

There were no lions it seems in the den, only lambs. The general's moment was a long one: in the meanwhile I pumped the young man. Despite his silly prattle he was no fool: I would find the army and the air force very eager to help us—the navy was different, snooty fellows, he said, but they would have to toe the line. With great satisfaction he rang up naval headquarters in Brindisi and had the admiral brought out of bed to be told that a British representative would call on him at three that morning.

The Germans, he thought, had pulled out of the province by now, but I had better be careful on the way to Brindisi not to fall in with their rearguard. They had a large technical staff who had been working on the airdromes, but few fighting troops. Somewhere in the north was the German First Parachute Division, perhaps in Bari, with which town telephone communication had been interrupted earlier that day.

He was happy and excited. The war was over—the bitterness of defeat had been swallowed, and he saw opening up a delightful era of collaboration with English gentlemen: he was a bit of a snob.

The general, having been given his instructions by me, said he would call on General Hopkinson first thing in the morning, and would arrange straight away for his divisional transport, such as it was, to report at Taranto during the day. (As to bringing his troops to fight with us, his only answer was a hopeless gesture of the hands.) Walking out of headquarters I was met by the sentry I had

CENTRAL
ITALY

Miles

0 10 20 30 40 50

disarmed; with tears running and heavy sobs he begged me
to return him his weapon.

Back with my men, I got Beautyman to put up his aerial
and try to get in touch with Brooks at divisional headquarters. I enciphered a message giving my first scanty intelligence—then we had a meal. Beautyman was a long time
tapping his key before he got a reply, so that, with one
delay or another, when we finally reached the outskirts of
Brindisi the time was, not three, but six o'clock in the
morning. The few people about fled when they saw us, and
we drove along the streets preceded by a clatter of shutters
hastily pulled to. The experts had promised us a friendly
welcome from the population, but it was through a hostile,
surly and silent town that we drove to naval headquarters.

Grimy and unshaven I padded in my slovenly desert
boots up a marble staircase into a vast and noble room:
through six crimson curtained windows the rising sun
shone from over the harbor onto a tubby figure standing
alone in the middle of the floor in gimcrack finery. The
admiral wore a sash, a sword, and many medals; he stared
peevishly out of a yellow, puffed face, for he had been
standing there three hours, and his first words were a
complaint about my delay.

I called to the orderly who had showed me in:

"Bring a seat for the admiral, immediately. Can't you
see that His Excellency is falling with weariness?"

The poor admiral, his surrender scene utterly ruined,
declined the chair, but led me into an office where he
sulked, puffed and objected while I talked. His head ached,
he said, and he would attend to business later in the day,
but I was in no mood to humor him, and twenty minutes
later we were driving out to view the harbor, the seaplane
base, and the airport. By nine we had finished, had
dropped him at his headquarters, and drove off through
the town on our way to Lecce.

Brindisi had in the meanwhile undergone a peculiar
transformation: Union Jacks, Italian flags, and carpets such
as are used for religious processions had been hung from
the house windows, stalls in the market square sold small
Union Jacks (some of them rather queer), and red, white,
and blue cockades; the streets were so packed that we
could hardly drive. Waves and waves of cheers enveloped
us: men climbed onto our jeeps, shook us by the hand, and

kissed us in ecstasies of enthusiasm. It seemed very odd:
two days before we had been still at war with these people,
and now they gave us a welcome that could not have been
exceeded had we been their own victorious troops returning home after the utter defeat of the enemy. They
longed desperately for a hated war to end, they cared not
if their country's military disasters were the price of the
peace we brought. To their simple minds we were allies
and friends, who had fought to deliver the suffering people
from their wicked rulers and to put an end to nightmares
of apprehension and terror: they loved us, their deliverers,
hysterically. They were not, as some may think, trying to
propitiate the new master, for their joy was uncalculating:
obscurely, in their poor hearts, they felt that we had won
the war for them.

I realized later that at our early arrival in Brindisi we
had been mistaken for a party of Germans.

In every village that we passed that day events developed along a similar pattern: as we reached the first houses
a wave of panic spread ahead of us, women gathered their
children and bolted for their houses, slammed the doors
and banged the shutters, carts backed up side streets, men
on bicycles slipped furtively away, and the main square
was empty when we arrived, except for two or three small
boys who, curiosity having overcome fear, remained to
watch us. As we drove by, their faces registered comically
in succession surprise—incredulity—hesitation and then,
suddenly, decision: off they darted, like mad, from house
to house; bang, bang, bang, on each door, piping shrilly:

"Inglesi, Inglesi, Inglesi!"

As if they had been massed behind the closed doors
waiting for the signal, crowds poured into the square and
the streets: we were enveloped, submerged, cheered, and
kissed. If we stopped long enough, and often we had no
other choice, locked as it were in the crowd, men of
importance forced their way to my jeep and delivered
speeches of welcome—offerings were brought: baskets of
grapes, almonds and apples emptied over our knees, eggs,
cheeses and loaves piled in the back of the trucks. Bottles
of wine reached us, from hand to hand, over the heads of
the people, glasses were produced and toasts proposed. In
one village an old woman came forward with a pitcher of
cool water and an egg, all she had, she said, for she was
very poor. I took a long draft of water and, not knowing

what to do with the egg, sucked it then and there. Everywhere the "Americani," elderly men who, having worked in America for a term, had returned to their native village with a small hoard of dollars, came up, called "'Ello, Boy" and then stood mute, for they had forgotten the few words of English they had ever learned.

The people who greeted us were all of the poorer kind, peasants and laborers, for in these parts the landed gentry and their satellites of the professions—doctors, lawyers and suchlike—don't mingle with the vulgar. The priests also kept aloof.

So much kindness might have overwhelmed us, but we managed to keep our heads, and during that day, our first in Italy, we visited all the landing grounds in Lower Apulia (Puglia). From them all the aircraft had been removed and attempts had been made by the Germans to destroy the ground installations, but they had left in a great hurry without achieving much damage. The Italian Air Force officers in charge fell over one another in their eagerness to help us, each commander endeavoring eloquently to persuade me that *his* landing ground was more suitable than any other to be occupied immediately by the R.A.F., and they made a great show of starting repairs even before we had left them. The keenness of these fighting men was different in my eyes from the singlehearted enthusiasms of the poor people and left a bitter taste: they showed, to my liking, too much eagerness to fall on their former allies, the Germans, now that we had proved to possess the greater strength. They liked to think that their behavior would commend itself to us, but I couldn't help feeling that their sudden change of face stank of treachery.

Toward evening I reached an airfield, near San Pancrazio Salentino, with which my review of the landing grounds south of a line running from Taranto to Brindisi would be completed. Thinking of my job for the morrow, I asked the local commander for information about the installations farther to the north, in particular about the airfield at Gioia del Colle—the only one of importance, according to my knowledge, for the ground becomes rough and rocky as you proceed north from Taranto and is generally unsuitable for landing aircraft. He described the facilities at Gioia and said:

"As to the present state of the ground I am not informed, but if you don't mind waiting a moment I shall ring up my colleague at Gioia and find out from him."

This very simple method had not occurred to me, as I had assumed, without giving the matter more thought, that all telephone lines to the north would be cut off. The colleague in Gioia said that German troops had occupied his airfield early that morning, coming from Altamura, their headquarters. A little later we heard German voices and he rang off. Encouraged by this success we telephoned to various other places, talking either to the local Italian military commander, or simply to the postmaster. Many of the telephone exchanges were still functioning with their civilian staff, and so little were they adapted to the new situation resulting from the armistice and our landing that no one questioned our business in asking for information; they had not realized yet that we had brought war to their peaceful backwater. I was enchanted by this easy method of getting inside the enemy camp. In less than two hours, just by sitting in an office and listening patiently on the phone over very faulty lines, I had been able to put the enemy on the map where before I had only a blank.

As a result of the talks, I had gathered that there were German troops to the north of Taranto and that they were concentrating in places of which I knew three: Gravina, Altamura and Gioia del Colle. Of their numbers, units and resources I was still completely ignorant.

By one in the morning on September 11 I was back in Taranto, twenty-nine hours after I had left it. Division headquarters were now in a building in the town; such troops as had so far disembarked held a perimeter around the town and they had been in contact with enemy patrols on the main road to Gioia. I gave verbally the general information I had collected, dictated a report on the airfields, told the general that I would try to reach Bari in the morning and thence go to the rear of the German positions on the Gravina-Gioia lines, and went to sleep for a couple of hours on the roof of headquarters building.

My heart was heavy with sad news: early on the tenth H.M.S. *Abdiel* had foundered in a few minutes after striking a mine in the outer harbor; there were few survivors of the crew or of the troops on board, and neither McGillavray nor Gaskell was among them—our first death casualties in P.P.A.

I had placed great hopes in McGillavray: gifted with courage, imagination, singleness of purpose and tremendously active, he was, I think, the most promising young officer I ever recruited for P.P.A. I was fond of the man and it was the friend that I mourned, not the loss of a useful officer. In our tense little world affection developed quickly, went deep and lasted; unexpressed ties of friendship held us together, a band of brothers who shared a taste for stenuous action, and our allegiance was to each other more than to a wider community. The inspiration of our enterprises was our common wish to perform well the difficult task which we set ourselves. As the general military situation became less acute the need to keep our country free from a foreign domination receded more and more into the background of our consciousness.

In our hazardous pursuits we suffered death and the loss of friends with an even mind, but it grieved me that this man should have been killed before he had given his measure, at the very moment when his toilsome preparation would have begun to bear fruit.

Early that morning our five jeeps were once more on the road, which climbed first to the top of the watershed and then looked down on Locorotondo and the Adriatic. The houses here are made of stone; circular and domed like beehives, they are spread over the countryside under clumps of trees. The landscape of gray rock and red soil adorned, but not clothed, with wild vegetation and very ancient olive trees, is so beautiful that driving down toward the Adriatic I fell into a dream and saw the whole of Italy stretched out before me.

"Jock, four hundred miles up this coast lies Venice, an island town of canals and narrow streets, where no wheeled vehicle has ever been seen. One day we shall land our jeeps on the main square, which is called Piazza San Marco, and drive them round and round, a senseless gesture no doubt, an empty flourish—but it has never been done before and at that time we shall be able to afford showing off because the war will be nearly over."

Cameron, who was watching the map, replied:

"No doubt indeed. The village we are coming to now is Fasano, on the main road. Hadn't we better slow down and inquire, or we may run into a German post? The war isn't over yet."

Fasano turned out to be unoccupied, and nobody stopped us till we reached the outskirts of Bari, where an

Italian guard on the road provided, at my request, a guide to corps headquarters. I left my men in the street and walked in to see the corps commander.

He was a fat, fussy little man in a state of considerable agitation, who said:

"I want immediate support from your troops. You have got a radio, haven't you? Then signal your headquarters in Taranto to send up immediately five squadrons of armored cars, ten batteries of field artillery, and two battalions of infantry. We have had a battle with the Germans in the harbor yesterday [a scuffle, as I found out, with some German engineers who wanted to blow up the port installations]. We beat them off—but this very moment they are coming back along the main road from Trani."

The poor man had in Bari three infantry divisions with their artillery and several squadrons of tanks, but he hadn't the faintest notion how to employ troops. He had not in his life held an active command, and was in fact no more than depot commander who had overnight, so to speak, found himself in command of front-line troops—he was in a panic and his headquarters, having none of the organization required for battle, couldn't help him at all. The whole staff was scared of the Germans. I refrained from mentioning that our forces in Taranto had no armor, no guns heavier than four-pounders, and no transport, but I agreed to refer his request to my headquarters and infuriated him by declining to give him any information.

Putting together the meager information I had, and looking at the map, I worked out a provisional picture of the German dispositions: they had forces based on Gioia del Colle, Altamura and Gravina, holding the crests of the hills, with a good lateral road. This line possibly extended to Potenza in the west and on to Salerno. The forces with which I was immediately concerned were supplied from Foggia along the road running to Gravina. As Bari was in Italian hands and the first place held by the Germans on the coast, to my knowledge, was Trani, they had from Gioia del Colle to the coast an open left flank forty miles long, which I presumed they guarded in some manner, either with detached posts or with patrols.

I made a plan to slip through this guard with my small

party the next morning, cross by night the Gravina-Foggia road, the main enemy lines of communication, and establish myself to the west of it, in what looked, on the map, a fairly remote hilly area. Being there well in the rear of the enemy and on the opposite side to his open flank, I thought it unlikely that we should be bothered by his patrols, and I hoped I should be able to investigate his positions in peace. I say in peace, for on this trip, I was out to obtain information, which might prove to be a slow business, requiring care and cunning, and I had no intention of giving myself away by indiscriminate shooting. We had larger issues at stake than the killing of Germans or the destruction of a few of their trucks. Consequently my orders were that once we had passed into enemy territory there would be no shooting except in self defense and when flight was impossible.

We left the Italian lines at Modugno and proceeded along the main road to Bittetto, ten miles from Bari. We were greeted by the usual crowds and pinned down in the center of the village. Picking out from among the frantic cheerers a man of more sober appearance, I asked him whether he had any knowledge of German troops.

"Of course," he replied, "there are two German armored cars in the village now," and laughed. What joke the yokel saw I don't know; we were caught in a compact mass of men, women, and children, and if it came to a fight, God help us.

We discovered the two German armored cars in the southern outskirts and chased them in the direction of Altamura. Where the road widened I spread out my jeeps to give a free field to each of our ten guns, and we let go with everything we had. One of the German cars stopped, but I let the other one go—it suited me well that the rumor should spread in the German camp that there were strong British forces in Bari.

I then retraced my way into Bittetto and left the village again to the west along a cart track. For two hours we wandered in a maze of tortuous lanes between high stone walls built to keep robbers out of olive groves. The map didn't help me much in this labyrinth but finally, unseen, we emerged where I wanted, in the foothills of the Murge, a barren plateau, forty miles by ten, stretching between the coastal plain and the valley in which runs the Gravina-Foggia road. Rising to fifteen hundred feet above the

plain, its rocky, broken surface intersected by low stone
walls, fit enough for sheep, would normally be considered
inaccessible to any vehicles, but, as I expected, we found
no great difficulty in driving our jeeps across it. When at
last we could see the German road, we had not been
detected and I felt that first the olive groves and then the
rocks of the Murge were, between them, a discreet back
entrance to enemy territory.

The road ran along a broadish valley, a thousand feet
below the edge of the Murge plateau where I stood. On
the far side rose the hills into which I wanted to go. Nearly opposite me was a hilltop village—Poggio Orsini, in
which through my glasses I could see signs of military
occupation. Between the foothills and the road there was a
flat stretch of dark green vegetation, supiciously swampy,
which would have to be avoided. A mile down the road,
toward Gravina, I spotted a small track leading off across
the suspected bog into the hills: this track I decided to
attempt after dark. The danger spots were: Poggio Orsini
on its hilltop across the valley, Gravina ten miles down the
road on our left, Spinazzola ten miles on our right, and of
course the road itself with its German traffic. I called the
men together, each one with his maps, explained the
situation, and told my plan. I then sent them in pairs to an
observation post on the edge of the plateau to have a good
look with their glasses at the country we were going to
enter.

When darkness fell we eased our jeeps down a very
rough gully into the valley, struck the road turned
into it, making for the side track. There was a little light
from the stars and we crept along, hugging the verge,
showing no lights whatever. Cameron, who was watching
the speedometer, warned me when we had covered a mile:
a moment later a high tension tower loomed out of the
dark, a landmark which I had seen from the top of the
Murge, and I realized that I had overshot the mark: the
turning into the track must lie a couple of hundred yards
behind us. I stopped, warned the next jeep and started
turning around. I was half across the narrow road when I
saw the dark form of a truck bearing down on me from
the direction of Gravina. I straightened out immediately
and pursued slowly along the road in our original direction: there was no time to give a warning and I had an
anxious moment wondering if the rest of my party would

guess what I was doing and follow me quietly, or if they would carry on with the original purpose and get entangled with the German convoy while they were turning their vehicles around.

A moment later Cameron reported the jeeps following on our tail and all was well. Twenty-eight ghostly German five-ton trucks crawled past our five jeeps, but their drivers, straining to keep on the dark road, took no notice, and our men had the sense not to open fire. A clash would probably have gone in our favor, but would have wrecked my chances of snooping into the German camp and discovering the information I required, for there would have been such a hue and cry the next morning that we should have had to leave the area.

When the convoy was past and out of hearing we turned round, undetected, found the side track and drove into it. I carried in the back of my jeep a man called Liles, a new recruit to P.P.A., whom I had taken with me on this operation for training, to give him experience in our ways. Liles fancied himself as an expert on all types of military vehicles, and after a while he said:

"I thought those trucks might be German five-tonners."

"So they were, Liles, you are quite right."

"What, all captured vehicles?"

"Not captured," I said. "That was a German convoy. I told you this road was German. We are now on the main German line of communication."

Liles adjusted himself to a new situation with a sharp gasp. At the same time I learned the lesson that infinite patience is required to make every man in a patrol listen to what he is told. We discovered that several of our new recruits were "followers" who drifted along, trusting that when the time for action came they would be told what to do: the army had trained them too well in unquestioning discipline, and we had to break them into a more lively awareness. Liles, by the way, was not a *congenital* follower.

The side track took us to a deserted farmhouse, then petered out. A moment later we had two jeeps wallowing in a morass. While we were pulling them out, Sanders, our New Zealand sergeant, found a firm route across the hidden stream. At the top of the rise we came upon a country lane, then upon a rural road which I identified on the map. We left Poggio Orsini on our right at a safe distance. I pushed on into the heart of the hills, along winding lanes, up and down, from crest to crest. At two A.M. I called a stop, after crossing a stream which I took to be the Basentello; according to the map we were now near the center of a group of hills and well away from the main roads. There was nothing more we could do before daylight, and having found in the dark a gully just deep enough to conceal our jeeps, we drove into it, set two men on guard to be relieved every hour, and went to sleep.

At five A.M. I was called to take my turn of guard duty. I posted myself under a tree with my glasses and waited for dawn to break. I had succeeded in getting my patrol undetected into enemy territory: the coming day would be the test of my ability to put this achievement to a practical purpose. Between me and our division in Taranto stood an unknown force of German troops; my object was to discover how many there were. To do so I should need help from the local civilians because, though undoubtedly I could, by surprise, fight my way into the rear enemy formations, such an action would in no way give me the information I required. From my experience of the previous days I knew that the peasants were favorably disposed toward us, but unlike the Senussi Arabs they were not a warlike people. During the next few hours it would be my business to find out: first, if they had enough self-control not to spread the news of our presence so widely that the rumor would reach the Germans; second, whether I would find a single individual among them with enough guts to give me practical help; and last, if their untrained minds would grasp the nature of the military information which was useful to my purpose.

My assets were: an imperfect command of the Italian language (but none at all of the local dialect), a certain confidence in my powers of persuasion born of past successes with other people in another land, and a long, long patience. Intensely curious about the way events would develop, I was looking forward to a test of my wits.

The sky lighted and I began to see the landscape: our gully was slightly above the Basentello: farther away from the stream bare fields rose to a crest on which I discerned a large group of buildings with a few big trees. Dim human shapes moved backward and forward from the buildings to a nearby field, but it was yet too dark to make out who they were or what they were doing: perhaps troops digging. The buildings, a large farmstead or a monastery, being on the skyline, seemed hardly suitable to be used as a strong point, but even Germans make mistakes, and I looked around to consider an eventual line of retreat for my party. There was time yet, however, and I waited for more daylight.

The troops digging turned out to be women, dozens and dozens of them, coming out of the farmstead for their morning squat. I could see them quite plainly now in my glasses, with their skirts up and gossiping, I guessed, actively. I made a note of this interesting local custom, and turned to other matters. I flicked pebbles at Bob Yunnie, who was sleeping below me in the gully, and asked him to rouse the men: I wanted them to wash leisurely and then to cook breakfast, without, however, showing themselves outside the gully. We still kept our desert habit of carrying our own water, so there was no need to go down to the river.

A small boy trotted past us, along a track that led from the farmstead to the road along the stream: I beckoned; he came over; I made sure he saw our company in the gully, gave him a piece of chocolate and finally dismissed him with a message for his father (whoever he might be) asking him to come and talk to me. The die was cast, I had made my first contact.

The boy's father drove down in a trap: he was the tenant of the farm, a middle-aged man of sober demeanor and good understanding, courteous but shy. I told him that we were an advance patrol of a large force of British tanks which would move down later from Bari to wipe out the Germans in Gravina. He saw our men stripped to the waist and washing—I hoped that the sight of our composure would banish the alarm he might have felt at our arrival.

I mentioned no more military matters for the time, but put him on to local gossip; he fell in readily with my lead and told me how, German troops having occupied Poggio Orsini the day before, the inhabitants had fled in fear: in his own farm up the hill he had at present over one hundred and forty refugees, mostly women and children. I told him not to worry, that we would clear the Germans out of the area in a few days—in the meanwhile how was he for food? He was all right he said, the refugees having brought some food with them, and his farm was well stocked.

Would I not, he asked, move up to the farm with my men and accept a meal?

I declined this offer; it might give him too much trouble, and if ever the Germans came out and fought us, I didn't want any of his people mixed up in the clash.

"It is better," I said, "that the Germans shouldn't know yet that we are here. The crowd up at your place might gossip."

He laughed. "We know how to keep our tongues. This is Basilicata, not Puglia. It is not such a long time ago that we had the bandits."

I offered him a packet of cigarettes, but he only took one, which he lit.

"There is some information I should like to have," I said. "If you have got any friends who would like to talk to me, please ask them to come down." He departed to reassure the crowd at the farm that we were not Germans.

The cat was out of the bag; there was no reason why we should hide any longer, so we moved out of our gully up the slope to a more open space among the trees, where I thought we couldn't be surprised, and where we had room to maneuver, and an open field of fire if ever the Germans heard of our presence and became inquisitive.

The farmer's friends soon came down in droves. They were very excited and all thought they had vital information to give me. I interviewed them in turn and spent hours listening to fatuous gossip. I heard the story of the occupation of Poggio Orsini ten times over, and what the grandfather had said, and what the sister-in-law had seen. My difficulty was that these farmers didn't know their area. Apart from their own farms, and the towns of Gravina and Irsina where they went to market, they knew less than I did with my map. They couldn't tell me who lived over the next ridge but one, and none of them have ever been to Genzano, five miles away. I got the most fantastic accounts of the troops in Gravina: two hundred tanks, guns larger than a railway train, seven generals and so many soldiers that they couldn't be counted. "Two thousand or thirty thousand, perhaps a hundred thousand!" Patiently I asked questions and listened: too often the talk digressed on to family matters and genealogies: these people were all related.

Still, a bit here and a bit there, I increased my knowledge—but by midafternoon I had a very poor showing for nine hours' work. I called to a little man who had been standing by for a long time waiting for his turn to speak, shy but less dim-witted than those other boobies. The first thing he said was:

"I know the quartermaster officer in Gravina, Major Schulz, the one who buys the supplies for the officers' mess. His office is in the piazza, the third house to the left of the trattoria, the one with the double brown door. My name is Alfonso."

His words gave new life to my poor brain, dazed by so many hours of fruitless gossip.

"Alfonso," I said, "please tell these people who are still waiting that I shall talk to them tomorrow." I took him by the arm and we sat down side by side on a stone. Alfonso had sold cheese, eggs and wine from his farm to Major Schulz; he had been in Gravina the day before and had noticed many things; he offered to go again and try and find out what I needed. Eventually we evolved another plan. First Bob Yunnie with four jeeps set off to watch the Potenza-Gravina road. He found a suitable hide-out on a height opposite the small mountain-top town of Irsina, close enough to the road to read the number plates of the passing vehicles. He organized the familiar routine of road watching, and I pulled back three miles to a deserted railway station on the Potenza-Gravina line. From the station telephone I called up Major Schulz. I had a long struggle to get through but eventually I got him. Speaking Italian mixed with a few words of German I told him, with a great show of secrecy, that I was the quartermaster sergeant of an Italian headquarters in a town which had recently been evacuated by the Germans. I had, I said, the disposal of eight cases of cognac which I would like to sell if he would offer me a good price. We haggled a good deal about the sum. When we had finally come to an agreement I said that for obvious reasons I didn't care to deliver the goods by daylight. If he would wait for me in his office that night at eleven o'clock I would drive up with the drink in a small captured American car. Would he give the word to the control post on the Spinazzola road to let me through without asking questions?

Major Schulz was a simple soul: he may have had scruples about buying stolen goods, but he wanted the cognac badly for the general's mess, and I had made free use of the name of his predecessor, Hauptmann Giessing, with whom, I said, I had in the past made several similar deals. (The relevant information came of course from Alfonso, a good schemer with an observant mind.) He agreed to my dubious request and promised to wait for me that night.

With Cameron we stripped our jeep and loaded in the back some compo-ration boxes, weighted with stones. At ten to eleven the guard on the road block lifted the barrier for us and waved us through, and at eleven exactly we pulled up on the piazza opposite Major Schulz's office. Cameron and I grabbed each end of one of our cases, went past the sentry, up the stairs straight into the office, where Major Schulz dozed at his desk. Wakened by the thump of the case on the floor, he opened bleary, drunken eyes and gazed at us uncertainly. Cameron didn't give him time to wonder at the nature of our uniforms, but hit him smartly on the head with a rubber truncheon*—a gift to us from S.O.E.** Schulz passed out and slumped in his chair. Cameron went down the stairs for another case—while I went through the papers in the room. By an amazing stroke of luck, open on the desk lay the ration strength of the units of the First Parachute Division and attached troops which were supplied by the distributing center in Gravina, dated September 12, 1943. While Cameron brought up the remaining cases I collected more documents out of the files. We placed a quarter-full bottle of whisky, uncorked, on Schulz's desk (the poor man deserved a reward), and walked out into the street. The German sentry was idly examining our jeep. Moved by an impish gust of Scottish humor, Cameron, the sedate, shook him by the hand, pressed on him a packet of "V" cigarettes, said:

"Good night, good German," and we drove off.

Two hours later, from a fold in the hills, Beautyman tapped out:

POPSKI TO AIRBORNE STOP TOTAL STRENGTH FORMA-
TIONS OUTSIDE TARANTO 12 SEP ALL RANKS 3504 RPT
THREE FIVE ZERO FOUR MESSAGE ENDS

*blackjack.
**Special Operations Executive.

On the 0900 call I received:

AIRBORNE TO POPSKI STOP PLEASE CONFIRM TOTAL
STRENGTH ENEMY FORMATIONS TARANTO PERIMETER
NOT MORE 3504

I knew that Intelligence had put the figure much higher.
Slightly piqued, I fell to the temptation of showing off and
having by now sorted out the papers I had stolen from the
unfortunate Schulz, I composed a lengthy signal which ran
to four or five messages and took the rest of the day to
encipher and to transmit. It went something like this:

POPSKI TO AIRBORNE STOP CONFIRM TOTAL STRENGTH
ENEMY 12 SEPTEMBER ALL RANKS 3504 RPT THREE
FIVE ZERO FOUR INCLUSIVE OFFICERS 441 STOP LOCA-
TIONS FOLLOW GINOSA OFFICERS 61 ORS 500 MATERA
OFF 72 ORS 570 ALTAMURA OFF 83 ORS 629 SANTERA-
MO OFF 58 ORS 469 GIOIA OFF 92 ORS 755 GRAVINA
OFF 75 ORS 140 STOP ORDER OF BATTLE FOLLOWS ONE
PARACHUTE DIV 19 RGT D COY O.C. LT. WEISS INITIAL
W.G. GINOSA B COY LESS ONE PLATOON O.C. HAUPT-
MANN SCHWARTZ INITIAL ILLEGIBLE GINOSA. . . .

and so on. Major Schulz had filed his strength returns with
care.

With this flourish I considered that my first mission was
completed, and I turned my mind to investigations much
further afield.

19

IVAN AND NIKOLAI

THE German First Parachute Division had its headquarters at Foggia two hundred and fifteen miles to the northwest: the importance of this town lay in the fact that it was the center of a large group of airfields spread in a plain. I knew that our command was anxious to secure possession of these airfields as a base for strategic bombings of southeastern Europe, and more particularly of the Rumanian oilfields, and I expected that the Germans would put up some resistance and try to deny us the use of the area. The next battle, I thought, would be around Foggia, and I wanted to investigate the place before the trouble started. The objective might seem a little remote to my friends in Taranto and beyond their scope—so, to avoid arguments, I resolved to keep my own counsel.

There was, however, a snag which prevented me from immediately undertaking a long reconnaissance: we were using Italian synthetic gasoline, and we had already found that with this fuel the performance of our jeeps was very poor and consumption thirty per cent higher than it should have been. I decided to return to our lines, fill up with our own brand of gasoline (there would by now be sufficient stocks landed at Taranto) and load an Italian truck with three tons of the stuff to make a few dumps in enemy territory.

The night after my visit to Schulz, I said farewell to my peasant friends and to Alfonso, told them I was going to Potenza and on to Salerno, and we started off along a country road leading to these places but, ten miles on, I cut northward across country in the dark, drove through plowed fields, circled a village, climbed a hill, discovered a ruined castle, and spent the rest of the night there. At first light we started off again, drove down into a valley and found a convenient camp for the day in a small wood. My idea was to create such a mass of conflicting rumors that the Germans would conceive an exaggerated opinion of the large number of enemy troops reported in their rear. In this I succeeded in a way other than I expected; for the local peasants reported to me that during the previous night the Germans had hauled up their heavy guns into the ruined castle (where we had slept) and that their tanks had been heard—and seen!—in several villages.

Two men came up to me while we were waiting in our grove to resume our wanderings after nightfall; they were dressed as the other peasants, but with an outlandish air that proclaimed them of some different race: squat and strong, with rugged features, tousled blond hair and tranquil blue eyes, they stood before me, not to attention, but yet with a nonchalant hint of military smartness. One of them did the talking, in broken Italian.

They were both Russian soldiers, captured together at Smolenski. They had been first held in a POW camp in Germany, then made to work with the Todt organization in France and later in northern Italy, from where, having escaped, they had found their way to the far south. They had worked in the fields with the Italian peasants who treated them kindly, but, now that we had arrived, they wanted to be allowed to join us and share our fortunes in fighting the Germans. The speaker's name was Ivan, his companion's Nikolai. I replied with a few Russian words to the effect that I was glad to have found them; in a few days' time our troops would liberate this part of the country and would look after them and send them back to their own people, but I had no room to carry passengers on my small jeeps.

"But we are soldiers," urged Ivan, using now his native tongue. "We want to fight with you now, and we can go back to Russia later. Please, please, take us with you: you speak Russian and you can give us orders which surely no other English officer could do. Please do not leave us with these peasants." Nikolai never said a word, but grinned and nodded in violent agreement. My words had been cold because Russian came with difficulty to my tongue: I had to choose what I said according to the words I could remember, but I was much shaken by the encounter; the two men were lovable and I could imagine only too well how they felt. It broke my heart to refuse them but I thought it would be inconvenient to carry them if we ran into a scrap, and also I was a little afraid of what Sergeant Waterson would think: there had in the past been much joking at my tendency to collect "pets"!

Finally I compromised and agreed to take Ivan: Nikolai, I said sternly, would remain behind. He walked away dejectedly like a beaten child. Ivan went and collected a little bundle of his possessions; I told him he would ride on the back of my jeep—Liles moved elsewhere. In the late afternoon we drove out. Passing a field where some men were working, Nikolai came running alongside us, saying good-by to Ivan. Tears were running down his face as he trotted to keep up with my jeep. I realized that, unless I relented, these two friends would never meet again, so I made a sign with my hand. Nikolai gave me a smile, slowed down till the second of our jeeps came bumping along; then he took a flying leap and settled on the back of the truck.

These two served with us until well after the end of the war and became the mascots of the unit.

So far, our first trip behind the lines in Italy had for me personally been satisfying. I had begun to learn how to handle the Italians and I had made a scoop that exceeded my hopes; for all the other members of the party (excepting Cameron) it had been dull and disappointing. I wanted to give them a reward for their patience and keep up their enthusiasm, as I could now afford to do. Instead of just crossing the main road after dark and disappearing immediately into the wilderness of the Murge, we stopped at a crossroad and laid an ambush: Bob Yunnie and Waterson posted one on each side of the main road, the remaining three jeeps strung out along a track which ran at right angles from the road over a railway line and away into the Murge: thus all our guns could fire onto the road together. I let Yunnie make the dispositions and he worked with so much certitude that I realized I had been wasting his talents dragging him around with me. I resolved to give him a patrol and let him operate independently as soon as the remainder of the unit had landed in Italy.

We were, however, out of luck that night for not a vehicle came our way. At three in the morning, with just time enough to cross back to Bari before dawn, we laid mines across the road, and, so that the Germans should not put the blame on the local civilians, Sanders, our New Zealander, who had a passion for heights, and, having

served in sailing ships, climbed well, swarmed up a tele-
graph pole and tied a Union Jack to the top crossbar. I
then pulled away my reluctant men and we drove up a
narrow valley rough with boulders: we were halfway to
the top of the plateau when, from behind us, came a flash
and a report, followed later by the red reflected glare of a
fire. When at a later date we revisited the spot we found
the burned-out remains of a gasoline tank and trailer and
two German graves by the roadside. But we got little
satisfaction from this achievement at second hand.

In this matter we were not consistent with ourselves. We
were opposed to any enterprise that smelled of glamor.
Out for results, to hurt the enemy and help our side, we
disclaimed any ambition to provide ourselves with exciting
adventures. We took pride in our businesslike methods,
expected a good return from each one of our operations,
and did not give a damn whether we cut a fine figure or
not. According to our standards of business, mines on the
read should have been considered a sound investment:
they caused the enemy to lose lives and equipment, shook
his morale, and gave us no risk whatever; and yet, in the
perversity of our nature, we didn't care to use them. We
had little scruple in shooting up unsuspecting soldiers if we
chanced to surprise them off their guard, but we found
something mean in leaving mines to do their beastly work
for us after we had gone: there are fine points of etiquette
in the conduct of the bloody business of war, and this was
one about which we had strong feelings. I can't remember
that we ever used mines again, except as a protection.

We made use, however, of gadgets which we christened:
"Turds mule, Calabrian," perfectly imitated turds made of
painted plaster which concealed a small explosive charge.
Strewn over a road they were indistinguishable from the
real article: a truck driving over one of these set off a
detonator and, the charge exploding, blew a large hole in
the tire.

A little later that same night Cameron taught me another subtlety of good fighting manners. When we
reached the top of the Murge plateau, deeming myself out
of any possible contract with the enemy, I turned on my
headlights to help me pick my way among the rocks and
the stone walls. The figure of a man appeared in my lights:
at first I thought he was a shepherd, but getting nearer I
recognized a German soldier standing with his rifle at the

ready against a low wall. Cameron, in his seat next to mine, cocked his gun and waited. At fifty yards I stopped, saw dim figures moving behind the sentry, and ordered Cameron to fire. He didn't. I looked at him, thinking he had not heard but he only shook his head ever so slightly, kept the man covered, and said nothing.

I changed my mind, swung out of the jeep and walked up to the German. He swayed slightly, stared, and let me pick his rifle out of his hands without resisting. Behind me I heard a slight shuffle: it was Ivan, who had come up carrying a tommy gun. He looked at the German with good-natured ferocity, but never used his weapon. I asked the German how many were with him. Eight, he said, and he would call to them to surrender with him. As in a trance he called out, but all the response he got was a scamper of hobnailed boots over stones. We let off a few bursts but made no attempt to round them up in the dark.

I entrusted the prisoner to Ivan on the back of our jeep, which pleased him as an auspicious opening of his association with us, and he chatted to his man in broken German. The latter, however, was so much shaken by his downfall that he mutely refused a cigarette and even a drink of water. He had been puzzled by our lights, for he didn't think cars could drive across the Murge. As, however, we came from the direction of his own lines he had assumed till the very last moment that we were a German patrol, and it was only when I walked up to him and he recognized my uniform that he realized his mistake.

The shock was so great that not till the next afternoon did he recover enough composure to take some food. This behavior distressed us all; we would have liked him to enjoy the breakfast we gave him, a very good one too, we thought, of scrambled eggs. We liked our first prisoner taken in Italy, a pleasant young man whom we were quite prepared to adopt, but we handed him in a few days later. We always had a friendly feeling toward our prisoners, particularly those we captured in battle, as if our recent endeavors to kill each other had created a bond between us.

We reached the coast shortly after dawn, slept for a few hours in an olive grove, then drove to Bari where we found a few of our troops, odd specimens like ourselves: Hugh Frazer with his "Phantoms" and also a detachment

of Second S.A.S. under Roy Farran, who had driven up
brazenly through the German positions in a train from
Taranto. They could deal with local reconnaissance and this
confirmed me in my resolve to penetrate deeper to the
north. I requisitioned a truck from the Italian command,
sent it with Waterson to Taranto and got it back loaded
with gasoline the following night. While Waterson was on
this job I established a rudimentary base in Mola di Bari in
a farm and country house, where I left Brooks with his
radio set, two men, and Nikolai the Russian. Ivan, dressed
up as a British soldier and armed, I took with me, third
man on my jeep.

Our Italian gasoline truck took some coaxing, but we
finally got it to Alfonso's *masseria*, near which we dumped
some of the load. From there we pushed on by night along
small roads well up in the mountains, lying up by day, and
dumping gasoline at intervals for future use. In this way
we reached the neighborhood of Bovino, ninety miles
northwest of Bari and only ten miles from Foggia. From
our mountain top we had a good view of the main German
lateral road running from Foggia to Salerno in the valley
at our feet, and in a village nearby I had the use of a
telephone.

The peasants were helpful: they had a very old tradition
of conspiracy, banditry, and secret societies, which made
them fall in readily with my spying schemes. Exploited for
centuries by the landowners and the Church, they were
accustomed to hold together in a dumb, resentful opposition to their oppressors: the mass of the peasants on one
side, the landlords with their scanty, middle-class followers
on the other, lived in separate worlds with contacts so
restricted that they might have been inhabitants of different countries.

Thus, although several thousands of peasants knew of
our presence, and scores of them were actively working
for me, no information ever leaked out either to the local
gentry or to the Germans. In the ignorant minds of the
poor peasants, the landlords and their bailiffs, the priests,
the lawyers in the small towns, the German command,
their own government, all belonged confusedly to a class
of people to be feared and mistrusted, natural enemies, too
powerful to be openly fought, on whom it was praiseworthy
to play secret tricks. They had no personal hatred for the
German soldiers and maybe they would have helped them

as well as us, if they had come as friends, for they had no idea of the wider issues of the war. Restricted by their wretchedness and their ignorance, their knowledge was limited to their own villages and starvelings and to their heartless overlords; beyond that familiar circle stood an obscure and hostile outer world.

I did not have to dissemble to pass myself as their friend; I liked the kind creatures. In spite of our rollicking assurance, they pitied us—weren't we poor soldiers torn away from our homes to fight a cruel war?—and they endeavored to comfort us with food and hospitality. Furthermore I cared little for their gentry, fawning and yet insolent, intolerable in their assumption that their possessions made us of one family, they and I. The war, the sordid extravagances of the rascals they had helped to power, and now forsook shamelessly, were mere accidents which should not be allowed to come between gentlemen: cynical, cowardly, vain, selfish and futile, they had the impertinence to treat me as an equal!

The enemy in Foggia turned out to be much weaker than I expected, and having got the news on our radio that contact had been made with the Canadians of the Eighth Army, I returned to our lines to talk to them about it. We followed much the route we had come up by, crossed once more the Murge and arrived in Bari.

We had found on the roads long columns of refugees. They were peasants dislodged by the recent battles and many thousands of people of all conditions displaced by the Facist government who now foolishly thought that, with the armistice, the time had come to regain their homes. They went in families, four generations together: great-grandmamas carried in chairs by their grandsons, sucklings in arms, tramping, tramping day after day, loaded with the bundles and the pathetic bursting suitcases which we came to recognize in time as the mark of the refugee all along the roads of Europe.

The compassionate peasants fed them as they could, but, poor themselves, they had already been eaten out. In every tumbledown farm hosts and guests starved together, and such was the press that many families had to camp out in the fields. The sudden impact of this misery shook us as the bloodiness of battle had never done, and we soon found ourselves out of rations. We gave a few lifts on our small jeeps, but the acts of mercy we could afford were of no avail in the immensity of the catastrophe. Distressed at my impotence, I thought of enlisting the help of someone better equipped to provide relief, and, on our way to Bari, I called at Andria on Conte Spagnoletti.

This nobleman had given us hospitality on a previous occasion when Andria was still in a dubious no-man's-land. He had put us up for one night in a country house of his just outside the town, and I had appreciated his pluck in taking the risk of being found out by the Germans at a time when, though they didn't actually occupy the town, their patrols visited it daily. This time, Andria being now in our hands, I called openly at his town residence, a large flat in the thirteenth-century family *palazzo*. Young, handsome and wealthy, recently married to a very beautiful girl, Spagnoletti had notions of domestic comfort far beyond the modest requirements of most of his friends. His flat contained two bathrooms, one of which, done up in black marble and filled with gadgets, was as impressive as any I have seen, and, furthermore, was perfectly functional. In a part of the world where a W.C. is considered an amusing toy, where indeed even outdoor sanitation is deemed superfluous when a garden is available, my host certainly possessed a progressive spirit.

We drank cocktails, ate a five-course lunch served by two footmen in livery and white gloves (to be fair, this is not, in Italy, the sign of opulence that it would be in England or the United States), followed by coffee—real coffee—got up, crossed three drawing rooms filled with gilt and scarlet Neapolitan furniture, and came to rest in a more intimate *salotto*.

I told the Conte about the destitution of the refugees: kindhearted, he was shocked and expressed his compassion for the unfortunate creatures.

"Beyond giving away our rations I can't do much to help," I said. "I have got my duties and they don't leave me much spare time. When our military government arrives in Italy, no doubt they will take the question in hand, but in the meanwhile it is a matter for people of goodwill. Your tenants are doing their best but, as you know, their means are small: they have no transport and, as to food, they are nearly starving themselves. Now you and your friends of the Landowners' Association—of which you are, I believe, president—if you get together..." I expected him to respond; to my dismay he only put on an expression of deep puzzlement and he said with hesitation:

"But—what has it got to do with me, or my friends? Surely it is a matter for the government?"

"Look, Spagnoletti," I replied, "you know perfectly well there is no government here at the present moment—neither Italian nor Allied. These refugees are of your own people, they are starving, dying of exposure and exhaustion on your land. Surely, now that you know the facts, you will want to help. In an emergency, such as the present, I would have thought that people of importance and power, like yourself and the other landowners, would like to come together and run the show for a while, till conditions get settled again."

Poor Spagnoletti was very upset. "We don't want these refugees here; they only bring trouble—why don't they stay at home? And there is nothing we can do, we have no gasoline."

"You have got horses and carts, haven't you?"

"We need them all for the work in the fields." He grew peevish. "I have got trouble enough of my own. Last year's crop of olive oil hasn't been all taken away yet. Where shall we put the new crop? And oil, which is worth twelve lire here, fetches eight hundred in the south, but we can't get it over. That is an urgent problem."

I gave up. After the war, I thought, the miserable people of this land will settle their accounts with their masters. Let us go now and beat the Germans.

The Germans by now had been pushed back, but they were by no means beaten. The Eighth Army, coming up from Calabria, had linked up with the Salerno bridgehead on the left and Taranto on the right, and on the Adriatic side it was moving up toward Cerignola and Foggia. General Hopkinson, who commanded the First Airborne Division, had been killed at Massafra, outside Taranto, on a visit to his outposts. He was a man who couldn't bear to remain behind when he had ordered his men forward, and a sniper shot him through the head. A well-beloved leader in his picked division, according to his men he was just what a general should be. It might seem a pity that he should have been killed, not on one of the airborne operations for which with great fervor he had prepared himself and his troops, but on a humdrum routine tour of inspection of his grounded troops; but it is a fit end for a soldier to lose his life in the punctilious performance of his less spectacular duties.

That was the way I hoped death would come to me—toward the end of the war preferably, as I wanted to see it through—for I never really expected to survive the war. (Even now, three years and more after the victory, I am still mildly surprised to find myself alive.) I didn't want to die, but, when I considered the matter—which was not often—it seemed unreasonable to expect my luck to hold through an indefinite succession of narrow escapes. This prospect didn't bother me at all but I preferred the end to be seemly and I often thought how annoying it would be if I got killed in a car crash, or, worse still, if I got caught by a bomb during an enforced visit to A.F.H.Q.

The days of our precarious isolation in Taranto were over; on every side the land was full of our troops (or so it seemed in contrast with our previous scantiness), the Germans in Altamura had been pushed back without great effort by the First Airborne and First Canadian Divisions; elements of the Seventy-Eighth Division and Fourth Armored Brigade, landed in Bari, were moving up the coastal plain. All was a-bustle and it seemed for a while that we were going to push the Germans right back to the Alps; but I was never very happy in a crowd and I longed to get back to the dangerous peace of our lonely operations.

Jean Caneri having landed in Taranto with the remainder of P.P.A. and all our vehicles, I could now give Yunnie a sensible job: we sorted out our men, he took command of the patrol he had trained in North Africa and, at the request of the Fourth Armored Brigade, he set off immediately to reconnoiter the Gargano Peninsula on the right flank of our advance. Bob Yunnie was remarkable, even in our very informal little group, by his complete rejection of the commander's aloofness. He lived with his men more intimately than any of us, shared their jokes and their escapades, and in return received their unreserved devotion. They called him Skipper and took the cue from him in everything they did. Ruthless in discipline, he never overlooked a fault, and yet, without effort, he created an atmosphere of adventure and high spirits. Where I was calculating, he seemed impulsive; although he laid his plans with care his mind worked so swiftly that he ap-

peared to make his decisions on the spur of the moment
and dashed into action with a flourish that concealed his
Scottish craftiness.

Although, with his patrol, he was engaged more continuously than any other—and only once did he fail to
achieve what he had set out to do—he suffered fewer
casualties than any. Himself, with a charmed life (bullets
he said bounced off his spare, bony form), he never
received a scratch.

In the selection of his men he was incredibly hard to
please; he rejected the reinforcements I offered him with
an exasperating regularity with the bare comment: "I don't
like him," or "He doesn't fit in the patrol," and preferred
to go into action undermanned than carry someone who
didn't suit his fancy. From the first his B Patrol became a
closed world, a crack unit, intolerable sometimes in their
assumption of superiority, and so pleased with themselves
that I could, at times, have wished that failure would teach
them a fairer appreciation of other people's achievements.

They enjoyed themselves so lightheartedly that no one
bore them a grudge for their occasional boastings; rather, I
think, the men who served under more sedate leaders, such
as myself, envied the privilege of those who were admitted
to B Patrol. Inspired with a sense of fun, they enjoyed the
traveling, the fighting, the unexpectedness and the hazards
of their roving life; as to hardships, they were generally so
clever at making themselves comfortable that when by
some chance they had to skip a meal or to sleep a night
in the mud, they could afford to laugh at the mishap and
treat it as a joke.

Bob Yunnie knew that to himself and his men danger
and labor were stimulating; but that hunger, cold, and
monotony (in that order) would inevitably get them down.
Thus it was usual to see fowls tied to his jeeps: sometimes
bought, more often "they had rushed under the wheels";
and on one occasion at least that I know, leaning out of his
seat, his corporal, Ben Owen, had caught a goose by the
neck as he drove by, an achievement we all tried vainly to
emulate. Whenever possible each meal was made a festive
occasion: bellies were filled and at the same time minds
were diverted from the boredom of waiting and watching.

Avoiding draughty castles on hilltops they put up at
night in a country house, if they could find one, or perhaps
only in a peasant hovel, or if nothing else was available

they would build themselves shelters, never contented to lie in the cold and the rain if, exerting themselves, they could keep warm and dry. Thus if they hadn't that day fought the enemy, they had at least defeated the weather, and they could slip into their sleeping bags with a sense of achievement. In this manner they endeavored to solve the problem of keeping the soldier comfortable and fit without pampering him, and they entirely succeeded in maintaining their keenness.

What was this keenness about? They didn't know, or at any rate if they did, they couldn't express it. Their standard answer was that they liked being with the boys and wanted to enjoy some fun, a statement which begs the question, as it does not explain the attraction of our peculiar form of fun. Considering that I selected each one of our men, watched over them and nursed them for years, and cast out so many whom I considered unfit, I fancy I know more about their motives than they ever did themselves. They will no doubt laugh at my presumption and affirm once more that they "liked being with the boys and wanted some fun and that was the long and short of it," but I think there was more to it and they can't prove me wrong.

I should say at once that each one of us had a set of private reasons for enjoying the continuous toil of our lives in the patrols: maybe escape from a domineering mother or an incapacity to submit to the formal discipline of orthodox units; with these incidental motives I am not concerned at the moment for I am trying to disentangle the common fundamental impulse which urged us all increasingly to greater exertions.

At the beginning of the war when we rushed into the army, peril threatened our land. We wanted to help, to lend a hand in the common danger, to follow our friends, to be active instead of sitting and waiting for disasters. Some of us felt moral indigation against the Germans and wished to punish them for their wickedness, perhaps a few dreamed of cutting a fine figure. This original impulse sank rapidly into our subconscious minds; after two years of soldiering we had stopped bothering about the broad issue; we had forgotten the time when we had been anything else but soldiers. Our life was in the army and our business to remain in it until the war had been won.

But obscure duties which had satisfied us at first were no

longer enough; a sense of unreality crept over us and bred in our hearts a desire to assert ourselves, to meet the enemy face to face, and to reach at the inner truth of a conflict, in which, although our uniform proclaimed that we were participants, yet we ever seemed to be hovering on the outer rim. We felt like a man in the back rows of a crowd watching an exciting game: he hears the cheers and the whistle of the referee but can see nothing. He presses his way forward and at length reaches a position where, through the eddies of the crowd, he can catch now and then a glimpse of the players. With effort he reaches the front row and he can now follow the game. But he is still unsatisfied, he feels the pride of his strength and of his skill, and, not content to remain a spectator, he will have no peace until he can also take a hand in the game.

From the moment a volunteer had been accepted into P.P.A., had passed his tests, and had been posted to one of our patrols, he was one of the team and out with the players. He had now to prove himself or his place would be taken by another and he would find himself back among the audience. More and more, as he got absorbed in the skillful practice of the game he ceased to be troubled by the confusing issues of the war. The vague, world-wide conflict had been brought down to his scale, to a manageable size, to something he could apprehend entirely. No more an obscure individual in an army of a million men, but one of a team of fifteen, he could apply himself to problems within his understanding. Failure or success depended on his own efforts and those of his few fellows. Thus he achieved a double satisfaction: he was at the very heart of the fight and he could affect the success by his own private exertions; the prize was well worth the risk and the effort.

Because fundamentally we considered our job to be a complicated, highly skilled game rather than a duty, we could afford to take it seriously without being self-conscious. It is permissible to be in earnest about football, cricket, or rock climbing, and to pursue these activities with a zeal which would be ridiculous and embarrassing if applied to business or the service of the government. The risks we ran (there were ugly prospects for any one of us who got seriously wounded) and the help which our achievements, such as they were, could bring to our main forces saved us from a feeling of futility. Thus we slaved away at our self-imposed tasks and, when circumstances forced us out of operations, we felt no peace till we had found some means of getting back to the battle. Twenty-nine months passed from our first starting from Cairo till the end of the war. During this period the time we were engaged in active operations totaled one year and eight months, the longest uninterrupted stretch being seven months. And we had no reserves—when the unit was engaged, the whole of its fighting strength was at work.

Our reward and our incentive were not so much our military successes—there is something deceptive about success so that somehow it fails to fill the heart—but the pleasure and the pride we took in the skillful performance of self-appointed and difficult tasks. We liked to think that not only were we good at the game, but we had invented it ourselves and only a few choice spirits, besides our favored companions, even knew the rules.

We thought at that time that the Fifth Army would be able to liberate Rome within a few weeks, an objective pursued for reasons more sentimental than military, and the advance of the Eighth Army up the Adriatic coast had as its main purpose to outflank the town and make its capture easier for the army on its left. At Army Group Headquarters I had heard the view expressed that the Germans would fall back rapidly on to prepared positions in the Alban Hills, a group of extinct volcanoes immediately to the south of Rome, and there, in this last bastion, make a desperate stand to cover the city. A study of the map would, I am sure, have convinced me that such a course of action was too childish to commend itself to the German command, for the high mountains farther south, extending as they did down to the coast, offered considerably greater facilities for defense than the hills of Albano. However, in my presumption I had not taken the trouble to examine the matter and I had given myself for this trip the task of investigating the formidable defense works which, I felt sure, were being carried out in the Alban Hills.

From Cassino northward we drove along Route Six. It was nearly deserted, which troubled me. Two hours before dawn we turned left and drove gallantly toward Velletri and Genzano. In these places undoubtedly German engineers would be working day and night. I would soon find out, but I didn't think we had more than a gambler's chance of coming back to tell. Round every winding of the mountain road I expected to fall into a hubbub. We were high up in the hills and on our left the ground fell sharply to the plain, to Anzio and the distant Mediterranean. On the slope where they should be building concrete gun sites, shelters, and trenches, strangely we saw and heard absolutely nothing. The autumn night was soft, crickets were busy, an immense peace was on the world: something had gone wrong with my appreciation of German intentions.

Apart from a few sentimental tourists I don't believe there was a single German in the whole of the Alban Hills, and the latest fortifications had been built in 1487. We spent the day in a vineyard and talked to the peasants. We saw a little military traffic on Route Seven, which runs to Naples, but the supplies for the troops in the south were carried by rail mostly and we found no occasion to break the peace. Toward sunset I climbed a hill to have a look at Rome on the horizon, then after dark we drove to the eastern side of the hills, where all also was peace.

I fancied I had discovered an important secret which might hasten the fall of Rome and shorten the war, but all it amounted to in fact was that the German command, at a time when it was still fighting to defend Naples, had not foreseen that we would land at Anzio four months later. Even for that operation my knowledge proved useless; for the planning staff, too timid to take advantage of the German unreadiness, sent our troops to a lingering stalemate which was not broken until after four months of bloody fighting.

Pleased with my illusory success and happily unconscious of its futility, but finding little more to do in this remote area, I took my patrol back into the Apennines, to the mountainous area bordering on the left flank of the Eighth Army. Traveling fast I had no time to make inquiries from the peasants: I followed the smallest mountain tracks on the map, thinking that the Germans would not bother to use them when they had the freedom of the main roads—our air force being still too scanty to worry them much.

Very early one morning we started winding up the narrow road that leads to Castel Vétera in Val Fortore and stops at this small town, two thousand feet up the mountainside. To the north of this road the map showed a patch of green, a wood, off the beaten track, in which I hoped we could shelter for a few days, make inquiries and lay plans for the future. The forest ran up a steep mountain and we could enter it nowhere, till we found a broad patch of fairly level ground. Here we plunged into the undergrowth and concealed our jeeps in a dark thicket between the hillside and a large boulder four or five hundred yards from the road. Day came, Sanders reconnoitered the neighborhood and found a mule track which climbed down six hundred feet to the valley bottom. I interviewed a few peasants, dull-witted boobies who helped me little with a confused (but alarming) story of German vehicles going up to Castel Vétera and back on the previous day.

We were all in our bower eating our midday meal when we heard in the distance tanks coming up. We put out our fire and waited. There was nothing else we could do: our fortress had no back door and we were trapped. Two German scout cars showed on the road and pushed on toward Castel Vétera. Ten minutes later they returned and stopped opposite our level patch of woods; one remained while the other drove down. Meanwhile the tanks had stopped out of sight; half an hour later we heard them grinding up. Time dragged on; a first tank came into view and was waved off the road into the wood by the men in the scout car; others followed clanking, to be dispersed to cover under the trees. By nightfall we had a squadron camped, somewhat uphill from our position, between us and the road. Just after dark more tanks arrived and these stopped below us.

These elements of the Sixteenth Panzer Division moving over from Salerno to the Eighth Army front, had, with motives similar apparently to our own, chosen this remote spot, well covered from the air, to camp in peace while the rest of their division moved to its concentration area.

The whole of that endless afternoon we kept ready to bolt up the mountainside, our weapons and emergency packs at hand, an incendiary bomb laid out on the seat of each jeep, but when darkness fell not one of the enemy had troubled to poke his nose behind our boulder. Hours of waiting in our trap, coming after all those days of snooping and hiding, had put us in a savage mood: we longed senselessly to hear loud noises and to feel our machine guns rattle in our hands—unfortunately, though our half-inch bullets might knock chips off the armor of

Mark IV tanks they couldn't penetrate it. We should have to use our wits and lay in turn a trap for the enemy who had so stupidly failed to catch us when he had us in his hand.

Pz. Kpfw. IV

The position of the German tanks in two camps—one on each side of our way to the road—made me think of a possible deception; I conferred with Sanders, then called the men together, and we laid our plans. We divided all the explosives we had—about sixty pounds—into four lots and fixed to each one a long fuse. At one in the morning we crept out and placed two charges about fifty yards apart toward A squadron on our left and similarly two charges near B Squadron on our right. At one-thirty the fuses had been brought back to our camp and five minutes later we detonated charge one. When the report went up and reverberated from the hills we started our engines and drove out between the trees toward the road, leaving one jeep behind to detonate the other charges at twenty-second intervals. I intended thus to cover the noise of our trucks and to distract attention from us altogether. Charge two went off, and as it had been laid at the foot of a tall, slender tree, brought it down crashing near the foremost tank of B Squadron. Charge three, on the other side, projected a clattering load of stones over a tank of A Squadron, then number four went off and brought down another tree.

We had now reached a position midway between the two squadrons, and while we waited for our last jeep to catch up we fired our only bazooka in the direction of A Squadron. The small rocket-propelled shell described a lovely parabola of fire and landed in a bush.

Now, at last, the enemy on both sides began to wake up: we heard shouts and the noise of a tank engine starting; but, puzzled as they must have been, they were not going to rush into action before they found out what was happening. We staggered our jeeps and fired a broadside of our ten guns toward A Squadron, then we moved on fifty yards and served B Squardron, moved again and sent streams of tracer toward A and B simultaneously. Most of our rounds hit the trees, a few reached their objectives, a lucky burst of incendiary hit a gasoline can and lit a dim glare in the lines of A. Then at last coming from my left I heard what I had been hoping for, the short, deep report of a seventy-five millimeter. Somebody in A had lost his temper. We concentrated our pinpricks on B till they also let off, and after that all we had to do was to poke the fire. After ten minutes A and B were at one another good and proper and we edged off toward the road, splinters and branches showering down on us as shells—which were not meant for us—hit the trees overhead.

I fired a German signal cartridge which I had carried with me many months. It generated a lovely shower of purple and silver stars, and was followed immediately— which rather startled me—by the deafening report of a seventy-five fired, it seemed, at point-blank range from an unnoticed tank. I thought it was time to say good-by, and I led my little company down the road, leaving the battle behind.

20

RECRUITS

CANERI had transferred our base to Lucera and there we all gathered. In his attempts to cross the lines in the northern sector, Bob Yunnie had found his progress stopped on the roads by demolitions, and across country by the weather. Half an hour's rain was enough to make even a moderately steep grass slope inaccessible: with no grip on the slippery surface the wheels spun, cut through the turf and churned the greasy loam underneath into mud. True a few hours' sunshine set it right again, but, until the following April, the sun seldom shone in the mountains for several consecutive hours. By the beginning of November the weather, the mountainous country, and the increased enemy resistance had nearly brought the battle to a standstill. The Germans, reinforced to about twenty divisions, now held a line practically continuous across Italy from the Volturno River on the Tyrrhenian to the Sangro on the Adriatic coast.

For two months, since our landing at Taranto, a fluid military situation and dry weather had presented us with golden opportunities for worrying the Germans inside their own territory, but I saw unmistakable signs that this period of easy chances had now closed down and that in the future we should find our work tougher than any we had done either in Italy or in the desert.

I had no doubt that we should still be able to outwit the Germans, but, faced with a situation entirely new to us, until we had invented fresh tricks the obvious move was to pull out from the line for a while, sit back and cudgel our brains. I feared a little that the Eighth Army might not share this view and assign us to routine duties for which we were unfitted, but I need not have worried. Major General de Guingand, Chief of Staff of the Eighth Army, had apparently reached the same conclusion as myself, but, in his pleasant manner he didn't wish to force a decision on me: he called for me a few days after my return and asked what were my plans. I had to tell him that, unless the weather improved, I saw no possibility of crossing the German lines by land, nor indeed, in the present static state of the battle, could I think of anything very useful we could do even if we managed to get ourselves behind the German lines by air or by sea. (If I had known then that some Italians were building up a partisan movement my reply might have been different.)

De Guingand then suggested that I should withdraw my unit to the rear and take advantage of the respite offered by the lull in the battle firstly to get a larger establishment sanctioned for P.P.A. and then to recruit, equip, and train additional men. I fell in with this plan and didn't tell him that if my men were to remain out of active operations for any length of time I would be hard put to keep them happy and in good spirits. That was my responsibility and I didn't expect him to alter the course of the war to suit my convenience. Even during our busiest periods some of my men felt that I wasn't giving them enough to do or that their tasks were too easy and not up to our standards, nor was this opinion always unexpressed. Yunnie, Curtis, O'Leary, Porter, Cokes, Cameron, Owen, Sanders seem to me, in retrospect, to have been much of the time hinting at the inadequacy of the opportunities I provided for their ambitions. Caneri, in closer touch with me, better informed of the general situation and with a Frenchman's acceptance of facts, took a more sober view. I had my share of frustration and, in common with many of us, I reached the end-of-the-war feeling that we had not really given our measure.

In November, 1943, we moved to billets in Bisceglie, near Bari.

I sat down with Caneri to work out a new establishment. I had long ago fixed in my mind an upper limit of 120, beyond which I didn't care to expand our strength: the reason being that I wanted to know the character, the capabilities, the background, and the personal history of each one of my men and to watch how he developed under the influence of his companions, and my brain was so made that I could not build up and keep in my mind a satisfactory picture of more than 120 men at a time. Only thus could I maintain the high standard of the individual members of the unit and the quality of their team work, in which lay our distinctive character and the justification of our existence as a unit. I saw no excuse for locking up in a specialized force more men than could be kept up to its highest standards. Furthermore, our *raison d'être* was that we achieved results out of all proportion to our numbers. This aim was furthered more by improving the quality and the experience of our men than by increasing their number. If, after we had done our best, it appeared that there was room for more work than we could do with a hundred men, let other troops follow in our footsteps and take on some of the jobs (they were welcome to our experience); we would remain free to lead the way in changing circumstances. Neither my ambition nor my inclination was to command large numbers, but to labor for perfection in a limited, pioneering field.

Yunnie and Caneri shared my views. When we were together, most of our time was spent discussing our men; we took infinite care over the composition of patrols, promotions, and dismissals, and over the training and testing of recruits. My two friends knew our men as I did and in a way, between the three of us, we ran P.P.A. as a family business. I reserved to myself the duty of recruiting —inconvenient as it was that I could do it only in my spare time (when I was not engaged in planning or on actual operations)—not that I mistrusted the judgment of my companions, but I found that their tastes differed from mine and the only way I could find of developing P.P.A. the way I wanted was to select the men myself. Yunnie, I thought, was too apt to be influenced by wayward feelings; Caneri, on the other hand, tended to disregard intuition and to judge a man according to his written record.

In December Caneri and I flew over to Algiers to put our case before the Establishment Committee. This ferocious body, we had been told at Army Group, cut down savagely all requests for increased establishments or even dismissed them flatly if they suspected that exaggerated claims had been made. Cautiously we asked that our original strength of twenty-three should be increased to seventy-odd (determined to go, in practice, well above that figure), but I found the devouring lions sweet and reasonable—to my amazement they pointed out that my figures were too low, particularly in signalmen and tradesmen (rare birds on the market in those days) and should be amended.

We returned with an establishment (NA/229/31) providing for eighty all ranks, including six officers, two warrant officers, four sergeants, five corporals, and five lance corporals, fitters, radio operators, radio mechanics, and armorers. The total strength was divided into four fighting patrols: B, R, S, and Blitz (H.Q.), administrative headquarters, signal section, and M/T section. We made the necessary promotions to provide the cadres for our new organization (Caneri became second-in-command and adjutant), and then I set about recruiting to make up our numbers.

The times were over when we had to live by our wits: we now had authority to draw volunteers from all units in the Central Mediterranean Force; in theory every commander could be compelled to hand over as many of his men as wished to join us and I was willing to take. In practice, I never drew a man from a *fighting unit* in this dictatorial manner, which I considered unfair and which would have given me a bad name with commanders with whom I had every reason to remain on friendly terms.

With base formations I had no such scruples, but my main source of supply was found in the reinforcement depots which had recently been transferred to Italy from the Middle East and North Africa, and held a large number of men who had fought with the Eighth and First Armies. Another useful privilege we were granted at that time was that those of our men who went on leave or were admitted to a hospital had to be returned to us in due course: in this way we suffered none of that draining away of experienced men, the plague of the ordinary unit, which breaks the heart of every company or squadron commander, liable as he is, at any moment, to lose his carefully selected NCO's as a result of a minor sickness or the normal rotation of leave.

I signaled the training depot newly established near Taranto asking them to call for volunteers among their men for fighting service with Popski's Private Army, a "special service" unit, and to have them ready for interview in a week's time. For reasons of security I could give them no other indication of the type of men I required (beyond the fact that they should be physically fit and experienced drivers with, if possible, battle experience), and also because I knew that the officers in the depot could have only a scanty knowledge of the big floating population that passed through their hands. When I arrived I found that one hundred and thirty men had put their names down. I got them together in an olive grove and addressed them in my loudest voice:

"The unit I command is rather secret—most of you will have never heard of it before—and I realize that you have volunteered mainly out of curiosity and because you are bored with life in the depot. A few of you, however, may have heard rumors about us: before we go any further I want them to know that everything they have heard is untrue. We do not go dashing about the streets of Rome kidnapping German generals right and left, we have not been parachuted in our jeeps into a POW camp in Germany, I am not an eccentric Polish millionaire, we don't get treble pay, in fact the men who join us drop their rank and their pay suffers accordingly; our other ranks are not privileged to dress up as officers when they go on leave, they are not even allowed a tie.

"For reasons of security I can't tell you as much about my unit as I should like you to know before you make up your minds, but I shall tell you this much: our service is mainly behind the enemy lines; it is not too uncomfortable but very, very tedious. Most of the time we wait and hide—often we have to run away. The virtue we require most is patience, patience and steady nerves. There are risks, of course, but I assume that you wouldn't mind that. I want you, however, to realize that if one of us gets wounded it is just too bad: there is no medical officer to look after him and no hospital to take him to.

"I have known very brave men, men who were never upset in an ordinary battle, and yet they could not stand the strain of our operations. If a man does not care for that kind of life he can't possibly be blamed. I want those who feel that our type of service is not in their line to stand down. The men who don't want to press their applications, please stand down."

Nobody moved. I did a little prodding: two or three overcame their self-consciousness and fell out—thirty other doubters followed the lead.

This preliminary weeding-out completed, I told the remaining ninety-odd men that the men I selected would first undergo training, and then be tried out on an operation before becoming full members of P.P.A. At any time during that period, as well as later, they were liable to be dismissed if I thought fit "and no blame attached." Conversely if for any reason they wanted to leave the unit they would be released at the earliest opportunity.

Sitting at a desk in a tent I then saw the candidates individually. Having made a note of name, previous service, driving proficiency and knowledge of weapons, I put away notebook and pencil and started a conversation. I took my time, for the best candidates and the most eager to be accepted came to the interview tongue-tied and in a state of nerves. When I felt the man had eased up I asked:

"Why do you want to join us?"

The replies I got fell into four categories. Many were diffident. "It might give me a chance to get on with the war." "I don't like to sit back and let the others do the fighting." "I am not particularly good at anything special but I should like to have a try at something difficult." These were the answers I liked best.

Then we had the glib and flattering replies which brought the interview to a sudden end. "I have an urge toward high adventure." "I hate the Germans." "I would consider it a great privilege to serve under such a distinguished officer as yourself, sir."

Some were sullenly aggressive and said: "I am browned off. I want to get away from the depot." A very feeble reason I thought, and generally sent them packing, though Ronnie Cokes, a thirty-year-old R.A.S.C. driver and one of my best recruits, gave me this type of reply with so much vigor and such a wealth of invective that I accepted him on the spot and made a damn good bargain.

Lastly, I got the fanciful replies. "Because I couldn't get on with the Guards officers in the Commandos," or "Because I want to learn Italian," or "My grandfather was an admiral." These in most cases I dismissed on the spot, although I accepted the man with the grudge against the Guards and he showed up tolerably well.

This concluded the preliminaries, and if I thought the candidate was worth the trouble I got down to business. I told the story of one of our operations—or of a blunder—produced maps and exposed problems of topography and of supplies. I talked and waited for questions and comments; when I got response I could build up in my mind a picture of the man's personality; when I didn't I cut the interview short. Whatever his hidden virtues, a fellow with no imagination could be of no use to us. The interviews were enjoyable for me; they required mental agility, for I couldn't afford to spare much time on each candidate. My judgment proved right for roughly half the men I selected; how many good elements I summarily dismissed I cannot, of course, tell.

On the third day I had interviewed everyone and made my selection. Out of a hundred applicants I had picked fifteen, and seven of them eventually remained in P.P.A. A good haul and above the average, for over the whole of our time we didn't retain more than 3½ per cent of the men I interviewed.

I don't think I was too fussy: for one thing, we couldn't afford to take on any but talented drivers. As it was, they required four or five months' training before they reached the proper acrobatic standard of driving over mountains, across rivers, in mud and snow. Fundamentally, success depended on our ability to take heavily-armed jeeps into improbable places—we could make no concessions on that score. Then our men had to have topographical intuition and the gift of finding their way in the dark. From among the men with the technical qualifications we had to pick out those who possessed the fundamental qualities of character, who were brave, sensible, patient, cool, resourceful, and determined. And if the poor blighters turned out to be real angels of virtue, still it wasn't enough; they had to fall in with the humors and the conceits of fourteen men in a patrol, who considered themselves the best men in the army and were not prepared to welcome newcomers except on their own terms.

Most of our men had a secondary school education, none had been at a public school or a university. With two or three exceptions they came from working-class families, mostly with an urban background; in politics they ranged from Tories to Communists (only the latter held their political convictions more than perfunctorily); according to the religion duly registered in their pay books, a majority belonged to the Church of England, with Roman Catholics, Presbyterians, Methodists, and Baptists following in order of numbers, also one Jew and one Atheist; none of them, however, as far as I could find out, had any strength at all of religious feeling. Neither in behavior nor in argument did anyone ever display any interest in matters of faith. They were not ignorant, for they all had had a religious upbringing, but so completely unconcerned that they could not legitimately be described as Christians.

We got on very nicely without religion. We preserved the decencies through the violence and the license of war: raped no women, tortured no one, looted in moderation and only from those who could well afford to lose, drank decorously (by soldierly standards), and refrained from bullying, went wenching only with the best, and, when we could, we looked after the girls we got into trouble.

As a matter of course, we helped a companion in trouble, took our duties to heart, looked after our men, loved our enemies (in the persons of the prisoners we took), and laid down our lives without making a fuss. Our behavior was modeled on that Victorian ideal of a gentleman, which has, in the course of time, drifted down from the class which first formed it (but has long since discarded it) to the bulk of the people for whom it is now the naturally accepted standard of conduct. There occurred many misdemeanors—mostly of a technical nature—for which I had to take sanctions, but the men themselves always saw to it that there should be no stealing, no lying, no quarreling, no bullying, no disloyalty, no cowardice, no shirking of responsibility, or any of those monstrous ill-defined crimes which come under the heading of "letting down the boys." I was well rewarded for the trouble I took in selecting our recruits and weeding out misfits.

By the end of December, after more recruiting trips, our numbers had reached a figure slightly above our new establishment, and Bob Yunnie got busy with the training. At the end of the war our numbers, exclusive of recruits in training, were 118.

I took our two Russians, Ivan and Nikolai, off battle duties because I thought they had done enough and I didn't doubt that they would receive bad treatment from the Germans if ever they were captured; it was unfair that they should run greater risks than the rest of us. Nikolai became cook to the unit and fed us remarkably, Ivan looked after me when I was at headquarters, where he had many other duties. They both learned Italian, but no English, worked all day and were never at a loss. When they ran out of firewood they took a few sticks of dynamite and blew down a tree. Ever smiling and ready with a joke, they became the pets of our men, who took a pride in their strength and their peculiar achievements. One of these was to drink at one go two gallons of wine out of a can.

I don't know why the British have a reputation for being bad linguists: it certainly did not apply to our men, who all learned Italian after a few months. Their grammar no doubt was sometimes atrocious but they had got well beyond mere cookhouse talk, and when we had been in Italy a year I could pick out any man at random, send him alone to the next village with a complicated message for the head partisan and be sure that he would bring back a complete and accurate reply.

The sober, competent officers whom I required existed no doubt, but they were all employed in fighting units, where they were quite happy, and anyway their commanding officers took good care that they shouldn't leave. On the other hand the depots bulged with thousands of nitwits who had been turned out by the Officer Cadet Training Units and were quite unemployable. Nor did they want to be employed—not in a fighting unit. They dreamed of a staff job and promotion; or, if they had not enough pull, they would be contented with a job as a town major or with AMG (Allied Military Government) where they could look forward to comfortable billets, an obliging girl friend, and reasonable profits on the black market.

Two officers I acquired at that time did not belong to this unsavory crowd. They were Reeve-Walker, a South African mining engineer, and Rickwood, a British tank officer.

21

A SHIPWRECK

IN the desert, where we had learned our trade, our operations were all of a pattern: we raided the enemy-held coastal area out of the inner desert (of which we had the freedom and the enemy had not)—we hit and hit again—then, before our supplies gave out, we vanished back into the waste and returned to a base securely held and supplied from our lines.

I had used the same pattern in our early operations in Italy, and successfully for a time, but the desert pattern was applicable only under freak circumstances, and both the topography and the shape of the Italian country were against it: if I persisted I should run into a dead end. So I had to set about to unlearn lessons and forget mental habits before I started on new plans.

I eventually decided to establish mountain bases well in the rear of the enemy line, supply them by air, and operate from them without attempting to bring my patrols back to our lines, either for supplies, refit, or reinforcements.

To bring my men with their jeeps and their supplies to the bases, the overland route being impracticable, I should have to fly them in gliders or land them from the sea. It appeared that all gliders had been moved to England from the Mediterranean, in preparation for the landing in Normandy, but a few landing craft were available. The sea route thus became the only possible choice. Once the bases were established and held, reinforcements and supplies could be dropped by parachute. This program involved the co-operation of the Navy for the landing; the R.A.F., No. 1 Special Force, a secret offshoot of S.O.E. which dropped supplies to partisans in northern Italy; A Force, another secret society, which rescued escaped POW's from the region of central Italy where I thought of making my landing; and the Italian partisans to guard my bases. I didn't like to be dependent on so many bodies, but I had no choice and I hoped that once I had bases established and well stocked, I would be my own master again, and so it turned out in fact.

Preparations for this operation, which received the code name of Astrolabe, took three months and involved much traveling between our base, Army Group at Caserta, the Navy at Taranto, Advanced A Force in Bari, No. 1 Special Force at Monopoli, the Eighth Army at Vasto and the Parachute School at Brindisi. The work fell mainly on myself, who did the general planning and the sales talk, and on Jean Caneri, who translated it all into practical arrangements. Caneri had a tidy mind and an unquenchable thirst for good administration. He had organized our headquarters on the best army model and made a point of carrying out all administrative orders, of which I had only a dim notion. The forms required were filled in and returned at the appointed intervals. He claimed that no division in the army had better-ordered affairs than P.P.A., of which I am no judge; but considering that I had no complaints from the men and few major "rockets" from our administrative masters, I presume that Caneri was not doing too badly.

Strangely this passion for order and legality went with an uninhibited gift for scrounging. He turned up at district headquarters and called on the A.Q.M.G.* (for his method implied striking at the head), very businesslike, with a briefcase full of documents and a deliberately assumed French accent, to complain of the delay in delivering our 399 Mobile Wireless Station. The A.Q.M.G., slightly taken aback, for these stations were scarce and only allotted to army headquarters and above, protested that P.P.A. had no authority.

Said Caneri: "But, sir, you 'ave given us authority yourself, 'ere is your letter, and 'ere is the authority from A.F.H.Q., and 'ere is our establishment and 'ere is G.R.O. 18/44 of last February: paragraph 9, as you know, deals with the allocation of W/T stations, and if you please, sir, you will sign 'ere and I can go to the Signal Stores and draw the set." And the A.Q.M.G., shamed by a display of erudition greater than he possessed himself, signed.

Bob Yunnie remained at home and trained the men. Our

---

*Army Quarter Master General.

base at that time was up a nearly vertical three-thousand-foot high mountainside. The access, the road having been blown, was either by a goat track, or by a funicular belonging to a hydo-electric plant, on which we managed to balance a jeep.

When we chose we could cut ourselves off from the outer world and enjoy as our own a hundred square miles of mountains and lakes and a peak six thousand feet high. In March there was plenty of snow; the Eighth Army provided skiing equipment for every man in the unit, and we recruited four instructors from an *Alpini* battalion. Later, when the snow melted, we practiced rock climbing, at which a few enthusiasts among our men became fairly expert—useful accomplishments as they proved more than once, but mainly intended, in my mind, to develop self-confidence in the men and to keep them interested and fit during the period of preparation. We practiced also other exercises which had a more direct bearing on our military activities.

One evening I came home from a trip to Caserta and found waiting for me a young captain, John Campbell, who had come from the I.R.T.D. (Infantry Reinforcement Training Depot) to offer his services. For the occasion he had put on his best clothes. Apart from his hair, which hadn't been cut for six months, he looked neat enough in a tunic, trews* (his regiment was the Argyll and Sutherland), and rather dainty shoes. Tired, hungry, and a little short in temper, I was not impressed; Campbell was tongue-tied, said the wrong things, and I turned him down. Caneri took me aside and said: "I would give him a try. I have talked to him this afternoon, he seems all right. You have frightened him."

I looked again at the big awkward lad in his tight clothes and told him: "We have an exercise starting in an hour's time. Without going into details now, it involves finding your way across country with a companion and walking about sixty miles carrying forty pounds in a pack and your weapons. The trip has to be done in record time, as it is by way of being a race. Go on the exercise—if you come back in good time I shall take you in P.P.A."

Later that evening Campbell, in borrowed boots and battle-dress, climbed into the back of a truck with the

---

*Closely fitted Scottish breeches.

other competitors. I had softened to the extent of giving
him as companion my gunner, Jock Cameron the gillie, of
all our men the cleverest at finding his way over mountain
ranges. They were driven out in the dark. In the early
hours of the morning the pairs were dropped a few miles
apart, given an escape map printed on a handkerchief, told
hurriedly where they were, and they pushed off to make
their way back to our base in San Gregorio in the Matese
Mountains. They were to avoid highways, assumed to be
enemy held, and to have nothing to do with the local
population, assumed to be hostile—which they had no
difficulty in doing as they were mistaken by the peasants
for German parachutists and created quite a scare. They
carried their own food, escape rations; their only compass
was of the kind that can be hidden in the stem of a pipe.

Cameron and Campbell arrived first, thirty-two hours
after they had been dropped and two hours ahead of the
next pair. The last pair, Duggan and a companion, turned
up on the fifth day, having walked all the time and crossed
the Apennines three times. Duggan lost whatever chances
he may have had to serve in a patrol, but found a job in
our headquarters as a cook—his companion, having failed
again on another exercise, was dismissed.

Campbell remained with us till the end of the war and
rose to be the fourth of us "Big Three." But he had a long
way to go before he took command of S Patrol, made a
name for it in cloak-and-dagger operations, and got himself two Military Crosses. I gave him first to Jean Caneri,
for whom he ran errands for several months. Following
the example of his boss he developed a masterful manner
with reluctant quartermasters. Thus he got his first training
fighting, not the Germans, but our rear headquarters in
Italy, where he came to be known and feared for an
awesome obstinacy.

At the end of May, 1944, many of our men, but not
myself, had graduated from the Parachute School in Brindisi; we had acquired the technique of receiving parachuted supplies at night, and we had learned to play with that
coy pair, Rebecca and Eureka, who between them, in
awful secrecy, guided planes on a radio beam toward the
dropping zones where we waited for the containers and the
men they would drop on us from the sky.

A Force had on three occasions taken off escaped
prisoners from a beach near the mouth of the Tenna River

on the Adriatic coast, sixty miles behind the German front
line as it now stood near Pescara. The naval craft they had
used had taken soundings, from which it appeared that
there was just enough water to sail a loaded L.C.T. over a
sand bar five hundred yards off shore and beach her on the
coast. From the beach there was easy access for vehicles to
a road.

No. 1 Special Force was in intermittent radio contact
with an agent they had staying with Italian partisans at
Cingoli, a town in the mountains thirty miles inland where
a hide-out could be arranged for us in the woods for our
first day ashore. These considerations made me pick on the
mouth of the Tenna as our landing point, the Navy agreed,
and it was arranged that the operation would take place
during the no-moon period in June, between June 12 and
17, three days each side of the new moon. I should have
liked to land on the twelfth, but there were several delays,
and the date finally agreed upon was June 15 at 11 P.M.

I should in fact have liked to land very much earlier, at
the beginning of June, but the Navy, having first agreed,
discovered a ruling that vessels should not be exposed on
an enemy coast except at night and during no-moon
periods, and none of the arguments I put forward could
prevail. Meanwhile the main battle, which had started
around Cassino on May 11, had succeeded in breaking the
German resistance; on May 23 the Anzio force broke out
from the beachhead in which it had been fighting since
January 18; on June 4 Rome fell and the Fifth Army
pursued the Germans in disorderly retreat beyond the
Tiber. On the Adriatic side of Italy there had been less
activity, but on June 10 the Eighth Army took Pescara, an
advance of ten miles which might be the first sign of a
German collapse in this area. Much greater actions were
taking place in Normandy at the same time, but, absorbed
in our own affairs, we took little notice of the opening of
the Second Front.

The earlier we got into our positions, the greater advantage we should be able to take of the German withdrawal;
for a retiring army was one of our natural targets—more
important still was it that we should land before our beach
was overrun by our own advancing forces.

On June 12 I sent an advance party to our landing
point. They sailed in a naval M.L. which made a landing
at midnight one thousand yards south of our beach. Bob

Yunnie with Gino Mifsud, the Italian anti-Fascist who had been with us for over a year, and accompanied by a local partisan leader known under the battle name of Quinto, whom I had seen at A Force headquarters, went ashore and walked away inland. I wanted Yunnie to get in touch with the partisans and obtain from them a picture of the situation from the coast up to Cingoli.

Three days later, unless in his view the situation was such that an attempt to land the main party could only end in disaster, he was to come down to the beach and signal the L.C.T. carrying me and the main party to the landing point. If on account of the weather or for some other reason we were unable to reach the landing point at 11 P.M. on the fifteenth, or if we didn't see Yunnie's signals, it was agreed that we would repeat the attempt on the sixteenth and the seventeenth. Quinto was to provide the contacts, Gino, in civilian clothes and with faked documents, was to tour the countryside on a bicycle and check the information given by the partisans, whose judgment I didn't trust too much. Sergeant Porter of P Patrol landed with Yunnie to reconnoiter the beach and its exits; he sailed back the same night on the M.L. to make his report to me on what he had found. Two naval officers landed also to reconnoiter the beach from the naval side. They were all back the next night in the port from which they had sailed, where a jeep waited for Porter and brought him to me. He had drawn a sketch of the beach. One hundred yards of firm sand led to the beginning of a good dirt track, which, passing under the railway, joined six hundred yards farther on with the main tarmac coast road. He had found neither mines nor vehicle obstacles and during the hour or so he had spent ashore he had seen no more than five or six German vehicles driving along the road.

The naval officers had taken some further soundings and reported everything in good order. They had made a note of landmarks on the coast which would make our approach from the sea foolproof.

The first success was a good omen. I still saw a number of possible snags for which I endeavored to make provision, but on the whole I thought the odds were in our favor: if Bob Yunnie had landed without trouble on the twelfth, we stood a good chance of doing the same three days later. I trusted the Navy entirely to see to their side

of the undertaking: I stood in such awe of them that I
wouldn't have dared to make a suggestion even if any had
occurred to me.

I collected my party and on June 14 we drove to
Manfredonia, a small port south of the Gargano Peninsula. After dark we moved into the harbor and drove our
twelve jeeps in reverse up the nose ramp into the L.C.T.
Four rows of three jeeps fitted snugly into the "Landing
Craft Tanks," and this consideration had determined my
decision to employ twelve jeeps. Having got them in, we
drove them all out again so that, each man knowing when
his turn came and where he had to drive, there should be
no confusion at the actual landing. Sergeant Porter had
paced out on shore a replica of our beach and the track as
he had seen them. He and Corporal Owen directed the
vehicles and got them lined up in the proper order. We
repeated the process a second time, then re-embarked and
the L.C.T. sailed.

H.M.L.C.T. 589, commanded by Lieutenant H. Dale,
R.N.V.R. carried a crew of eleven. The strength of my
party was thirty all ranks. We couldn't fit more than that
number into twelve jeeps—that L.C.T. could not take more
vehicles, and the Navy couldn't spare a second L.C.T.—
for the time being I had to be contented with this small
party.

We carried in addition a detachment of four officers and
sixty-nine other ranks of Ninth Commando. They had
offered to hold the beachhead for us while we landed, and
although I didn't think I needed them, I hadn't liked to
refuse them a chance of taking part in an operation; for
the poor lads had been sitting inactive for over eight
months. They were to re-embark and sail back with the
L.C.T. after seeing us ashore.

Our total complement thus was one hundred and fourteen.

Our craft was only a floating box, an unarmed, rectangular, flat-bottomed hull with the engine room, the tiny
bridge, the chart-room-cum-ward room, the ratings' quarters in the stern, and a swinging ramp in the bows, over
which, when let down, vehicles could be driven. She was
escorted by two naval vessels of another kind: one was an
M.F.V.—a Motor Fishing Vessel. Deceptively in appearance like a wooden sailing craft, with stumpy masts and a
dirty gray deckhouse, it could travel at a fair speed,

carried a Bofors in the deckhouse and was fitted with some
new navigational device which computed, so I was told, a
dead-reckoning position unaffected by drift or current.
The other escort was an M.L., a Motor Launch, which
looked quite openly like a tiny destroyer.

My men, happy and excited, lay on deck between their
jeeps and talked in whispers throughout the night while
our ship plodded over the quiet sea. Their time for the last
two months had been full of new activities, followed by a
week of ceaseless work, to get themselves ready for an
unspecified expedition in which, as they feared in their
hearts all the time, their place might be given at the last
moment to a more lucky companion. This night, for the
first time, they had nothing to do or to worry about till the
morning, when I would tell them where we were going and
what I expected to do. Meanwhile they floated in a void,
suspended between the world they had left behind and the
strife they would face the next day. For a few hours they
were free to dream of adventure.

I was in the same mood, but before letting myself sink
into blissful inactivity there was one more little job I
wanted to do. Two photographic reconnaissances had been
flown the day before by the Desert Air Force to cover the
various roads we could follow between our landing point
and our first hide-out in the woods near Cingoli, and the
photos had reached me just before embarking. In the chart
room, as a last and rather superfluous precaution, I set
about checking my maps by the air photos, in case they
were inaccurate in some detail. As I did so I noticed that
one of the bridges we would have to cross appeared on the
photo to be destroyed. A shadow of anxiety disturbed my
inner quiet. Then I discovered another bridge, unmistakably blown. As there were no signs of bomb craters it
could not be the work of the air force—who anyway had
agreed to keep off our area till we had gone through
(except for the main coast road).

I concluded that the partisans had been active—were
probably active again this very night—and the peace of my
mind went like a soap bubble. My trouble was that if,
starting from the coast at about midnight, we did not
succeed in reaching the mountains before dawn, our presence would be discovered by the Germans before we had
time to get organized, and my long-range schemes would
fall to the ground. Three rivers stood across our way: if

the bridges had gone, the streams would have to be forded, not an impossible task in June, but a slow one that I could not hope to complete in time with twelve jeeps, at night and in a hurry.

I succeeded in working out two routes along which, according to the photos, the bridges were intact. They were longer by half than my original one, running to about sixty miles of tortuous going: I marked them in blue and yellow respectively on twelve sets of maps, then I tore up the photos and threw the bits overboard.

As there was nothing more I could do, I dismissed my plans from my mind and walked out on to the bridge to talk to our young, black-bearded skipper. Sailors have a serenity denied to ordinary men; in the company of Dale the last vestiges of concern evaporated and I lightly laid aside my responsibilities until the time came to land.

Dawn found us sailing northwest by north up the Adriatic, out of sight of land, a clear sky and no sea.

After breakfast I gave out my instructions, to each patrol in succession:

"Tonight at 2300 hours we shall make a point on the coast, one thousand yards south of the mouth of the Tenna River. Bob Yunnie will be on the beach from 2200 hours to 0100 hours. If conditions are right for us to land, he will flash at intervals the letter R, dot-dash-dot, on a red torch, during the whole of that period. If we don't pick up his signal we shall put out to sea and try again on each of the two following nights.

"Our landing point is sixty miles in the rear of the German line. According to my latest information there are few German forces inland, though they have some military traffic on the coast road, and they may have control posts on the roads and guards on the bridges. Bob Yunnie will give me fresher information, as it is possible that the situation has altered during the last few days.

"There are some friendly partisans in the area of whom we shall get to know more than we do now. Our code name with them is supposed to be 'Banda di Pappa.' I am not very sure that they know it.

"My intention is to establish a base in the mountains, supplied from the air, from which we shall operate as long as conditions remain suitable. When necessary we shall move to other bases, always keeping to the rear of the enemy.

"As soon as we touch ground the ramp will go down and the Commandos will disembark to form a beachhead for us. The jeeps will not land till I give the order.

"Our objective tonight will be Cingoli, which we shall reach before dawn, following the route marked in yellow on the map."

Technical details on disembarkation and the mode of travel followed.

"You will all memorize the yellow route and be able to follow it without reference to the map—as we have done on exercises before. It is a long route, over sixty miles, with forty-four crossroads, and it goes through four small towns, of which I have made sketches from the air photos." I explained about the bridges which compelled us to take a devious route. "If the bridge over the Tenna near Fermo has been blown since my photos were taken, we shall follow the blue route, which you will also memorize. This evening you will hand over the marked maps to me to be destroyed."

I fixed the rendezvous in the woods northwest of Cingoli, about which there would be no difficulty, for however well we might be hidden from the Germans, every peasant would know where we had gone.

"The main point to remember is that we must be well clear of the last main road south of Cingoli before 0500 hours, lest all our future plans go by the board. We shall travel fast and anyone who takes the wrong turning will be R.T.U. the next morning. [R.T.U. stood for 'Returned to Unit'—dismissed from P.P.A.—our one and only punishment.] If we meet resistance we shall fight our way through, and all the Germans we may meet will be killed. This means that we shall take no prisoners and we shall finish off the wounded. Thank you very much. Good luck to us all." This was as much feeling as I dared put in my speeches, anything more would have been considered incongruous by my audience.

I then made arrangements with Captain Long of the Ninth Commando for guarding the beachhead. We had Porter's sketch to work on and we marked out the posts. I asked his permission to say a few words to his men. I put them in the general picture, told them what was expected of them, and, in a more florid speech than I had used with my own men, thanked them for their help. I then stood by while Long and his officers briefed their NCO's.

I spent the remainder of that day in a delightful stupor, although I came back to the world twice to rehearse my route. I would be leading the party and I didn't care to disgrace myself, but in fact I relied entirely on Jock Cameron.

Before sunset we changed our course to the west and the mountains of Italy rose out of the sea. Before leaving port the skippers of our three ships had decided that, disregarding the Admiralty instructions not to come within sight of the coast by daylight, they would make sure of their landfall before dark. I liked to see that the Navy had as few scruples about disobeying orders as we had ourselves.

At dusk we hove to, with the M.F.V. standing by; the M.L. opened up her engines with a roar and sped toward the coast. An hour later a dark smudge appeared on our port bow, the launch back, having picked up her landmarks. The M.F.V. parted company and with three hours still to go we started the run-in, dead slow, without a ripple. At 10 P.M. the coast showed up. At 10:30, watching through the glasses to pick up Bob Yunnies's red signal, I saw uncanny lights flitting here and there over the beach. I couldn't account for them; car headlights couldn't move that way! Could they be hundreds of men brandishing torches, excited partisans come down to meet us? Blast them, blast Bob for letting them come! At 10:45 I ordered all jeep engines to be started up.

At 10:50 the skipper by my side said: "Look, exactly over our bows." In the glasses I saw a small red glow, strangely immobile and dull among a myriad darting points of greenish fire, blinking slowly dot-dash-dot, pause, dot-dash-dot, pause, dot-dash-dot, pause. There was nothing in a silent world but those weird lights and the friendly red torch. On the deck below me Owen muttered "Bob is still alive."

The L.C.T. put on speed, lurched, scraped the bottom, pulled herself off. We were over the bar, in clear water; then another lurch on an uncharted sand bank, and clear again. At 11:30 the anchor chain rattled down, the bows slid up the beach, the L.C.T. stopped with a jerk, and the ramp went down. Below me on the sand stood Bob Yunnie, in a cloud of fireflies.

He came on board as the Commandos filed out without a sound. Leaning against the bulwarks we stood talking in whispers: the situation ashore had deteriorated during the last two days. The German Army was in retreat, its transport covered the roads and there were troops in the villages. I went down to the beach and talked to Gino, who had cycled halfway to Cingoli during that day. He had seen long traffic jams on the roads inland and machine-gun posts on the bridges, but no preparations yet for demolitions.

I had to make a decision and I turned arguments in my mind while Bob Yunnie talked: I was tempted to let my twelve jeeps loose among the German Army, but I didn't want my men to lose their lives in one silly blaze of glory.

Perhaps the next day the troops would have moved on and we might be able to nip in before the rearguard came up—a very long chance, if it was a chance at all. I walked up to the main road, six hundred yards away, and saw a convoy of trucks, armored cars and guns in a jumble creeping along head to tail. I came back still undecided: I had but to lift my hand to Porter, waiting at the foot of the ramp, and the jeeps would drive up the beach. If I didn't opportunity might never come again. The temptation was great, but common sense prevailed in my mind. Our chances of fighting our way to the mountains before dawn were slender: caught by daylight in the plain we would have to abandon our vehicles and slink away on foot—a band of refugees. I said to Porter: "Landing canceled. Pass the word along," and walked aboard to warn Dale, our skipper. Bob and his party came aboard also; the Commandos were called in, the ramp went up, the engines started astern and the L.C.T. prepared to put out to sea.

Fast aground, she didn't move. The crew hauled on the anchor cable astern and using the engines alternately, then together, the craft backed two yards, then stuck with the stern slowly swinging to port. Dale tried vainly to check the drift with the full power of his engines. At 12:45 he reported that he was aground, his anchor had dragged, and a coastal drift, helped by a northerly breeze, was gradually bringing the L.C.T. to broach to. Apologetically, for I hated interfering but after all Dale was very young, I suggested that he cast another anchor—if he had one— some distance out to starboard. "I know," he replied, "I have got an anchor all right, but no boat to take it out."

I went into the bows and had the ramp let down again.
It now ran parallel with the coast and five yards off it, into
five feet of water and a soft bottom. The two girders we
had brought with us could not help us to land the jeeps
now. We might drive one jeep into the sea, perhaps two, to
lighten ship, but lying on the bottom they would prevent
any forward movement of the L.C.T., and astern we were
against a shallow sand bank.

At 1 P.M. Dale with a lamp signaled the M.L. which was
standing out at sea, invisible in the dark, asking her to
come in and try and tow us off. He got no reply. The
M.F.V. had left us, bound for the Dalmatian coast, two
hours previously.

At 1:15, wrecked on an enemy coast, with our escort
out of contact, we decided to abandon ship and take our
men ashore. My men could look after themselves, and I
trusted the naval crew to be just as good, but I had on my
hands seventy-three Commandos. Tough fighters as they
were, they would be a raw crowd to take across forty miles
of open plain, filled with enemy troops, to the comparative
safety of the mountains. They were not trained for such an
expedition. The prospects of survival were unpromising; I
had no choice but to make the attempt. Sitting in the tiny
ward room with Rickwood, Long, and Bob, exhausted,
asleep on a locker, with the nominal rolls before me, I split
up the one hundred and sixteen men we had to get off into
twelve groups, each one including three members of
P.P.A., one of whom would be in command. I appointed
myself commander of a Commando group and put Rickwood in charge of the sailors. My plan was to put the
parties ashore at intervals, and walk them inland along
three separate routes, lie up during the day, walk again at
night, and so on until we reached the mountains, to wait
there for the Eighth Army to come up.

I detailed Sergeant Curtis to lay demolition charges on
each jeep, and on the engines of the L.C.T., and called
for the leaders I had appointed to the escape parties to
come with their maps for their instructions: meanwhile
Long got his groups of Commandos organized. Weapons
and ammunition to be carried—no food except escape
rations.

At 1:35 Dale, who had been on the bridge, reported
signal contact made with the M.L., which, coming in to us
had run aground on the sand bar, five hundred yards out

at sea. I allowed for seven more men to be taken off: the crew of the M.L.

At 2:00 the M.L. signaled that she was afloat once more, to seaward of the sand bar, and that she could stand by till daybreak to pick up as many men as could be ferried across to her. I decided to take my chance of a sea rescue, canceled the landing parties, and asked Lieutenant Dale to attend to the ferrying, for this was a naval matter. The order of evacuation was: Commandos, then P.P.A. less rear party (Cameron, Curtis and myself), lastly the crew of the L.C.T.

I woke Bob Yunnie and asked him if he would care to take ashore a small foot party with a radio set and remain in the area to give the Eighth Army general intelligence and bombing targets until he was overrun or I succeeded in joining him overland. His reply was: "If you say so, Popski," for he never expressed any approbation of the nice jobs I selected for him, and he went off to select his party. He intended to take two men only; after some argument, finding that every man in his patrol wanted to go with him, he took four: Sloan radio operator, Owen, O'Neil, and Gino. They took a radio set, batteries, their weapons, and ammunition, slid overboard, waded ashore and out of sight, accompanied by Quinto, the partisan. In my present position there was nothing more I could do to take advantage of our presence on the flank of the enemy.

The skipper of the M.L. paddled across to us on a Carley float to discuss the position. The draft of his craft being too great to allow her over the sand bar, our men would have to cross somehow the five hundred yards of water that separated us from the M.L. Between us we had one rubber dinghy carrying six, and two floats carrying three each: allowing for one man to bring the craft back, we could ferry eleven men across on each trip. A first batch of eleven Commandos turned up in battle order, carrying weapons, ammunition and full kit. My orders had been "Bodies only to be saved," and we had to strip them before lowering them overboard on to the flimsy craft. Later on a few Commandos succeeded in slipping away in full kit, with a disastrous effect on the overloaded floats— the only acts of indiscipline which occurred.

The position of the Commandos was trying, for apart from waiting to be carried off they had absolutely nothing to do, and most of them didn't know what had happened.

My own men were busy and several of them secretly hoped that, not being taken off in time, they would have a chance of joining Bob Yunnie's shore party. The crew of the L.C.T. worked quietly, cheerful and absolutely unmoved.

On first coming on the coast, being very conscious of the enemy on the road a few hundred yards away, we had talked in whispers and moved on padded feet. While Dale tried to wrench his craft off the sand banks the roar of the engines made us forget caution, and while the first party was leaving there was even some shouting over the dark water. At that moment a British plane flew overhead and dropped flares half a mile away, pulling off our blanket of darkness. Bare and exposed, we froze in our places: a hush fell over our company, and in the sudden silence the hum of the traffic and the German voices on the road appeared to be heading directly at us. Without a word our men picked up their weapons and manned the port bulwarks—the L.C.T. was too deep for us to use the jeeps' guns. Nothing happened. (I heard later from Bob Yunnie that when the flares dropped the Germans abandoned their vehicles and took cover off the main road.) We waited an eternity for the whine, the crash, and the boom of bombs dropping on the road and rail bridges over the Tenna, a thousand yards away. Then the flares floated down to earth and darkness fell over us once more.

The Commandos were awkward on the water and few of them could swim. Finally the dinghy towing the two floats with their human loads vanished in the dark and we settled down to wait for their return. I distributed to my men and to the crew the contents of two boxes of cigars I had—a gift from Egypt—and went into the ward room where Dale was tearing up documents and charts. I felt the same elation of spirits I had experienced while we were extricating ourselves from disaster at Qaret Ali, and not a shadow of regret.

A simple calculation showed that ferrying eleven men at a time we could not possibly take off everyone before daybreak: on the suggestion of Sanders I set our men to extract the inner tubes from our twenty-four spare wheels and inflate them to make life buoys.

The dinghy did not return for an hour: the Commandos, attempting to get out of it in military formation, had stepped together on the gunwale and capsized it and the

crew of the M.L. spent much time fishing them out of the
sea and bailing out the dinghy. The time was three in the
morning: with two hours to go till dawn when we should be
in full view of the Germans on the road we had still one
hundred men to take off. We made ten Commandos slip
an inflated inner tube under their armpits, tied the men on
to a line and lowered them into the water. As none of the
Commandos could paddle we had to put a rating on each
float and off they went: the dinghy and the two floats
towing the men on the line behind them; nineteen Commandos ferried over at each trip.

With a glow of dawn showing in the eastern sky, the
dinghy and floats came back for the last batch of Commandos; I saw them go without sorrow. We had still on
board nine of the crew and twenty-seven of P.P.A.—they
would have to swim for it. Rickwood stripped to the skin,
sprang on to the bulwark and with a "Yo-ho" went into the
sea head foremost. The others followed yelling and laughing—their bobbing heads disappeared toward the small
light which the M.L. showed over her side. Sanders, a pistol
belted around his bare body, swam carefully on his back in
the quiet water, smoking a cigar. Only our rear party
remained on board. With Curtis I went round the charges
he had laid and we poured gasoline over the jeeps and the
torn-up papers in the chart room.

We gathered on the bridge waiting for the dinghy.
Lieutenant Dale said:

"Never mind my L.C.T. She is expendable. But all those
nice jeeps!" We had spent much labor and much love on
them and I felt a pang.

"Don't worry," I replied. "War is wasteful. We shall get
some more."

But although we equipped many more jeeps before the
war ended, we never brought them again to the same pitch
of perfection.

Darkness lifted. A bank of white mist spread over the
sea, hiding the M.L., but to landward we began to discern
through the trees the slow-moving column of traffic on the
road. The dinghy bobbed up. Curtis having set the delayed
fuses, we climbed down into the small craft and threw in
the clothes left behind by the swimmers. Sitting on the bow
thwart I picked up my sculls, a rating sat in front of me,
Curtis and Cameron in the bows. We held the stern of the
dingy against the side of the ship for Lieutenant Dale to

come in. Erect in the stern, his log book under his arm, he saluted his ship: then he turned around and sat down, and we pulled away.

We floated a long time in a milky whiteness. A voice hailed us impatiently: suddenly we came out of the mist and there was the M.L. above us. It got under way as we were pulled aboard. The skipper was in a hurry: he had heard a train coming up the line and didn't want to miss it. He sailed a quarter of a mile along the coast, then stopped; the train came into view, and he opened up with the Bofors. The tracer curved toward the land—after a long while there was a cloud of steam and the train stopped. Bob Yunnie, sitting under a haystack two hundred yards from the railway line, cursed us abundantly.

Stern down and bows out of the water, the M.L. made for home with a roar of her twin engines. She rolled abominably. One hundred and eighteen men on board a craft designed to carry seven in very moderate comfort were somewhat cramped. Somehow the sailors managed to give us all hot coffee and whisky, which made us very brave for a while—then we began to fight seasickness. I held out till I saw Dale go under; my honor safe, I pushed my way through the crowd and was gloriously sick overboard.

We reached Manfredonia that afternoon at four. Our only casualty was a Commando who, having been ducked when the dinghy capsized, was feeling a little drowned, but the N.O.I.C. entertained us as genuine shipwrecked mariners. On landing I signaled instructions to Jean Caneri: he wasted no time and early the next morning we were on our way to San Gregorio in our own three-tonners which he had sent for us. At our base I found everyone a-bustle equipping the ten battle-worthy jeeps which remained to us. The whole of that day we worked and through the night and through the next day. At 3:15 on June 19, seventy hours after abandoning the stranded L.C.T., we were on the road with much the same party, in ten jeeps, driving northward in an attempt to take advantage of the German confused withdrawal and cross their lines in the mountains. None of us had had time to brood over our ill luck and our spirits were high.

Yunnie's radio had opened up at ten o'clock on the sixteenth from a position in the Tenna Valley, and every few hours since then he had been giving bombing targets.

So good was the coordination with the air force that he was able, after giving the new target, to report on the results of the bombing of his previous one. His messages were received by our radio station in San Gregorio, and retransmitted to our station at the Eighth Army where our liaison officer, Lieutenant Costello, then called up Headquarters Desert Air Force, who got on to their bombers.

I signaled Yunnie that we were on our way and would pick him up. I considered he had a two to one chance of remaining alive till that time.

At dawn we stopped on a mountain pass and looked once more on the Adriatic. We bought a basket of seventy-two eggs from an old woman and finished them off on the spot among the nine occupants of the three leading jeeps. For my share I sucked twelve.

At Chieti we entered no-man's-land: the Germans were on the run, and when we bedded down in a wood that night, sixty miles farther on, they were still two days ahead of us.

The next morning, outside a mountain town of the Abruzzi, we were met by strange creatures riding thunderous motor tricycles: they wore shiny black satin slacks and blouses, pink caps, and orange neckerchiefs, and suspended about their persons were hand grenades and daggers. They dashed about in a frenzy, yelling orders at one another, and did nothing—with hysterical earnestness: my first experience of "partisans of after the liberation." By a precipitous diversion, which hundreds of their more sober companions in ordinary peasants' clothes were digging out of the mountainside to by-pass a viaduct blown by the Germans, they led us to the town hall, where I found their head man. His name had been given me by my friends in A Force—he was a man who had helped many hundreds of our escaped POW's to rejoin our lines. A little, round man with an earnest countenance, he had appointed himself mayor and was furiously signing passes as I came in. He dropped his pen, came up and embraced me; he had obviously not slept for three days but his mind was clear. The Germans, he said, were somewhere beyond Sarnano, a town fifty miles ahead, and he gave me the name of a partisan friend of his who could help me. We drove out of the town through a dense crowd who did their best to induce us to stay with them and celebrate.

In Sarnano by four o'clock the crowd was even more

excited than usual as the Germans had left only the day
before. My partisan friend was not in town but at a small
village eight miles farther on on a side road. We pushed on
until I found him, dour-faced and hard-eyed: I didn't like
him much, but he seemed more businesslike than his
fancy-dress companions. He undertook to send men to
Tolentino, a town on the river Chienti fourteen miles
forward, to see if they could confirm the rumor that it had
been evacuated. Traveling in a cart they would be back by
ten o'clock that evening. Would we accept, all of us to
dine with the partisans in the village inn, while we waited
for his patrol to return?

We were all pretty well done in: I had pushed on since
early morning without stopping for a meal (for every hour
counted), and the excitement in all the towns we crossed
had been exhausting. I accepted the offer. On the evening
call we had news from Bob Yunnie. He was now five miles
inland, not more than twenty miles due east from us—as
the crow flies—and doing well. His area, still congested
with troops, was much harassed by our air force, which,
guided by his messages was doing useful damage. He
stated that the German rearguard was thirty-five miles to
the south (as we were level with Yunnie's position it
seemed that the withdrawal inland, where we were, had
been more rapid than on the coast). The intention of the
Germans, he said, was to make a stand on the river
Chienti, the one I intended to cross that night. If his
information was correct, I didn't have a chance.

The partisan dinner was slow in coming. At ten we had
not yet sat down and I got very impatient with the partisan
leader, who, very apologetic, remarked that, as his men
had not yet returned from Tolentino, nothing was lost.
When it was served the meal turned out to be worth
waiting for. Cameron, talkative for once, entertained us
with very funny stories.

The leader of the partisan recce party came in at last.
He had been right over the river into Tolentino with his
cart and had not seen a German till he had reached the
market square. He offered to guide us into Tolentino along
country roads, and would be ready as soon as he had had a
bite.

At midnight, with the partisan guide on the back of my
jeep, I led our column in the dark. As our forward troops
(along the way we had come) were still 150 miles behind

us, I thought that the Germans, lulled into a false security, had failed to organize their defense of the river. If we succeeded in crossing it, by the morning we would be deep in the enemy territory.

We were coming down the hills into the river valley about a mile and a half from the bridge, when a burst of automatic fire came from a farmhouse on the left, my side of the road. Some bullets hit the floor of the jeep between my legs and drew sparks: I wondered how they had got there without first going through me. I stopped the jeep to give Cameron, who was sitting on my right, a chance of answering the fire with his gun, and at the same time I turned round to warn the following trucks. Sergeant Mitchell, who was next to me, opened up, and Sergeant Beautyman, who drove the third truck, did the same. More bursts came from the farmhouse but the half-inch gun on my jeep didn't fire—surprised, I turned toward Cameron to see what stopped him, and found he wasn't there.

I walked round and found him lying on the road, wounded and unconscious, where he had slipped out of his seat. With Sergeant Riches, who had some understanding of first aid, I laid Cameron in the ditch, undid his clothing and began to dress his chest wound by the light of a torch; but he was far gone and after a few rattling gasps he gave a deep sigh and died in my arms. Meanwhile our men had stopped firing from their jeeps, and, led on foot by Beautyman, had entered the farmhouse and were apparently clearing it with their tommy guns. A moment later they reported two Germans killed and some others escaped.

We put Cameron on the back of my jeep (from where our guide had vanished). I sent for Corporal Taylor to be my gunner and we drove on. Less than a mile down the road we drew heavy fire from the bridge, and I turned back. The Chienti was guarded and my second attempt to cross the lines had failed.

We stopped outside a graveyard, where there was a plot of level ground, and bedded down. I stretched myself in my sleeping bag, Cameron alongside me, and woke up at dawn, holding his cold hand. I rose covered in white down from my bag, torn by bullets where it had lain in the back of my jeep. Twenty rounds or more had hit my car and apparently had traveled around me to go and hit Cameron on the far side. He had been killed by bullets meant for me, who had led him into the ambush. The kind wife of the gravedigger stitched up my kit, while her husband dug my friend's grave. He made me choose a plot, offering me the best of his lovely graveyard, on a slope looking onto soft hills. I strolled around, looking at the tombs; in the mortuary I saw a body laid out. Coming around once more to the gravedigger I found him making a wooden cross, and he asked me what inscription I wanted painted on it. Having written it out, I talked with him for a while, then said idly:

"You have, I see, another body waiting to be buried."

"It is my son, sir; he was with the partisans; the Germans killed him yesterday morning." He said no more; I fell silent, wondering at the humility of these people who took trouble with our dead and never mentioned their own so much more grievous loss.

I refused the offer to have a coffin made, for a soldier should be buried with no other covering than a blanket, in the bare earth on which he died. Thus we lowered Cameron in the grave, our men standing around and a detachment of the partisans. I read a short service and said:

"I want no other end than Jock has had: a quick death under the sky, with no fuss and no tears, among the friends with whom he had toiled for so long. Let us now carry on with our work." "Amen," said Sanders, and we filled the grave.

I sent Rickwood and Reeve-Walker separately with their patrols to reconnoiter fords across the Chienti, and I drove westward with "Blitz" to find a way over the five-thousand-foot range which ran north and south on our left. The partisans had tales of a band established in a mountain valley on the other side of this range, but they knew of no path leading to it; in this part of the Apennines there is still little travel between the valleys, where small communities live without contact with the world.

Toward evening I discovered a valley which seemed to afford a possible access to the ridge. It was too late, however, to press on and I returned to our camp. S Patrol with Reeve-Walker returned, having found several fords too strongly guarded to be attempted. Later R Patrol turned in; they had run into trouble and Rickwood had been shot through the body. Our rough knowledge of practical surgery was of no help in such a case: we covered him up, injected as much morphine as we dared, laid him on a stretcher, and drove him to the village doctor, who suggested, not hopefully, that we try the hospital in Sarnano. Unless he was operated on within two hours, he said, he was lost.

Morphine did not relieve his great pain: he grinned and joked when he could, but mostly his jaws were locked so as not to cry out. The hospital turned out to be a broken-down, one-man institution, run by a dejected surgeon-cum-G.P.-cum-obstetrician, with a diffident manner and a Sicilian accent. One of the three nuns who helped him to run the hospital combined the functions of anesthetist and operating-room assistant. I gave the doctor some ether and sulfanilamide, for he had no drugs. We had to wait three desperate hours while, judging by the noises I heard, the surgeon was attending a confinement. At last, in his spotted black coat, he came to fetch Richwood and wheeled him into the room himself. The operation lasted two hours—he had to open the abdomen from the navel to the pubis and patch up eighteen perforations of the intestines. When it was over he wouldn't say more than that in three days' time he might be able to judge if the patient had a chance of surviving. He seemed so unsure that I gave up all hope. He refused to take a fee but accepted the few drugs and rolls of bandages that I could spare and some tea for his patients. "There is so little a man in my position can do to help," he said, and added: "Don't worry, if the Germans come back while you are away they won't get him," and his dour face painfully cracked into a smile.

I left Rickwood (with Riches) in the care of the brooding old man, certain that I wouldn't see him again. And yet he recovered, and our surgeons, when eventually he came into their hands, said that the operation had been brilliantly performed. And—as in a tale—the dejected village doctor turned out to have been a well-known surgeon and a professor at Palermo University, until the Fascist government had exiled him to a mountain village.

The next day Sergeant Sanders, now in command of R Patrol, found a way across the range. Having climbed four thousand feet up rocky stream beds he was stopped, six hundred feet below the ridge, by a grass slope too steep for his heavy vehicles: he unloaded, dismounted the guns and, everyone pushing, succeeded in driving the empty jeeps in reverse to the top of the pass. They ferried up the loads on their backs.

Summoned by two of his men, who walked all the way down in the night, I joined him on the ridge the next morning with Blitz Patrol. On the far side we slithered down loose rock and terraces, that put a return journey out of the question, to the head of a secluded valley and an Alpine village of wooden chalets such as I had never seen in the Apennines. A track led us down the valley to a larger village; here we were stopped by a powerful, middle-aged man of a rugged countenance, armed with a German automatic rifle and wearing a German camouflaged jacket over his homely peasant clothes. He saluted, introduced himself as a detachment leader of the Brigata Sparsico, and said that his orders were to lead us to the brigade commander, Major Ferri. By the roadside six of his men stood in silence. Although their arms, clothing, and trappings—all taken from the enemy—did not match, there was about them an air of subdued soldierly alertness which I interpreted hopefully as a sign that the enemy was still with them, and active.

22

DECEPTION OF A DIVISION

MAJOR FERRI confirmed my hopes. His mountain valley ran northward ten miles to debouch through a narrow gorge into the valley of the Chienti. Down to the gorge was his secure domain, his little liberated kingdom —beyond it and across the Chienti German reserve troops were stationed with a divisional headquarters in a town six miles north of the river. They had built no defensive positions and it seemed that they had not realized that with their armies retreating along the coasts on both flanks, they, in the center, might soon find themselves in the front line.

I had got at last what I had been seeking: a mountain fastness opening into enemy territory, and (an unexpected blessing) I found myself also provided with a force to defend it, for Ferri and his brother Giuseppe, formerly professor of history at Pisa University, commanded three hundred men whom they had collected around a nucleus of refugees, escaped internees, and soldiers who had taken to the mountains after the Italian armistice nine months previously. The peasants of the valley fed them as a matter of course; from the Germans they had captured arms and ammunition and even two cars; some of the supplies dropped by No. 1 Special Force had also found their way into their hands; thus equipped, they had been raiding German road traffic and damaging bridges and railway lines, always at some distance from their valley.

The Germans knew there were "bandits" in the valley, and a few months previously had attempted to round them up. They had suffered heavy casualties forcing the gorge, and when they were finally let through and they drove up the valley, they found the villages empty, partisans and civilians having taken refuge in the forests. The Germans

301

burned several houses, looted the others, shot an old man
and his wife who had refused to go into hiding, and
withdrew. The inhabitants came down again, counted their
losses, painfully set their houses in order, and gave more
support than ever to the partisans, for such is the spirit of
the Italian peasants. Tenacious and long suffering, they
never blamed the partisans for the reprisals they brought
upon them—besides, many of their own youths had taken
arms with the bands.

Totally different from the hysterical popinjays in their
fancy clothes on the other side of the range, Ferri's men
lacked experience, to be sure, but they were fighters. Their
administration was adequate; the troops were fed regularly
and well; discipline, though quite informal, was such that
each man, having received orders, carried them out to the
best of his ability, but cadres were weak and the lower
formations too fluid for really efficient operations. Subor-
dinate commanders, instead of being in charge of units of
their own, were liable to receive an order such as, "Go up
to Fiastra, pick out ten men and take the bridge." Enthusiasm had to supply the lack of efficient teamwork. In his
planning, Ferri, in common with most partisan leaders in
those early days, made the mistake of overestimating the
possibilities of his troops. Engaging them in pitched battles, he had suffered heavy casualties with little compensat-
ing advantage, but at the time I met him he had already
realized the value of hit-and-run tactics and of small night
operations in which knowledge of the terrain and ability to
fade away and regroup elsewhere gave his men a marked
superiority over the more cumbersome regular troops of
the enemy. The majority of his men were recruited locally
and knew from childhood the ground on which they
operated.

I suggested to Ferri that joining forces we could,
between us, achieve great things. He agreed with enthusiasm: and that afternoon we drove together in a civilian car
down the valley, over the Chienti (at last) and reconnoitered the ground. Ferri's intelligence was well organized: he had several small detachments posted far out,
watching the Germans. We went around his posts, collected information, and when I returned after five hours'
driving I had in mind a fair picture of the situation over
one hundred square miles.

That evening I called for R and S Patrols and sent out

two signals: one to Jean Caneri to send up supplies for ourselves and bren guns, Stens and ammunition for Ferri; the other one to Yunnie in the Tenna Valley to join us as soon as he considered his job completed, for I had work for him. The rendezvous was at the foot of the range, from where we could ferry them across.

By crossing the range I had not only secured at last a base in enemy territory, but I had at the same time found on my doorstep an enemy I could worry. A weak German mountain division (without artillery) was stationed a few miles away in a small town, surrounded by fifteenth-century stone walls, rising on a knoll in the center of a cup-shaped circle of wooded hills. Under cover of the trees we could, without being seen, bring our guns within range of the city walls along nearly the whole of their circuit. To the rear, the Germans in the town were linked with the outer world by a single precipitous road over the mountains; to reach their troops on either flank they had only a road that followed the Chienti, a mountain torrent which here flows through narrow rocky gorges both up and down stream.

We mined these gorges and set partisans high up in the rocks. Having lost several vehicles and a few men, the Germans gave up the daily patrols they had been running along the river road and restricted themselves to the use of their line of communication in the rear. Then one night we

Sten Gun

switched over to this road and blew up the bridge over the river Potenza seven miles to the rear of the town. Deliberately we did no more damage to the bridge than could be repaired in a couple of days so as to give the impression that the demolition was the fumbling work of partisans— we wanted the Germans to get worried about their communications, but not to the extent of building a diversion, for if they took the trouble to dig approaches they could ford the river two hundred yards below the bridge.

The bridge was duly repaired and two nights later we ambushed and burned a ration convoy three miles from the town. To make the supply position more alarming, I set Ferri's men to harry the German foraging parties who went out daily into the countryside for cattle, pigs, and poultry. All the time I took care that none of my men should be seen by the Germans and that no weapons were used but such as could normally be in the hands of partisans. In my mind the knowledge of the presence of British troops should come to the Germans only as an unexpected and overwhelming blow, which would induce them to withdraw.

The day after the ambush we opened up with two radio sets, giving the call signs of several of our armored units. By the next night we had six sets each sending spurious messages at the rate of two or three an hour. The range of our sets, reduced by the high range, was too short to interfere with the real communications of the units we were impersonating, but we hoped that to the Germans it would seem as if all these Bristish tanks and armored cars had moved up the coast and had overrun their left flank.

Ferri was an exceptonally humane partisan leader. Although the best his men could expect was a swift death if they fell in German hands, he had captured a number of German prisoners and kept them in a cave up the mountainside. Most of these men were Austrians of an unwarlike disposition; being well fed and well treated they showed no inclination to escape. Among them, however, we discovered two NCO's, fanatical Nazis, who I hoped would serve my turn. The first one proved a failure: in spite of his high talk to his companions, he declined the opportunity of escaping to his own side when it was offered him.

The second fell into my trap in this manner: he was brought to me after dark to be interrogated in a room where I had set up a faked office (I preferred to have my real headquarters in the open). While we talked in English, two of our signalers came in and set about marking unit locations on a map on the wall, from a situation report they were supposed to have just received from the Eighth Army. When they had finished, the map showed our forward positions running from the coast to some distance inland along a line well in the rear of our friends in the town. The signalers went out and, as arranged, I was then called away, leaving the German alone in the room with the map, under a partisan guard.

I came back after ten minutes, and, being unable to get any information out of my pig-headed customer, I pretended to lose my temper and said that I would take him with me over the range the next day to our headquarters, where means would be found to make him talk. He was then marched out and locked in a room downstairs for the night. There he found he could slip through a small back window and he disappeared in the night. In the early morning the partisan guard on the Chienti bridge heard someone splash through the stream, and, in spite of heavy but deliberately erratic fire, scramble out on the far side and away through the woods.

While we were playing these games Yunnie and his four men were completing a much tougher work in the Tenna Valley. Behind hedges, under haystacks, lying in the standing corn, in the midst of the retreating German Army, he had missed little of what was going on on the two roads that crossed the Tenna. The enemy, fearful of our aircraft, lay up during the day; but however carefully they camouflaged their positions, our planes, guided by Yunnie's messages, always seemed to know where to drop their bombs and which woods they should spray with gun fire. When our troops got nearer he concentrated on saving the bridges. When the German sappers had laid their charges, he opened up on them and with the help of a handful of halfhearted local partisans, whom he had somehow goaded into action, chased them away before they had set their fuses, and held the bridge till the first Polish armored cars rumbled over. He then packed himself and his men into a captured German car and joined me where I was waiting for him at the foot of the range. I don't suppose I said a word of praise, for such was not our way, but when I saw his bony frame and his thin, dirty, weather-beaten face tumbling out of the car, and Owen, Sloane, O'Neal, and Gino following, I felt a relief and a pride that I should have been embarrassed to express. I believe I said something like: "Come in, you bloody ghosts, and have a drink," and we walked silently into the village *trattoria*.

We got more talkative after dinner: of all their achievements the one that struck them as being most worth recounting was how they had induced a German sergeant not only to exchange their exhausted radio batteries for fresh ones, but also to carry them to their hide-out where they then held him prisoner. Fooling the enemy was a legitimate subject of boasting—of danger and fighting little was said, or indeed, I believe, remembered.

I gave them one night's rest and then we crossed the range together: the prospect of being once more with their friends and of fighting in jeeps, in the proper manner, instead of hiding in ditches, was enough to dispel their weariness. Sergeant Curtis, however, who had come over with me to greet his leader, unexpectedly showed signs of strain. As we were nearing the top of the range he called my attention to a suspicious-looking vehicle on a hilltop two thousand feet below us. I pointed my glasses:

"Looks to me like a hay cart," I said.

"I thought it might be a German armored car."

I looked again. "More like a hay cart. Even if it is an armored car, there is nothing we can do about it. Let us push on."

A moment later he stopped again, with a queer look in his eye.

"I think it is an armored car. Hadn't we better get off the skyline?"

In my mind an alarm bell rang: Curtis was cracking. This strange disease overtook the strongest of us. Waterson, Locke, had gone under. I told Yunnie I would give his sergeant a period of change, looking after our supply line—he would have to replace him; Riches was the man we had had in mind for such an eventuality. A fortnight later Curtis thanked me and asked to be posted back to a patrol; I appointed him to my own Blitz and found him once more cool and solid. I wondered if it would also happen to me.

I gave the German commander twenty-four hours to digest the news brought by the returned prisoner, while we kept up our fancy signaling and jammed his own messages; then the next morning I staged my show.

During the preceding days, with the help of over two hundred peasants to fell trees and cut the undergrowth, we had cleared tracks through the woods surrounding the town. Along these tracks we now drove our jeeps divided into two patrols, and, having stationed them half a mile apart in camouflaged positions from which, quite invisible, they had a view of the city walls, we opened up toward the town with every gun we had. Through our glasses we could see tracer bouncing off the walls and shattering tiles on the housetops, a sensless performance which set a few roofs on fire but otherwise could do no damage.

Ten minutes later we rushed one patrol over to another position, from which it again opened up; later we moved the other, and repeated these antics throughout the day—with intervals to saved ammunition—until we had fired at the town from every angle and from many different positions. I intended that the German commander, seeing fire come from woods which in his mind were inaccessible to vehicles, should assume that the weapons were fired by infantry. With this notion in his head he would naturally assume that the several positions from which we opened up were occupied by us simultaneously—as no man can run a mile in five minutes carrying a heavy gun. Finally multiplying the number of guns firing from each point by the number of these points, he would, I hoped, inevitably come to the conclusion that, being encircled by the troops of two infantry brigades or more, the best course of action for him to take was to get out before he was destroyed. On the other hand, there was the possibility that he might think that an enemy who wasted his time—and his ammunition—firing his machine guns at stone walls the whole day long was too foolish to bother about. Mortars would have been more sensible weapons for us to use in this case than guns, but we had lost all ours in the L.C.T.

Until an hour before sunset we drew no response whatever from the town. During the morning we had seen soldiers moving in a street, but from noon onward not a soul. The place might have been evacuated, but I couldn't think how the Germans could have slipped away without being seen as we had an observation post covering their main road of retreat.

I lined up my ten jeeps on the main road and led them toward the town, determined to draw fire, and to give an extra headache to the German general by showing him that, in addition to the infantry troops crowding the woods, vehicles had now been brought against him in some inexplicable manner.

The road came out of the woods, dipped into the open fields, and wound its way among low hills, alternately discovering and masking the southern gate of the town, now considerably above us. I thought how embarrassing it would be for me if I drove right in to the town square and found the German general waiting to surrender. How could I bluff him to believe that, apart from the twenty-five men on my jeeps, I had a few thousand in the woods?

I had nearly reached the foot of the ramp leading up to the gate, when a black mushroom of smoke and dirt sprang up in a field to the left of the road ahead of me, then some more on the other side and behind me. Taylor, from his seat next to me, leveled his gun and fired at where he thought the enemy mortars were. I stopped by the side of the road: the other jeeps, staggered behind me, all opened up. After a while the mortars got our range and plastered us pretty freely. In a moment our position became so alarming—at any instant I expected a direct hit on one of my jeeps—that I decided to pull out. Weaving between the bursts I drove back to the tail of the column, signaling each jeep to turn back as I drove by. Then I stopped and when the jeeps came up to me in their original order, firing back as they went, I waved them on, for instead of leading the column I wanted now to take the rear position and try the smoke generators I carried at the back of my jeep—a new gadget we had not used yet in action. Yunnie, coming up last in his jeep, misunderstood my intention and waited for me to take the lead of the column. Two mortar bombs bracketed his jeep and hid him from my view; slowly the cloud dispersed: he was still alive and grinning, his face plastered with black mud. Above the din I shouted:

"Carry on, I want to lay smoke." He made a gesture of incomprehension. Taylor shouted: "Smoke," and put his hand to his mouth as if smoking a cigarette. Yunnie pulled his long legs out of his jeep and walked over: another burst hid him—then he was by my side, offering me a cigarette!

Off we drove, the column ahead of me, the nine jeeps still all going. I pressed down a switch on the dashboard: with a fizzling noise a cloud of white smoke rose behind me, spread and filled the narrow valley, like a curtain drawn up, hiding the town. The mortars stopped dead, the men feeding them must have thought that a happy hit had blown us all up.

Nobody was hurt, although there were a few dents in the jeeps. We stopped in the woods and waited for our observation post to come up on the radio. Just after dark it reported a short column of trucks heading north from the town, and, later, marching troops: the German general's mind had functioned as I intended and he had fallen into my trap.

I instructed Ferri to take his men into the town as soon as the Germans were out and round up stragglers, but to avoid street fighting which would be to no purpose. Then we took two partisans each on the back of our jeeps and drove slowly along a mountain track which joined on to the main road halfway between the town and the bridge over the Potenza. We had time to spare: I had no intention of taking on the whole of the German division with my twenty-five men. We dropped the partisans, who trotted off in the dark toward the bridge, under which we had laid charges with an electric detonator and a very long cable, and we waited off the road while the German troops marched by, their kit, carried in bullock carts, following behind.

There was a long gap in the convoy; then, as our observation post had announced, came a last column of staff cars and troop-carrying trucks, presumably headquarters with the rearguard. We tailed onto them and when the road, with the mountainside on the right and overhanging a ravine on the left, took a long bend out of sight, we opened up. There was some confusion and for a while we had it our own way as the troops at the head of the column were quite a long time before they realized their tail had come to grief. Eventually we broke off and the remnant of the column put on speed, with us in pursuit.

When we judged we were a mile from the river we fired a prearranged signal, two red and two green Very lights;

the partisans pressed the plunger and the bridge went up
with a bang. The Germans abandoned their trucks and
bullock carts, and splashed across the Potenza in good
order on foot. Although we fired at them from higher
ground and with weapons heavier than theirs, they never
broke, but organized a rearguard which kept us at a
distance till the last survivors had crossed the river.

We had no casualties, the partisans lost two men, the
Germans about a hundred, most of their precious vehicles and nearly all their equipment, which fell as booty to
the partisans. Civilians reported that the German general
had been found among the dead, but I didn't see the body
myself. We kept his staff car, bullet-ridden but still in
running order, as a souvenir.

The bullocks were driven back to their former owners,
the trucks that had not been burned were driven off and
hidden in the woods, the dead were buried. By noon the
next day the road and the river bank were tidied up.

I drove my party back to the town, for I didn't care to
sleep close to the enemy with the partisans too excited to
give us protection, and also because we were nearly out of
ammunition. At dawn I sent Reeve-Walker, the South
African, with S Patrol to recruit labor and dig approaches
to the ford below the blown bridge. He got about one
hundred men, but being much pestered by German snipers
he could not complete the work much before dark.

I stayed the day in town to lay the basis of a civilian
administration. I appointed Giuseppe Ferri, the university
professor, civilian governor, with his brother, the major,
under him to command the troops. Neither they nor their
men were coming on with us: they had liberated their
district and as far as active fighting was concerned the war
was over for them. I did not press them, for I thought they
had done enough, and I wanted them to keep the town tidy
and enforce law and order till our military government
took over. At noon the civilian governor had a problem
for me: he had, he told me, about a dozen of Mussolini's
Republican Fascists locked up in the town hall. What was
he to do with them: shoot them or keep them to be handed
over to our authorities? Knowing too well the tenderness
of certain A.M.G. officers for former Fascists, I replied:

"When I leave tonight I shall have forgotten about your
Fascist prisoners. Till our military government officers

Sniper Rifle

arrive you are the master and you do what you think best."
It would save trouble and bitterness for the future if these
men got killed in the confusion of liberation. And if two or
three innocents perished with them, by mistake or as a
result of private feuds, well, war is wasteful of lives and
many good men are killed in it every day.

Similar situations often occurred, and whenever I had at
hand a sensible fighting partisan leader I made it my policy
to leave matters to his discretion: if I could have guessed
then what situation would develop in Italy after the
liberation and in the following years, I might have been
much more explicit in my suggestions.

That evening we had a dinner party with two hundred
guests in the town hall, followed by speeches. I did my
stuff and went to work again with Ferri in the mayor's
office. The town was my prize and I wanted to give it a

good send-off; in a way it was to give these poor people a
fresh start that I was fighting the Fascists and Nazis who
preyed on them.

Ferri alone could not do all the work: his small band of
municipal servants could not help him much in this emergency. I suggested that we set up a committee of citizens.
Ferri thought they might be elected—he was a student of
political economy and a great admirer of the British
Constitution.

I said: "You wouldn't have to hold proper elections.
This is what we shall do: we shall select the members
together tonight. Then I shall nominate them according to
the authority I hold from the Allied commander-in-chief,
and as I shall leave tomorrow morning, nobody can undo
it till A.M.G. arrives and you all go home anyway."

We made out a list of possibles and called them for interview: we got a young doctor, the dean of the university, three shopkeepers, three farmers, a schoolmaster, a
priest, the widow of the man who had run the local bus
service and who had been shot by the Germans, and five
partisans, including of course Major Ferri as "head of the
police." Representatives of the local gentry also came; they
asked for improbable favors, such as to be given a car to
take them to Rome, murmured names of duchesses and
princesses, but refused to volunteer to do any work and
then, illogically, left in a huff because they were not
selected.

At five in the morning I swore in the new councilors and
dismissed everyone. I was tired: these people talked so
much. I embraced Ferri, had a cold bath and drove away
with my men to the ford over the Potenza.

Out on the mountain road, quickened by a cool and
lovely dawn, I reverted in my mind with pleasure from
politics to considerations of war. Turning over the things
we had done since we had first crossed the range, I
realized that there was an inescapable lesson to be drawn
from our success: it was that operations *behind* the enemy
lines, which had been for two years my main concern, had,
for the present, become obsolete. No doubt, if I pursued
my old plan and penetrated deeply into enemy territory, as
I believed I could now do, I might enjoy an easy time in
areas of relative tranquillity, and at the same time earn for
myself and my men (from the uninformed) an undeserved

reputation for spectacular daring. But I would be wasting
my opportunities and shirking my duties, which, as I saw
them, lay in remaining *in* the disrupted German front line
to harass and hound the enemy: a policy both arduous and
unspectacular, accompanied by many risks, but the only
one likely to bring in dividends in the shape of military
advantages. During the short drive to the ford I scrapped
all my previous arrangements and made new plans for
immediate action.

Two German snipers, who on the previous day had
inflicted several casualties on Reeve-Walker's working party, were still hiding in the willows on the far bank: they
fired at us with their rifles as we approached the ford,
delaying us for a while. The determination of these men
was a demonstration to us of what could be achieved
by small means cunningly used. Under a different uniform,
we would have been glad to count them in our party.
When, chased off by our overwhelming fire power, they
took to the open, we let them escape.

Towed by bullocks, our sodden jeeps, the water rippling
over the hoods, made the far bank of the Potenza. Here we
separated: I sent Yunnie with B Patrol to the northwest, S
and R Patrols to the east; with Blitz Patrol I followed the
second party later in the day, with the supplies we had
accumulated carried in captured German transport.

My instructions were that they should operate in the
high mountains, fifteen miles on each side of the watershed
of the Apennines. Along this front, roughly equal to
one-quarter of the width of Italy from sea to sea, and
working to a depth of twenty to thirty miles into enemy
territory, they were to seek out the Germans and harass
them in every manner local circumstances and their own
ingenuity would suggest. My intention was to compel the
enemy to withdraw more rapidly in the center than on
either flank. I expected that his main forces in the coastal
sectors, feeling their inland flank uncovered, might open
their minds to suggestions of withdrawal (to keep in step
with their light troops in the mountain) and offer a less
stubborn resistance to our Eighth and Fifth Armies. We
were the only Allied troops in the central mountains; on
either flank we were supported by armored-car regiments
with whom we made occasional contacts. For the next few
months, let loose among the enemy in the mountains, we

carried out, on the whole successfully, this plan conceived on my morning ride to the ford.

Our men were happier than at any time since we had left the desert. Engaging the enemy day after day was more on the scale of their understanding than long-range raids during which they were little more than bodyguards to their leader. Constant fighting called for individual action, and their personal success could be measured unmistakably by the number of villages they liberated. They developed an enthusiasm for their work, a sense of personal achievement and an attachment to their friends in the patrol which they had never known before in their lives. Every day each one had to use his ingenuity to discover means of worrying the enemy. If they ran into danger, their companions helped them out of trouble; and, the day's work over, they rejoiced together over their narrow escapes, their stratagems and the discomfiture of the enemy: for they proved more than a match for the bewildered Germans. In seventy-eight days, although our numbers never exceeded fifty at any one time, P.P.A. cleared sixteen hundred square miles of mountains, enticed several thousand Germans sixty miles back, killed over three hundred, and yet lost ourselves but one man killed, and three wounded who recovered and rejoined the unit.

As there were in this area few organized partisans, our first task was to provide our own intelligence. Four or five days afer crossing the Potenza, B Patrol had pushed on fifteen miles to the neighborhood of Fabriano, and the remainder of the unit was in the mountains southwest of Cingoli. We found that the enemy controlled with a Jaeger Division the four main roads, had a strong garrison with artillery in Fabriano and kept detached posts in isolated villages. The forested mountainside was ours: the ranges rose to four thousand feet, with peaks over five thousand, and were not everywhere so steep that with infinite labor we could not drive our jeeps over them. The mountain villages were often linked by extremely rough and narrow tracks used by the villagers for their bullock-drawn sledges, and running at improbable angles up the slopes and through the forests. His jeeps crawling along such tracks, Bob Yunnie reached a village which he used as his headquarters for a while. From there he undertook to chase the Germans out of a town in the valley below, between him and the front line. To shake their nerves he marched his men under cover to fire Very lights from many positions, simulating preparations for a night attack. At dawn, when he expected them to have relaxed after the anxieties of the dark, he engaged them with his jeeps, rushing from one position to another to give the impression of a large force; finally in the twilight he charged up the main street with three jeeps and set the enemy on the run.

The same day he appeared in another valley over a mountain range and raided a village; the following night he captured a mortar post outside yet another village. This deception work gave his men hardly a chance to rest. When they were not fighting they were hauling their vehicles over mountain ranges. The success of these schemes was based on striking at places far apart in such quick succession that to the puzzled German commander, reading the reports from his several posts, it seemed that they had all been attacked simultaneously. Three days went by, and the Germans, thinking that their positions had been penetrated by overwhelming enemy forces, called in their outposts and withdrew altogether from these valleys.

The following day Yunnie had one of his hunches, that his position was no longer secure. He suddenly took his patrol right over the ridge of the Apennines in the most difficult climb ever made by our jeeps, and descended on the other side on a small town called Gualdo Tadino, surprised and beat away a large party of foraging Germans, and, establishing himself in the neighborhood, started operations in virgin country. Four days later, Gino, who, sick with malaria, had had to be left behind in the original village, joined them by a devious route, in civilian clothes, driving a bullock cart in which he carried some gasoline jettisoned before the climb. He brought the news that after the patrol's departure the enemy had turned up a battalion strong, and made directly for a ruined monastery, Yunnie's former headquarters (informed no doubt by some Fascist). Disappointed, they had turned on to the village and captured and shot a small group of partisans who had befriended our men. Gino had escaped disguised as the village idiot. A few days later B Patrol recrossed the Apennines by another route—they preferred that the same

tracks should never be used twice—surprised and destroyed a battalion headquarters, then pushed a reconnaissance to within sight of Fabriano, which they found too
strongly held to be attempted before the Germans' will to
resist had been further softened.

Yunnie crossed the Apennines once more—three days
of hard work this time, rolling boulders and cutting tracks.
Traveling along the hillside, one jeep, a rock giving way
under its offside wheels, turned over sideways and rolled
down the mountain till fortunately stopped by a tree. The
gunner, Stewart, was thrown clear; the driver, O'Neil,
pinned underneath, was recovered with a broken back.
The jeep, its frame warped, was still in running order but
too weak to be used on patrol work. They tied O'Neil to a
plank, and, while the two jeeps remaining in the patrol
pushed on, the third one drove him back along the road,
through a German post and twenty miles back to where
they knew of a position held by the Twelfth Lancers, who
took charge of the casualty. Three months later he was
back with us, weak but indomitable. I appointed him
armorer, for he was not fit to go into action.

Fortunately, I succeeded in getting through to Yunnie
three new jeeps manned by members from his patrol and
two recruits.

Meanwhile the two other patrols operated together farther east. Sometimes driving, at times on foot, we pushed
our way up toward Cingoli. S Patrol, the latest born of
our patrols, was taking shape under the leadership of
Reeve-Walker. The partisans here were divided into rival
bands, with no strong leaders. They had a few Jugoslav
members who did all the work while the others sat back
and quarreled. As a result we had to do much slow
reconnaissance ourselves. We decided to capture some
prisoners for information from a small village in which the
local peasants reported a German post. Reeve-Walker with
O'Leary and Hodgson of his patrol, Sanders, the New
Zealander, and Porter of R Patrol, set out on foot about
ten in the morning. They worked their way into woods
above the village, where Reeve-Walker, rather rashly, told
them to wait while he went to reconnoiter. Later they
heard some firing, and fearing their short South African
leader had run into trouble, walked into the village. The
time was noon on a very hot July day, the streets were

empty, the inhabitants in hiding and the Germans at their meals in the coolness of the houses. They looked into several houses and finally walked into the signalers' office where three Germans were lunching. Our men held them up and made them walk away with them, carrying their radio sets.

Halfway down the street, fun started: shot at from above, they fired back and started running along the sun-scorched street. One of the Germans was hit and fell; our men, with their two remaining prisoners, darted down an alley, out of the village into a dry stream bed where they lay low till the hue and cry died down. Sending Hodgson on with the prisoners, Sanders, Porter, and O'Leary walked back into the village in search of Reeve-Walker. The dead German had been removed, but they picked up his set, and having got engaged in a second street fight, gave up their search and returned.

Sitting with the jeeps half a mile away, we had fired a few bursts of intimidation in the direction of the village when we heard the rumpus. Then, quiet falling, we had waited a long time. Finally Hodgson and his two prisoners arrived; half an hour later Sanders, Porter and O'Leary, sweating under their load of radio sets, reported their failure to find Reeve-Walker. We were getting together a relief party when he too appeared down a dry watercourse, kicking a stone and whistling to himself. He had waited to see the Germans pack up and leave the village.

The prisoners, interrogated while they were still flustered, talked willingly, and, being signalers, knew the location of the German units in and around Cingoli. With this useful information we succeeded a few days later in pushing the enemy out of another village just short of Cingoli, but the town itself we found too hard a nut to crack and gave it up for the time being.

From the reports of Yunnie, I judged that the time was ripe to make an attempt against Fabriano, and accordingly I joined him with all my men at Gualdo Tadino.

Harrying the enemy daily, Yunnie had pushed them back ten miles along the road leading north from Gualdo Tadino, and had thus cleared the way to the entrance of a railway tunnel which, passing under the ridge of the Apennines, joined our valley with that of Fabriano. The road which passed over the mountain had been blown by

the Germans and could not be made practicable without
considerable work. In the tunnel seven railway cars had
been crashed together and then blown up, bringing down
part of the roof.

The Germans in Fabriano thought themselves secure
from that quarter and concentrated their defenses in other
directions. They had some field artillery as we found out
when, to confuse them, we staged diversionary attacks
from the north and the east. I recruited local labor and
cleared the tunnel: we had discovered an oxy-acetylene
torch and a few cylinders of gas in a workshop in a small
town called Nocera Umbra, which enabled us to cut up
the tangled remains of the trucks in the tunnel.

While we were thus getting ready, Yunnie switched over
his activities to Gubbio, fifteen miles to the northwest, and
harassed the Germans there, crossing the mountains every
day by a different track, his object being to deceive the
enemy into believing that he had lost interest in Fabriano.
Meanwhile I had observers in the town, in particular a
partisan called Gigi Cardona, a former regular officer in
the Italian Army, whom Yunnie had recruited earlier and
who had become a brilliant member of his patrol.

One night, when I judged by his reports that the time
had come, I sent S and R Patrols through the cleared
tunnel: before dawn Reeve-Walker had ten jeeps in the
main square and had set fire to German headquarters; by
midday the town was ours, and by the next morning all
German troops lying south of Fabriano had been withdrawn, leaving the way clear for our orthodox troops to
come up and take over the town from us.

Two days later the Household Cavalry, an armored
regiment freshly arrived from home and, I believe, in
action for the first time, made its way cautiously up the
road. Either our intelligence reports had not reached them
from the Eighth Army, or they had disbelieved them.
Coming within artillery range of Fabriano they sited their
field guns and opened up. Reeve-Walker in the town,
finding himself under fire from our own troops, drove out
to regimental headquarters and demanded to talk with the
commanding officer. An angry interview developed between our cocky little South African and a supercilious
colonel of the Household Cavalry, who found it hard to
accept the claim of a scrubby, unshaven ragamuffin of a

lieutenant to have liberated with twenty-two men a town which he was planning to reduce according to the rules with an armored regiment. At one stage Reeve-Walker came very near to being put under arrest, but eventually the South African made his point and led a patrol of armored cars into Fabriano.

During these operations we were much dispersed. Scarcely a day passed without an engagement of which no more than the result was reported to me on the radio. When we came together, like all soldiers, we talked of the fun we had had, the girls, the food and the wine, but very seldom of fighting: thus I have no knowledge, or only at second hand, of scores of actions in which our men were engaged.

What made their life bearable was that engagements were short and they could pull out to comparative safety, and the comfort of peasant hospitality. Thus the tension was broken, and although for three months they were not one day out of danger they showed little signs of strain. The successful soldier forgets unpleasant experiences very quickly; if he doesn't he is not a successful soldier: he finds his way to a hospital as a psychiatrist's case. Brave men experience fear—only morons are never afraid—but they forget it, forget it again and again.

Breaking a long spell of administrative duties, Jean Caneri took over command of P.P.A. when I went to the hospital for some weeks.

Bringing fresh ideas to the game, he led his patrol at a furious pace and extended the activities of P.P.A. over a wider territory than we had ever covered. By some accident he never even got a wound.

We pursued our games till the Germans retired behind a line of prepared positions stretching from Pesaro on the Adriatic to Pisa on the Mediterranean (which we called the Gothic Line). We then pulled out and drove to a castle near Perugia, whence Caneri had transferred our base. We stayed there a few days to refit.

As I thought that the Eighth Army would shortly break through the Gothic Line, I wanted to have our patrols equipped with fresh jeeps and ready for the final chase across the Po plain up to the Alps. This done we would, I thought, transfer ourselves to another theater: I wrote to friends I had on the planning staff, asking them to include

P.P.A. amongst the groups to be sent out to the Far East.

Curtis had been sergeant in my H.Q. Patrol ever since I took him out of Yunnie's patrol, when he had given signs of battle weariness. Recovered very rapidly, he had been indefatigable with me ever since. He had to serve the other patrols—repair and replace the jeeps and the radio sets, supply them with ammunition and with gasoline, and at the same time fight our own battles. He was at that period the busiest man in the unit and the most exposed. He stepped on a mine while clearing a ford, lost a foot, and died in a hospital a few days later. He was a quiet little man with an irrepressible cheerfulness, and the most entertaining manner of turning his narrow escapes into funny stories. One of the pillars of P.P.A., he could not be replaced.

Sam Taylor was not happy with me as my gunner, although I liked him and trusted him. Perhaps, taking over from Cameron, he felt his position difficult, as between Cameron and myself there had been a deep friendship; more probably Taylor didn't like me and preferred to be with his own friends in his original patrol. I made him sergeant in R Patrol when Sanders left us to go back to New Zealand, and I chose for my companion an untried newcomer called Charles Burrows, a butcher from Plymouth, a plain and rather shy lad of twenty-three. Yunnie had rejected him from his patrol but I fancied there were signs of valor in him and gave him a try. I did well for myself with this choice, for a little more than two months later he brought me out of a scrap in which, but for his steadfastness, I myself, along with thirty other men, would undoubtedly have perished.

Reeve-Walker left us about this time and I appointed John Campbell to command S Patrol in his stead.

Sergeant Beautyman's turn came to go home under the "Python" scheme. At first he was disposed to let another go in his stead, then he changed his mind and asked to be released. He had not been on home leave for over five years, and yet I was surprised that he should wish to go, for I had cut my ties so completely that I had no life of my own outside the army. However, we were always ready with a substitute for any of us who might fall out: Brooks took command of the signal section, and, sorrowfully, I let

Beautyman go. He went home, got married to a girl he had known all his life, served for a while in England, didn't like it, and wangled his way back to P.P.A. six months later.

23

CLOAK AND DAGGER

THE Eighth Army forced the Gothic Line and reached Rimini, the gateway to the plain.

We waited, poised for the chase—then after three days we knew there would be no chase.

Intersected by a network of rivers and drainage canals, deeply set between banks sometimes fifty feet high, the Po plain was even less suitable for a pursuit than the mountainous country we had left behind. The map had told us this all the time, but we had hoped that the enemy would lose heart after the breach of the Gothic Line and run for the Alps. He didn't. He blew the bridges and held us up every few miles behind a canal bank. Our air force destroyed all the bridges over the Po; at night the Germans swung pontoon bridges across the river and drove bullock carts laden with supplies over to their troops farther south.

It was a cruel anticlimax to the hopes of every man in the Eighth Army: wondering if the war would be settled in Germany (where our troops were nearing the Rhine) before they even reached the Po, they applied themselves once more to pushing the enemy back from one river to the next.

I told my men that the pursuit was off, and went in search of a new role for P.P.A.

On November 1, 1944, I crossed the Savio River on a Bailey bridge just put up by the sappers, and from the high bank looked northward on to a desolate landscape. Rain had been falling for some days; the river in spate rushing through a breach in its bank had flooded the flat countryside as far as the next canal, its banks just visible through the mist. A few farmsteads stood out, in water up to the window sills. Bob Yunnie and five of his men walked away along the submerged road, up to their waists in the turbid

flood, looking rather unheroic. When they reported back
four hours later, we lifted each of our jeeps into a Duck
and drove the amphibious trucks down on to the water. By
nightfall we were settled on the dry edge of a pine forest
stretching from the main road three miles to a sandy sea
coast.

Some partisans were camped in the wood; they told us
that the next canal, one mile to the north, was held by
German troops. We pushed the jeeps a hundred yards
distance from a keeper's lodge which served the partisans
as a headquarters, and, taking turns on guard duty, settled
down to an uneasy night's rest under the rain amid the
creaking trees. The Ducks were sent back to Savio.

DUKW

The partisan leader asked me to join him at supper in
the lodge. He had in two rooms some thirty men and three
girls. The rest of his detachment, eighty-odd, were out on
duty. Wearing the red scarves of the Garibaldi Brigade
over their civilian clothes, armed with German weapons,
they looked wild but their speech was low and their
manners subdued, for they were weary. They had fought
the Germans continuously for the last four months in the
flat country around Ravenna and finally, being overrun,
their detachment was separated from its brigade and left
in no-man's-land, where we had now joined them. I had
for some time been in radio contact with their brigade

commander, who went by the name of Bulow (a battle
name derived from the word for bull in Romagnolo
dialect), and I had on three occasions put out to sea in an
Italian motor launch to visit him in the marshes north of
Ravenna, and been forced back by the weather every
time.

The leader of the detachment was a burly stonemason
of thirty-four years of age called Ateo, Atheist. The name
was not a battle disguise but his own by right, for he had
been thus named at birth as a token of his father's
anticlericalism. His speech was rough and mixed with no
little of harsh Romagnolo dialect in which, when I got to
understand it, I found he expressed himself with a richness
of homely imagery.

After the Italian Armistice, the Romagnoli, trained to
administer their own affairs in the co-operatives, and helped
by the sound organization and the strong discipline of the
Communist Party, soon ran the most efficient partisan
formation in Italy.

Ateo was a Communist and so were the majority of his
men—but by no means all. The officers were elected by
their men: the appointment had to be confirmed by higher
authority, who held also the power to dismiss. A political
commissar in each detachment was responsible for the
morale of his unit and instructed it in political doctrine,
and also took his share of the normal duties of a fighting
officer.

I knew nothing of the things I have just related at the
time I first met the detachment; considering them with a
professional eye I soon perceived that they were good
soldiers and of a quality quite new to me in my experience
of partisans. I decided to take them under my command
and make them fight alongside my own seasoned warriors.

My first favorable impression came in this way: I
obtained for them British weapons, clothing and equipment and asked Ateo what in his opinion would be the best
way to issue these to the men so as to avoid waste. His
answer was that his quartermaster, a medical student
called Camerani, would take charge and I could rest
assured that there would be no wild scramble such as I had
witnessed with other partisans in other places. And so it
turned out: Camerani locked his new stores in a room of
the lodge and entered them in his books. When he had
done, he issued each man with his needs and no more; he

had a nominal list of deficiencies and asking for additional items was a waste of time. Ida, our leading girl, having been fitted with a battle dress, wanted also an automatic; when she couldn't get one—indeed Camerani had none to issue—I am sorry to say she swiped one from John Campbell, but returned it when she was made to understand that the young captain could be court-martialed for losing his pistol. Ida, in spite of her love of weapons, was not supposed to take a hand in the fighting; she was our chief spy and messenger. Tough but comely in her usual appearance, she dressed up for her errands as a dirty and repulsive old woman; no German soldier ever looked at her when she shuffled past him carrying a bundle of sticks. She was then indeed, to all practical purposes, invisible.

The two other girls cooked and washed for the detachment and occasionally took their turn on guard duty. They were nice, simple, hard-working peasant girls, who never thought they had done anything out of the way in joining the partisans; the same applied to the men, who were remarkably free from heroics. Camerani was the only intellectual in the detachment: Taschiero, Guberti and Rafuzzi, the three company commanders, and Dario Gradi, the political commissar, were stonemasons or mechanics, the rest also stonemasons or agricultural laborers. In born within fifteen miles of Ravenna in peasant homes. In the fertile Romagna plain every foot of land is cultivated: apart from the strips of pine forest and marsh along the coast, it provides no hide-outs, and partisan fighting had perforce been interwoven with the lives of the peasants. Their troops came out at night from the farms to raid traffic, dumps, and German headquarters, and relied on their fathers, their mothers, and all their elderly relations to give them refuge again until their next operation, so that there was actually no real distinction between fighters and civilians. Arms and ammunition were concealed under haystacks and in barns; when the Germans went out foraging for food the farmers' wives, who were compelled to entertain them, kept a serene face, for if they aroused the suspicions of their guests there would be no escape from the shooting party. By the time we arrived, however, the German withdrawal had filled the land with troops and pushed the partisans into the coastal strips, giving a precarious ease to the farmers.

To test my partisans I gave them the most unpalatable task of all: guarding us and our jeeps while we slept at night. They acquitted themselves of their duty so conscientiously that I decided that it would be safe to trust them further, and soon I had them attached in groups to each of our patrols. I tried to give them a defensive role, not because they lacked aggressive qualities, but I had scruples about exposing them in such actions as might cause them to be captured by the enemy: the difference in the treatment by the Germans of British and partisan prisoners-of-war was never out of my mind.

The equanimity with which the Italians exposed themselves to the risk of an ignominious end by torture, which *we* would have been reluctant to accept, showed how much more passionate than ours was their determination to fight. They had emotional motives with their roots in hatred and revenge, fundamental human impulses which played but a small part in our lives; they fought in their own villages for their own homes, which had been ravished not only by a foreign enemy but by some of their own traitorous people, Mussolini's Fascist republicans, whom, as is natural, they held in extreme contempt. Lastly they were animated by a passionate desire to redress social injustice and establish a new rule in their own country, when freed at last of its hated tyrants.

Although they took care not to let themselves be diverted from the task of beating the Germans, their fight was fundamentally a civil war. We, on the other hand, had been away from our country for several years, fighting in strange lands, and though our families had also suffered from the violence of the enemy, it was through the anonymity of bombing aircraft, and not the personal assault of a ruffianly soldiery. Such are human feelings that the loss of relatives crushed to death under a crumbling house is easier to bear than the knowledge that an insolent *feldwebel* has laid his dirty hands on their bodies and dragged them to a cold-blooded execution. We saw this strange discrimination in the behavior of the Italians themselves, who accepted resignedly, as an act of fate, the terrible losses inflicted by our bombing but shook with rage at the forcing of their homes by marauding Germans.

In spite of all this it must not be thought that the partisans behaved as bloodthirsty fanatics: cheerful and good-humored, they were soon adopted by our men as friendly companions. Each one of our patrols came to be affectionately proud of their own Italians and boasted of their high deeds and of their tricks. The partisans, on their side, ceased to feel that we were a superior kind of people and joked and fooled about with their English comrades in the perfect equality of soldiers fighting together the same battle.

Rain-drenched and half-flooded, the Pineta di Classe (a pine forest of Byronic fame) and the sand dunes on the coast were our battleground.

We had a good time in our forest. With good cover and ferrying our jeeps over the floods into unexpected positions, we soon had the Germans puzzled and nervous. We pushed them out of the positions they had occupied when we first arrived, and as soon as we were comfortably established halfway up the forest, we undertook to out-flank them by landings on the coast. To do this we loaded our jeeps in Ducks—one of which was fitted with a crane for this purpose—and sailed them at night from a beach in our rear. When the distance was too great to be covered by the slow-sailing Ducks, whose speed in the water was under five knots, we loaded the amphibians (each carrying a jeep) into L.C.T.'s, and, having reached a position off our chosen landing beach, drove them out of the landing craft into the sea and made the land under our own power. Thus we avoided the need to beach the L.C.T. such as had brought us to disaster at the mouth of the Tenna. The Ducks ashore, we lifted the jeeps out of them and proceeded on our business. The empty amphibious craft sailed back and by a tricky maneuver drove up the ramp from the water into the waiting L.C.T.'s. Sergeant Porter became our chief expert on those operations, for he liked to turn fanciful projects into practical realities. He worked hard and long at his undertakings; when he was ready he demonstrated his results with a boyish smile and tremendous confidence. We all thought how easy it all really was.

After many practice exercises we thought we had fairly mastered the elaborate technique of these operations, but one night I got into trouble when I was taking back two empty Ducks from a landing point on the enemy coast to a beach in the rear. The distance being but ten miles the trip was to be done by the Ducks under their own steam. We sailed at dusk: our course was to hug the coast for twelve

minutes, then out to sea, due east, for twenty minutes, then
seventy-five minutes on a bearing of 170° magnetic; finally
a run in of a few minutes due west would take us to the
beach at Cesenatico. The second Duck ran aground on a
mud bank a few minutes after we had left, just as a thick
fog descended on the sea, and my own craft also got
entangled. We floundered for a quarter of an hour before
we both got clear, when I made directly for the open sea.
To avoid losing my escort in the fog (she was manned by
two R.A.S.C. drivers who were not very good at navigation) I had to slow down to a speed that I could only
estimate very approximately, thus putting out my calculations. When I thought I was two miles at sea, I turned
south. There had been no wind and no sea until now, but
as we turned we were struck head on by a squall, and a
few minutes later the sea was covered with foam with high
waves running.

Even in calm water a Duck with its tiny rudder tends to
yaw as much as thirty degrees and you have to keep
playing on the wheel to keep her on a course. In the gale
that was now blowing we found it a problem to keep our
head into the wind. Spray and rain soaked us and got into
the prism of my service compass, which was all I had to
steer by. I handed over the wheel to the driver while I
crouched under the dashboard, trying to find a dry piece
of cloth to clean the compass. I told him to keep her head
into the wind; either he misunderstood me or he gave the
wrong turn on the wheel, for a moment later we had
broached to and were rolling in the trough of the waves,
with the sea pouring over our sides. When we finally
succeeded in getting her head back into the wind we were
nearly waterlogged and our escort had vanished. Any
precaution against being seen being now pointless, we
turned on our headlights and were relieved to see our
escort do the same about a quarter of a mile ahead: better
sailors than we were, they had kept on their course. For
two hours we remained hove to, the engine dead slow,
struggling to keep in the wind. With the compass out of
action I had no idea from which quarter the wind was now
blowing and for all I knew we might be heading for the
Dalmatian coast. In any case there was nothing we could
do about it: if we had tried to steer off the wind we would
inevitably have foundered. Then the gale dropped suddenly, and though the sea was still running high, the craft

became more manageable and I could devote myself to the
compass and wipe the prism dry. By a coincidence, for my
navigation had been pure guesswork, our wheels touched
the bottom less than a mile from the spot on the coast I
was making for.

After this escape I got myself a proper ship's compass
and had larger rudders fitted to our sea-going Ducks.

Successive landings allowed us to outflank the Germans,
who were trying to hold us on the streams which intersected the forest, and in due course we squeezed them out into
the open and in view of Ravenna. They never realized how
we managed to get behind them and they thought that the
coastal strip of dunes was still theirs; one afternoon a
patrol of theirs commanded by a lieutenant walked into
the camp R Patrol had made in a hollow and were all
captured. The officer was sent back to my H.Q. in Savio.
Judging him to be a vain man and very much of a Prussian
officer, I treated him with a ceremonial courtesy that broke
down his defenses. I told him in French, which he spoke
elegantly:

"It is the fortune of war that you should have been
captured. Will you please do me the honor to dine with
me?" Ivan, scowling and with rage in his heart, served us a
very special meal and plenty of drinks. My guest, a
fanatical little Nazi, had absorbed the ferocious teachings
of his masters and had expected to be jeered at and
played with. When instead he was treated as a gentleman,
which he certainly didn't deserve, and entertained to dinner by a (to him) high ranking officer, his vanity went to
his head and he talked more than any prisoner-of-war I
have known. I couldn't stop him. When, bowing and
thanking me for my "correct attitude," he finally left for
the cage, I knew as much as he did of the defenses of
Ravenna. I knew also that the German Army, in spite of
their reverses in Russia, in France and in Italy, had no
idea that they were beaten, but were sustained by an
unshakable faith in Hitler's secret weapons, and I guessed
that they would go on fighting till they were on their
knees.

I, on the other hand, felt that the end of the war was in
sight and as a consequence I relaxed somewhat from the
extreme caution with which I had, for years, weighed
risks and husbanded our strength. With victory assured,
our lives were no longer so valuable and we could allow

ourselves to attempt some of the wilder schemes with
which we had toyed in imagination for a long time but
which I put aside, thinking that the risk was not justified
by the results we could hope to achieve. We could now
relax somewhat from our austerity of purpose.

As it happened our most precious lives were not lost in
acts of daring. The day after my party with the German
lieutenant, R Patrol was relieved by S on the coast and
sailed back to Savio for two days' rest. George Lee, a
young Canadian, who now commanded it, reported very
sadly that laying mines across a ford so as to protect their
position, his sergeant, Dave Porter, had unaccountably
blown himself up, together with Trooper Croghan who
was assisting him. It was a great loss to all of us. Porter had
been with P.P.A. since our early days in North Africa and
was part of the very framework of the unit. Tall and burly,
resolute and reliable, unmovable by fear or by excitement,
I had always thought him, of all our men, the most
comforting to be with in a tight spot. Whatever happened
he was tranquil and assured, his orderly brain working in
advance on problems that might crop up; he was never
caught unprepared. He came the nearest to being the ideal
type of soldier we tried to turn out in P.P.A., lovable and
by far the most popular man in the unit. Croghan, a
newcomer, was not very well known; a quiet little man,
Porter had taken him under his wing and had thought
much of him.

With Waterson, Locke, Sanders, and Beautyman gone,
Cameron, Curtis and Porter killed, the group of men who
had given its character to our unit was thinning out. Their
successors, didn't seem to me to have the same stature, the
same solidity, their personalities seemed paler; but I was
under the usual delusion of the older generation when it
begins to feel lonely in life—that the giants they have
known in their youth can't be equaled. For, three months
later, they in their turn had graduated into the old guard.
In the meanwhile, with Sergeant Brooks, S.Q.M.S. Davies,
Stewart, Barnes, I would chat about the old days, only
two years gone at most, but time moved fast with us.

Pushed out of the forest, the Germans blew the bank of
the last river which stood between us and Ravenna and
flooded the land. They kept only a chain of strong-points
in farmsteads and ricks which they could reach by raised
paths: they mined all other approaches and sat pretty.

Before tackling these we joined with the Twenty-Seventh Lancers in an operation against a village called Fosso di Ghiaia, which, strongly held, prevented their advance along the main road to Ravenna. The Lancers put in fifteen minutes' concentrated shelling, while we opened up from the flank with twenty machine guns, then we moved in along a canal bank in our jeeps, the Lancers coming in on foot from another direction. There was a tense moment which we approached Fosso di Ghiaia, our vehicles much exposed on the high bank to fire from the sunken village; we had two men wounded but a moment later we rushed the houses on foot and the Germans gave up. As we came out with fourteen prisoners (the Lancers got the rest), mortars and 88 mm. guns opened up on us. It was a narrow squeak but we brought the prisoners into the forest into comparative safety and lined them up to be searched and interrogated. Rather dazed at first, they suddenly realized that the war was over for them, and, with hoarse jokes, they unbuckled their leather belts and threw down on the ground these symbols of military servitude.

We loved these men who, ten minutes previously, we had been trying to kill—as they had been trying to do to us. They were offered cigarettes, and Burrows, my gunner, produced a *fiasco* of wine and a mug to give them a sip each. While I interrogated them one by one, I noticed that those I had done with were taken away to where tea and breakfast was cooking for them. No orders had been given, it seemed a natural thing to do to men who had just been through a heavy ordeal. We delighted to find that the enemy, whom we so seldom saw alive at close quarters, were persons like ourselves. The partisans looked on, disapprovingly. Later in the day I had a request from Sergeant Davies, who had received a slight wound, that he be allowed to keep the prisoners for a few days as they had already proved themselves so helpful with the building of a bridge over the canal: the unit was trying to acquire fourteen more pets.

John Campbell, who now commanded S Patrol, had shed his inhibitions and developed a reckless personality. Stationed in a farm called La Guaiadora, he had as next-door neighbors a German post in a farm called La Favorita. Several days running he sent one of his partisans, unarmed and in civilian clothes, with a can of milk to

German 88

sell to the soldiers at La Favorita. Having thus obtained knowledge of the post and of its approaches through the mine fields and the floods, as well as of the habits of its inmates, he made a plan to capture them all. At first I forbade the attempt, but he pleaded so urgently that I saw it would be hard on him and his men to prevent them from carrying out an enterprise on which they had set their hearts, and I let them go.

It must be remembered that Campbell had only been in action with his patrol for a short time and had not yet proved himself. I knew he could be foolish and he had an irritating weakness—he kept losing his guns, his mortar and even his own money; but I was impressed to see that he was backed by Sergeant Sizer, O'Leary, and Hodgson, sensible and experienced men. Obviously if he had won their confidence there was more in Campbell than I sus-

pected. Anyhow I let them go. They set out on foot very early one morning, guided by the milkman; creeping along in the dark on padded feet they reached a barn outside La Favorita and concealed themselves. The Germans were nearly all on guard duty round the farm at night, for they were fearful of being surprised, yet Campbell and his men came in so discreetly that nothing was heard. At dawn the Germans, relieved that another long night was over without an alarm, walked back to the house to breakfast and rest, leaving one sleepy man on guard at the door. Campbell gave them an hour to relax and then issued from the barn with his men and rushed the farm. The sentry was overpowered before he could realize what had happened; the others, some in bed, some drowsing over their breakfast, were disarmed without a shot fired or anybody hurt. O'Leary, swift and powerful, got six men out of the loft all

by himself. They tidied up the farmhouse, left everything
shipshape, and returned to La Guaiadora with their prisoners. When the German ration party came to La Favorita
the following night they were deeply puzzled: there were
no signs of a struggle, half-eaten food was still lying on the
table and yet the whole complement of the post had
vanished. I don't know what report they made to their
headquarters, but no attempt was made to re-occupy the
farm.

Such was the first of John Campbell's cloak-and-dagger
operations. He made several more with equal success, till
nearly all the posts on our side of the Fiumi Uniti, the
river covering Ravenna, had been captured. The prisoners
told us that wild spooky rumors were going around the
German troops: the strange fact was that none of the posts
thus captured were ever replaced. The other patrols also
ran cloak-and-dagger operations, and a competition developed between them on which I kept a watchful eye. Plain
and sober as most of our men were, they had this weakness: that they tended to develop a jealous pride each in his
own patrol. In our early days I had played the patrols one
against the other in emulation. I had soon become very
careful to do exactly the opposite, for fear that they might
become too rash, trying to overbid their companions or
even be carried away to play tricks on each other.

One farm, the Casa del Guardiano, was so well covered
by floods and mines that we never managed to get near it.
Rickwood, fairly recovered now from his stomach wound
and, at his request, once more in command of R Patrol
(against my better judgement for he was still far from
well), tried to find a way into it by daylight, disguised as a
shepherd—the only instance I know of any one of us
operating in civilian clothes. He looked pretty convincing
to me and had quite a manner with sheep, but he was
greeted by bursts of machine-gun fire and had to retire,
having lost five sheep. We got the Lancers to shell the
place, but the Germans had shelters inside ricks which
were immune even against a direct hit.

I had made friends with the pilot of an artillery observation plane, and Bob and I flew several times in his tiny
Auster over our area. Then we had an idea, and getting
from the R.A.F. a load of small obsolete twenty-five pound
bombs, we practiced hand bombing on a deserted beach.
When I thought I was sufficiently expert, we took off one

morning with nine bombs all over us in the cockpit. We had some difficulty in taking off with the extra load, but with a very long run we managed to become airborne. We circled the Casa del Guardiano, then ran in at sixty feet: I held a bomb out of the window and let it go when I thought the distance was correct. I overshot with the first one, undershot with the second, and got a direct hit with the third. As usual the Germans had not shown themselves at first, for no one cares to give away a position to an observation plane; our strange behavior must have shaken them—nobody had ever heard of an Auster dropping bombs—so it was not till after the fifth drop that they opened up. Being unused to these things, though I heard a distant rattle of guns over the noise of the engine, I didn't realize at all that we were the target. I asked my friend the pilot to run in once more as I had still four bombs to dispose of, which he did and I quietly took aim and dropped bomb number six, which missed, then round again and got a hit. Said the pilot: "Do you want to go in again?"

I said: "Why not?" and in we went.

As we came out he drew my attention to certain holes which had appeared in the wing above us. I said: "Our last one, what do you think?" He was a little thoughtful but came round again and flew over the farm at twenty feet. I thought we would hit the roof and was so alarmed that I pulled in my bomb and only dropped it when we were well beyond the target. I enjoyed the party more than my friend, who was a bit worried how he would account to his commanding officer for the bullet holes in his plane. I made a clean breast of the affair to his commander, who, being a sportsman, overlooked our misuse of the aircraft and allowed us to use his planes on other occasions.

One night I received a visit from Bulow, the partisan commander of the Twenty-Eighth Garibaldi Brigade. He had sailed at night in a fishing smack from his headquarters in the marshes beyond Ravenna and landed at Cierva, in our lines. He was a little man of great vivacity, born in Ravenna, who before the war had been a student at an agricultural college. He had fought in Albania (a second lieutenant in the Royal Army) until he returned to Ravenna, after the Italian Armistice, to join the partisans and the Communist Party. Discovered by Longo, the head of the Italian resistance movement, who picked him out from

Auster AOP-1

among the others for no other reason, I believe, than his experience in the army, he was given command of a brigade that didn't yet exist. He raised it, trained it, and led it into action, and developed an ability for partisan warfare and an outstanding gift of leadership which surprised his countrymen, "for," they said, "he cannot talk"; and indeed, by Italian standards, he was no speaker. He had disrupted the German communications in Romagna and speeded up their withdrawal; now, having concentrated his forces in the pine forest and the marshes on the coast north of Ravenna, he prepared for an attack on the town concerted with our own advance. After the liberation of the town his brigade became a unit of the Eighth Army and took part in the final rout of the Germans.

We struck up that night a friendship that has lasted and

increased to this day. Not that the little man had at that
time anything pleasant to say to me: he was rightly
indignant that the supplies which had been promised had
not yet been delivered, and the purpose of his visit was to
tell all of us what he thought of our negligence. He had
been to Eighth Army headquarters before coming to me;
he had received promises, and I undertook to see that they
were kept. We made plans for a concerted attack on
Ravenna, arranged radio communications and such details,
then we went and visited Ateo's detachment, which was
part of Bulow's brigade. I was able to give him a very good
account of the work done by Ateo since he had been with
us. His partisans had indeed done extremely well, fighting
not only with bravery but also with skill. They had lost
several men killed and made no fuss about it. Bulow,
whose real name is Arrigo Boldrini, left that same night
and sailed back to his watery headquarters.

The civilians made no more fuss than the partisans
about their dead. A peasant woman asked to see me and,
after an apology for taking up my time, told her story:
during the battle which had led to the liberation of Savio
she had found herself with her family between the two
armies; their village being shelled, they had taken shelter
in the fields under a haystack. A shell unfortunately had
burst quite close killing her husband, two of her daughters,
her sister, and an uncle. She herself and other members of
the family had escaped unhurt and had been evacuated by
us behind the river Savio. "This happened ten days ago,"
she said. "It is not fit that our dead should remain any
longer unburied. I have come to ask your permission to
cross the Savio and collect the bodies." She stood, dignified
and very quiet, without tears, waiting for my answer. I
offered to send a truck to recover the corpses, but she
would have nothing of it. "I don't want to cause any
inconvenience. I can get a horse and a cart and that is all I
need. My brother will go with me."

A high medieval tower at the mouth of the Fiumi Uniti,
occupied by the enemy, gave us great inconvenience as it
compelled us to put out far to sea in our navigations along
the coast, and it prevented a landing we wanted to make
on the far bank of the river, where a convenient road led
into Ravenna. We had tried to shell it but the walls were of
stone and ten feet thick so Campbell offered to capture the
tower by a crowning cloak and dagger.

We dropped him and his party on the coast, out of sight of the tower, and off they marched in the sand dunes, to spend two days snooping and observing. When they thought they knew enough they concealed themselves at night in a shed, a hundred yards from the tower, the only cover there was—for the tower stood on a bare knoll. After dawn, as usual, the Germans retired inside the tower and closed the door, a heavy affair of oak four inches thick. Our men waited in their shed, there was nothing else they could do. At last at eight-thirty a German came out to relieve nature, leaving the door ajar. Our men sprinted, unperceived by the lookout on top of the tower, floored the piddler, dashed up the winding staircase and captured the whole garrison. At nine I got a radio signal that all was well.

We sailed from down the coast and landed five jeeps and twenty partisans at the foot of the tower. The partisans took it over, Campbell concealed his jeeps in the sand dunes to give supporting fire if needed and promptly went to sleep, while the prisoners were shipped away. At eleven o'clock the German officer's orderly came along the path carrying his master's newly pressed coat, entered the tower and was suppressed. At one a man came to look for the orderly, and never came out again. At four a patrol of six who came to look for the orderly and for the man were let in by our partisans, and remained in. At sundown a patrol of eighteen under a captain came to look for everybody. This time there was a bit of a fight; two Germans were killed, the sixteen others joined their companions in the dungeon.

There were no more visits that night and the next morning we found the last posts south of the Fiumi Uniti all evacuated.

24

WHEELS IN VENICE

RAVENNA was entered two days later by Porter Force from the south, Canadian troops from the west, Bulow from the north, and P.P.A. last of all from the east, for we had lingered by the way. Bulow was wounded in the arm: I had him attended to and took him to stay with me the night. If we had formed our opinion of Italian soldiers from the behavior of the Royal Italian Army or from that of the fancy-dress partisans farther south, Bulow would have upset all our notions. Here he was on the day of his victory, a wounded hero in his liberated native town: would he stay and enjoy his triumph? Active and restless as usual, he had no peace till he left once more for his marshes, where he had led so long the life of a frog. They lived there in clumps of muddy reeds, hardly a few inches above the water: all their movements were in punts, following invisible channels. They issued to raid the Germans every night, during the day they lay in the mud.

He left me the following night: the Germans still held in strength the port of Ravenna, and their supplies, coming along the beach, were a tempting target for Bulow's forces in the marshes.

I promised to join Bulow with a patrol of P.P.A. in three days' time, and in the meanwhile I pushed R Patrol up a road leading north from Ravenna till they made contact with the Germans. They found them halfhearted, and after a few shots had been exchanged, they withdrew. The next day our patrol was relieved by two troops of the Twenty-Seventh Lancers and fell back two miles to the rear in support. There was another pine forest here, and I put a post of Ateo's partisans under the trees to cover a bridge over a canal half a mile to the right of the Lancers.

Back in Ravenna I made arrangements with an aged

expert to take me round the churches, which for many years I had wanted to visit. A few days previously I had had the luck to save from our shelling the church of San Apollinare in Classe, outside Ravenna. I had dimly remembered that it was decorated with sixth-century Roman mosaics of great beauty, and I had prevailed with the gunners to postpone the shelling twenty-four hours while I sent a party to visit the bell tower in which the Germans were believed to have an artillery observation post. I proved the rumor to be unfounded and saved the church. This act of virtue, the first in a long career of destruction, had left me so self-satisfied that I wished to visit the other monuments of Ravenna.

My appointment being at eleven, I got up early and drove out in my jeep with Charlie Burrows, before breakfast, to visit the Lancers' post on the main road and the partisans in the wood.

The road rose on a ramp to be carried by a stone bridge over a canal, which ran to the sea between banks ten feet above the sodden plain. Just beyond the bridge a Lancer sergeant with three men had sited a bren gun in the middle of the road. The two troops were on the near side of the canal with a few bren guns under the canal bank on each side of the road, and the remainder of the men on the left of the road in a hut down in the fields, against which they had driven a scout car. Unused to infantry fighting they were ill at ease without their armored cars. They had seen no enemy when I arrived. I thought the Germans were on the run—there had been little fight in them during the last few days—and I made a plan to reconnoiter forward on the next day with R Patrol. I left Burrows with my jeep on the road eighty yards from the bridge (on our side), made him turn it around facing home (the only sensible thing I did that morning), told him I would be back in an hour and strolled away along the canal bank to the right toward the next bridge on which the partisans were on guard. With me was Gigi and one of Ateo's company commanders who had come to meet me. I found the partisans happy and much better organized than the Lancers, for the job was more in their line of business. They had patroled forward as far as the next canal in the early morning and seen no enemy.

We made our way back to my jeep, Gigi and I. As the weather was fine for the first time in a month, we walked slowly along the bank discussing the possibility of finding guinea fowl in this forest as we had done in the Pineta di Classe. The road with the jeep on it came in sight; a hullabaloo broke out on our right, in the forest on the far side of the canal. Many guns were fired, mostly German by the noise, but we discerned also the fast, dry rattle of a bren.

Gigi said: "A counterattack?" I nodded and we both slid down the bank into the field below, which was covered in a foot of water. Gigi ran splashing toward the road, I plodded along sedately: somehow it seemed undignified to run. As I got nearer, things began to whistle and whine over my head: I saw broken twigs showering down from the trees beyond the canal bank. Three Lancers came running, head down, over the bridge carrying a bren and plumped down out of sight on the far side of the road; the fourth, the sergeant, had been killed. Burrows was crouching by the side of the jeep, his shoulders hunched up. I felt guilty that I had left him there, eighty yards from the front line, with no other instructions but to wait for me on the road, and there he was, waiting patiently when he could have taken cover.

Hoarse cries came from the bridge: German soldiers were pouring slowly over it, six abreast, between the parapets, yelling all the time to keep up their spirits. They were in no hurry: I fancied the men behind were pushing and those in the front row were holding back hard. Burrows, seeing at last somebody to fire at, came to life, got up, stretched himself, leveled the big gun at the back of the jeep, and fired: the tracer plunged into the solid human mass on the bridge, some men fell, the others drew back beyond the bridge.

At that moment something hot and very noisy whizzed past my head, very close. I put my hand to my right ear and brought it back bloody, but the ear was still there. Perhaps my duffel coat made me conspicuous, for much stuff seemed to be coming my way, but I was not going to take it off, and plodded on, worried a little that if I was hit I might fall and drown in a foot of water!

Gigi now was by the jeep and firing the second gun. When I climbed up the bank onto the road he was gone; Burrows was there, still firing a burst now and then, and looking most serious. I couldn't see anything to fire at and waited with the butt of the gun in my hand. The air was thick with whistlings and whinings. An old man came riding up the road in a donkey cart; he must have been double deaf not to have heard the racket. I waved him off the road but he noticed nothing till he arrived within four yards of me, when he uttered an imprecation, jumped off his cart, pushed the donkey down the bank and toppled over, shot through the head.

The Germans came over the bridge once more in a pack, yelling as before. I could see their open mouths. When we fired they stopped on the bridge, somewhat thinned out. One of them leaned against the parapet, stuck a rifle grenade into the muzzle of his rifle and took a slow aim at us. I tried to get him with careful bursts: three times he fired and missed and still I couldn't get him. I walked round the jeep to get a new belt of ammunition, when something that made no noticeable noise squashed and shattered my left wrist. The bones and the flesh of the wrist and the forearm were in a pulp, the hand was sound but hung livid and deadlike, with darkening nails, and there was no doubt that it would have to come off.

I was pleased to be wounded in this manner—more than pleased; I was filled with a joyful peace, a tranquil certainty of fulfillment. I had been chasing a phantom right through the war and now, at last, I had come on to something solid: my wound was real and nothing could take it from me.

I pushed my mangled hand into the breast of my battle dress and asked Burrows to fit a new belt into my gun. He did so, still looking most serious, and went back to his own gun. The Germans came over a third time, at a run this time, filling the whole width of the bridge. A few got across and dropped promptly behind the canal bank, the others either fell or crawled back over the bridge. Though I hadn't done much good, firing with one hand, I went and sat in the jeep waiting for the next attack. After a good while the German fire eased a little; I thought they had had enough and wouldn't attempt to come over the bridge for some time: now was the moment to go and get reinforcements, or the Lancers in the hut and down the bank would all be slaughtered. I called down for any wounded men to come up to be evacuated. One man only, with a bullet through his shoulder, crawled up the bank and into the jeep. He was upset and whimpered, "I have lost my arm, I have lost my arm."

"So have I," I said. "There's nothing to make a fuss about." He brightened up immediately.

Burrows drove us to where R Patrol was, a couple of miles down the road. I told Rickwood to move up and keep the bridge covered until I could send B Patrol from Ravenna to support him. At first I had expected a hemorrhage, but seeing that blood was no more than oozing from my arm, I dropped the wounded Lancer at the hospital and went to find Jean Caneri in Ravenna to tell him to take over command of P.P.A. from me as I would be some time in the hospital. His first job would be to extricate the survivors of the two Lancer troops and our partisans, and he jumped to it. I then told Burrows to drive me to the Canadian Casualty Clearing Station: I walked in and, feeling a bit weary, lay down on a stretcher. The duty surgeon lit a cigarette for me, injected penicillin, then looked at my hand and asked:

"Any other damage?"

"Right ear split, that's all."

"What about the blood on your right hand?"

"Oh, that is only blood. " I looked again. No, by God, it wasn't. There was a bullet hole through the palm and the fourth finger was broken. That's why I had been clumsy with my gun.

He then asked a question that shattered my wonderful peace: "How long have you been wounded?" I lifted the smashed wrist where the watch should have been: it was gone—my excellent Swiss watch which I had carried throughout the war, a watch that varied less than two minutes a month.

That afternoon B Patrol, with R in support, drove one of its six jeeps on to the bridge where it fired all its ammunition at the Germans on the far side, then another took its place, then another for over an hour, keeping the Germans fairly quiet while the marooned Lancers were extricated. Gigi was with them, having been wounded in the shoulder and through the chest while he was firing the second gun on my jeep that morning. Sergeant Galloway of B Patrol was hit in the thigh while he was carrying a wounded Lancer out of the canal; he then went back to his jeep and went on firing till he fainted from the loss of blood. The Germans put up a heavy barrage of mortars and artillery, but our men were too close to the enemy positions to be much affected. Three Canadian Honey tanks down the road gave artillery support to our side. Ateo's partisans on their bridge had had two men wounded whom they brought back walking through the forest.

"Honey tank"

The Germans withdrew that night, leaving thirty dead behind. They were two companies of an S.S. Battalion, arrived the day before, fresh from rest, to relieve the tired troops we had been fighting so long.

This happened on December 9, 1944. Two days later Caneri and Campbell with S Patrol joined Bułow in the marshes, where they stayed till the nineteenth. Then the whole of P.P.A. was relieved and drove back to its new base near Rimini. They had been in action continuously since June 16 for six months and three days. Aggressive operations stopped for the winter along the whole of the Italian front.

I woke up from the anesthetic that evening. My left hand was gone above the wrist, the right one was in plaster, leaving only the thumb and the tops of the second and third fingers free. I had two stitches in my right ear and I felt wonderfully hungry. There were no more than three other patients in the C.C.S. so only our ward was open, where all the sisters gathered round the stove, talking and knitting. I was fed an enormous dinner by a kind Canadian sister, after which I fell off to sleep. All was peace and kindness, I had absolutely nothing to worry about and I was completely happy. The next morning Ivan came to keep me company: he had put on a strenuously cheerful hospital face, but when he saw the stump of my left arm with its little bloody dressing, the tough Russian warrior burst into tears and I had to comfort him, which was pleasant. A sister brought him a cup of tea, patted him on the back and told him sweet things, of which he never understood a word but they made him smile through his tears. These Canadian girls were the kindest in the world and they spoiled me thoroughly.

Most of the men in the unit came to see me during the next three days, after which I was driven to a General Hospital in Rimini. I woke up in the morning in a huge ward quite full of patients. A very busy sister brought me my breakfast on a tray; later, seeing I was not eating, she asked what was the matter. Somewhat abashed I made a helpless gesture with my stump and my plastered hand. She laughed and said:

"But you can feed yourself you know. Just try. I'll help you if you like, but I'm very busy."

The lesson was good—I never felt sorry for myself again.

I was flown from Rimini to 104 General Hospital in Rome, where I was operated on by a woman surgeon, Barbara Stimson, an American, but a major in the R.A.M.C. Head of a hospital in New York, she had joined the British Army long before her own country came into the war, and she now commanded an orthopedic unit to which special cases were directed. She operated eight to ten hours every day in the theater, and found time to visit the wards at some time of the day or the night. We all loved her; the female staff, sisters, nurses, and V.A.D.'s adored and worshiped her; the doctors and surgeons danced around her when they could and praised her professional skill when she was out of hearing. She looked rather severe in uniform, her hair cut straight and her manner brisk which suffered no nonsense, for she was a busy woman and very clever; but one day I called on her in her quarters, where she was confined by a bout of flu, to find her dressed in a soft flowery gown, and knitting! We talked of books, pictures, people, and children—she was a very human and very remarkable person.

On previous occasions when I had been in the hospital I had always had one of our radio sections at hand and kept on fussing P.P.A. at a distance, but now, for the first time, I was without any responsibilities. It was pleasant for a few days; then when my stump had healed and the pleasure of having lost my hand had worn off, although I had dear friends in Rome, I became anxious to be back at work.

On January 11, just over a month after being wounded, I was in Viserba, worrying Jean Caneri about his plans for keeping the men happy during the winter, for we were told at the Eighth Army that no operations were contemplated till the final battle in March or April. I stayed three days, during which I interviewed a number of recruits, then drove back to Rome and Naples and sailed for Liverpool in a hospital ship to be fitted in England with an artificial hand: I was told it would take six months, but I pestered the War Office so much that by the middle of April I was back in Italy.

During my absence Caneri had kept his men busy indeed. Apart from our routine training, he sent them to follow a course of parachute jumping, and, after that, for a month at Terminillo on a mountain warfare course, skiing, climbing, and handling mules. In spite of these activities the men had grown restless and a little out of hand.

Bob Yunnie had left P.P.A. for good in the middle of April 1945. Perhaps he too, like others before, had borne as much strain as he could stand, but he would have fought with us the last battles of the war but for the tragic, sudden death of his only son, a boy of eight, who lived with his wife in Aberdeen: the disaster broke his determination. Although I had seen him in England with his wife and son, when he came on his first leave since the beginning of the war, I had inhumanly taken it for granted that his allegiance was only to us. When, arriving in Italy, I read in a letter he had left for me that he had accepted not leave but a permanent home posting, I remained for a long time unbelieving and heartbroken.

Caneri's patrol commanders were now Captain John Campbell, promoted to the old guard, Lieutenant Steve Wallbridge, a newcomer of great achievement, and Lieutenant McCallum, a very young officer transferred from the Twenty-Seventh Lancers. I liked him so much that I thought I had found in him at last a young man I would be able to train to perfection in my own manner and I took him in hand—but a few days after he joined us, I was wounded. He now succeeded Bob Yunnie in command of B Patrol. Rickwood, disguising very gallantly the painful disorders resulting from his wound, was second-in-command of P.P.A. He exerted himself against terrible odds when, by all standards, he should have been resting in a convalescent home. The other officers we had were useful in many ways: they did not take part in the fighting. George Lee had unfortunately been recalled by the Canadian Army, and his experience was lost to us.

Thus shorthanded Caneri had every excuse to follow his bent and take the field himself. He organized his own H.Q. as a complete fighting patrol, and on April 21, when the Eighth and Fifth Armies attacked after the winter pause he went into action with the whole fighting strength of P.P.A. For seven days they fought around Lake Comacchio, with the Twenty-Seventh Lancers and the Twenty-Eighth Garibaldi Brigade. On the twenty-third McCallum, leading his patrol into a village, ran into an ambush and was killed with his gunner, McDowall, by a *panzerfaust* which completely destroyed his jeep. Sergeant Galloway brought the patrol back, together with twenty-two prisoners.

Panzerfaust

On the twenty-sixth Caneri embarked his jeeps in six
R.C.L.'s and sailed with a mine-sweeper escort to the
mouth of the Po. R.C.L.'s were craft designed for inland
waters, but they had been proved to be seaworthy in the
course of numerous exercises during the winter. From that
day P.P.A. operated in its own watery domain, on the
canals, river deltas, and lagoons which stretch from the
mouth of the Po to Venice. The R.C.L.'s commanded by
Lieutenant Thomas, R.A.S.C., became part of the unit;
they ferried the jeeps across the water, brought up supplies
and evacuated casualties and prisoners.

The main branch of the Po was crossed the same day,
and P.P.A. established beyond it with the support of local
partisans. On the twenty-seventh they crossed the Adige
and the Brenta, and appeared before Chioggia, a small
fishing town at the south end of the lagoon of Venice,
where the Germans had seven hundred men with two
batteries of 88 mm. field guns, one battery of coastal
defense guns, one hundred and twenty heavy machine
guns, much ammunition and supplies for three months.
The commander thought himself secure behind three rivers and innumerable canals on which all the bridges had
been blown. Jean Caneri sent Wallbridge to him under a
flag of truce, with a request to surrender within twenty-
four hours, failing which he would be bombed out of the
world by the air force. Concealing the fact that his whole
force on the spot consisted of nine men in three jeeps,
Caneri received the representative of the German commander and in five hours' talk bluffed him so successfully
that he returned to his commanding officer to recommend
an unconditional surrender, for Caneri would accept nothing else.

Meanwhile the other patrols had fanned out to the
northwest. On the twenty-ninth John Campbell charged a
battery of 88 mm. guns while they were firing on our
troops outside Padova and captured them intact with three
hundred prisoners, whom he handed over to the partisans;
he pursued his way toward Padova and entered the town
where partisans, having risen in force, were disarming the
Germans. On the same day Sergeant Galloway with B
Patrol, making its way toward Venice, engaged the enemy
in the morning, capturing ten prisoners. Later in the day
they entered a small town where the Germans, barricaded
in houses around the square, opened up on them from the

windows. In the fierce engagement which followed, Rogers was killed, Sergeant Galloway was wounded a second time and a gunner, Brown, also grievously wounded. Corporal Sonley took command of the patrol, fought in the square for forty-five minutes, killed seven Germans, captured fifteen, exhausted his ammunition and withdrew with the wounded and the dead.

On the thirtieth R and B Patrols sailed (in R.C.L.'s) across the Gulf of Venice and landed well beyond the town, just in time to chase the Germans out of Iesolo.

When I arrived in Chioggia the poor German major, who had declared that he wouldn't surrender to anything smaller than a battalion, had realized that he had been tricked by a handful of men—but it was too late: his men were disarmed, his officers all put under guard and he consoled himself with the brandy bottle. Steve Wallbridge had spent twenty-four hours in the town before the surrender, at the German H.Q.; he had cleverly played on the dissensions among the German staff some of whom, against the views of their commander, wanted to resist to the last round, and he had somehow succeeded in suggesting that he had several battalions just across the Brenta. I believe that an important element in the success of his negotiations took place on his first night in the town, when, being entertained in the German mess, he drank the whole staff under the table. Of this, however, I have no other evidence but the word of an enemy.

In the course of the last few days P.P.A. had captured thirteen hundred and thirty-five prisoners, sixteen field guns and many smaller weapons. I felt that the war in Italy would end in a few days and that the time had now come to carry out the plan I had told Cameron about when we were on our way from Taranto to Bari a year and a half earlier—a purposeless piece of swagger, indeed, but a flourish can be an end in itself.

We loaded five jeeps in three R.C.L.'s and, young Thomas leading recklessly among the German mines, we sailed from Chioggia to Venice up the lagoon, entered the Canal San Marco and moored our craft on the quay. I started my jeep and, trembling with excitement for the one and only time during the war, drove into the Piazzetta, passed between the columns, turned left into Piazza San Marco, and, followed by the others, drove seven times round the square. This was my hour of triumph.

Eight days later we were in a deep Alpine valley below Tarvisio waiting morosely for the war to end. Lazy rumors went round the camp. At six o'clock I received a slip from Sergeant Brooks, Germany had surrendered.

The next day, driving in Austria, we met a group of three hundred creatures, bare-footed, in white and gray striped pajamas, heads shaven, faces gray, eyes glazed, bones protruding, corpses that moved in fours and shuffled painfully in a ghostly semblance of soldierly order. When they reached our convoy, which I had stopped, uncomprehending, they raised croaking voices in a manner of song, a rustling Marseillaise, no louder than a whisper. They were French political prisoners, and this indignity had been done to them by their German keepers in a concentration camp up in the mountains. If this, I thought, is what the Germans really are, we shall have a long job to cure them.

Two days later again we were driving eastward from Klagenfurt in Austria with a detachment of the Twenty-Seventh Lancers. At Wolfsberg the road climbs up a narrow mountain gorge: it was filled from parapet to wall with routed German troops. For eight hours we forced our way through three divisions, mostly on foot, some on bicycles, some on horseback. They had broken-down trucks, ox carts, horse carts, and donkeys; no officers; the men, haggard and panicky, plodded blindly on, terrified of the Russians in their rear. At intervals, when rumors spread among them that the Russians were catching up, they broke and stampeded into the fields or up the hillside —then, the panic over, they took to the road again.

At dusk the last Germans thinned out. In the valley below we saw Very lights fired. It was nearly dark when, having reached the valley, I saw the mass of a tank ahead of me, covered with a red Soviet flag. It stopped and so did I. Major Lykov climbed out of the turret, we walked toward each other and clasped hands. Then the Russian stepped back, stood to attention and delivered a speech. He ended: "There is nothing that can destroy our solidarity."

The war being over, I thought, I might well now see to that.

BANTAM IS PROUD TO PRESENT A MAJOR PUBLISHING EVENT

THE ILLUSTRATED HISTORY OF THE VIETNAM WAR

Never before has the Vietnam War been so vividly presented. Never before has a full account of the controversial war been available in inexpensive paperback editions.

Each Volume in the series is an original work by an outstanding and recognized military author. Each volume is lavishly illustrated with up to 32 pages of full color photographs, maps, and black and white photos drawn from military archives and features see-through, cutaway, four-color paintings of major weapons.

Don't miss these other exciting volumes:

Special Offer
Buy a Bantam Book
for only 50¢.

Now you can have Bantam's catalog filled with hundreds
of titles plus take advantage of our unique and exciting
bonus book offer. A special offer which gives you the
opportunity to purchase a Bantam book for only 50¢.
Here's how!

By ordering any five books at the regular price per
order, you can also choose any other single book
listed (up to a $5.95 value) for just 50¢. Some
restrictions do apply, but for further details why not
send for Bantam's catalog of titles today!

Just send us your name and address and we will send
you a catalog!